The Nationalism of the Rich

Based on rigorous analysis of the propaganda of five Western European separatist parties, this book provides in-depth examination of the 'nationalism of the rich', defined as a type of nationalist discourse that seeks to end the economic 'exploitation' suffered by a group of people represented as a wealthy nation and supposedly carried out by the populations of poorer regions and/or by inefficient state administrations. It shows that the nationalism of the rich represents a new phenomenon peculiar to societies that have set in place complex systems of wealth redistribution and adopted economic growth as the main principle of government legitimacy. The book argues that the nationalism of the rich can be seen as a rhetorical strategy portraying independent statehood as a solution to the dilemma between solidarity and efficiency arisen in Western Europe since the end of the Glorious Thirties. It further suggests that its formation can be best explained by the following combination of factors: (1) the creation, from the end of the Second World War, of extensive forms of automatic redistribution to a scale previously unprecedented; (2) the beginning, from the mid-1970s, of an era of 'permanent austerity' exacerbated, in specific contexts, by situations of serious public policy failure; and (3) the existence of national/cultural cleavages roughly squaring with uneven development and sharp income differentials among territorial areas of a given state.

Emmanuel Dalle Mulle is a post-doctoral researcher and project coordinator at the Graduate Institute of International and Development Studies, Geneva.

Routledge Studies in Modern European History

The Nationalism of the Rich

Discourses and Strategies of Separatist Parties in Catalonia, Flanders, Northern Italy and Scotland

Emmanuel Dalle Mulle

Routledge
Taylor & Francis Group

LONDON AND NEW YORK

First published 2018
by Routledge
2 Park Square, Milton Park, Abingdon, Oxon OX14 4RN

and by Routledge
711 Third Avenue, New York, NY 10017

Routledge is an imprint of the Taylor & Francis Group, an informa business

British Library Cataloguing in Publication Data
A catalogue record for this book is available from the British Library

Library of Congress Cataloging in Publication Data
Names: Dalle Mulle, Emmanuel, 1985– author.
Title: The nationalism of the rich : discourses and strategies of
separatist parties in Catalonia, Flanders, Northern Italy and Scotland
/ Emmanuel Dalle Mulle.
Description: Milton Park, Abingdon, Oxon ; New York, NY :
Routledge, 2018. |
Series: Routledge studies in modern European history ; 51
Identifiers: LCCN 2017029283 | ISBN 9781138066885 (hardback :
alkaline paper) | ISBN 9781315158952 (ebook)
Classification: LCC D1058 .D25 2018 | DDC 324.2/183094–dc23
LC record available at https://lccn.loc.gov/2017029283

ISBN: 978-1-138-06688-5 (hbk)
ISBN: 978-1-315-15895-2 (ebk)

Typeset in Sabon
by Wearset Ltd, Boldon, Tyne and Wear

Printed and bound by CPI Group (UK) Ltd, Croydon, CR0 4YY

To my family, my friends and Cassandre for their endless support

Contents

Figures

Tables

Acknowledgements

This work would have never been possible without the help of several people. Unfortunately, I will not be able to thank all of them here, but I will at least try to give due credit to some. My apologies in advance to those that I will forget below.

My first acknowledgements go to Professor Andre Liebich for his endless patience in carefully reading earlier versions of this study and for the invaluable advice that he has given me in the last few years. Then, my sincere gratitude goes to a number of scholars who have provided me with useful feedback and encouragement, notably: Michel Huysseune, Liah Greenfeld, John Breuilly, John Hutchinson, Montserrat Guibernau, Annabelle Littoz-Monnet, Anwen Elias, Davide Rodogno, Velibor Jakovleski, Koen Abts and Jurgen Nagels. Yvette Issar deserves special mention for her precious linguistic guidance.

The research required to write this book received the generous support of the following institutions: the Swiss National Science Foundation (grant n. P1GEP1_148782), the Swiss Academy of Humanities and Social Sciences, the International History Department of the Graduate Institute of International and Development Studies (IHEID) and the Pierre du Bois Foundation. I would like to thank all of them for their vital help. My sincere gratitude also goes to the IHEID's Publication Department and the team of International Development Policy, as well as to the foreign institutions that have hosted me during my research, notably: the Political Science Department of the *Vrije Universiteit Brussel*, the Government Department of the London School of Economics and Political Science, the Sociology Department of Boston University, the *Instituut voor Sociaal en Politiek Opinieonderzoek* of the KU Leuven and the Political Science Department of *Universitat Pompeu Fabra*.

More fundamentally, this work would have never been possible without the personal support of my closest friends, notably Simone Bianchi, Valentina Collazzo, Samuel Colle Dominguez, Francesco De Bortoli, Davide Lessi and Andrea Luchetta. My endless gratitude goes to my family for everything they have done for me. Finally, I want to say 'thank you' to Cassandre for making my life happy so naturally and so completely every day.

Acronyms

CD&V	*Christen-Democratisch en Vlaams* (Christian-Democrats and Flemish)
CDC	*Convergència Democratica de Catalunya* (Democratic Convergence of Catalonia)
CiU	*Convergència i Unió* (Convergence and Union, Catalonia)
CSU	*Christlich Soziale Union in Bayern* (Christian Social Union in Bavaria)
CUP	*Candidatura d'Unitat Popular* (Popular Unity Candidacy, Catalonia)
CVP	*Christelijke Volkspartij* (Christian Social Party, Belgium)
DC	*Democrazia Cristiana* (Christian Democracy, Italy)
EEC	European Economic Community
ERC	*Esquerra Republicana de Catalunya* (Republican Left of Catalonia)
ERDF	European Regional Development Fund
EU	European Union
FI	*Forza Italia* (Go Italy)
GDHI	Gross Disposable Household Income
GDP	Gross Domestic Product
GERS	Government Expenditure and Revenues in Scotland
GVA	Gross Value Added
ICPS	*Institut de Ciencies Politiques i Socials* (Institute of Political and Social Sciences, Barcelona)
IMF	International Monetary Fund
LN	*Lega Nord* (Northern League, Italy)
MP	Member of (national) Parliament
NAFTA	North American Free Trade Agreement
NATO	North Atlantic Treaty Organization
N-VA	*Nieuw-Vlaamse Alliantie* (New Flemish Alliance)
OECD	Organisation for Economic Co-operation and Development
Open VLD	*Open Vlaamse Liberalen en Democraten* (Open Flemish Liberals and Democrats)
PCI	*Partito comunista italiano* (Italian Communist Party)

PdL	*Popolo della Libertà* (People of Freedom, Italy)
PDS	*Partito Democratico della Sinistra* (Democratic Party of the Left, Italy)
POS	Political Opportunity Structure
PP	*Partido Popular* (People's Party, Spain)
PS	*Parti socialiste* (Socialist Party, Belgium)
PSC	*Partit dels Socialistes de Catalunya* (Socialist Party of Catalonia)
PSI	*Partito Socialista Italiano* (Italian Socialist Party)
PSOE	*Partido Socialista Obrero Español* (Socialist Labour Spanish Party)
SME(s)	Small and medium-sized enterprise(s)
SNP	Scottish National Party
SSAS	Scottish Social Attitude Survey
UCD	*Unio de Centro Democratico* (Union of the Democratic Centre, Spain)
UK	United Kingdom
US	United States
USSR	Union of Soviet Socialist Republics
VAT	Value-added tax
VB	*Vlaams Blok* (Flemish Bloc)/*Vlaams Belang* (Flemish Interest)
VEV	*Vlaams Economisch Verbond* (Flemish Business Organisation)
VNP	*Vlaamse Nationale Partij* (Flemish National Party)
VU	*Volksunie* (People's Union, Flanders)

Introduction

'Every generation has its own preoccupations and concerns and therefore looks for new things in the past and asks different questions' (MacMillan 2009, p. 38). Academic interest in specific subjects waxes and wanes, influenced by those events that shape our present and urge us to seek explanations. Nationalism is no exception. After a period of neglect, due to a prevalence of Marxist and modernisation-theory approaches predicting the disappearance of nationalist conflicts, research on nationalism has experienced a burgeoning revival. The demise of the Soviet Union, followed by an outburst of nationalist sentiments in many of its former republics, mainly accounts for such a renewed interest. The end of the Cold War inevitably caused shifts in the balance of power among and within existing states, sometimes leading to the redefinition of borders. It is in this context, marked by gruesome conflicts in former-Yugoslavia, Rwanda, Azerbaijan and Georgia, among others, that the literature on nationalism, whose premises had been laid down at the beginning of the 1980s, exploded. While focusing mainly on the spread of nationalism in Central and Eastern Europe, scholars also began taking into serious account those stateless nationalist movements that, since the end of the 1960s, had begun voicing their calls for self-determination in Western Europe. Here, the resurgence of nationalism was much more challenging from a theoretical perspective because, in the second half of the twentieth century, nationalism in Western Europe seemed an exhausted force. During the process of decolonisation, Western Europeans could look at nationalist conflicts in Africa and Asia as outbreaks of chauvinism and irrational violence endemic to 'backward' societies. Eastern Europe posed more of a problem, since socialism had been looked at by a number of Western scholars as an attractive alternative to liberal capitalism. But, after its demise in the early 1990s, one could point to the chaos triggered by the fall of the USSR and the so-called 'return of the repressed' in order to explain nationalism's resurgence in the area. The growth of nationalism in the 'advanced West', however, was totally unexpected.

Yet, in the time span going from the late 1960s to the early 1990s, nationalist parties in Catalonia, Flanders, Northern Italy and Scotland, among others, gathered momentum. Their rhetoric was one of economic and cultural victimisation. Centralising states were accused of financially overburdening them to the advantage of a lazy bureaucracy and of poorer regions. They also referred to the incipient process of globalisation to make their arguments more solid. They saw globalisation as a new stage of modernisation in which advanced regions compete with each other beyond and regardless of state borders and in which economically dynamic nations cannot afford to be hampered by inefficient state structures and by underdeveloped areas. Perceptions of increasing economic power and political marginalisation went hand in hand, setting the ground for what I have called the 'nationalism of the rich'. In this book, I argue that this is a new phenomenon in Western Europe, peculiar to societies that have set in place complex systems of national redistribution and have adopted economic growth as the main principle of government legitimacy.

The nationalism of the rich is the subject of this book. I define it as a type of nationalist discourse that aims to put an end to the economic 'exploitation' suffered by a group of people represented as a wealthy nation[1] and supposedly carried out by the populations of poorer regions and/or by inefficient state administrations. The core elements of this rhetoric are: a claim of economic victimisation, according to which a backward core area holds back a more advanced periphery; and a denunciation of political marginalisation. Here, the term marginalisation points to the fact that, despite sometimes indulging in colonial metaphors and statements about foreign occupation, its purveyors, in fact, more consistently point to subtler forms of subordination linked to: the lack of recognition of the relevant community's special status as a nation (Catalonia); the strings imposed by a consociational system over the political latitude of a demographic majority (Flanders); a mismatch between the economic power of the relevant community and its actual political representation (Northern Italy); the neglect felt by a demographic minority as a consequence of the economic and social policies implemented by its senior partner in a majoritarian union state (Scotland).

I do not argue at all that the nationalism of the rich is only about the economy. On the contrary, cultural and political arguments are fundamental, but, as I will try to show, compared to the bulk of the nationalist propaganda of the nineteenth and early twentieth century, the economic dimension has acquired an unprecedented primacy. In this connection, a remarkable feature is that the 'economic prowess' of the members of the nation has not only become a source of national pride, but also a marker of the national identity setting it apart from the other groups inhabiting the parent state. Apart from the deviant case of the Scottish National Party, the rhetoric of the other parties analysed in this study features a focus on the entrepreneurial spirit and hard-working ethos of the national community and its small and medium-sized enterprises (SMEs); hence, this rhetoric could also be dubbed 'the nationalism of the producing people'.

But, above all, the nationalism of the rich is peculiar because the claim of economic exploitation is framed as coming from a privileged – both in objective and subjective terms – community. In this connection, it should immediately be made clear that the adjective 'rich' in the title of this book does not refer to individual citizens, but rather to the collective level of the nation as a whole. In other words, it is a discourse that deals with the socio-tropic (Kinder and Klewiet 1981) plane of the national community, not the individual one of its single members.

This book thus has three main objectives. First, to show that the nationalism of the rich represents a novelty in the history of nationalism. Second, to write a comparative history of the evolution of the nationalism of the rich as formulated by the parties analysed in the case studies. Third, to identify explanatory factors for its appearance and evolution.

Nationalism: between form of consciousness and form of politics

Nationalism is considered here first as a form of consciousness – or 'a way of seeing the world' (Brubaker *et al.* 2004, p. 47) – that 'locates the source of individual identity within a "people", which is seen as the bearer of sovereignty, the central object of loyalty, and the basis of collective solidarity' (Greenfeld 1992, p. 3). This definition may seem parasitic on the term 'people', but the reason for the association between the nation and the people is historical. The word nation used to designate an elite, while the term people referred to the plebs, with a clear derogatory meaning. Their equation signalled the transition from a society segmented into orders to one composed of, at least formally, equal and sovereign members.[2] This 'light' definition accounts for nationalism as a general phenomenon that is very protean and pervasive. The other side of the coin is represented by the great many particularistic nationalisms that can possibly be formulated around a specific set of ideas defining a nation as a unique and monolithic entity. Apart from the elements of (formal) equality and sovereignty common to all nationalisms, these may be characterised by social, cultural, ethnic, political or moral elements in varying combinations that cannot be predicted or reduced to a recurring pattern. These self-understandings are social constructions – that is, symbolic and inter-subjective works of several individual minds – which prevalently take, at least when they are not yet institutionalised, a discursive form. Of course, there is much more than discourse to the creation, and especially the institutionalisation, of these national understandings. As Thomas Eriksen (cited in Özkirimli 2010, p. 215) correctly pointed out the '"sense of being in the same boat and living in the same world, with a shared destiny" results from "regular interactions, small exchanges and mutual courtesies, webs of kinship and neighbourly relations", not from some unaccountable feeling of attachment to the "imagined community" of the nation'. Yet, nationalist discourse is a fundamental component of a national self-understanding, of a narrative that helps make sense and organise the social world. It provides a frame to interpret those 'regular interactions, small exchanges and mutual courtesies' according to a specific conception of the community one lives in.

Recent advances in the research on ethnicity and nationalism propose to look at these two related phenomena as specific forms of social categorisation that allow individuals to simplify social reality through the classification of human collectivities into fixed and homogenous groups (on social categorisation see Tajfel 1978). This 'stereotyping' would thus be a natural device used by the (limited) human brain to make wide inferences about the social word on the basis of scarce information, in accordance with a principle of 'cognitive economy' (Brubaker *et al.* 2004, p. 38). Nationalism (and ethnicity more widely) can thus be seen as a cognitive device – as a kind of 'instinct' – that by reducing complexity, notably regarding other groups, makes action possible. In this perspective, nationalism would mostly act at an unconscious level and form the basis for rational action. It would be pre-rational, rather than irrational, and become salient only in specific situations, when issues of material or symbolic importance for the relevant group are considered as being at stake (Hale 2008, p. 52). This understanding is very useful because it allows explaining the persistence of ethnicity and nationalism, as well as the strength of so-called 'participant primordialism' (the belief in the nation as a community of descent), without resorting to socio-biological arguments (such as Van den Berghe 1981). Yet, at the same time, we must not lose sight of nationalism's constructed nature. While social categorisation as such might be a permanent cognitive device of uncertainty reduction, historical evidence suggests that the specific forms that such categorisation can take – nationalism among them – are contingent and come about, as well as are reproduced, through complex processes of symbolic communication. This is true not only for nationalism as a general phenomenon, but also – and more importantly – for the construction of the great many particular nationalisms that carry with them specific descriptive and normative representations of the national community influencing individuals' perception and behaviour. In other words, while an understanding of nationalism as a cognitive device for complexity reduction in situations of uncertainty can enable us to avoid the excesses of some theories of social identification, its representation as an 'instinct' should not lead us to conclude that it is an innate feature of the human brain. Historical and sociological evidence rather points to the conclusion that it results from the open system of cultural symbolic communication, rather than the closed one of biological evolution (Geertz 1964, p. 11).

One of the main consequences of a constructivist interpretation of nations and nationalism is that researchers should avoid 'groupism', i.e. 'the tendency to treat ethnic groups as substantial entities to which interests and agency can be attributed' (Brubaker *et al.* 2004, pp. 31–32). Unfortunately, many recent comparative studies on stateless nationalism have focused on nations (or regions) as units of analysis in themselves (Harvie 1994, Keating 1996, 1998, Guibernau 1999).[3] What instead should be sought is a focus on specific actors and this for two main reasons. First, an actor-centred approach helps avoid idealism, i.e. an approach to the history of ideas and identities whereby these originate at some point in time from other ideas and the retrospective look of the historian make them necessary without accounting for alternatives, inconsistencies or variation, and, especially, without consideration for human agency (Greenfeld 1992, p. 19). Second, nationalist discourses are certainly the result of complex inter-subjective symbolic processes involving wide groups of individuals and reflect their interests and existential problems, which are shaped by, as much as they shape, the social contexts in which these individuals live. But some actors play a more important role than others in crafting, modifying, spreading and activating national narratives. This is also true for the practical implementation of nationalism's political implications, be they connected to the need for nation-building and national integration in the case of state-led nationalism (Weber 1976, Billig 1995, Birch 1989), or to the wish to achieve varying degrees of self-government in the case of stateless nationalism (Breuilly 1993). Looking at nationalism in this perspective means to account for its role as a form of politics and a tool of political legitimation (Breuilly 1993, Abulof 2015). More specifically, in the stateless nation context of my case-study parties, nationalism can be seen as a form of 'remedial political action' based on a discourse expressing variations of the single core lament 'that the identity and interests of a putative nation are not properly expressed or realized in political institutions, practices, or policies' (Brubaker 1996, p. 79).

The constructivist approach described above can therefore be usefully complemented by a moderate ethnic entrepreneur perspective. According to this, political parties can establish themselves 'as poles of attraction acting as professional brokers of ethnicity' (Lipset and Rokkan 1967, p. 3). As suggested by Anthony Smith (1999, pp. 174–180), they are like 'archaeologists', who put together past and present cultural elements into a coherent narrative that they use to mobilise people. Yet, ethnic entrepreneurs are 'both dependent variables influenced by their environment and independent institutional forces affecting political development' (De Winter and Türsan 1998, pp. 6–7). Research on ethnicity and nationalism as cognitive devices confirm that while framing – meant as the 'conscious strategic efforts by groups of people to fashion shared understandings of the world and of themselves that legitimate and motivate collective action' (McAdam *et al.* 1996, p. 6) – is often an elite-driven process, ordinary individuals are not passive sponges ready to absorb whatever is thrown at them. On the contrary, the degree of fit to perceived social reality of any framing strategies is a key factor in determining whether individuals will accept it as valid or not (Kuzban *et al.* 2001).[4] In other words, frames are effective only if they are perceived as helping to make sense of social reality (for a similar argument see Breuilly 1993, p. 13). Therefore, in this book I will look first at the narratives crafted by the case-study parties, examining the specific version of the national self-understanding they have provided, the problems they have pointed at and the solutions they have proposed. In this way, I will look both at their contribution to the development and reinforcement of the national consciousness and at the ways in which they have cued it for mobilisation purposes. I will then evaluate the degree of fit of their arguments to the socio-economic context in which these have been elaborated.

The need to account for human agency in the formulation of national self-understandings pointed out above has led some to advocate a form of methodological individualism (Greenfeld 1992). This is certainly a very powerful strategy in exploring the personal motivations and the cognitive processes that lead single individuals to beget new identities and the set of ideas that underlie them. Yet, it is much less capable of accounting for their spread, political implementation or failure to do either, since it cannot but focus on a limited number of individuals. An analysis based on political parties as primary actors can help cope with this shortcoming because, while still being made up of individuals and thus reflecting their own anxieties and interests, parties are collective actors that claim to represent a community and are determined to have a direct political impact. Hence, analysing them may help bridge the gap between the individual, the social and the political dimensions. This involves looking not only at their formulation of national identity, of political problems concerning the national community and of solutions to solve these latter, but also inquiring into the growth of party support, party strategies, the opportunity structure in which they act and the impact of their action on the wider social body.

However, looking at specific actors also means clearly distinguishing between them and the wider society. While nationalism is certainly a pervasive phenomenon that has become one of the founding elements of modernity and, therefore, affects virtually all members of – at least European and Northern American – societies, we cannot expect its intensity and salience to be the same for all individuals. It is more fruitful to think of it as a property that is certainly widely distributed, but varies from one individual to another (Sperber 1985) along a continuum going from total indifference to total commitment to the national cause. While we can expect members and militants of such parties to be closer to the latter pole of the spectrum, we cannot attribute the same profile to the rest of society. We must thus be careful to generalise conclusions on the basis of the material produced by these actors and rather confront their assertions with trends concerning support for independence, the reasons for such support, subjective national identity and stereotypical representations of the parent states and/or other regions functioning as the main relevant Other in the wider social body.

What parties and how to study them?

This book relies on the comparative study of five political parties located in four Western European regions. They are: *Esquerra Republicana de Catalunya* (ERC, Catalan Left of Catalonia); the *Vlaams Belang* (VB, The Flemish Interest); the *Nieuw-Vlaamse Alliantie* (N-VA, The New Flemish Alliance); the *Lega Nord* (LN, The Northern League); and the Scottish National Party (SNP). These five parties were selected after a preliminary analysis of a wider pool of nationalist movements voicing serious economic grievances in Western Europe. Following the suggestions of several authors who have worked on stateless nationalism (Birch 1989, Keating 1996, De Winter and Türsan 1998, Keating *et al.* 2003), I privileged an in-depth contextual examination of a limited number of units to favour thick description and accuracy over generalisation, hoping that my conclusions may generate insights to be applied more widely. As the willingness to disengage from the system of national solidarity of the parent state lies at the core of the nationalism of the rich, I have decided to focus on separatist parties, which display a stronger commitment to this goal, through the pursuit of independent statehood, than autonomist ones. Also, it is this separatist version of the nationalism of the rich that is of greatest empirical interest because it threatens the stability and integrity of the respective parent states. Of course, the distinction between separatism and autonomism is often not so sharp and, as we will see in the next chapters, my case-study parties have followed gradualist strategies that have taken advantage of such ambiguity. However, all the parties in the sample have, from a certain moment on in their history, declared independent statehood as their official aim, if not in the near future at least in the long term.

It should be immediately pointed out that the SNP is a rather deviant case and this for two main reasons. First, Scotland's wealth did not accrue to Scotland but could have done so had the country seized the revenues (or a bigger share of them) of North Sea oil. Without oil, Scotland did not stand out if compared to the British average income. Moreover, had it been fully realised, this wealth would have come from the exploitation of a natural resource, thus substantially diverging from the manufacturing model prevalent in the other case studies. Second, and as a consequence of the different context in which it was operating, the SNP has consistently had to confront the accusation of Scotland being subsidised by the rest of the UK, which other case-study parties have instead made against other regions of their parent state. What, however, makes the SNP worth being included in the study is the economic case for independence made by the party, whereby this has consistently depicted Scotland as a rich, advanced nation mismanaged by successive London governments. Also, Scotland did have an evolved industrial structure, albeit a declining one, and there has been a long tradition of depicting the Scots in popular discourses as skilful and hard-working – what is often defined as the myth of the 'lad o' pairts' (McCrone 1992, pp. 182–183).

Each case study is conducted according to a two-step procedure. The first consists in the dissection of the arguments of economic victimisation and political marginalisation making up the nationalism of the rich and their evolution over time. It relies on a wider study of these parties' propaganda (Dalle Mulle 2015), which was based on Mudde's approach (2000). This entails the clear identification of the body of literature to be analysed; the construction of categories, or dimensions, within which party arguments can be organised; and the reconstruction of the 'causal chains' of concepts making up the ideological arguments under study. With regard to the dimensions of the analysis, the original study looked at the economic and political relationship of the relevant community with the parent state, the definition of the nation, the ideological profile of the party, the position on immigration, and attitudes towards Europe and the EU. Here, the emphasis will be on the first two dimensions, since they are the most relevant for the purpose of this book, but I will integrate elements of the others whenever appropriate.

Before moving to the second step of the case-study analysis, it is necessary to briefly clarify the definition of discourse used here. Discourse can be interpreted in two different although related ways. On the one hand, it can be seen as a paradigm, or better a social consensus, structuring the social world and constraining the possibilities of human imagination and understanding until new discursive formations come to upset the boundaries thus fixed.[5] According to Laclau and Mouffe (1985, p. 108), for instance:

> an earthquake or the falling of a brick is an event that certainly exists, in the sense that it occurs here and now, independently of my will. But whether their specificity as objects is constructed in terms of 'natural phenomena' or 'expressions of the wrath of God' depends upon the structuring of a discursive field. What is denied is not that such objects exist externally to thought, but the rather different assertion that they could constitute themselves as objects outside any discursive condition of emergence.

On the other, we can refer to discourse – or rather discourses – as 'ways of representing aspects of the world – the processes, relations and structures of the material world, the "mental world" of thoughts, feelings, beliefs and so forth, and the social world' (Fairclough 2003, p. 124). Different actors beget different discourses that reflect and shape their positions within society and relations with other members. Hence, 'discourses not only represent the world as it is (or rather is seen to be), they are also projective, imaginaries, representing possible worlds which are different from the actual world, and tied in to projects to change the world in particular directions [...] discourses constitute part of the resources which people deploy in relating to one another' (Fairclough 2003, p. 124). I suggest that these two definitions of discourse roughly coincide with the two aspects of nationalism discussed above. While the first meaning, which operates at a more general and abstract level, squares with nationalism as a general phenomenon – i.e. the idea of national societies as sovereign communities of equals that has progressively become hegemonic in Western Europe since at least the French Revolution – the second one, to be used mostly in the plural, refers to the construction of particularistic understandings of a specific national community.[6] It is this second meaning of discourse that will be used here.

The second step of the case-study analysis provides an inquiry into the socio-economic contexts that have favoured the formation of these arguments and their success, focusing, again, on the core claims of economic victimisation and political marginalisation. There, I try to explain why the nationalism of the rich arose at a specific point in time in the propaganda of the case-study parties and what has been its evolution. As the case studies are quite different in terms of historical evolution, institutional representation within the parent state, national traditions and cultural features, the discourse of the nationalism of the rich is the only variable shared across the sample. Hence, dissecting the narrative might lead to finding similar underlying conditions. The questions that guide such examination are: to what extent do the parties' claims correspond to the available evidence? With what cultural, socio-economic and political materials have these claims been constructed? In other words, what is the context in which they have come about and upon which they have had an impact? The purpose is not to prove the frames used by these parties to be right or wrong according to objective standards, but rather that one can examine their consistency and plausibility (see Breuilly 1993, p. 54). In other words, by comparing them with existing historical and socio-economic data, one can eventually evaluate their degree of fit to 'perceived social reality', which plays an important role in explaining whether the local population would find them useful in making sense of the social world.

There is however a third step, that goes further than the formation of the nationalism of the rich and focuses on party success as measured mainly by two variables: first, as these parties aim to convince voters of the merits of radical institutional change, a discussion of trends in support for independence and other constitutional options will help gauge their effectiveness on the attainment of this outcome; second, as political parties, they naturally strive to maximise their electoral power (either in terms of votes, or in terms of seats), hence a focus on their electoral results is necessary. This additional level of analysis – which will be carried out in Chapter 9 – is required because by stopping the study at the identification of the factors explaining the formation of the nationalism of the rich, I would leave the reader with the incorrect impression that these factors fully explain electoral outcomes. Such an effort entails the integration of insights from electoral studies, notably from the literature on sovereignty-association in Quebec (which constitutes a key precedent for my case-study parties), but also a party politics approach.

Studies on support for sovereignty-association in Quebec provide useful tools to analyse similar trends in Western Europe. Pinard and Hamilton (1986), for instance, developed a model that explains attitudes towards sovereignty-association not so much with reference to grievances – against the central government or other relevant Others in the parent state – but rather to the existence of positive or negative incentives. At the same time, they conclude that, although they are not sufficient to mobilise people in favour of constitutional change, feelings of deprivation seem necessary to determine the perception of positive incentives. Blais and Nadeau (1992) later found national identity to be the main predictor of support for sovereignty followed by the economic prospects of independence, while Howe (1998) convincingly suggested that national identity and support for sovereignty are more likely to influence an individual's evaluation of sovereignty's consequences for the economy and the French language than the other way around (or in other words one's evaluation of the structure of incentives). Hence, those Quebeckers declaring dual or intermediate national identity would be more influenced by rational considerations over the prospects of independence than those with strong Quebecois or Canadian identities. This in turn would explain both the higher stability of support for sovereignty as compared to party voting and sudden changes at specific points in time. The former would be due to the existence of a core of unconditional 'sovereigntists', while the latter is to be attributed to the capacity of political parties to convince conditional voters of the soundness of their arguments about the prospects of sovereignty, or to changed conditions in the structure of grievances and incentives. These insights will therefore be used to examine trends in support for independence in the regions where my case-study parties have operated.

In Chapter 9, I will also take a look at the political opportunity structure (POS) faced by these parties, using a modified version of the conceptualisation developed by Kriesi in the context of social movements. This mainly looks at three major components: the political system's formal institutional structure, the informal strategies used by established parties against challengers and the configuration of power among actors in the political arena (Kriesi 2005, p. 83). However, as political challengers are not passive actors, but adjust to the surrounding context, one also needs to take their adaptive strategies into account (Hepburn 2009a, Elias and Tronconi 2011b, Alonso 2012). As we will see in Chapter 9 more in detail, these strategies, along with the presence of devolved legislative and executive institutions, are the most important factors explaining the electoral evolution of my case-study parties.

Overall, the book tries to strike a middle ground between a functionalist, constructivist and actor-centre approach. It starts from the assumption that structural factors, and the change arising thereof, have a fundamental impact on human behaviour, but they are never 'objectively' and 'homogenously' understood. Thy are rather perceived in specific cultural contexts and interpreted through multiple discursive frames constructed through social interactions in which some actors play a more important role than others. By focusing on some such actors, I aim at finding the structural factors that might have influenced the formation of a new discursive formation – the nationalism of the rich – using their arguments as hints of the social problems arising from structural change. In other words, I aim at finding the factors that created a window of opportunity for such actors to arise (or reorient their discourse) and provide diagnostic and prognostic frames to identify pressing social problems and to propose specific solutions (Benford and Snow 2000, pp. 615–618). Once these actors have established themselves in the political arena, however, the elements explaining their rise are not necessarily the most useful in accounting for their electoral performance. In this respect, the rules and circumstances of the political game, along with the strategies developed by them, often provide a more fruitful ground for inquiry.

The welfare state and the dilemma between solidarity and efficiency

The main conclusion of this book is that we can interpret the nationalism of the rich as a rhetorical strategy portraying independent statehood as a way out of the dilemma between solidarity and efficiency that arose at the end of the Glorious Thirties.[7] This conclusion, which is discussed more fully in Chapters 6 and 7, is based on four main pillars, two of which are structural, while the other two are cultural.

The first pillar lies in the progressive creation in Western Europe, after the Second World War, of mechanisms of social solidarity and state involvement in the economy of unprecedented magnitude. The establishment of the welfare state has been a major transformation in the experienced reality and normative structure of Western European societies. It has led to an unprecedented level of mass wellbeing, while economic management and the efficiency of welfare service delivery have become the main principles of government legitimacy (Postan 1967, p. 25, Poggi 1990, p. 114, Mau 2003, pp. 1–8, Bommes 2012). The establishment of welfare arrangements however happened in a phase of exceptional economic growth, the so-called Glorious Thirties, during which expansion could be achieved on the basis of a policy of 'more for everybody' (Heclo 1981, p. 397). In such a context, 'private affluence and public generosity could go hand in hand' (Mishra 1984, p. 4) and questions about reciprocity, sustainability and the costs of welfare more in general, which lie at the core of welfare arrangements, could be almost completely shunned. Yet, when, from the mid-1970s on, the growth engine slowed down, and even halted at times, the costs of welfare, along with some of its inefficiencies, became much more salient and visible. In the era of 'permanent austerity' (Pierson 2001a), Western European governments began facing a dilemma almost unknown in the previous three decades, that between social solidarity and economic efficiency. This is mainly due to a structural feature of modern welfare arrangements, whereby 'the welfare state, rather than being a separate and autonomous source of wellbeing which provides incomes and services as a citizen's right, is itself highly dependent upon the prosperity and continued profitability of the economy' (Offe 1984, p. 150). An increasing portion of Western European publics began perceiving the fiscal burden of welfare arrangements as excessive, while, at the same time, support for welfare arrangements has kept showing considerable resilience, thus ruling out radical welfare reform (Taylor-Gooby 1988, Pierson 2001a, Roosma *et al.* 2013). In specific places, dissatisfaction was fuelled by mismanagement of public finances, perception of welfare fraud, corruption and inefficiency in the delivery of welfare services.

The second pillar is uneven territorial development. Sharp income differentials among different areas of the same country do set the ground for the territorialisation of claims concerning such unequal distribution of resources and burdens. While welfare arrangements automatically redistribute on the basis of individual incomes without taking into account where such individuals reside, the concentration of relatively richer individuals in some areas and relatively poorer ones in others can generate visible inter-territorial transfers.[8] Yet, inter-territorial transfers as such need not be problematic. Not only within virtually every European country are there transfers between richer and poorer areas that do not generate major political controversies, but also one might find major imbalances (and thus resource transfers) between different areas within rich regions themselves.

Here is where the first cultural pillar comes in. It consists in the existence of national – or cultural/ethnic cleavages – squaring with the territorial income differentials mentioned above. Such a coincidence allows interpreting inter-territorial transfers in nationalist terms: as *transfers between different groups* inhabiting different areas of the same state, rather than as *transfers between members of the same group* inhabiting different areas of the same state. In other words, it explains why, while the welfare state is usually 'colour-blind' in its redistributive functioning, recipients and contributors are not. This links back to an important feature of welfare arrangements more in general, that is, their bounded nature. The Western European welfare state has been created around and consolidated through a process of internal bonding through external bounding and this because, more generally, social sharing builds upon social closure (Ferrera 2005, p. 2, Bommes 2012, p. 28). In light of these considerations, it is easy to understand how the existence of sub-state national cleavages can threaten the capacity of the state to legitimately extract the considerable resources necessary to sustain solidarity – especially in times of slow growth and austerity – from certain sections of the population on account of 'national' solidarity (McEween and Moreno 2005, p. 6). At the same time, this assertion should be nuanced. The context in which my case-study parties have operated have been characterised by dual identities and discourses of partnership between the relevant community and the other populations of the parent state. Therefore, identity alone is not sufficient to justify a rejection of solidarity with the parent state. Other arguments, referring to the principles of reciprocity, trust and fairness underlying welfare provisions, are widely used to warrant a redefinition of the community that can legitimately deserve solidarity. In this connection, the list of deservingness criteria proposed by Wim Van Oorschot (2000, 2006) and the ideas about conditional solidarity elaborated by Abts and Kochuyt (2013, 2014) constitute very useful analytical tools that I will briefly introduce here and further expand in Chapter 6.

Van Oorschot (2000, 2006) identified the following five criteria used by European publics to judge the legitimacy of social support:

- *identity*: members of the relevant community (usually the national community) are seen as more deserving than outsiders;
- *control*: the more recipients are seen as being responsible for their state of need, the lower their deservingness;
- *attitude*: recipients should, at least symbolically, pay back the support they receive, for instance, by not demanding it and making a good effort to get out of their needy situation;
- *reciprocity*: people who contribute more to the system should receive more once in need;
- *need*: the more needy a person is the more it deserves help.

My case-study parties draw extensively on different combinations of such criteria to reject solidarity with the parent state. Two combinations of such criteria elaborated by Abts and Kochuyt (2013, 2014) are particularly relevant to my analysis: welfare producerism and welfare chauvinism. The former can be defined as a conditional conception of solidarity prevalently based on the criteria of control, reciprocity and attitude, while the latter as a conditional conception of solidarity prevalently based on identity. Although these two are not mutually exclusive, it is useful to distinguish them because the identity criterion works in a fundamentally different way from the others. First, it is often – although not always – linked to an ascribed criterion (origin) rather than a behavioural one. Second, it is logically prior to the others since it relates to the determination of the 'legitimate community of social sharing' to which specific principles of justice and deservingness criteria apply (see Deutsch 1975, p. 142, Opotow 1990, pp. 1–4).

Furthermore, the welfare producerism formulated by my case-study parties has undergone a peculiar process of 'culturalisation' – which constitutes the second cultural pillar. By means of a cultural-determinist explanation of the region's socio-economic development as primarily, if not exclusively, deriving from the hard-working ethos, entrepreneurship and thrift of the local population, these parties have been able to make the 'imagined community of welfare producers' discursively coincide with the imagined community of the nation. The advantage of such a culturalised form of welfare producerism lies in that it can be interpreted as a less divisive discourse than a 'culturally neutral' producerist rhetoric and these for two reasons. First, the self-understanding of the nation as a community of people endowed with an exceptional hard-working ethos and entrepreneurship conveys the image of a society naturally producing surplus resources that could be used to improve welfare without affecting the competitiveness of the national economy. Second, and especially for those parties that have openly used stigmatising language against welfare recipients in other areas of the parent state and, at the same time, called for austerity measures to reduce the fiscal burden of welfare, the identification between the nation and the community of producers suggests the 'externalisation' of the negative effects of austerity on the dependent populations of the parent state. In such a discursive context, austerity and solidarity are compatible, since austerity will rebalance the distribution of benefits and burdens between the recipients (to be found outside the in-group) and the contributors (made up of the members of the in-group).

Sources and structure of the book

This book is based on the study of primary sources encompassing the parties' internal and external propaganda. They include: party programmes, campaign material (party posters and leaflets), thematic brochures and party papers. The material collected covers most of the manifestos and papers published by the parties analysed during the time frame of study, i.e. between the appearance of the arguments of the nationalism of the rich – which varies from one case to another – and 2015, when the analysis stops for reasons of feasibility. The only major gap concerns the SNP which, in fact, did not consistently publish a paper until 2000 when it started distributing 'Snapshot' and, later, the 'Saltire'. Minor problems in collecting party papers have been encountered with regard to the LN, for the period 2004–2012 because of the closure of the party's archives in Milan after my first visit. I was later able to collect copies of the party daily newspaper *La Padania* from the digital newspapers archive of the University of Padua – equal to two months' worth of daily publications before each national and regional election between 2003 and 2012 – while from 2012 to its closure in December 2014, digital copies of *La Padania* where available on the party's website. I thus selected a random sample of them equal to about four issues a month. I also used a series of editorials from the journal republished on the party's website and covering the period 2008–11. Similarly, I was not able to consult copies of the VB's monthly magazine for the period 2003–06. Also, for reasons linked to my limited proficiency in Dutch, I have consulted only a randomly selected sample of VB's papers equal to about four issues per year. Likewise, as

ERC's monthly turned briefly into a weekly for the period between March 2008 and December 2011, I randomly selected an issue a month for that period. On the contrary, I was able to consult all copies of the N-VA's monthly magazine because they were spread over a much shorter period of time. The research on which this book is based has also entailed semi-structured interviews with 21 elected politicians from the case-study parties (the list is available in Annex 1).

The book is divided into nine chapters according to the following structure. Chapter 1 provides a historical survey of nationalist discourses in the nineteenth and twentieth centuries in order to look for precedents of the nationalism of the rich. Chapters 2 to 5 present the case-study analysis, each focusing on a single party except for Chapter 3, which treats the VB and the N-VA together on account of their common context. Chapter 6 discusses comparatively the discourses of the case-study parties, while the following two chapters draw together the main findings concerning the factors explaining the rise of the nationalism of the rich. More specifically, Chapter 7 deals with domestic factors and also provides a wider comparative framework, bringing illustrative examples from other contexts not covered in the case studies. Chapter 8, instead, takes a brief look at external phenomena such as globalisation and European integration that hover in the background in the central chapters without being treated in-depth. Chapter 9 looks at the evolution of support for independence in these regions and the electoral results of the case-study parties, trying to explain these with reference to the POS in which the parties have operated, as well as to the specific strategies that they have adopted.

A final note: this book does not aim at explaining why nationalism, in general, has regained life in the last quarter of the twentieth century in Western Europe, but it rather strives to inquire into the sources of a specific nationalist self-understanding that developed during the same period. Yet, when looking at Europe since the mid-1970s, with the only exception of similar forces in the Basque Country and, perhaps, Northern Ireland, the separatist parties analysed here have been among the most active and successful in the entire continent, while, in recent years, a subset of them – ERC, the N-VA and the SNP – have been leading one of the most formidable challenges to state integrity in the history of Western Europe since the end of the Second World War.

Notes

1 The definition of the nation as wealthy is first and foremost based on the self-understanding of the community developed by the case-study parties themselves.
2 Although there is huge disagreement in the literature about the timing of this transition (timing that does not concern us here), the fact that such a transition did happen sometime in the past in most of Western Europe is agreed upon by several authors (see Anderson 1983, p. 16, Gellner 1983, p. 73, Greenfeld 1992, pp. 2–4, Brubaker 1996, p. 85).

3 This is also true of Gourevitch's (1979) pioneering study of the 're-emergence of peripheral nationalism' in the West, which provides insights into the importance of the mismatch between the economic and political power of the relevant region analysed here more in detail.
4 The study referred to racism rather than to nationalism, but these can be seen as related forms of social categorisation (see Brubaker *et al.* 2004).
5 This is especially the case with some post-structuralist interpretations of Foucault (1972). See for instance Özkirimli (2010, p. 206).
6 See Calhoun (1997, p. 6) for a similar line of argument. I am fully aware that discourse is not limited to 'what is being said', but extends to who speaks, when, where and how. However, I cannot apply here the same methodological focus on the micro-level required by this more extensive definition of discourse (see Fairclough 2003, Schmidt 2008). My concern rather is with an analysis of the construction and evolution of my case-study parties' nationalist arguments over an extended period of time, which clearly requires a macro-analysis.
7 This conclusion is in line with – but further specifies – Keating's (1996, p. xii) argument that 'minority nationalism may be a mechanism for problem solving, in particular for reconciling economic competitiveness and social solidarity in the face of the international market'.
8 The visibility of inter-territorial transfers also depends on the level of knowledge about them. As we will see in the case studies, the spread of academic works on inter-territorial redistribution largely contributed to their increased political salience. On the role of improved knowledge about redistribution in undermining (under some conditions) its legitimacy see Rosanvallon (2000, p. 4).

1 The nationalism of the rich

A new phenomenon

The rise of sub-state nationalism in Western democracies from the late 1960s onwards was shocking for mainstream theorists who had long predicted the disappearance of such 'primitive' reactions in the developed world. As Anthony Smith stated in the late 1970s:

> these autonomist movements have arisen this century in their political form, in well established, often ancient states, with clear and recognised national boundaries, and with a relatively prosperous economy. While not minimising considerable differences of degree, all these states are fairly industrialised, and much of the population is literate and even quite well educated. And yet, despite all these advantages, which led theorists to postulate the early demise of nationalism, the ethnic minorities seem more discontented than before, and some even wish to go it alone.
>
> (Smith 1979, p. 153)

Along the same lines, Anthony Birch (1989, pp. 37–39) pointed out that between, roughly, 1850 and 1960, European political theory had been dominated by the assumption that progress and historical necessity required the expansion of units from smaller to larger scales, and especially from more backward to more developed institutions. After all, this had been the way national development had been pursued in most of the western part of the continent, i.e. through the slow integration of diverse pre-existing human communities into the wider nation-states of England (and later Great Britain), France, Spain, Germany and Italy. As confirmed by Eric Hobsbawm (1990, pp. 32–33), in the nineteenth century 'the building of nations was seen inevitably as a process of expansion [...] it was accepted in theory that social evolution expanded the scale of human social units from family and tribe to county and canton, from the local to the regional, the national and eventually the global'. This opinion held sway among liberals and Marxists alike. While John Stuart Mill (1988, p. 363) argued that 'nobody can suppose that it is not more beneficial for a Breton, or a Basque of French Navarre, to be brought into the current of the ideas and feelings of highly civilized and cultivated people – to be a member of the French nationality', Marx and Engels suggested that the fate of cultural minorities in the newly formed nation-states 'was to be consigned to the rag-bag of history' (quoted in Birch, 1989, p. 38). In the following section, I will look in more detail at such processes of territorial aggregation.

The formation of national states in Western Europe: a tale of advanced expanding centres

The process of progressive territorial consolidation that occurred in most of Western Europe began in the late Middle Ages at the edges of the so-called 'trade route belt', that is, the stretch of independent and confederated city-states roughly extending from Central and Northern Italy to the North Sea and the Baltic, through Western Germany and Eastern France. As argued by Stein Rokkan (1973, p. 79), 'the great paradox of European development is that the strongest and the most durable systems emerged at the periphery of the old Empire'. The disintegration of this latter brought about the creation of a series of dynastic units that started competing for the creation of new 'centres'.[1] The creation of 'monopolies of power' was harder in the more densely populated and richer urban trade belt, where many resourceful centres competed with each other, which explains why dynastic territorial consolidation mostly started in the periphery. Military force played a major role in the process of centre-formation. In the early phase, it acted as a primary source of economic improvement. The division between the political and economic spheres is indeed something of a recent invention. In most societies based on bartering systems – and to some extent even in later ones – force is a key instrument of economic development (Elias 1975, p. 88). The late Middle Ages were no exception: land was the major source of power and conquest the major source of honour. Thus, military territorial acquisitions entailed improvements for both the economic resources and symbolic status of kings and their vassals (Blockmans 1994, pp. 224–225).[2]

However, war was expensive and became increasingly dearer through the centuries, because of technological progress and international competition. The monetisation of the European economy that occurred between the fourteenth and sixteenth centuries initially tipped the financial balance of power in favour of the rich urban centres of the trade belt. Rulers willing to expand their domains looked with greed at cities and city-states, either as allies from which to receive loans, or as subjects from which to extract the necessary resources through coercion. As argued by Stefano Bartolini (2005, p. 73):

in early modern Europe, states and capitalism seemed to develop according to different preconditions and prerequisites [...] The most highly developed market forces and infrastructures of merchant capitalism flourished in the area of low hierarchical control from Central Italy to the Flanders. By contrast, the most developed state hierarchical infrastructures consolidated in the relatively poorer and also culturally peripheral areas, and were often heavily indebted with the city-belt lending institutions.

Yet, the early divorce between territorial expansion and capital was quickly reversed. In the longer run, the monetisation of the economy opened up the possibility to turn the military monopoly established by a ruler over a specific territory into a fiscal one through the collection of taxes (Elias 1975, pp. 36–37). The 'fiscalisation' of territorial rule had another major consequence for the consolidation of royal possessions: in the feudal economy rulers were forced to compensate their allies by giving away parts of their territory; in the monetary one, they could simply pay them through the income coming from the realm (Elias 1975, pp. 179–181). The growth of trade and the later rise of new industries allowed territorial centres to further expand and consolidate their military-administrative machineries without exhausting their resource base (Flora *et al.* 1999, p. 130). Size mattered not only for military purposes, but also because it played a key role in the profitability of 'national markets'. From 1600 onwards, the newly formed and enlarging territorial states progressively adopted mercantilist and protectionist economic policies that considerably harmed the trade activities of city-states. More generally, such policies decisively contributed to the 'nationalisation and territorialisation of capitalism' (Bartolini 2005, p. 73).

Hence, while in the early phase of monetisation city-states enjoyed an edge over less developed territorial peripheries – and although many city-states survived well into the nineteenth century – 'the increasing scale of war and the knitting together of the European state system through commercial, military, and diplomatic interaction eventually gave the war-making advantage to those states that could field great standing armies; states having access to a combination of large rural populations, capitalists, and relatively commercialised economies won out' (Tilly 1990, p. 58).[3] Alternative combinations of capital and coercion between the capital-intensive pole represented by city-states and the coercion-intensive one of some eastern empires existed throughout the period between the late Middle Ages and the triumph of national states in the nineteenth and early twentieth centuries. In the long run, however, most converged, through a kind of 'natural selection' by means of war and institutional imitation, towards a 'capitalised coercion' model best embodied by the examples of France and England. Indeed, these two countries largely managed to make their respective territorial cores coincide with important urban systems of high capital concentration – Paris and London – that progressively consolidated their domain over adjacent areas (Tilly 1990, pp. 38–66).

This kind of pattern is visible in the formation of Portugal, where the early creation of a modern territorial state in the seventeenth century coincided with the rise of Lisbon in the role of a commercial capital of continental pre-eminence (Hespanha 1994). Italy and Germany, on the contrary, were late-comers in this process. High urban density and territorial fragmentation, especially in Northern Italy and Western Germany, largely contributed to the delay in territorial consolidation. Yet, the emergence of two territorial states, the Kingdom of Sardinia (also know as Piedmont-Sardinia) and the Kingdom of Prussia respectively, combining high capital concentration, military force and administrative capacity – relative to the rest of the area – constituted the prelude to the unification of Italy and Germany respectively. Territorial conquest and agglomeration under the leadership of these two cores played a key role. Piedmont clearly led economically and politically, retaining decisive political influence for a long time even after the capital moved to Rome. By contrast, Germany showed a much more pronounced polycephalic character and Berlin had to compete with the strong economic centres of the western part of the country (Rokkan 1973, pp. 79–80, Rokkan and Urwin 1983, pp. 37–38). Around the mid-nineteenth century, Prussia was one of the richest states in the German confederation. With the exception of Saxony and the city-states of Hamburg and Bremen, the richest provinces in terms of GDP per capita were to be found in the Hohenzollerns' territory. This provided the Kingdom with the means – and the interest – necessary to lead the process of German unification. The Kingdom, however, owed its dynamism and prosperity to its Western possessions – Rhineland and Westphalia – acquired at the Congress of Vienna in 1815. During the nineteenth century, these two areas underwent a process of rapid commercialisation, and later industrialisation, that accounted for much of the economic vitality of the state (Ziblatt 2006, pp. 32–56). After unification, the polycephalic reality of Germany came to be reflected in the institutional architecture of the country, which respected the economic strength of the western areas, as well as the identity of the kingdoms absorbed between 1866 and 1871, through a strategy of territorial federalisation. As Rokkan (1973, p. 211) pointed out:

> the great difference between the German and the Italian unification processes reflected this contrast in the balance between central and peripheral forces. In Germany the highly urbanised western regions were unified from a military periphery: Prussia. In this situation, federalisation was the best strategy of unification. In Italy, the unifying power had its base in the highly urbanised north and the state builders did not need to resort to a federalising strategy to gain control of the southern periphery.

The strength and resistance to territorial integration of the non-territorial trade belt, however, should not be exaggerated. Two of its core areas indeed merged quite early on through processes of consolidation that, although of a peculiar consociational nature, did lead to the formation of modern territorial states: Switzerland and the Netherlands. While Switzerland probably represents the best embodiment of a well-balanced polycephalic federation with no true core area, the Netherlands turned into a much more centralised federation in which the economic dominance of Holland went along with its political centrality (Flora *et al.* 1999, pp. 176–179).

The gravitational pull of strong centres, both in military-administrative and economic terms, was accompanied by nation-building processes that took advantage of state institutions to promote cultural and national homogeneity, although to different extents in different places. While France is often considered the epitome of such a process (Weber, 1976), similar policies were adopted all over Western Europe, with the only exceptions – arguably – of the multilingual Swiss federation, where cantonal mono-lingualism was enforced, and, to a lesser extent, the United Kingdom, where Scotland enjoyed a high degree of cultural autonomy (Flora *et al.* 1999, pp. 170–190).

The formation of Spain, however, only partially mirrors the general tendency – described above – of economic and political centrality to coincide in processes of state formation in Western Europe, or, where policephality prevailed, to lead to well-balanced federal structures. Whereas the union of the Crown of Castile and that of Aragon did coincide with the economic decline of Barcelona and the rise of Castile and its thriving urban centres, the unification of its different components into a modern centralised territorial state occurred only from the eighteenth century onwards, when Castile's economic fortune was steadily declining. The simultaneous slow economic revival of Catalonia, later to become a true industrial power-house paralleled only by the Basque Country, further complicated the picture (Elliott 1963, pp. 1–21, 2002, pp. 361–386).

The trajectories of progressive territorial consolidation of the major Western European countries seen above seem to confirm Charles Tilly's (1994, p. 22) assertion that, as centres of concentration of capital, 'important trading cities managed to build into the state apparatus more of their local and regional power structures than did local and regional market centres'. In this framework, the nationalism of the rich is interesting for two main reasons. First, as we will see in more detail in the case studies, this nationalist discourse in part arose as the result of changes in the economic relationship between different areas within consolidated territorial states that did not lead to an immediate adjustment in their political representation – or at least to the perception of a deficit of political representation. The economic rise of Catalonia between the end of the nineteenth and the beginning of the twentieth century can be seen as an early example of such a dynamic, thus accounting for the pioneering role of the Catalan nationalist movement of the time. The outstripping of the Walloon economy by that of Flanders, the rise of what has been called the 'Third Italy' and the discovery of North Sea oil are later instances of a similar phenomenon.

Second, war making is generally considered as a major factor explaining centre-formation and state-building. Yet, since the end of the Second World War – and progressively so after the end of the US-USSR confrontation – war has become ever less a priority for most Western European states, as also evidenced by dramatic reductions in military spending. This does not mean the demise of the sovereign territorial state. On the contrary, as the following chapters will show, what my case-study parties seek is precisely a sovereign independent state, although they are open to accept the constraints of the contemporary interdependent world on par with all other existing states. Yet, the nationalism of the rich does reflect a lower degree of concern with size and military might, as sources of power in the contemporary world, and a more pronounced focus on economic capability, whereby a smaller size can even turn into a competitive advantage. While this lower concern with size does not only depend on security aspects – see Chapter 8 – and it might still be a temporary phenomenon due to the peculiar circumstances of the last 70 years, it does mark an important change in Western European history.

Minority nationalism: the rebellion of the backward periphery?

In the 1960s and 1970s, a revival of nationalist, ethnic and cultural conflicts spurred a turnaround in academia. Several authors started questioning not only the efficacy, but also the necessity of processes of national integration for the functioning of democracy (Birch 1989). The most interesting reactions in the field of the study of nationalism came from Michael Hechter and Tom Nairn. With his 1975 *Internal Colonialism*, Hechter criticises 'diffusionist' theories of national integration and proposes to explain the rise of peripheral nationalism in the UK with the 'internal colonialism model'. According to this framework, the homogenisation of peripheral areas into the dominant culture of the core, due to the increased contacts between the two under conditions of modernity that the diffusionists postulated, did not come about because the more advanced group instead tended to institutionalise its position of domination over the periphery. This institutionalisation would not only concern the economic dimension, but also the cultural one and the prestige associated with each culture. The result would be a stratification system that he calls the 'cultural division of labour', leading to different ethnic and national identifications in the two groups (Hechter 1977, pp. 1–14).

Hechter's theory has been criticised on different accounts (see Page 1978), the most important being that the data he uses does not fit the facts (Kendrick *et al.* 1985). What is interesting, however, is Hechter's suggestion that nationalism would arise out of the cultural division of labour imposed by the core-periphery relation of domination. Since the core is not interested in acculturation:

> to the extent that social stratification in the periphery is based on observable cultural differences, there exists the probability that the disadvantaged group will, in time, reactively assert its own culture as equal or superior to that of the relatively advantaged core. This may help it conceive of itself as a separate 'nation' and seek independence. Hence, in this situation, acculturation and national development may be inhibited by the desires of the peripheral group for independence from a situation perceived to be exploitative.
>
> (Hechter 1977, p. 10)

In *The Break-up of Britain*, Nairn takes issue with Hechter as far as the revival of nationalism in Scotland is concerned, but at the same time agrees with him on the idea implicit in the model – i.e. that nationalism comes about in exploited and disadvantaged peripheries. Nairn even turns this idea into the pillar of a general theory of nationalism. Nationalism, he writes, 'arose out of a host of earlier phenomena as the protest of under-developed peoples. It became their way of mobilising, and trying to catch up with already industrialised areas. Over much of the world, too, it was an ideological weapon of liberation from dominance by the latter' (Nairn 2003, p. 172).[4] However, in accordance with his claim that Scotland does not fit this description, he points to the existence of another, 'neglected but significant', category of peoples who

> turned nationalist in order to liberate themselves from alien domination – yet did so, typically, not from a situation of colonial under-development but from one of relative progress. They were nationalities that struggled to free their own strong development from what they had come to perceive as the backwardness around them – from some larger, politically dominant power whose stagnation or archaism had become an obstacle to their farther progress.
>
> (Nairn 2003, p. 172)

Nairn has been widely criticised by later authors, especially on account of the presumed functionalism of his theory (Orridge 1981a, 1981b), as well as because locating the origins of nationalism in the periphery of the most advanced European countries would simply not square with historical events (Breuilly 1993, p. 413). What concerns us here, however, is not the validity of Nairn's suggestions as a general theory of nationalism, but rather the fact that he identifies Scotland as a case of 'overdevelopment nationalism' and that this is seen as somewhat of an exception in the history of nationalism. Even more interestingly, looking for precedents of such 'overdevelopment nationalism' in the past, he mentions Belgium,

Bohemia, the Basque Country, Catalonia and Croatia as kindred cases. Let us thus proceed to analyse these more closely.

With its wide array of minority nations and nationalities, the Habsburg Empire is a good place to start an inquiry of possible precedents of the nationalism of the rich. Nairn mentions Bohemia and Croatia as regions that could show the kind of 'overdevelopment nationalism' that he attributes to Scotland. In his critique of Nairn's model, Breuilly also added the Magyars, as an example of a privileged group within the empire, rather than a dispossessed one, which developed strong nationalist feelings. In economic terms, as late as 1910, the most industrialised areas of the empire were parts of Austria, notably Vienna, and the Czech lands of Bohemia-Moravia-Silesia, with 46 per cent and 51 per cent of the population employed in industry. The relative figures for Hungary and Croatia were 23 per cent and 13 per cent respectively. As far as GDP per capita is concerned, while the Austrian-Bohemian area was close to the average of Western Europe, Hungary's reached about 57 per cent and the Balkan countries did not go beyond 40 per cent (Berend 2003, p. 179). As a matter of fact, 'the Austrian and Czech lands emerged as an industrialized regional core with agricultural peripheries within the monarchy and in the neighboring Balkan countries' (Berend 2003, p. 150). Yet, the economic relationship between the Czechs and the Germans was not one among equals. Most of the industry was controlled by the Germans, who also constituted the overwhelming majority of the Austrian bureaucracy. Despite the growth, in the last quarter of the nineteenth century, of a Czech middle-class that by 1914 managed to own a quarter of the textile industry, an Austro-German still earned on average 25 per cent more than a Czech (Rudolph 1976, p. 19).

But what about their claims? Before the 1867 Austro-Hungarian compromise, the main demand of the Czech national movement consisted in the reintroduction of the Bohemian 'state right' (*Staatsrecht*), i.e. the legal status of the Czech kingdom under the monarchy. This would have entailed some form of autonomy, recognition of the Czech nation and equal status for the Czech language in the education system and the government (Berend 2003, pp. 102–105). The Czech were disappointed by the 1867 compromise, as they saw themselves deserving equal status with the Magyars. From the 1870s on, the political struggle focused on language rights, which the emergence of the radical Young Czech Party, in the late 1880s, tied to demands for universal suffrage. The nationalism of the Young Czechs mainly consisted of resistance to Germanisation and the continued demand for Bohemian state right (Winters 1969, p. 430). The party advocated socio-economic reforms, but these mainly concerned employment opportunities in the lower ranks of the administration for Czech people, defence of small farmers from foreign competition and a ban on discriminatory practices on the part of German cartels in the industrial and banking sectors (Winters 1969, pp. 433–442). Such an account is also confirmed by Breuilly, who points out that Bohemian cities became the stage for a confrontation between an advancing Czech lower middle-class and the Germans occupying the upper strata. He stressed that 'small Czech merchants, retailers and manufacturers objected to liberal economic policies which seemed to favour larger German competitors' (Breuilly 1993, p. 133) and this, in turn, brought about a mobilisation of the Germans who fought harshly against competition from Czech labour willing to work for lower salaries.

The positions and arguments of the Magyar and Croat national movements seem to conform even less to the rhetoric of the nationalism of the rich. Economically, the areas in which these two movements acted occupied an intermediate position between the industrialised West and the most backward rural areas of the South and the East. The Magyar landed aristocracy enjoyed a high standard of living due to its hold over the rich agricultural production of the large Hungarian estates. Furthermore, both the Magyar and Croat elites were politically privileged, although to different extents. The Croats enjoyed a special relationship with the Hapsburg Crown and, although to varying degrees, they benefited from some form of autonomy under Hungarian control, which was officially recognised by the 1868 Croatian-Hungarian compromise. Yet, despite such agreement, the Croats of Croatia-Slavonia were not spared the harsh policy of Magyarisation that gave renewed strength to the idea of 'Trialism', i.e. the transformation of the empire into a federal union of Germans, Magyars and South Slavs. Thus, the main claims of the Croat national movement were based on the recognition of the historic rights of the Croat kingdom, first, and the project of unification with the Southern Slavs, later, rather than on any specific socio-economic platform (Kann 1950, pp. 233–259).

Before the 1867 compromise, the Hungarian upper nobility consistently opposed the modernisation policies promoted by the Hapsburg monarchy since the end of the eighteenth century. It especially resented the abolition of serfdom, the attempts to introduce German as the only language of the empire and, more generally, the trend of political centralisation that threatened its historical rights. In the first half of the nineteenth century, national demands revolved around linguistic legislation. An economic agenda did blossom under the leadership of Lajos Kossuth, but reflected the primitive development of the Hungarian economy. Kossuth called for protective tariffs against Austrian competition and urged his compatriots to buy only Hungarian industrial products in order to boost the infant local manufacturing sector (Berend 2003, pp. 105–111). However, the economic balance progressively swung to favour the Magyars. As argued by Andrew Janos (1982, p. 321): 'while Hungarian nationalists never stopped complaining about the depredations of Austria [...] the economic relationship between the two halves of the realm was gradually reversed, until it had reached the point where it could be safely said that Hungary exploited Austria, by refusing to pay her fair share of common defense and overhead expenses,

and by forcing upon the empire a system of protective tariffs, highly injuri-
ous to Austro-German and Bohemian industrial interests'. The 1867 compromise elevated the Magyars to a status unrivalled by other nationalities
in the empire. Austria and Hungary were de facto independent except for a
common ruler, army, ministry of foreign affairs and a financial contribution to these two activities. The Magyar political elite enjoyed full powers
over the relationship with the nationalities inhabiting its territory and consistently applied a policy of cultural assimilation and economic discrimination. Thus, until the turn of the twentieth century, the Magyars were
among the strongest supporters of the empire. Things began to turn sour
with the rise of the Independence Party in 1894, which, emboldened by
Hungary's good economic performance, mainly due to the tariff system,
believed that Hungary could stand alone. However, although there were
some clashes over the periodic negotiation of the common expenditures,
the real bone of contention related to the military, where the Magyar
nationalists demanded an independent militia with Magyar as the official
language (Mason 1997, pp. 16–45).

An interesting case not mentioned by Nairn and, yet again, part of the
Habsburg Empire is Lombardy. The Risorgimento's historical tradition
portrayed the Habsburg policy as discriminatory and detrimental to the
interests of the Lombard economy. Such a view, however, has been largely
reconsidered. First, while being one of the richest territories of the empire
between 1815 and 1859, and enjoying a buoyant export-oriented economy,
Lombardy's per capita GDP was still about half that of Lower Austria and
mainly derived from an over-reliance on the rather primitive silk industry
(Pichler 2001, pp. 35–38). The myth of an unbearable Austrian taxation
was mainly based on the high revenues deriving from export duties on silk,
which did not negatively influence trade and were offset by disproportional
levels of public spending. Second, although there were tensions between
the economic interests of the Lombards and the rationales guiding imperial
economic policy, there was no formulation of a clear Lombard common
economic interest, but rather a constellation of varying interests often at
odds with each other. What is most striking in this connection, is that
within the general debate on whether or not to industrialise the Lombard
economy as a step towards the modernisation of the whole of Italy that
took place in the Lombard press in the first half of the nineteenth century,
not only was the empire not the object of scorn and loathing, but it was
not even taken into consideration. As made clear by Kent Greenfield (1965,
p. 267) 'the Lombard journalists did not oppose the Austrians; they
ignored them'.

Similar arguments about an unbearable fiscal burden as lying at the
roots of the Belgian secession from the Kingdom of the Netherlands in
1830 have been made by some early nationalist historiography. Leon van
der Essen (1920, p. 151), for instance, mentioned the fact that the Belgians
were asked to pay for the debts incurred by the Dutch Republic, as well as

for the defence of the Dutch colonies from which they did not derive any advantages, as a reason for the failure of the union of the Low Countries. Yet such a claim is nowhere to be found in more nuanced treatments of the subject. Els Witte (2009a, pp. 21–28) points out that the 1830 revolution stemmed from a strange alliance between a liberal, upwardly mobile, intellectual middle-class that had no specific economic grievance, but simply wanted to see recognised its new status by pressing through political and social reforms, on the one hand, and the landed gentry that, along with the clergy, was dissatisfied with the religious policies pursued by William I, on the other. Ernst Kossmann (1978, pp. 130–131) provides further details of the economic situation of the Kingdom of the Netherlands. The malaise of the early 1820s gave way, for the rest of the decade, to slow but constant growth. As compared to the period of French occupation, taxation decreased and it was in any case higher in the North, where per capita contributions averaged 17 guilders, than in the South, where they reached only 11 guilders. All this left the dominant economic elites quite content with their prosperity for the entire period. Kossmann (1978, pp. 133–147) did point out that, despite lack of clear evidence, some of the Belgian liberals were convinced that the young and vigorous Belgium would take over the stagnant and immobile Northern Netherlands as the leading force within the Kingdom and when they realised that this would not happen, opted for secession. Yet, this did not clearly figure in their programme, which was rather geared around demands for wider liberties including, free press, free education and linguistic freedom, thus largely ignoring social and economic problems.

About a century later, however, Belgium did show signs of fiscal grievances coming from the economic core of the country (back then Wallonia) against the fiscal exploitation of the poorer periphery (Flanders). In 1930, the government announced that it wanted to establish a provincially based system of child allowances with a compensation mechanism whereby provinces with a surplus – i.e. with a lower amount of large families – had to pay half of that to a national fund supporting those in deficit. As families tended to be larger in Flanders, the project sparked protests in Wallonia. The proposal was modified in 1935, when the government limited the amount that deficit provinces could receive to a 25 per cent contribution on top of the allowance that they had to pay to families resident on their territory. Yet, the debate went on and ended only with the onset of the War. Léon-Eli Troclet calculated in 1939 that the system cost Wallonia 200 million francs, or 3.75 per cent of the Walloon wages (Boehme 2008b, pp. 475–481). Although the imbalance was in fact one between industrial centres and the country-side, it was interpreted as leading to inter-territorial transfers between Flemish and Walloon provinces and, since the debate coincided with the first sign of industrial slowdown in the south of the country, some concluded that Wallonia could better use the resources going to Flanders to put its own unemployed to work. As argued by Olivier Boehme (2008b, p. 481), the child allowances debate suggests that 'as soon as the government created new financial mechanisms for social and economic purposes, the resulting "profit-and-loss" calculations became a new bone of contention between two separate and rapidly "consolidating" regional communities, which became ever more tightly-knit by the very process of calculation' (see also Van Goethem 2010, p. 175).

This conclusion is in line with the main argument of this book about the formation of the nationalism of the rich, i.e. the establishment of substantial forms of automatic redistribution – albeit incipient ones as was the case in Belgium during the interwar years – in countries characterised by territorial identities squaring with uneven development are likely to lead to interpreting fiscal issues in inter-territorial terms. Yet, the child allowance debate remained a very limited issue in the politics of the time in Belgium and never led to a coherent set of nationalist arguments deprecating the fiscal exploitation of richer Wallonia by poorer Flanders. This is also confirmed by an analysis of similar conflicts about another important measure introduced in the same period, i.e. unemployment benefits, which however, were not interpreted along territorial lines (Boehme 2008b, pp. 480–481). The incipient nature of the social policy of the time along with the weakness of the Walloon identity – which could hardly be defined as a full national one back then – certainly constrained the formulation of a fully-fledged nationalism of the rich in interwar years Belgium.

Catalonia and the Basque Country: forerunners of the nationalism of the rich

There are two cases, however, among those mentioned by Nairn that can, to a large extent, be considered forerunners of the nationalism of the rich. They are represented by the nationalist movements that arose in Catalonia and the Basque Country between the end of the nineteenth and the beginning of the twentieth century.

Analysing the then Catalan-Spanish relationship, Joan Culla (1999, p. 41) argued that 'for the greatest majority of Spanish politicians, it was incomprehensible and unacceptable that Catalonia, the strongest, most prosperous, and most European territory would demand autonomy to a state within which it enjoyed economic hegemony. Somebody expressed it in the form of a joke: "It is the first case of a metropolis that wants to emancipate itself from its colonies"'.

The rise of nationalism in Catalonia, in the second half of the nineteenth century, coincided with a spectacular economic development accompanied by limited political power, which encouraged the Catalan industrial bourgeoisie to abandon any attempt to take over the Spanish institutions and rather focus on regional autonomy (Vilar 1962, pp. 144–158, Linz 1973,

p. 63, Giner 1980, pp. 8–10). Furthermore, the development of the region coincided with the contemporary decline of the rest of Spain, except for the Basque Country. Even more interestingly, Catalan nationalism, as formulated then, contained, among others, a socio-economic argument whereby 'Catalonia's subordination to Castile was thwarting the enterprising spirit of the Catalans at a time when Catalonia was recovering from centuries of decadence' (Llobera 2004, p. 66).

From around 1820 to 1885, in the wake of the spread of romantic nationalism, a Catalan national identity, which did not present itself as incompatible with a Spanish identity, began to develop. Yet, during this period the interests of Catalan and Spanish economic elites started diverging, as the former was increasingly willing to protect its industry from foreign competition through high tariffs that the latter considered harmful to its agricultural exports.[5] This clash led to a steady conflict over trade policy that, despite having been won by the Catalan bourgeoisie in many instances, nourished anxiety among its members and anti-Catalan feelings among big landowners in other Spanish regions. The process was accelerated by the Spanish loss of its remaining colonies at the end of the Spanish-American War of 1898 (Conversi 1997, p. 26). The defeat brought home to the Catalan economic elites that they belonged to an inevitably declining power, whose decadence was much more evident when compared to Catalonia's rise. As argued by a then Catalan MP, if Spain had been a successful nation, there wouldn't have been any attempt to put its legitimacy into question (quoted in Vilar 1962, p. 144). The *Lliga Regionalista* (Regionalist League), founded by the multimillionaire industrialist Francesc Cambó in 1901, was the best embodiment of such a move towards Catalan autonomy (Giner 1980, pp. 17–25).[6] On the other hand, Spanish neutrality during the Great War decisively advantaged the Catalan textile industry unleashing an extraordinary wave of prosperity that made the Catalan upper classes more assertive (Conversi 1993, p. 263). Most Catalan nationalists, however, remained loyal to the Spanish framework and this for two main reasons: Catalonia needed the Spanish market; independence would mean violence and the Catalan society, being wealthier than the Spanish one, had too much to lose from a violent rebellion (Linz 1973, p. 55, Culla 1999, p. 40).

The loss of Cuba also triggered one of the most interesting early cases of fiscal protest in the region. Facing the need to reduce the gigantic deficit generated by the war effort, the Spanish Government of Francisco Silvela imposed a dramatic increase in taxation that caused discontent throughout Spain, but especially in Catalonia, where demands for fiscal powers that had been formulated in a prototype statute of regional autonomy drafted a few years earlier (the *Bases de Manresa* of 1892) were simultaneously rejected by Madrid. The protest took the form of a generalised closure of businesses (especially by tradesman and craftsmen) aimed to avoid paying the taxes due for the second trimester of the year without formally violating the law. The *tancament des caixes* (the closing of the cashboxes), as it was called, went along with demands for a fiscal pact along the lines of the *concierto economico* (economic agreement) granted to the Basque Countries in the 1870s (Camps i Arboix 1961, Balcells 1991, pp. 42–111, Fontana 2014, pp. 320–321). Yet, after that the stern opposition of the central government had broken the resistance, the issue of the *concierto economico* de facto disappeared from the political agenda until late twentieth century. As argued by Culla (2017, p. 9), from the end of the *tancament* onwards, 'Catalan demands were going to be of a political, cultural, linguistic or social nature and learning centres, libraries, routes, houses and gardens were built and designed, but the issue of how to finance that, the self-government that was claimed, remained in limbo'.

The Basque case shares many of the above elements. Both industrialisation and the formation of Basque nationalism began slightly later than in Catalonia but developed very rapidly. The bases of a modern Basque economy, centred around heavy industry and, later, the financial sector, were laid down between 1876 and 1898. During this period, iron production increased 20-fold and at the turn of the century 30 per cent of Spanish banking investments were concentrated in the Basque Country. Similarly to Catalonia, Spanish neutrality in the Great War favoured the development of the local economy and already in the first months of the conflict, 80 per cent of Spanish steel was produced in the region (Payne 1975, pp. 61–94). From the late 1880s on, a young Basque intellectual, Sabino de Arana i Goiri almost singlehandedly formulated the ideological basis of the Basque national identity and founded the Basque Nationalist Party. This was radically separatist at the beginning, but turned more conciliatory and autonomist from the early twentieth century onwards. In this formulation not only the Basques and the Spaniards were thought of as being two completely unrelated peoples, but the Basques were also considered as considerably more advanced (Sullivan 1988, pp. 1–26). As Stanley Payne (1975, p. 107) pointed out: 'in Vizcaya and Guipozcoa [the two most important Basque provinces] nationalists considered Basques the economic elite of Spain, which, rather than providing new opportunities, was holding them back'.

Yet, there is a major difference between Catalan and Basque nationalism. As a consequence of the suppression of the *fueros*[7] after the Carlist Wars, in 1876, and with the aim to appease the Basque elites, the then Spanish President of the Council of Ministers, Antonio Cánovas offered a very favourable regime of local fiscal autonomy called *concierto economico*, which remained in place until 1937. As a result, the inhabitants of the Basque provinces were subjected to about half the tax burden borne by the rest of the population of Spain. Furthermore, the industrialists were able to secure high custom tariffs to protect their activities. This had two consequences. First, the industrial and financial elite was satisfied with its position within the Spanish Crown and did not aim at either challenging the regime or at taking it over. Second, economic issues became salient only on those few occasions when governmental policy threatened the privileges secured through the *concierto economico* (Fusi 1979, pp. 17–19). Also, in its early separatist phase, Basque nationalism did not really bother with this kind of economic struggle, but rather left it to spontaneous organisations – called *Ligas Forales* – for the defence of the *concierto* that nationalists regarded as examples of short-sighted regionalism (Payne 1975, p. 89).

Overall, these two cases are certainly of great interest as forerunners of the nationalism of the rich and should be analysed further in-depth in future research. However, a number of elements suggests considering them precisely as forerunners rather than fully-developed cases: their association with a single parent state, Spain, which does not allow a cross-country analysis; the weakness of clear separatist forces within them, which limits the scope of a study of the redefinition of national identity as incompatible with membership of the parent state and with the existing national solidarity; and, above all, the dubious economic grievances in the Basque case as well as the mainly traditional character of the Catalan ones, based more on skirmishes over tariff walls rather than on unfair redistribution. In this connexion, it is important to note that one of the main changes introduced in the debate over the economic relationship between Catalonia and Spain by economists conducting the first scientific studies over inter-territorial flows, in the 1960s, was a shift from the internal balance of trade – whereby Catalonia was often accused to 'exploit' the Spanish 'captive' market to sell its products thanks to the protection of trade tariffs – to fiscal flows between the region and the central administration (as well as within the banking sector), which were considered by part of the Catalan public opinion as detrimental to the region (see Hombravella and Montserrat 1967, p. 33). While in the first perspective Catalonia 'depends' on the rest of Spain, in the second it is held back.

Notes

1 Rokkan defines a centre as 'a privileged location within a territory' or, more specifically, as a 'location within a territorial system where the largest proportion of economically active are engaged in the processing and communication of information and instructions over long distances'. On the contrary, a periphery is mainly characterised by its subordinate position to the centre or 'more concretely, we can say that a periphery is dependent, with little control over its fate and possessing minimal resources for the defence of its distinctiveness against outside pressures' (Flora *et al.* 1999, pp. 110–113).
2 This logic outlived the feudal system and has informed the process of state formation through the centuries.
3 For a more nuanced interpretation of the reasons why national states prevailed see Spruyt (1994, pp. 151–180).

4 Albeit not so explicitly, a similar idea can also be found in Gellner (1964, p. 168).

5 In fact, protectionism mostly harmed the export-oriented agricultural industry in Andalusia and around Valencia, but favoured agricultural regions producing for the home market such as Castile-Léon (Tortella 2000, p. 436).

6 Yet, the *Lliga*'s attitude, as well as Cambó's, was much more ambiguous and still expressed, at times, a willingness to exercise greater influence over Spanish politics.

7 These were a series of administrative and fiscal customary rights that had granted a varying degree of autonomy to the Basque provinces since the Middle Ages.

2 Catalonia
Fiscal plundering and the end of federalism

Origins and evolution of ERC

Esquerra Republicana de Catalunya (Republican Left of Catalonia, ERC) was founded in 1931 with the goal of establishing the independent Republic of Catalonia. It immediately became the dominant party in the region and remained such until the Civil War. Francisco Franco's harsh repression of *Esquerra* contributed to transforming it into a symbol of the regional struggle for autonomy and democracy (Alquezar 2001). During the dictatorship, however, ERC grew out of touch with the changing Catalan society and slowly turned into a prestigious, but unimportant actor. As a result, in the mid-1980s the party was close to extinction (Segura 2001). Things changed radically in 1986–87, when a group of young separatists led by Josep-Lluis Carod-Rovira and Angel Colom joined it with the goal of rejuvenating it and making it clearly separatist and left-wing. In 1992, ERC became the third force in the Catalan Parliament and kept growing until an eventful change of leadership, in 1996, stopped this first expansion (Culla 2013, pp. 297–350). In the early 2000s, under Carod-Rovira's direction, it scored its best results in the post-dictatorship period (around 16 per cent of the Catalan vote, see Figure 2.1) and joined two successive regional government coalitions (2003–06 and 2006–10) (Argelaguet *et al.* 2004, Culla 2013, pp. 580–666). During the first, the party played a crucial role in putting the reform of Catalonia's Statute of Autonomy on the agenda, with the aim of transforming Spain into a pluri-national federation (Orte and Wilson 2009). After the ratification of the new Statute, in 2006, however, *Esquerra* entered a new phase of internal dissent and change of leadership – with Joan Puigcercos replacing Carod-Rovira – that harmed its electoral performance (around 7–8 per cent at the Catalan and Spanish elections of 2008 and 2010 respectively). This decline was even more striking as, from 2009 on, Catalonia experienced the rise of a grassroots movement advocating the organisation of a referendum on the independence of the region, which, in June 2010, was further fuelled by a ruling of the Spanish Constitutional Tribunal declaring unconstitutional some articles of Catalonia's Statute.

On 11 September 2012, during the celebration of Catalonia's national day, more than a million people joined a demonstration in favour of the 'right to decide'. In the following weeks, the President of the *Generalitat* (the Catalan executive) and leader of the Catalan nationalist party *Convergencia i Unió* (Convergence and Union, CiU), Artur Mas, decided to call an early election on the issue of an independence referendum. Having solved its internal disputes and found a new skilful leader in Oriol Junqueras, ERC capitalised on growing demands for independence and became the second force in the regional Parliament (with 14 per cent of the Catalan vote) (Culla 2013, pp. 667–732). Despite remaining in the opposition, *Esquerra* offered its support to CiU's government in exchange for the promise to hold an independence referendum. As the Spanish Government refused to allow such vote, in November 2014, ERC and other forces defending the right to decide organised a mock referendum. About 35 per cent of Catalan voters participated in the poll, with 80.7 per cent choosing an independent state. In the face of the Spanish Government's continuing opposition, Mas called early elections again (held in September 2015) and framed them as a 'plebiscite on independence'. On this occasion, ERC ran

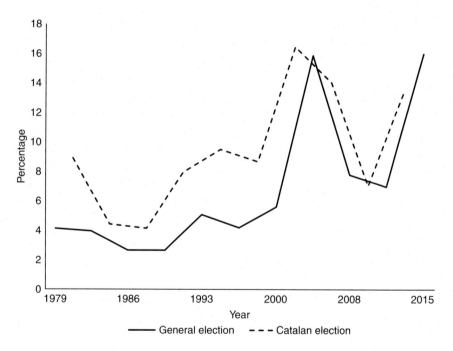

Figure 2.1 ERC's electoral results, 1980–2015 (regional vote).*

Source: my elaboration on Generalitat de Catalunya 2017.

Note

* The 2015 Catalan election was not included because ERC ran within the *Junts pel Sì* coalition.

in a coalition with *Convergencia Democratica de Catalunya* (Democratic Convergence of Catalunya, CDC, previously part of CiU) called *Junts pel Sì* (Together for Yes) that obtained 39.6 per cent of votes. Another separatist party, *Candidatura d'Unitat Popular* (Popular Unity Candidacy, CUP), received 8.2 per cent. Taken together, the votes for these two pro-independence actors fell short of an absolute majority (47.8 per cent), but translated into 53 per cent of the Catalan Parliament's seats. *Junts pel Sì* and CUP thus claimed to have the legitimacy necessary to begin a process of 'disconnection' from Spain. In January 2016, the new President of the *Generalitat*, Carles Puigdemont – a member of CDC – vowed to realise the region's independence according to an 18-month roadmap, a commitment later changed into that of organising an independence referendum. This time, ERC joined the government (Martì and Cetrà 2016). The agreement came after the Spanish general elections were held in December 2015, in which ERC won 16 per cent of the regional vote and nine seats. Although it had obtained a similar score in 2004, this time, *Esquerra* became the first nationalist party in Catalonia and was thus set to play a leading role in the implementation of the pro-independence roadmap.

ERC's nationalism of the rich

In the first years of the democratic transition, ERC's main objective consisted in the re-establishment of the *Generalitat* of Catalonia (ERC 1977, Front d'Esquerres 1977). The party extensively used its glorious past to present itself as the most reliable actor to carry out the process of devolution of powers, but, at the same time, struggled to formulate detailed and comprehensive policy proposals. All this was very different from the organisation that Carod-Rovira depicted in an article published in the Catalan daily *L'Avui* in November 1986 and become famous as the *Crida a Esquerra* (Call to *Esquerra*). There, he argued that ERC should exploit its 'Catalanist' and reformist traditions to modernise left-wing separatism and make it appealing to the masses (Carod-Rovira 1986). The rise of Colom as the head of the party a few years later consolidated ERC's separatist profile, which was formally confirmed when *Esquerra* amended the first article of its Statute to declare 'the territorial unity and independence of the Catalan nation' (ERC 1992a) as its over-riding goal. In those years ERC also became the main referent of a new 'economic nationalism' (Alimbau 1995, p. 72) based on the perception of Catalonia as a distinct economic unit within the Spanish state and, more specifically, a fiscally exploited one.

L'espoli fiscal

At the core of ERC's claim of economic victimisation lies the assertion that the Spanish Government has consistently extracted more resources from the Catalan economy than those spent in the region. As clearly explained in the 1992 manifesto for the Catalan Parliamentary elections: 'the process of economic depredation of the Spanish State is constant [and] translates into a steady increase of the fiscal pressure without any significant improvement either in public services or in infrastructures' (ERC 1992b, p. 47). A year later, in the midst of economic recession, the party launched the first campaign centred around the fiscal deficit under the title '*Solidaritat si. Robatori no. Els nostres impostos a Catalunya*' (Solidarity yes. Larceny no. Our taxes in Catalonia) (ERC 1993a). From that moment on, the argument of economic victimisation – generally referred to as *espoli fiscal* (fiscal plundering) – has remained a pillar of the party's propaganda and, in recent years, has become a key claim of the wider movement for Catalan independence.

Estimates of the fiscal deficit have varied. In 1989, *Esquerra* asserted that each Catalan was robbed of 180,000 pesetas a year (about 1,380 euros)[1] (ERC 1989a, p. 5). In the mid-1990s, it calculated the deficit at 12–13 per cent of Catalan GDP (ERC 1995, p. 23), while, in 2008, it concluded that the state was siphoning off 2,622 euros per Catalan each year (ERC 2008a). In the context of the recent economic crisis, it decried that since 1986 Catalonia had been deprived of about 8 per cent of its GDP every year (Sol 2012).

ERC has consistently argued that this fiscal assault against Catalonia is deliberate and perpetuates the 'dependency' of the region on the Spanish state. The use of the term 'dependency' stresses that Catalonia is forced to transfer its abundant tax revenue to Madrid and then to hinge on insufficient funding from the centre to finance its services. In this way – *Esquerra* has asserted – the most efficient territories, like Catalonia, are penalised (ERC 2000a, p. 18, 2008b, p. 43), while, at the same time, financial autonomy is not a solution, because the periodic renegotiation of the bloc grant to the autonomous communities, and the conservative estimates of the central government, leaves Catalonia's funding at the mercy of Spain's decisions (Camps Boy 1990a, 1990b, ERC 2006a, p. 55).

According to ERC, one of the main causes of the *espoli fiscal* lies in the 'appalling inefficiency' of the Spanish administration, which is described as parasitic and oversized (ERC 1992b, p. 47, Colom 1995, p. 12). Such inefficiency makes that, as the party stated in 2003, 'we [the Catalans] pay taxes like a social-democracy and we receive public spending like an ultraliberal country' (ERC 2003a, p. 5). Similar claims have become especially relevant during the euro crisis. In this context, *Esquerra* has argued that an independent Catalonia could escape painful austerity measures (Aragones 2012) and criticised Madrid's imposition of draconian spending limits to the already cost-effective peripheral administrations, pointing to the central government's enormous potential for savings: 'the absurd thing about the policy of the Spanish Government is its inefficiency. It ignores the mass of the deficit, which coincides with the central administration, and forces to cut where we have already reached the bone. In return, it maintains a sumptuous spending policy that continues to waste enormous resources' (Sol 2013).

The consequences of all these forms of fiscal discrimination against Catalonia are deemed by ERC to be serious not only per se, but also because of the high potential of the Catalan economy. Here, two elements are outstanding in the party's rhetoric: the role of claims concerning the need for market efficiency in justifying the call for self-determination and the impact of the Spanish incorporation into wider international markets. With regard to the former, the party has consistently stressed that a robust economy is necessary to provide quality services to the national community and, simultaneously, it has consistently extolled the modernity of the Catalan economy relatively to the Spanish one, identifying the region with the rest of Europe and arguing that its shortcomings derive from the flaws and discriminatory practices of the Spanish state (ERC 1989b, p. 56, 1993c, p. 14, 1996, pp. 11–13, 2006b, p. 2, 2012b, p. 41, Colom 1995, p. 20). However, its discourse has been contradictory because *Esquerra* has at times stressed the Catalan economic success, while, at others (especially in the late 1980s and the early 1990s), it has underlined the gap with the richest continental countries (ERC 1989a, pp. 14–15, 2000a, p. 19, Colom 1995, pp. 19–20).

The most important element of ERC's rhetoric of economic victimisation lies in a culturally-determinist explanation of the socio-economic difference between Catalonia and the rest of Spain. The party has consistently portrayed the Catalan nation as composed of hard-working, entrepreneurial and productive people (ERC 1993a, p. 14, 1994, p. 26, 1996, p. 12, 2001a, p. 13, 2003a, p. 4, 2008b, p. 10, Junts Pel Sì 2015, p. 18). This representation has not been accompanied by racist or xenophobic arguments against other Spaniards, though. On the contrary, the party has been very careful to direct its accusations against the Spanish Government, described as dominated by an oligarchy of bureaucrats, landlords and speculators. In 1993, for instance, the party openly denounced the 'subsidy culture promoted for electoral reasons by any incumbent Spanish government' (ERC 1993c, p. 18). Such a Madrid oligarchy has thus been the main negative 'Other' in the party's construction of the Catalan self. This is clear from Angel Colom's (1995, p. 55) definition of Catalan society as one that 'has a good potential to find itself among the most advanced in Europe. Values such as freedom, effort, initiative, solidarity that make us a society open to change are prevalent'. By contrast – he continued – 'Spain remains an archaic state, unable to catch up with Europe, in which a political class originated in territories and environments that have only knowledge of the rules of the speculative and financial economy' (Colom 1995, p. 52). The connection with the dense network of SMEs characteristic of the region has been especially important in the party's discourse, since they are deemed to embody the Catalan values of hard-work and entrepreneurship (ERC 1996, p. 3, 2000c, 2003a, pp. 4–5).

Yet, it should be noted once again that *Esquerra* has also been very careful to talk about institutions and specific classes rather than using sweeping generalisations about wide cultural aggregates. Interviews with current and former members of the party confirm this aspect.[2] While all interviewees agreed on the existence of cultural differences between Catalans and other Spanish peoples (and on the economic consequences thereof), they also made clear that, according to their left-wing thinking, such features should not be essentialised. This, however, reveals an underlying and unresolved tension within the party's discourse.

Therefore, in *Esquerra*'s rhetoric we find elements of the producerist discourse mentioned in the introduction, although the party has carefully targeted the Spanish political elite rather than the populations of poorer Spanish regions and thus put more emphasis on the criterion of need as compared to other case-study parties (see below). The conditionality of its 'welfare producerism' (Abts and Kochyut 2013, 2014) is clear when analysing the arguments it formulated to reply to the accusations of selfishness made against it in the early 1990s. ERC has suggested that what the rest of Spain calls for is not solidarity, but dependence. Colom's (1995, p. 21) words clearly illustrate this: 'Catalonia is willing to be solidary with the other peoples of the state that are in need, especially those from which many Catalans come. Nevertheless, we are not willing to confuse solidarity with charity'. He further argued that, instead of redistribution, Catalan taxes were used to feed clientelism by financing jobs in the public sector, which did not help the endogenous development of the beneficiary regions. As a consequence, Spain was stifling the industrial engine of the country – Catalonia – to fund unproductive activities in the rest of the state. By contrast, the party later asserted, solidarity should target endogenous growth, be limited in time and amount, and be directly managed by the *Generalitat* (ERC 1999b). In more recent proposals for a reform of the financing deal between Catalonia and Spain, the party proposed contributing 2.5 per cent of its GDP to a fund of inter-territorial cohesion for a decade (ERC 2003b, 2006c, p. 6). After that, however, solidarity with Spanish regions would not be different from that with other nations of the world, many of which are much more in need of help. As argued by Carod-Rovira, 'we want to exercise solidarity, but not in a compulsory and unjust form. Not with the Andalusian gentry or the Madrid bourgeois who travel by high-speed train, but rather with Central America and the countries of the Sahara' (ERC 1999a).

The party has thus clearly relied on principles of welfare state deservingness in its criticism of Spanish solidarity, notably the criteria of: need, whereby solidarity should be proportional to the level of neediness of the recipient – the Madrid oligarchy clearly does not deserve Catalan solidarity; control, whereby those who are seen as being responsible for their neediness are deemed to be less deserving – the poverty of other Spanish regions is due to the misled clientelist policies of Spanish parties and, although they are not directly accused of profiting from it, the populations of such regions are at best seen as passively accepting such clientelism; and reciprocity, whereby those who contribute more should also to some extent receive more – the Catalan population pays too much and receives too little. Such welfare producerism is further 'culturalised' since the 'cultural-determinist' interpretation of Catalonia's socio-economic development seen above has allowed the party to make the 'imagined community of welfare producers' coincide with the entire Catalan nation. Although the party has widely used such criteria to justify its rejection of solidarity with the rest of Spain, identity remains a key underlying criterion, since the 'relevant community' to which the term solidarity refers clearly is the Catalan, not the Spanish, nation.

La mentalitat radial

In ERC's discourse, the economic exploitation of the Catalan nation is nothing but the direct consequence of its political marginalisation within the Spanish state. The two claims therefore must be considered in conjunction. In the late 1980s, *Esquerra* often described Catalan history as a tale of occupation and repression (ERC 1989b, p. 4, Colom 1989). Such rhetoric was later toned down, but the argument remained in the idea – popular during the entire Colom period (1989–96) – that the democratic transition had failed and the state had remained anchored in the previous Francoist establishment (ERC 1990, Colom 1995, p. 51). This was deemed to be reflected in the persistent centralist mindset of the Spanish bureaucracy and political class (ERC 1989b, p. 21, 1993c, p. 11). As a consequence, Catalonia remained 'a nation separated into two states, economically plundered, culturally subjugated and, what is most important and that determines the rest: politically subordinated' (ERC 1992b, p. 13).

In the early 1990s, the party was critical of representative democracy and campaigned for a higher involvement of citizens in the democratic process (ERC 1989b, pp. 20–22, 1992b, pp. 23–25, 1993b, p. 14). Such a critique resembled that of European populist movements arising in those years in the wake of corruption scandals that undermined citizens' confidence in traditional parties (Mudde 2004). Corruption scandals were frequent in Spain as well. In this context, ERC tried to present itself as the only 'clean' Catalan party and called for a renewal of the political class that had managed the transition (ERC 1992b, 1993c, p. 1, 1995, pp. 20–21, Colom 1995, pp. 42–43). At a closer look, however, in the party's discourse, Spain's purported lack of democracy is not so much linked to the malfunctioning of the political system described above, but rather to the lack of recognition of the Catalan nation as a constituent unit of the country endowed with a right to self-determination. In other words, Spain's anti-democratic character does not derive from democratic theory itself – which is silent about the boundaries of the self-governing community (Dahl 1982, p. 98) – but it rather hinges on the principle of national self-determination. Accordingly, under the leadership of Angel

Colom, the party argued that Spain was not a true democracy because the political system should allow for the possibility to redefine minority-majority relations at any time (ERC 1992b, p. 23).

From the turn of the century on, these arguments were adapted to the new reality of the *Partido Popular*'s (People's Party, PP) absolute majority in the Spanish Congress[3] and, later, to the debate about the reform of the Catalan Statute of Autonomy. *Esquerra* denounced an attempt on the part of the PP to re-centralise powers that was deemed to reflect its *mentalitat radial*, i.e. the idea that everything must emanate from and pass through Madrid (ERC 2000b, 2001b, 2002, 2003a, p. 6). As ERC made clear in 2000: 'the PP unleashed again a clear reactionary offensive, based on the claims of the stalest Spanish-centred mentality and the return to the unitary state, thus stigmatising democratic peripheral nationalism and rejecting any proposals of plurinational structure' (ERC 2000a, p. 7). Although I have mentioned that *Esquerra* has been very careful in directing its accusations against the Spanish state and its political elite, in the context of discussions concerning the democratic nature of the country, one can see references to the wider Spanish society as being less democratic than the Catalan one. For instance, in the manifesto for the 2004 general elections, the party claimed that Catalonia would be willing to share its democratic achievements with the rest of Spain with a view to triggering 'a general process of improvement of the democracy and the quality of self-government of the nations and regions making up the State' (ERC 2004, p. 6). Although the text mentions only the state, the image is that of Catalonia as the leading region in the democratisation of the country – and thus implicitly more democratic and modern than the rest.

The debate about the place of Catalonia within the Spanish state became especially heated during the reform of the Statute of Autonomy of the region. ERC demanded it as an intermediate step in the transition to full independence, but also because the model of the State of the Autonomies established by the 1978 Constitution had grown to limits in terms of regional self-government. With the reform *Esquerra* aimed to achieve a new constitutional balance based on a 'real' recognition of the differential identity of the peripheral nations (ERC 2000a, p. 7). The Statute was approved by the Catalan Parliament in 2005 and then transmitted for approval to the Spanish one, as foreseen by the Constitution. When the Spanish Parliament heavily modified the Statute, ERC defined this act as 'an authentic democratic scandal' (ERC 2006d) and stressed that 'the non-recognition of Catalonia as a nation means the perpetuation of the contempt of the country [Catalonia] on the part of Spanish nationalism' (ERC 2006b).

Although since 1987–89 the solution proposed by the party to free Catalonia of its subordinated condition has unambiguously been independence, the concrete formulations and strategies for achieving it have varied over time. In 1991, writing the first blueprint of the party's programme for constitutional change, Carod-Rovira suggested that independence could be achieved through a unilateral declaration to be issued after a majority of the Catalan population had voted for a separatist party. Meanwhile, Catalonia should try to get as many powers as possible within the existing political framework (Carod-Rovira 1991, pp. 1–6). Colom accepted this gradualist strategy towards independence, although Carod-Rovira pursued it much more consistently once at the head of the party (ERC 1992b, p. 16). Therefore, ERC has consistently advocated the renegotiation of the relation with Madrid into one between equals, either in the form of the transfers of all powers to Catalonia except for foreign policy and defence, or as a federation of freely associated but sovereign states. This conception of the Spanish state also entails the possibility that the Catalan people can express at any time their willingness to become a separate country, either by electing a pro-independence party – as above – or through a referendum, with the latter option replacing the former in the party's propaganda since the second half of the 1990s (ERC 1998, 2000a, p. 28, 2003a, p. 6, 2005).

This has however changed with the onset of the constitutional crisis triggered by the 2010 ruling of the Spanish Constitutional Tribunal over the Catalan Statute of Autonomy. In this context, the right to decide became the main theme of the party's campaign for the Catalan election held in the same year (Pagès 2009, Agudo 2010). In the manifesto for the 2012 election, which was centred around the idea of an independence referendum, *Esquerra* further argued that the poll would be an occasion for Spain to show its commitment to the principle of democracy. Yet, in case Spain did not recognise the validity of the vote, the party declared itself open to the possibility of a unilateral declaration of independence, which it would carefully portray as the last resort of a national community that was deprived of its right to self-determination (ERC 2012b, pp. 6–9). A few years later, the stern opposition of the Spanish Government to any such referendum despite substantial support for its organisation in the region, led the party to conclude that: 'the State is a wall that refuses recognising the sovereignty of Catalonia. No Statute, no *concert econòmic*, no 9N [a short-hand for the independence referendum] [...] we have been enduring for 10 years a democratic involution and a reduction of rights and liberties that jeopardise the welfare of the people' (ERC 2015, p. 2). Hence, the party proclaimed the end of federalism as a feasible constitutional scenario, the reality being that 'it is easier to make the Catalan Republic than to reform the Spanish Monarchy' (ERC 2015, p. 2).

El catalanisme del benestar

The will to combine Catalan nationalism and left-wing progressivism lay at the very core of ERC's rejuvenation in the late 1980s. Carod-Rovira's *Crida a Esquerra*, specifically decried the dissociation between the struggles for national dignity and social justice, calling on ERC to provide the necessary third way between the regionalist conservative Catalanism of CiU and the bureaucratic 'Spanish-subjected' Left represented by the *Partit dels Socialistes de Catalunya* (Socialist Party of Catalonia, PSC). Since then, the party has consistently claimed to embody such a 'third way'. The theme of the *catalanisme del benestar* (welfare Catalanism) has been the key discursive tool in the construction of such a model. This can be defined as the idea that national self-determination must be achieved not because it is important per se, as a principle, but because it will improve the quality of life of Catalans. Already Colom had declared that the nationalism of ERC was 'an economic and social separatism' (ERC 1989a), yet Carod-Rovira formulated the concept more in detail. In his 1991 *La via democratica a la independencia*, he advocated combining 'a patriotic separatism – valid only for patriots – with a pragmatic separatism – useful to the entire society and all economic sectors. A separatism in touch with the needs of the people, that has an impact on the daily routine and people's lives, and, what is most important, that offers guarantees of being able to make life better' (Carod-Rovira 1991, p. 6). Thus, the project devised by Carod-Rovira aimed at abandoning the strictly culturalist rhetoric of small cliques of committed nationalists to embrace a wider positive message of material and spiritual prosperity that would enable the party to gather an electoral majority and bring about constitutional change.

As the party recently argued, 'the most convenient option for Catalanism is that of economic growth. The demand for more self-government and sovereignty will grow if we manage to make people understand that this will entail more economic growth and, as a consequence, more welfare' and, it continued, 'for all one thing is clear: Spain today is a brake that prevents us from obtaining the prosperity that we deserve on the basis of our effort' (ERC 2008b, p. 7). What is very important to notice, here, is the contrast stressed by the party between the prosperity that the Catalans enjoy and that which they would 'deserve' on the basis of their 'effort', which refers, again, to criteria of deservingness and notably to that of reciprocity.

In this framework, *Esquerra* has portrayed the welfare state as a fundamental pillar of the legitimacy of the state vis-à-vis the national community. According to the party, independence and the establishment of Scandinavian-style welfare depend on each other, as the hostility of the Spanish state makes using Catalonia's resources to bring about 'the Scandinavian utopia' impossible, while a strong Catalan welfare is necessary to convince the people about the merits of independence (ERC 2012b, p. 111). Hence, in the context of the euro crisis and the austerity imposed by the Spanish Government, *Esquerra* made a clear connection between the *espoli fiscal* and the *espoli social* (social plundering) caused by the government's budget cuts, asserting that, without the fiscal plundering, Catalonia would be the 'Sweden of the Mediterranean', would much more easily get out of the economic downturn and would even be one of the few countries in Europe to record a budget surplus (ERC 2011a, 2011b, 2012a, 2015, p. 21, Aragones 2012). Such an instrumental argument, which relies on the representation of the Catalan nation as made up of hard-working and entrepreneurial people naturally producing surplus resources seen above, has enabled the party to convey a positive message of change framing independence as a tool to preserve and improve the welfare of the national community, and ultimately as a way out of the dilemma between solidarity and efficiency posed by international competition and the economic crisis.

At the roots of ERC's discourse

In Chapter 1, I argue that the Catalan nationalist movement of the end of the nineteenth and the beginning of the twentieth century can be considered as a forerunner of the nationalism of the rich. This has been implicitly suggested by Juan Linz (1973, p. 67), who, pointing out that 'in many other European societies the linguistic, cultural, peripheral oppositions challenging central power emerged in agricultural, economically underdeveloped regions', concluded that Catalonia constituted a noticeable exception. Let us now have a look at this argument more in detail.

Spain: economic and political power divorced

Linz defined Spain as a case of early state-building and late nation-building. Although Spanish unification was completed through marriage policy and conquest by 1512, the Kingdom was composed of very different and largely autonomous entities. The constituent parts of the Crown of Aragon – the kingdoms of Aragon and Valencia and the Principality of Catalonia – maintained their own political institutions until the eighteenth century. Economically speaking, in this early phase, thanks to its explorations in the Atlantic, Castile enjoyed an advantage over Catalonia, which entered a phase of recession. Yet, Spain did not embark on any process of national homogenisation, although attempts at administrative centralisation came about in the seventeenth century (Elliott 1963, pp. 1–22). The persistent imperial effort and reduced colonial revenues induced successive kings from Philippe II to Philippe V to adopt a more efficient system of taxation. The autonomous institutions of the constituent parts, though, stood against their efforts, leading, in the case of the Principality of Catalonia, to the wars of 1640–52 and the conflict with the Spanish Crown in the War of Spanish Succession (1701–14) (Linz 1973, pp. 38–47, Culla 1999, p. 36). Ironically, Catalonia's economic revival began soon after the loss of the Principality's autonomous institutions. As argued by Vilar (1962, p. 555), this occurred before large-scale participation of Catalan merchants in the colonial trade and was mainly based on improvements in the agricultural sector that made the capital accumulation necessary to invest in manufacturing possible. The development of the region and the contemporary decline of the rest of Spain – except for the Basque Country – heavily impacted on the formation of the Spanish national identity in the nineteenth century.

Spanish and Catalan nationalism developed abreast during the nineteenth century, especially from 1840 on. In Catalonia an old territorial identity slowly turned into a national one, although it remained fundamentally compatible with the Spanish framework until the interwar years. The diverging interests of the Spanish and Catalan economic elites, on the one hand, and the failure of the Spanish liberals to propose a non-organic definition of the Spanish nation, alternative to the conservative one and open to the integration of peripheral nationalism, paved the way for a strengthening of autonomist and even separatist tendencies in the region. This was favoured by the weakness of the Spanish state institutions. While the conservatives mainly followed a Jacobin model of state centralisation, they lacked both the material and ideological resources that other European countries used to lead a modernising process of economic development and cultural homogenisation (Sahlins 1989, pp. 279–298, De Riquer 2000, p. 14). The Spanish state could not, for instance, enact a truly comprehensive and compulsory education system – in 1900, 63.8 per cent of the population was illiterate against only 16.5 per cent in France (Culla 1999, p. 38). Furthermore, as suggested by Llobera (2004, p. 66), among the arguments used by Catalan nationalists in the second half of the nineteenth century, there was one 'of socio-economic rationality: Catalonia's subordination to Castile was thwarting the enterprising spirit of the Catalans at a time when Catalonia was recovering from centuries of decadence'. This suggests a dynamic realised in the other case studies – although much later – whereby a change in the economic balance between centre and periphery spurred calls for a similar change in political relations. Hence, the inefficiency and declining influence of the Spanish state in the nineteenth century, combined with the existence of an old territorial identity in Catalonia and the latter's exceptional modernisation, go a long way to explaining the growth of a strong national identity in the region and the moderate success of Spanish nation-building.

The clash between competing Catalan and Spanish nation-building projects reached a climax in the first half of the twentieth century. Primo de Rivera's dictatorship, first, and Franco's regime, later, embodied the imposition of the latter project over the former. Franco, in particular, hit the Catalan movement very hard and actively repressed Catalan identity. Yet, from an economic perspective, Catalonia experienced impressive economic development. Between 1960 and 1973, the region amassed a disproportionate share of foreign investments entering Spain and its GDP grew 8 per cent a year on average (McRoberts 2001, p. 92). As a consequence, in the late 1970s, Catalonia enjoyed a per capita income 30 per cent higher than the Spanish average and, while inhabited by 16 per cent of the population it accounted for 20 per cent of Spanish GDP and 26 per cent of industrial production (Giner 1980, pp. 51–54). The fiscal relationship with the rest of Spain has however remained strained.

The fiscal transfers

Fiscal imbalances in Spain existed much earlier than the late 1980s, when ERC began formulating the rhetoric of the *espoli fiscal* (see Balcells 1991, pp. 41–111). Nevertheless, in the late nineteenth and early twentieth century, the debate over the economic relationship between Spain and Catalonia mainly concerned trade flows. Free-marketers (often represent- ing the Spanish agricultural export-oriented sector) argued that the trade tariffs demanded by industrialists disproportionally favoured Catalonia by creating a 'captive' market for its industrial products, while this region, in return, did not buy a sufficient share of the agricultural produce of the rest of the country. The protectionists, by contrast, tried to show that Catalo- nia did consume a substantial share of Spanish products and that its balance of trade with the rest of the country was basically in equilibrium (for a summary see Petit Fonseré 1965, p. 68, Hombravella and Montser- rat 1967, p. 33). From the 1960s, however, the focus started to move from trade to financial flows. An important role was played by the economist Ramon Trias i Fargas. Not only was he the first to attempt to carry out an analysis of the 'balance of payments' of Catalonia (i.e. including trade and financial flows), but he also ran a centre for economic studies at the Barce- lona office of the Urquijo Bank that focused on regional economics. He thus decisively contributed to increasing knowledge about the Catalan fiscal deficit, promoting the idea of Catalonia as an economic unit distinct from the rest of Spain, and to form several young economists who will later work on similar subjects (see Amat 2009, pp. 151–185).[4]

From the end of the 1970s, economic studies of the relationship between Catalonia and the Spanish administration began to be produced quite sys- tematically and regional data to be more refined. At the same time, state expenditure went from 20.1 per cent of GDP in 1970 to 42.7 per cent in 1990, recording one of the highest percentage progressions among advanced economies over the same period (Comin and Diaz 2005, p. 877). As a consequence, during the 1980s, Spain's tax revenue, as a percentage of GDP, grew faster than in any other Western European country (see Tanzi and Schuknecht 2000, pp. 6–7). Such evolution should not be seen as a sign of deterioration of public finances. It largely represented a 'nor- malisation' compared to neighbouring countries that had created complex welfare systems and expanded state intervention into the economy well before. Nevertheless, the change was radical and carried out in much more unfavourable conditions than those of the Glorious Thirties (Comin and Diaz 2005, pp. 893–894). This led to consistent budget deficits and rising debt throughout the 1980s – although debt remained low relatively to the European average. The rise of state spending therefore increased the saliency of the transfers in the political debate.

Estimates of the fiscal transfers have varied widely according to the methods adopted. The most common methods are the monetary flow and the benefit flow ones. While the former attributes expenditure to the region where public goods are produced, regardless of who are the true beneficiaries, the latter allocates general services, such as foreign policy or defence, often geographically concentrated in some areas but, at least in principle, for the benefit of the entire population, on a per capita basis. There is no agreement on which of the two is sounder. While general services clearly cater for the entire population, the concentration of such services in specific areas can have disproportional positive effects on the local economy, and sometimes function as a subsidy (see Barberan 2010, Vaillancourt 2010).

Table 2.1 provides a summary of the main studies on the fiscal deficit. Three considerations can be made. First, already in the first half of the 1980s the study of Castells and Parellada (1983) provided evidence of the existence of substantial transfers. Although these had been suggested before, such detailed information was then disseminated in a democratic context and after the successful establishment of the Autonomous Community of Catalonia, which substantially increased its salience and usefulness for local political actors. This was especially the case in the second half of the 1980s, when the renegotiation of the funding agreement between the region and the central administration came for the first time on the political agenda. Second, while calculations vary widely, when taking into account only studies using the same method, divergences shrink. Since the 1980s, the Catalan fiscal deficit has averaged between 3–6 per cent and 6–9 per cent of its GDP according to the method used. Hence, there is little doubt that substantial transfers between Catalonia and the

Table 2.1 Estimates of Catalonia's fiscal deficit, selected studies (average yearly values as a percentage of regional GDP)

Author	Year of publication	Years studied	Monetary flow (%)	Benefit flow (%)
Castells and Parellada	1983	1975–79	7.3	–
Bosch *et al.*	1988	1980–85	–	2.76
Colldeforns	1991	1986–88	9.2	–
Castells *et al.*	2000	1991–96	6.4	4.6
Pons and Tremosa	2000	1985–2000	7.5	–
Uriel and Barberan	2007	1991–2005	–	5.2
GTABFC	2008	2002–05	9.0	6.6
Generalitat de Catalunya	2012	2006–09	8.2	5.7

Sources: see reference list.

rest of Spain exist and have persisted over the last three decades. Third, the deficit does not seem to have substantially worsened in recent years, as confirmed by data provided by Uriel and Barberan (2007, p. 303). The variability shown in Figure 2.2 is in large part due to the authors' decision not to neutralise the Spanish budget deficit and to distribute it to each region proportionally to their GDP. If one excludes the 1993–97 years, when Spain's budget deficit worsened considerably, the Catalan fiscal deficit remains circumscribed within the 5.2–6.7 per cent range. This means that variations in support for separatist parties and/or for independence cannot be explained with reference to a deterioration of Catalonia's fiscal deficit. It is for this reason that in Chapter 9 other factors will be analysed. On the other hand, the persistency of the transfers could clearly be used by ERC as evidence that, despite major reforms, the system did not fundamentally change. Furthermore, the lack of a consensual methodology allows for varying interpretations of the transfers' extent and causes.

However, Catalonia is not the only net contributor to the Spanish redistribution system. Almost all studies show that, when using a benefit flow method, the biggest deficit is held by the Community of Madrid. This, however, is in part due to the role of Madrid as capital, since when using a monetary flow perspective the deficit decreases considerably (Barberan

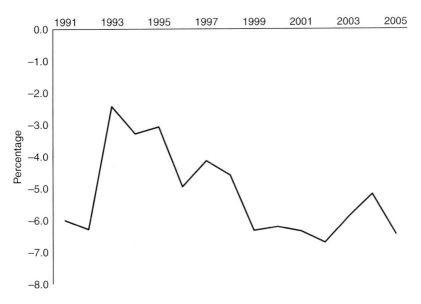

Figure 2.2 Catalonia's fiscal deficit with the central administration, 1991–2005 (percentage of regional GDP).*

Source: my elaboration on Uriel and Barberan 2007.

Note
* Benefit flow method.

2006, pp. 71–72, Espasa and Bosch 2010, p. 164). Sizable transfers, equal to 4.3 per cent of regional GDP on average for the period 1991–2005, have been recorded in the Balearic Islands as well (Uriel and Barberan 2007). Yet, despite the existence of regionalist parties there, the centre-periphery conflict has never escalated as much as in Catalonia,[5] nor have claims of fiscal exploitation become nearly as vocal. The reason for this certainly has to do with the fact that, despite being considered as part of the Catalan cultural area, for about 60 per cent of the Islands' population Spain, rather than Catalonia or the region, is the main referent of subjective national identification (IBES 2012b). This suggests that it is the idea of being a different community in the first place that sets the ground for the nationalism of the rich.

Beyond the transfers

The formation of ERC's claims of fiscal exploitation and their degree of credibility also depend on other factors than just the existence of a fiscal deficit with the central administration. While the 'adequate' level of social redistribution is a political question that does not concern us here, what can be discussed from a technical perspective is whether there are major flaws in the system that might nourish discontent with concrete forms of social redistribution. Ways of looking at this include the evaluation of: overcompensation effects, considerations of efficiency and regional economic convergence, trends in taxation and public finances, and the overall evolution of the economy.

A minimal definition of fiscal redistribution entails that regions should contribute in accordance with their income but receive equal per capita spending. Hence, those with a higher than average income should be net contributors and those with a lower one net recipients. Uriel and Barberan (2007, p. 412) show that, in the period 1991–2005, Catalonia's position was in line with this assumption. Yet, there also are some overcompensation effects,[6] although their precise size is unclear. Using data for 2005, Espasa and Bosch (2010) argued that Catalonia received between 12 per cent and 14 per cent less than the Spanish average. Yet, De la Fuente (2005) calculated the same amount at 6 per cent below the average for the period 1990–97. Furthermore, this has affected other contributory regions and not exclusively Catalonia (Tortella 2016, pp. 441–443). What, instead, seems to be uncontroversial is the disproportionately low amount of infrastructural investment received by Catalonia. De la Fuente – who has otherwise provided very conservative estimates of the fiscal deficit (e.g. De la Fuente 2001) – has pointed out that the *Generalitat* received less investment than all other autonomous communities during the 1990s. Such spending represents a small share of the deficit claimed by ERC, but it probably had a sizable negative impact on the development of the Catalan economy in recent years.

Despite occurring, economic convergence among Spanish regions slowed considerably in the 1980s and it was virtually absent in the 1990s (Goerlich *et al.* 2002, Mas *et al.* 1994). Some works further suggest that the increase in income per capita in the poorer regions was largely driven by public sector employment and emigration, rather than by endogenous growth (Garcia-Milà and McGuire 2001, p. 283). Furthermore, the perception of a 'doped' development in Spain's poorer areas was favoured by the wide array of corruption scandals that affected the *Partido Socialista Obrero Español* (Socialist Labour Spanish Party, PSOE) in the early 1990s. Overall, they evoked the existence of clientelist networks of voters supporting the Socialists in exchange for subsidies (see, for instance, the notorious case of the *Plan de Empleo Rural* – Plan of Rural Employment), public employment and investments, especially in the community of Andalusia, thus reinforcing existing stereotypes of this region as a 'land of idlers' (Cazorla 1994, pp. 5–7, Heywood 2005, pp. 52–53). Yet, clientelist practices in Spain seem to have remained limited in scope, especially if compared with similar dynamics in Italy (Pujas and Rhodes 1999, Hopkin 2001).

The presence of sizable and widely studied fiscal transfers, coupled with the perception of widespread corruption and the hike in government debt, budget deficit and taxation registered since the late 1980s (Figure 2.3) offered a fruitful ground for *Esquerra*'s claims of Catalan fiscal exploitation and its welfare producerism. This seems to be confirmed by public opinion data. Already in 1988, 56 per cent of the Catalan population thought that the Spanish Government was little or not at all concerned with the economic progress of Catalonia and 59.6 per cent believed that the public works and services provided by the central administration were not sufficient in light of the taxes paid by the community (Estrade and Treserra 1990, pp. 77–85). Thus, at the time of the formulation within ERC of the rhetoric of the *espoli fiscal*, this idea was already quite widespread among the general population. The activity of the party has therefore profited from 'cultural resonance' (Gamson and Modigliani 1989, p. 5), as *Esquerra* seems to have amplified beliefs already diffused in the reference society. Later surveys confirm such impression. In the 2001–10 period, 76.5 per cent of the Catalan population on average thought that the Spanish Government favoured some autonomous communities over others and 51.4 per cent that Catalonia received worse treatment (ICPS, 1991–2016).

Since the late 1980s, *Esquerra* has been the main purveyor of the rhetoric of fiscal plundering, using it as a legitimising argument for its project of radical constitutional change. Its role, however, must also be evaluated against the activity of its major rival in the Catalan nationalist camp, i.e. CiU. *Convergencia* has certainly been the main defender of the Catalan economic interest in Madrid, obtaining some modifications of the region's fiscal deal with the centre. Yet, only very recently has the party fully

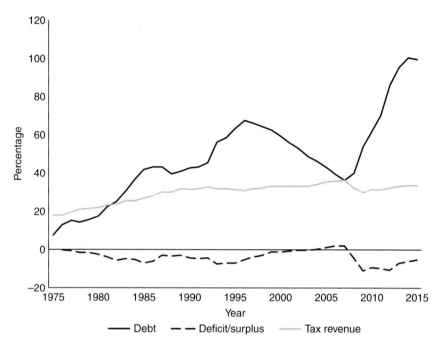

Figure 2.3 Spain's public debt, budget balance and tax revenue, 1975–2015 (percentage of GDP).

Sources: my elaboration on IMF-FAD 2012, Eurostat 2017c, 2017d, OECD 2017a.

embraced the rhetoric of the '*espoli fiscal*' promoted by ERC. In the 1980s, CiU was mostly focused on the task of *fer pays* (nation-building) after the trauma of the dictatorship (Dowling 2005, pp. 108–110). Furthermore, the party strove to consolidate the existing institutions rather than seeking a frontal clash with the Spanish administration on the fiscal issue. After having failed to project its modernising thrust in the rest of Spain through the so-called *Operacio Reformista*, CiU successfully implemented a policy of 'constructive opposition' to the PSOE and the PP whereby, relying on its regional electoral clout, it extracted concessions from the centre. In this way, it stood out as a nationalist opposition, but a responsible one, which prevented it from making radical claims of fiscal exploitation. A clear example is provided by the refusal to fight for a substantial reform of the fiscal deal with the central government at the time of its first renegotiation in 1986 (Lo Cascio 2008). Also, in the 1980s, the fiscal issue was overshadowed by the debate over linguistic policy and the process of transfer of powers to the autonomous communities (see below). The fiscal imbalance began gaining central place only between the late 1980s and early 1990s, coinciding with *Esquerra*'s new rhetoric.

Until the financial and euro crisis, however, *Esquerra*'s claims coincided with a period of prolonged and sustained growth. Per capita GDP has steadily expanded at 2.6 per cent per year in real terms between 1982 and 1995 and 3.5 per cent from 1995–2007 (my calculations on INE 2017a, 2017b, IDESCAT 2017a, World Bank 2017, see also Boix 2012). Hence, overall, in the three decades following the end of the dictatorship, most of the Catalan population achieved an unprecedented standard of living. This is in part reflected in opinion polls. Each year since 1991 the *Institut de Ciencies Politiques i Socials* (Institute of Political and Social Sciences, ICPS) has asked the Catalan population whether they think Catalonia's situation has improved, remained the same or worsened in the previous two years. The average figures for the entire decade of the 1990s were 50 per cent, 26.4 per cent and 22.4 per cent respectively. Skirmishes with the central government over infrastructural investments in the region probably account for a reduction in the number of Catalans who, from 2000–07, thought that the situation had improved (40.1 per cent) (ICPS 1991–2016). The picture changed considerably with the onset of the economic crisis. Between 2008 and 2013, Catalonia's real per capita GDP decreased by 1.6 per cent on average, recording three years of recession out of five and unemployment shot up from 7.5 per cent to 24.4 per cent (INE 2017c and my calculations on IDESCAT 2017a, 2017b, World Bank 2017). Accordingly, although the situation began improving from 2014 on, the average number of people who believed that the region's situation had worsened in the previous two years shot up to 73.7 per cent between 2008 and 2015 (ICPS several years) and coincided with a major radicalisation in grassroots support for independence. Yet, the economic crisis is not the only factor accounting for such a change.

Catalonia's political marginalisation until the democratic transition

Especially in its first years, ERC described the history of Catalonia within the Spanish state as a tale of subordination and repression. From a historiographical perspective, such a picture is one-sided and simplistic. It is true, however, that the history of the Iberian peninsula and the relationship between Catalonia and the rest of Spain has been more problematic than, for instance, that between Scotland and the rest of the UK (see Chapter 5). A key event in this connection is represented by the adoption of the Decrees of *Nueva Planta* (New Foundation) by King Philippe V in 1716, since they mark the first major attempt to transform Spain into a centralised country on the French model. Unlike its Habsburg predecessors, after having re-conquered Catalonia from its defection in the War of Spanish Succession, the new Bourbon King stripped the Principality of its autonomous institutions and imposed Spanish as the language of government (Elliott 2002, chapter 10.2). The Decrees are therefore often mentioned as the beginning of Catalonia's cultural and political repression. Yet, with regard to the use of language, as Laitin *et al.* (1994) have shown, the Catalan upper classes had already switched to Spanish in their appeals to the King, and in other official uses, about a generation earlier. Hence, the Decrees mostly acknowledged an already established custom. Martinez Shaw (1985, p. 122) even observed that, during the War of Spanish Succession (1707–14), 90 per cent of the anti-Philip propaganda in Barcelona was published in Spanish, while Vilar (1962, p. 160) suggested that Catalan was spoken without any political meaning until the mid-nineteenth century. More in general, for much of the eighteenth century, in the wake of Catalonia's renewed prosperity, a genuine sense of 'Spanishness' spread among the Catalan merchant and industrial classes, which probably account for the durable coexistence of Catalan nationalism and ideas of membership of the Spanish state (Vilar 1962, pp. 158–160).

Furthermore, the rise of peripheral nationalism in Spain occurred much later and can be described as a process of *longue durée* whereby old identities were given new meanings (Fusi 2000, pp. 21–23). In Catalonia, the process began with a cultural movement for the promotion of the Catalan language and culture – the *Renaixença*. This movement assumed a more modern profile with the work of Valenti Almirall and his 1886 *Lo Catalanisme* (Catalanism). Almirall was able to rally the bulk of the Catalan industrial bourgeoisie that, despite remaining pro-Spanish in essence, saw Catalan nationalism as a useful tool for bringing forth its protectionist demands and, more generally, claiming more political power within the Spanish state (Conversi 1997, pp. 15–18). In the following years, the Catalan national identity was built around the region's vernacular language, its institutional history, its bourgeois civil society and the belief in the hard-work ethic and industriousness of its people. It was also strongly influenced by Romanticism, the existence of a national Church and the weakness and inefficiency of the Spanish state (Llobera 2004, pp. 16–18).

It is at this time that the idea of Catalan political marginalisation was born. As argued by Llobera (2003, p. 66), 'the image of the spirit of Catalonia subjugated within the Spanish state was dear to the ideologists of Catalanism'. There is some statistical evidence of such political marginalisation. In the 1815–99 period, out of 850 Spanish ministers only 22 were from Catalonia, or 2 per cent, while the region accounted for about 10 per cent of the total population of the country throughout the century (De Riquer 2000, pp. 62–67). Between 1902 and 1930, the Catalan representation in government improved a little (13 ministers out of 182, or 7 per cent), but the Catalans were fairly represented (14 per cent against a share of the population of 13 per cent) only during the Second Republic (1931–36) and the Civil War (1936–39) (Llobera 2004, p. 151). And yet, this underrepresentation seems to be more the result of a deliberate choice of the Catalan elites, rather than a Castilian initiative. As Llobera (2004,

p. 150) suggests 'in the second half of the 19th century, Catalonia, despite being the most economically developed area of Spain, refused to participate in political life, hence abandoning the running of the state to elites from other areas'. This was mostly due to the diverging agendas of the Catalan and Spanish – especially from Andalusia and Castile – elites, which frustrated Catalan attempts at modernising the country. In this connection, the loss of the colonies at the end of the Spanish-American War in 1898 was a key event. It made the decadent state of Spain so obvious that 'Carlists, conservatives, liberals, republicans, radicals, socialists, anarchists and Catalan regionalists all developed opposing projects of "national regeneration"' (Balfour and Quiroga 2007, p. 27). While Catalan nationalists founded the *Lliga* (a powerful regionalist party), Spanish conservatives intensified the nation-building effort and set out to fight peripheral nationalism. The first application of such programme came under the dictatorship of Primo de Rivera in the interwar years; the second, and most brutal, with that of Francisco Franco.

The State of the Autonomies

The repression of the Catalan language and culture during the dictatorship, as well as the persecution of Catalan nationalism, are incontrovertible facts on which there is wide consensus. Ironically, however, in the long run, the regime both weakened the Spanish national identity and reinforced the association between peripheral nationalism and democracy (Balfour and Quiroga 2007, p. 1). Such a coincidence of the fight for democracy and that for autonomy meant that the transition could not but entail a decentralisation of the Spanish state.

In the early 1990s, ERC declared the failure of the democratic transition on account of the continuity of the political system with the past regime. In terms of bureaucratic staff, such continuity is a historical fact. Among the political elite, however, renewal was more substantial,[7] although, in general terms, the transition was carried out with the deliberate intention to avoid a sharp break with the past. All actors involved in the political process committed to prevent the country from falling back into the violence of the Civil War. A 'pact of silence' was tacitly signed by the main political parties, which agreed to work by consensus on the new constitution (Colomer 1998, p. 44, Pellistrandi 2006, p. 23). This, however, does not mean that Spain has not become a democracy. The country is often quoted as an example of successful democratic transition (Guibernau 2004, p. 4). It is true, however, that the opposite perception has been strong in Catalonia. From 1992 to 2006, 56.7 per cent of the population of the region, on average, found that Spanish democracy had not reached the level of other European democracies (ICPS 1991–2016).

Furthermore, the process of devolution of powers has been problematic and its outcomes contested. Because of wide discrepancies in the ideological positions of its drafters, the Constitution was ambiguous about the limits of devolution. The *Unio de Centro Democratico* (Union of the Democratic Centre, UCD)[8] wanted to keep power at the centre as much as possible. Basque and Catalan nationalist parties, on the contrary, sought to obtain recognition of their differential status and maximise their competences. The Socialists were open to federalisation, but according to a symmetric model. Each got something. The old Napoleonic provinces – seen as a tool of centralised control of the periphery – were left untouched and the unity and integrity of the Spanish nation was openly proclaimed in the Constitution. The Basque Country, Catalonia and Galicia were defined as 'historical nationalities' and allowed to immediately initiate the transfer of powers. All the other communities were given the possibility to obtain similar competences, even if at a later stage (Colomer 1998, pp. 40–42).

The fundamental trait of Spanish devolution has been the *principio dispositivo*, whereby the process has been driven by the periphery that could decide to access different degrees of autonomy (Fossas 1999, p. 6). Being open, it ensured flexibility, but at the same time made the system prone to a self-reinforcing competitive dynamic whereby the advances of the strongest communities, willing to mark their differential status, have fuelled demands for equality on the part of the other Spanish regions on the basis of a principle of 'comparative grievance' (Moreno 2001, p. 97, Colino 2009, p. 264). In this context, the negotiations for a better fiscal treatment have held central stage. Overall, there have been five major reforms of the financing system of the communities. At the 1993 and 1996 elections the PSOE, first, and the PP, later, needed the legislative support of CiU to have a majority in Parliament. This gave the Catalan party considerable bargaining power, which it used to obtain substantial fiscal concessions at each round. The absolute majority gained by the PP in 2000 put an end to the Catalan favourable position and, after a minor redefinition in 2001, the party opposed any further devolution. In 2009, a new negotiation involving all ordinary communities brought about a rise of the communities' share of income tax and VAT to 50 per cent, plus 58 per cent of special fees. As a consequence, about 40 per cent of state spending is now managed by the communities, while in 1980 the state controlled 90 per cent of it (Monasterio Escudero 2002, p. 181, Keating and Wilson 2009, pp. 540–541, Sala 2014, p. 123).

Four major flaws have, however, marked the devolution process, influencing fiscal claims in Catalonia. First, until 1997 fiscal autonomy progressively shrank since the communities gained financial (over spending) but not fiscal (over revenues) powers and thus increasingly depended on resources coming from Madrid. Second, few incentives for financial responsibility were given to the regions, which competed for demanding more resources rather than for making their spending more efficient. Third, the concrete meaning of the constitutional principle of equal fiscal treatment was not defined – for instance, equal spending per capita. Fourth, a specific stream of revenues to finance investments in non-needy regions like Catalonia was not foreseen. More generally, politics and contingency have largely determined the course of events, more than principles and any kind of model of federalisation (Monasterio Escudero 2002, pp. 158–169).

Nevertheless, asserting that the State of the Autonomies has been a failure would be a retrospective and mechanical argument. The relative peace and prosperity enjoyed by the country until 2008–10, after 40 years of a dictatorship that had dug deep fractures in its social fabric, is enough evidence of its success. Devolution of powers to the communities was conceived of as a device to ease conflict and assure state legitimacy in the periphery after the repression of the Francoist period. At least until the mid-2000s, devolution went along with a positive increase in dual identity (Spanish and Catalan). Therefore, as an attempt to accommodate difference, it was an effective nation-building tool (Martínez-Herrera 2002, Guibernau 2006). At the same time, however, devolution has inevitably offered structures from which nationalist and regionalist parties and organisations – CiU above all – could carry out nation-building activities (Balfour and Quiroga 2007, p. 137, see also Chapter 9). As a result, knowledge of Catalan has improved considerably (Roller 2001, p. 42) and has been accompanied by an increase in the strength of the 'predominantly' Catalan identity – from 26.6 per cent to 38.6 per cent between 1979 and 2009 (Argelaguet 2006, p. 437, ICPS 1991–2016).[9]

That notwithstanding, Catalonia experienced no nationalist radicalisation until the end of the 2000s, when the most important institutional conflict of the democratic period began. This has centred around a reform of the Statute of Autonomy of the community long advocated by ERC. Such reform became a possibility when, in 2003, *Esquerra* joined a regional government coalition led by the socialist candidate Pasquall Maragall, who had pledged to modify the Statute – perceived as being outdated – during the electoral campaign.[10] Despite being heavily amended in the Spanish Parliament, the final version of the Statute was then ratified by the Catalan population with a more than 70 per cent majority. Shortly after its ratification, however, the PP appealed against the Statute to the Spanish Constitutional Tribunal, asking the court to rule over the accordance with the Constitution of 187 articles. Four years later, in a judgment that is considered as the main trigger of the recent confrontation, the Tribunal found parts of 14 articles unconstitutional and gave constraining interpretations of another 27 (Guibernau 2013, p. 382). The Tribunal's clarification that the definition of Catalonia as a nation – made in the preliminary paragraphs of the Statute – is void of any legal value has probably been the sourest point. It nourished support for a grassroots movement for the 'right to decide' that had organised unofficial referenda in several Catalan municipalities in 2009 and early 2010 and that later promoted giant demonstrations in Barcelona (Subirats and Vilaregut 2012). The ruling openly rejected any plurinational interpretations of the Spanish state, stressing that, according to the Constitution, Spain is the only nation of the country. In this way, it shattered a 'constructive ambiguity' that had lain at the core of the constitutional pact and that had accommodated opposing views of the status of Catalonia and its relation with the rest of the country. Furthermore, despite being in line with legal practice, the ruling was perceived as inherently undemocratic because it invalidated parts of a text that had been approved by two parliaments and ratified through popular referendum (Fossas 2011).

In other words, the process of modification of the Statute of Autonomy of Catalonia opened a controversy about the place of the community within Spain that fuelled already existing perceptions of political marginalisation. These did not have so much to do with the democratic institutions of Spain as such, but rather with the type of democracy that they embody. For instance, while Catalan parties have consistently been underrepresented in the Spanish Congress and government since the democratic transition – they hold 13.5 per cent of seats while Catalonia accounts for 16 per cent of Spain's population, and have only held five ministries between 1982 and 1996 (Llobera 2004, pp. 156–157) – this has not been a major argument in ERC's, or even in CiU's, rhetoric. The bones of contention have rather been the fiscal deal and the recognition of Catalonia as a nation endowed with a right to self-determination. The claim of political marginalisation therefore depends on the definition of Catalonia as a distinct political community that deserves recognition on a par with Spain (Fossas 1999, p. 10).

Conclusion

Broadly speaking, ERC's argument of economic victimisation goes as follows. The Catalans are deprived of about 8 per cent of their GDP each year and such capital drain prevents them from improving their welfare and competing with more advanced foreign regions in continental and global markets. The transfer of resources to the rest of Spain is not legitimate on grounds of solidarity, since it has been used to nourish dependence in poorer regions, prop up the inefficient Spanish bureaucracy and fund the wastages of a corrupt political class. The rejection of solidarity is also warranted on account of the nature of Catalan wealth, which mainly derives from the effort of its entrepreneurial and hard-working people. The party has thus articulated a form of 'culturalised welfare producerism' that has, however, been very careful to direct against the Madrid establishment and the state administration rather than the populations of other Spanish regions. Always according to the party, if kept in Catalonia, those resources would afford a generous and efficient welfare system for all Catalans. For that to happen, however, the Catalan nation needs an independent state. In ERC's narrative, the Catalans have tried unsuccessfully for centuries to change the backward and authoritarian Spanish state as well as to be treated as an equal nation endowed with a right to self-determination. Until the recent constitutional crisis – from 2010 on – the party was open to a gradualist strategy whereby independence could be achieved in stages. Yet, the prolonged confrontation between the *Generalitat* and the central government over the holding of an independence referendum seems to have ruled out such a scenario for the foreseeable future. What has remained, however, is the theme of the *catalanisme del benestar*, which has emphasised the instrumental character of the struggle for independence, as a means to achieve a better standard of living and better welfare, rather than as an end in itself. The *catalanisme del benestar* has also entailed a stronger emphasis on catering for the everyday needs of the people, on engaging with and providing sound policy-making with regard to all areas of government action. In this way, *Esquerra* has 'normalised' separatism and turned independence into a goal that can be democratically achieved from within the Catalan political institutions.

Apart from this recent change away from gradualism, ERC's rhetoric has shown surprising stability. In recent years, dramatic change has been brought about by the process of reform of the Statute of Autonomy and by the economic crisis, but, their true impact seems to have consisted in making ERC's existing rhetoric more suitable as a diagnostic and prognostic frame for the Catalan population, rather than in urging any major adjustment in the discourse and strategy of the party.

As argued in Chapter 1, the Catalan nationalist movement of the late nineteenth and early twentieth century can be considered as a forerunner of the nationalism of the rich and this mainly on account of the coincidence of uneven economic development and the rise of peripheral national identities in Spain. The main difference between the debate over Spanish-Catalan economic relations that unfolded back then and that arisen since the 1960s consists in a switch in focus from trade to fiscal flows. From the early 1980s, several academic studies confirmed the existence of substantial fiscal transfers from Catalonia to the rest of Spain. Yet, the issue did not flare up until the late 1980s, when ERC began formulating the rhetoric of the *expoli fiscal*, because the main concern of the Catalan political elite up to that period was the consolidation of Catalonia's political autonomy and the protection of the Catalan language. The relevance of the claims of Catalan fiscal victimisation was heightened by the steady rise of state spending, taxation and debt, coupled with widely broadcast corruption scandals. They also enjoyed 'cultural resonance', since they tapped into older narratives depicting Catalonia as an advanced periphery that was being held back by a more backward Spain. While CiU had embarked in a policy of 'constructive opposition' that entailed a compromising attitude, ERC could take the lead in denouncing the *expoli fiscal*.

Nobody can deny the role of generous contributor that Catalonia has played in the Spanish fiscal system. Substantial flows have persisted for at least three decades, convergence has been only partially achieved, overcompensation effects have been documented – although estimates vary widely – especially with regard to infrastructural investments, and corruption scandals in the early 1990s contributed to spreading the perception that Catalan resources were being siphoned off for clientelist purposes. The fiscal imbalance calculated by the party, however, is compatible with academic studies based on a monetary flow methodology that underestimate the distribution of general expenses. Furthermore, other communities account for similar levels of solidarity – notably Madrid and the Balearic Islands. The example of the Balearic Islands suggests that the perception of being a different community plays a key role in the formation of the nationalism of the rich, since the reason why similar claims have not developed in the Islands seems to lie in the largely Spanish-oriented national identification of the local population.

This brings us to the historical relationship between Catalonia and Spain, which certainly offers a number of events that can be interpreted as evidence of Catalonia's oppression. Some, such as the persecution of Catalan culture and language under Franco or the abolition of the Catalan Parliament after the War of Spanish Succession, are incontrovertible facts. Others, such as the imposition of Spanish with the Decrees of *Nueva Planta* lie on shakier grounds, without being for this reason less effective. Furthermore, there is statistical evidence of underrepresentation of Catalan politicians in Spain's central institutions for much of the period from 1875–1930, as well as in the post-dictatorship era. Curiously, however, this has rarely been mentioned in the party's rhetoric. What has, on the contrary, been much more vocally decried is Spain's rejection of the plurinational character of the state and of the recognition of the right of self-determination of its constituent nations. Until recently, a frontal confrontation had been avoided mostly thanks to a 'constructive ambiguity' at the core of the model of the State of Autonomies adopted in 1978, especially through the use of the term 'nationality' to indicate the Basque Country, Catalonia and Galicia. This 'constructive ambiguity' has however been shattered by the 2010 ruling of the Constitutional Tribunal.

Notes

1 My calculations on Eurostat 2017a.
2 A list is provided in Annex 1.
3 From 1996 to 2004, after about 20 years of socialist rule, the PP won two consecutive elections, enjoying an absolute majority in Parliament during its second time in office (2000–04).
4 He later started a political career and took part in the negotiations on fiscal autonomy between the central government and the Catalan *Generalitat*. He was a strong advocate of the *concierto economico* and in the 1980s published books and gave speeches denouncing Catalonia's fiscal treatment (see Trias 1985).
5 In 2012, 78 per cent of the population of the islands was against a referendum on independence (IBES 2012a).
6 There is overcompensation when equalisation goes beyond ensuring equal per capita spending in all regions by providing more than average resources to the regions that contribute less and less than average in those that contribute most.

7 In the 1977 elections 56.6 per cent of the votes and 168 out of the 350 seats went to parties that had opposed the dictatorship (Hopkin 2001, p. 118).

8 This was a self-declared centrist party, which however included several members of the former regime.

9 By 'predominantly' Catalan national identity, I mean the sum of the percentages relative to the 'more Catalan than Spanish' and 'only Catalan' answers to the standard five-choice Moreno question on subjective national identification.

10 For more information on the process of modification of the Statute (see Keating and Wilson 2009, Orte and Wilson 2009, pp. 424–430).

3 Flanders

Inter-regional transfers and the powerless majority

Origins and evolution of the VB and the N-VA

The *Vlaams Belang* (the Flemish Interest, VB)[1] and the *Nieuw-Vlaamse Alliantie* (the New Flemish Alliance, N-VA) are late offshoots of the Flemish movement, i.e. a set of organisations fighting for the emancipation of the Flemish people that arose in Belgium in the second half of the nineteenth century and that here, for reasons of scope, I can only treat cursorily (for more detail see Wils 1992, De Schryver *et al.* 1998, Wils 2010). Both originated in the *Volksunie* (the People's Union, VU), a party founded in 1954, which, from 1961 on, began an electoral progression peaking at the 1971 election, when it polled 19 per cent of the Flemish vote (Witte 2009b, pp. 361–369). In 1977, the VU entered a government agreement aiming to achieve a federal reform of the country called the Egmont Pact. A substantial share of its militants however rejected this decision and some founded the *Vlaamse Nationale Partij* (Flemish National Party, VNP), led by Karel Dillen (Delwit 2009, pp. 188–189). At the general election held a year later, Dillen managed to obtain a seat in the Senate and changed the name of the VNP into *Vlaams Blok* (Flemish Bloc), which set out to fight for the establishment of a Flemish Republic from a right-wing platform based on anti-communism, solidarism and demands for amnesty for Second World War collaborators (Erk 2005a, p. 496).

In the mid-1980s, Dillen decided to broaden the appeal of the organisation by co-opting members from satellite student organisations who emphasised the party's attention on problems such as immigration, multiculturalism and security (Mudde 2000, pp. 83–84). Shortly afterwards, in 1988–89, the party made its first breakthrough outside the city of Antwerp – until then its cradle. When, in 1991, with 10.3 per cent of the Flemish vote it overtook the VU, all the other parties agreed not to enter into government coalitions with it at any administrative level, setting up a cordon sanitaire that has lasted until today. This notwithstanding, the VB continued to grow, obtaining the support of roughly a quarter of Flanders' electorate in 2004 (Figure 3.1) (Govaert 2001, Pauwels 2011, pp. 61–62).

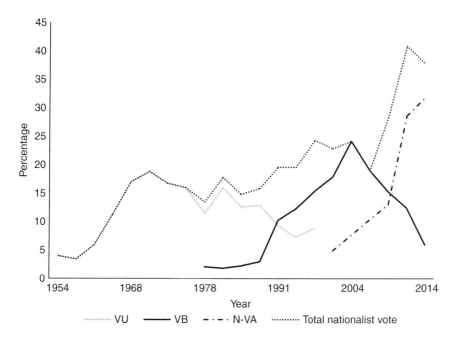

Figure 3.1 Evolution of the nationalist vote in Flanders, 1954–2014* (percentage of regional vote, main parties).

Sources: my elaboration on Van Haute and Pilet 2006, Pauwels 2011, Beyens *et al.* 2015, Chamber of Representatives of Belgium 2003, 2014.

Note
* The 2004 and 2007 N-VA's results have not been taken into account because obtained in a coalition with the CD&V.

At the peak of its popularity, however, the party was disbanded. Three organisations affiliated with it were brought to court on charges of racism and xenophobia. After a series of trials, the Flemish Court of Appeal ruled that, to remain eligible for public subsidies, the VB should reorganise itself with a programme in accordance with the law. The transition to the new *Vlaams Belang* was quite smooth though, as the party had previously toned down some of its harshest stances (Erk 2005a, pp. 494–495). In the following years, the rise of a strong competitor in the Flemish nationalist camp – the N-VA – undermined the electoral success of the party (Pauwels 2011, pp. 61–62, Swyngedouw and Abts 2011), which began a downward trajectory ending in the 5.9 per cent of the Flemish vote obtained at the 2014 regional and federal elections.

While the VB emerged as a reaction to the VU's drift towards a 'neither left nor right' moderate nationalism, the N-VA represents its transformation into a separatist and conservative party. As a reaction to the VU's decline, during the 1990s two factions arose within the Union: one willing to move to a post-nationalist platform; the other convinced that the nationalist agenda should be radicalised. After a long series of clashes, the fate of the party was decided in 2001 through an internal referendum. The group in favour of a more nationalist agenda won a relative majority and founded the N-VA, which declared itself to be separatist, republican, liberal and opposed to the ethnic nationalism of the VB (Govaert 2002, pp. 5–32). After a poor performance at the 2003 federal election and the introduction of a 5 per cent threshold to access the Flemish Parliament, the N-VA entered into an alliance with the *Christen-Democratisch en Vlaams* (Christian-Democrats and Flemish, CD&V) for the 2004 regional election. It obtained six seats (out of 124), became part of the regional government and largely radicalised the alliance's demands (Delwit 2009, pp. 266–267). The two parties ran together again in the 2007 federal election, scoring 31.4 per cent of the Flemish vote. The N-VA's demands though made the negotiations for the government agreement quite difficult and the party eventually withdrew its passive support to the government formed in March 2008 only a few months later (Sinardet 2008a).

In the meantime, in 2004, Bart De Wever became party chairman, an event that, according to some, explains much of the party's electoral breakthrough. In the 2009 Flemish election, the N-VA ran alone and won 13.5 per cent of the regional vote, a result that it more than doubled (28 per cent) at the federal election held a year later, thus becoming the leading party in Belgium. The party's extreme demands and electoral clout made the negotiations to find a governing coalition very difficult, leading to the world record deadlock of 541 days. The party's primacy was then confirmed after the 2014 general and regional elections, where it secured 32 per cent of the Flemish vote (Rochtus 2012, Beyens *et al.* 2015, pp. 2–3). This time the N-VA agreed to join a 'Flemish-dominated' federal coalition with the CD&V and the Flemish Liberals (*OpenVLD*) along with the francophone liberals of the Reform Movement.[2] By contrast, at the same election the VB scored one of its worst performances in the last two decades. What has not substantially declined, however, is the overall nationalist (and, after the demise of the VU, separatist) vote in Flanders (Figure 3.1).

The VB's and the N-VA's nationalism of the rich

Claims of economic exploitation were not new in Flemish politics. The myth of *Arm Vlaanderen* (poor Flanders), whereby Northern Belgium was being kept poor by a francophone-dominated state, was already widespread before the reversal of the economic relations between the two halves of the country (Bochme 2008a, p. 558, 2008b, p. 148). However, at the end of the 1970s the subject took on a new life and the economic victimisation of the region began being centred around a narrative of fiscal exploitation carried out by lazy, socialist Walloons and inefficient Brussels-based institutions (see also Quévit 2010, p. 3).

The cost of Belgium

Although the VB has engaged in a much more principled rhetoric than the N-VA, the economic argument has lain at the core of its discourse. As recently recognised by the party itself: 'Flemish nationalism is not to be reduced to a mere issue about pennies. Nevertheless, social security, public debt, prosperity, taxes and unemployment are important matters about which most Flemings feel directly concerned. The financial transfers therefore regularly form the core of the Flemish national argument' (VB 2009a, p. 3). This theme was already prominent at the first Congress of the party in March 1980. There, making extensive reference to academic studies on the fiscal transfers conducted in the late 1970s (see below), the VB attempted the first calculations of the *geldstroom* (the flow of money) from Flanders to Wallonia, estimating it at roughly 50 billion Belgian francs a year for the period 1974–78 (about 2.7 billion 2010 euros) (Van Gorp *et al.* 1980, pp. 1–4).[3] The figure has varied overtime with the most recent estimates reaching 16 billion euros per year, tantamount to 7 per cent of the Flemish GDP (VB 2007, p. 4, 2009b, Slootmans 2015a).

In 1992, the VB published its most complete brochure on the subject under the eloquent title *De kostprijs van België* (The Cost Price of Belgium). There, the party argued that the transfers from Flanders and Brussels to Wallonia amounted to 418 billion francs (about 13.7 billion 2010 euros), which meant that each Walloon received 130,000 francs per year (or 4,200 2010 euros).[4] This figure was broken down into the following components: social security, interests on the public debt, and other grants, mainly supposed to concern subsidies to 'uncompetitive' Walloon companies. The brochure concluded that 'the Belgian Treasury and the Belgian social security are a kind of efficient draining system for Flemish resources and Flemish energy'. It then continued: 'add to this the incredible arrogance of the Walloons, in particular their Socialist Party. They are not satisfied with Flemish pennies, but on top of this they want constant Flemish genuflections, humiliations' (Annemans and Smout 1997, p. 15). The brochure was republished, with basically the same structure and only updated data, in 2003 and 2009 (Joseph and Leen 2003, VB 2009c).

In the first years of the party's existence, the claim against state subsidies to southern enterprises featured quite highly in its propaganda, since the crisis of the so-called national sectors (coal, steel, glass, shipbuilding and textile), some of which were concentrated in Wallonia, was a burning issue at the time (Favere 1979, Laitem 1980). Similarly, and along the lines of the older narrative of *Arm Vlaanderen*, the party spilled much ink denouncing the economic consequences of the political dominance of the francophone elite, especially in the government and banking sectors (Laitem 1980, see also Annemans and Smout 1997, p. 14). These concerns, however, lost salience over time while issues linked to the skyrocketing public debt and the costs of social security became preponderant, especially amid the corruption and policy failure scandals of the 1990s (on such scandals see Maesschalck and Van de Walle 2006, pp. 1012–1014). In 1992, for instance, the party condemned that: 'Belgium has a dazzling national debt of 300,000 million US$. The traditional parties' politicians are not servants of the people. They primarily serve their party, their clan, their trade union. Political appointments of civil servants, embezzlement of public funds and other malpractices are rampant' (VB 1992, p. 17). A year later, it concluded that 'from its original function of guarantor, the state has become a kind of exploiter' (Annemans 1993, p. 19) and, while the party often generally referred to 'traditional parties' when identifying the main responsible of the corrupt state of Belgium, it also clearly asserted that Wallonia did have a dirtier political culture, largely implying that an independent Flanders would be a cleaner country (Annemans 1994, Van Hauthem 1996).

Although corruption and policy failure scandals later abated, the inefficiency of the Belgian state remained a key argument in the party's rhetoric. In 2005, the VB (p. 21) reported the findings of a study of the European Central Bank concluding that the Belgian Government was 20 per cent less efficient than the European average and that the same services could be provided with 35 per cent fewer resources. Then, with the re-emergence of issues related to budget deficits and the public debt in the wake of the financial and euro crisis, it started anew predicting a financial doom scenario and describing independence as the only way out of the 'suffocating Belgian straightjacket' (Pas 2009, VB 2010a, Valkeniers 2011).

The Belgian state, however, has not been the sole culprit in the VB's narrative. As previous quotes have shown, the Walloons, and the francophone *Parti Socialiste* (Socialist Party, PS) in particular, have been deemed responsible for the Flemish fiscal exploitation because they have deliberately lived on the Flemings' back. In 1983, Dillen claimed that 'Flanders thus becomes ever more the milk cow of a Wallonia that [...] seeks all its welfare in a wasteful statism' (see also Laitem 1980, Peeters 1982). What the VB has consistently implied with this account is that the economic difference between the two regions is culturally driven and Wallonia's future lies in the Walloons' hands: if they drop their socialist mindset and work more, they will be better off eventually (Penris 1994, Annemans and Builtinck 1997, pp. 21–22, Van Overmeire 2002, p. 10, VB 2005, p. 21, Valkeniers 2011). In this narrative, Flanders, in contrast, has been the engine of the country's economy, thanks to its hard-working population and its competitive small and medium-sized enterprises (Vanhecke 1979, Annemans and Builtinck 1997, p. 15, VB 2005, p. 6, VB 2009a, pp. 54–56). As asserted in the 2014 election manifesto, 'the work ethic and the spirit of initiative form the goodwill of the Flemish labour market' (VB 2014, p. 13). Nevertheless, Flanders 'gets poorer because of an excessive "solidarity"' (VB 2010b, p. 32). As a consequence, the party has consistently declared itself not to be against solidarity in principle, but rather lamented that 'the Wallons are deaf to the Flemish requests. They take always more, never give anything. This is no solidarity, but brutal theft' (Annemans and Builtinck 1997, p. 22, see also VB 1989, Vanhecke 2000, VB 2014, p. 7). The fact that the transfers have not helped the Walloon economy to become competitive again has often been mentioned as an additional reason to scrap them altogether (Van Hauthem 1989, Annemans 1993, p. 21, D'Haeseleer and Builtinck 2003, p. 5, VB 2009a, pp. 3–4, Slootmans 2015a).

Some have argued that Flanders was and currently is paying a 'debt of honour' to Wallonia, because the former profited from the latter's support in the nineteenth and early twentieth centuries. Already in the early 1980s, the VB dismissed this as 'a shameless lie' (Decoster 1980) and, in more recent years, they have quoted academic studies (see Hannes 2007) suggesting that, in fact, Flanders had been fiscally exploited already in the nineteenth century (Joseph and Leen 2003, VB 2009c). More fundamentally, according to the party, the idea that Wallonia was generous with Flanders 'is nonsense' because 'in that past social security did not exist and there was even less mentioning of the effect of the public debt' (Annemans 1993, p. 20, see also Annemans and Builtinck 1997, p. 23, Leen and Van den Troost 2005, p. 15).

The Walloons are therefore deemed to have violated the basic principles of trust, fairness and reciprocity that undergird welfare arrangements and, for this reason, not to deserve Flemish support. At a closer look, however, in the VB's mindset, true solidarity is possible only within the national community, where people are more ethnically homogeneous. In its formative years, the VB openly claimed to defend an 'ethnic solidarity' embodying a third way between Marxism and liberalism (Truyens 1980, VB 1983), while a decade later, it loudly asserted the social dimension of nationalism arguing that nationalism 'deems solidarity with the family and, thus, with the people, central' (Annemans 1993, p. 14). In this framework, true solidarity is only, or chiefly, possible within the 'cosy' limits of the ethno-national community – seen, as the above quote suggests, as an enlarged family – in accordance with a welfare chauvinist outlook concisely conveyed by the slogan '*eigen volk eerst*' (own people first) (Annemans 1993, p. 15).[5]

In the late 1990s, the then leader Frank Vanhecke (1998) tried to further reinforce the image of the VB as a 'social party' that, contrary to the traditional trade unions, knew the real problems of the people and catered for them, thus making the national and social struggles coincide (see also D'Haeseleer and Bultinck 2003, p. 5). In the context of the euro crisis, the party has again emphasised this profile and, after the 2014 election, it strongly criticised the austerity measures proposed by the N-VA-led federal government, thus portraying itself as a more social party than its main adversary within the Flemish nationalist camp (VB 2013a, Slootmans 2015b, Van Osselaer 2015).[6]

Since, in the party's view, the Belgian state remains the main obstacle to the implementation of a true and effective Flemish solidarity, 'any social policy in Flanders can only be aimed at the dismantling of the transfers and the transition to an independent Flemish state' (Annemans 1993, p. 20, see also Favere 1979, Vanhecke 2000, VB 2005, Dillen 2012). The abolition of the transfers has thus been used by the party as a 'trump card' that would allow the Flemish Republic to reduce taxes and labour costs without entailing an equal reduction of social services. As argued in the context of the euro crisis, for instance: 'without the transfers Flanders could let taxes structurally decrease and record a surplus of 3.5 per cent [of regional GDP]. As a result, we could eventually follow a social policy tailored around the Flemings' (Slootmans 2015a). Here, one finds an idea similar to the *Catalanisme del benestar* seen in Chapter 2, since independent statehood is proposed as a way to ensure the material prosperity of the Flemish nation.

Since the late 1990s, this discourse has been enriched by a further argument that we find in nearly all the other case studies, i.e. the idea that an independent Flanders will be as successful a community in the globalised economy as many other small states (Wienen 1998). Thus, in 2005, one could read in a VB brochure that 'small economies with international ambitions perform well. They are often more competitive and creative than big states which, because of their size and cultural diversity, can pursue no coherent policy' (VB 2005, p. 7). In other publications, the party also recalled that on a GDP per capita basis, Flanders would rank sixth in the World (Leen and Van den Troost 2005, p. 7), while, by contrast, 'one constant is clear from all recent economic reports and rankings: Belgium's economic decline' (VB 2005, p. 13).

The Flemish milk cow and the Walloon poverty trap

The arguments concerning economic victimisation made by the N-VA are very similar to those of the VB, although they are often more moderate and sophisticated. Like the VB, the N-VA has claimed that about 7 per cent of Flemish GDP is transferred from Flanders to Wallonia, through social security, interests on Belgian debt and the regional budgets. The party has likewise dismissed the argument whereby this would be a payment of honour to Wallonia for her previous solidarity with the Flemings, as it has argued that this never occurred. Thus, the transfers are deemed to be an injustice and Flanders 'a milk cow' that pays to maintain undemocratic and opaque subsidies that only help to prop up a clientelistic socialist state in the south of Belgium (N-VA 2002a, p. 4, 2003, p. 19, 2004a, p. 4, 2007b, p. 11, 2014a). The N-VA has also pointed out how Wallonia benefits from a wider public sector (about 40 per cent of the population) and free-riding practices, such as laxer controls on unemployment benefits (N-VA 2004b; see N-VA 2012b with regard to unemployment in Brussels).

These resources – the party has argued – could be used to finance better social policy and investments in Flanders. For instance, at the beginning of the 2000s, the N-VA claimed that, contrary to common wisdom, Flanders did not have the capital required to adapt to the transition to a knowledge economy, because this was being siphoned off by Wallonia (N-VA 2002b, 2004c, p. 27). In more recent years, it has rather underlined the management prowess of the Flemish Government as compared to the profligacy of the rest of Belgium and pointed to an increased urgency to bring about reform to avoid being dragged down by Wallonia and Brussels in the context of the financial and euro crisis (N-VA 2008, 2009a, pp. 4–7, 2009b, 2012a, 2014a).

The key argument made by the N-VA, however, is that the transfers have made Wallonia fall into a poverty trap whereby 'instead of stimulating the endogenous Walloon development, the flow of money keeps Wallonia stuck in the role of eternal beggar' (N-VA 2002a, p. 4). While solidarity per se, even in extreme forms, is not seen as a problem by the party, it should never turn into dependence (see also N-VA 2008), all the more so given that 'social security systems already lack the support of important groups of the population' (N-VA 2010, p. 25) because costs increase but performances do not improve. Hence, according to the N-VA, in the face of no substantial Walloon economic progress, worsening and more expensive welfare services in Flanders have dramatically affected the legitimacy with which Flemish residents view the continuing solidarity with the south of the country. Therefore, the N-VA declared itself willing to conclude 'a new socio-economic agreement with Wallonia, whereby we make measurable and time-bound commitments to bring employment to a higher level and within which we organise solidarity' (N-VA 2010, p. 14).

More fundamentally, the N-VA – like the VB – has consistently argued that the diverging economic performances of Flanders and Wallonia result from their cultural differences. As pointed out by Bart De Wever (2009): 'there is a communitarian difference, as so often in our country. On the one hand, people in the north of the country want to go to work much more rigorously, are much more concerned with healthy government finances. On the other hand, in the south of the country – and that has always been pretty much the case – they look at that with indifference' (see also De Wever's declaration in Cobbaert 2014). The logical conclusion drawn by the party is that Belgian solidarity, in its current form, has failed and Flanders is therefore justified in seeking independence – or confederalism in the short term – as an alternative way to remain among the richest and most economically efficient regions in Europe (N-VA 2007b, p. 6, 2009a, p. 4, 2014b, p. 2).

Furthermore, quoting the Harvard economists Spolaore and Alesina, the N-VA has suggested that globalisation, aimed at providing economies of scale, goes together with localisation, as a means to reduce heterogeneity costs, which means that Belgium no longer makes sense, because scale problems can be moved up to the EU, while heterogeneity costs can be reduced by transferring competences to Flanders (N-VA 2009a, p. 68, 2010, p. 8). In this perspective, Wallonia would also profit from an economic policy more tailored to its own characteristics. According to the N-VA, indeed, the two regions have very different industrial structures and, therefore, it does not make sense to apply homogenous solutions. While, in the short term, this would require devolving labour and fiscal policies along with the social security system to the regions – otherwise Wallonia would keep suffocating the productive Flemish economy (N-VA 2003, p. 16, 2007a) – in the long term, the true solution is Flemish independence. Hence, independence, and state reform more generally, has been portrayed as a tool to improve the lives and welfare of the Flemings, in a similar manner as the *Catalanisme del benestar* discussed in Chapter 2. As repeatedly argued by the party ahead of the 2014 elections: 'the N-VA does not want to "split for splitting's sake". Instead, a different approach is needed to secure the prosperity and wellbeing of all Flemings and Francophones. For that we need a new direction. And confederalism is about this. Hence confederalism is not a story of institutional reform, but is about our future and that of our children' (N-VA 2013b, see also N-VA 2014c).

Both the VB and the N-VA have thus clearly subscribed to a conditional conception of solidarity in which the deservingness criteria of control, attitude and reciprocity have played a key role, since the Walloons are believed: to be responsible for their protracted state of need by sticking to (wrong) statist economic policies;[7] not to make enough of an effort to get out of their situation of need, but rather to take advantage of Belgian social security (paid for by the hard-working Flemings); and to receive more than what they have contributed, while the Flemings receive less than what they deserve. This welfare producerism (Abts and Kochuyt 2013, 2014) is powerfully culturalised, since the portrayal of the Flemish nation as made up of hard-working and entrepreneurial people allows the two parties to make the 'imagined community of welfare producers' discursively coincide with the entire Flemish nation.

Both parties have also made consistent, albeit often implicit, use of the criterion of identity in their reasoning about redistribution, since the community of solidarity to which they have made reference is undoubtedly the national community. Yet, the VB and the N-VA have conveyed two different interpretations of membership in the national community, as well as given different emphases to the identity criterion. While, as seen above, the VB has claimed that solidarity is only possible within the strict contours of the ethno-national community – a claim in line with the wider ethno-pluralist outlook of the party (see Mudde 2000, pp. 99–101) – the N-VA's position has been more nuanced. Although it has rejected multiculturalism and shown clear assimilationist tendencies, the party has defended a more open and civic conception of the Flemish nation and identity than the VB (see N-VA 2002a, p. 7, 2004c, p. 15, 2009a, pp. 34–35). This does not mean that identity has been neglected in the N-VA's discourse. On the contrary, referring to the scientific literature on nationalism, the party has stressed the importance of national identity and tried to 'normalise' nationalism (see Maly 2012, 2013). It has also openly upheld the legitimate 'boundary-setting' role of national identity in carving out discrete communities of social sharing. As argued by De Wever in 2009, 'it is good to feel equally connected to everyone in the world so long as you are not asked to share your income with anybody and so long as you need not accept that through a democratic vote poorer citizens of the world could compel you to do something' (N-VA 2009c). Yet, as compared to the VB, access to the community of sharing is less influenced by one's origin than by the three principles of control, attitude and reciprocity.

The powerless majority

As in the other case studies, the VB's arguments about economic victimisation have been accompanied by accusations of political marginalisation. The peculiarity of Flanders is that such claims concern a demographic majority. In this context, the VB's starting point has been the artificial nature of the Belgian state, which the party has deemed to be the result of a historical accident: the decision of the European major powers to put together two different peoples (the Flemings and the Walloons) in a new state on the French centralised administrative model (VB 1980, Van Overmeire 2002, p. 9, Van Hauthem 2007). A compendium of the VB's interpretation of Belgian history can be found in a text issued from the 1990 congress 'Independence: We Must and Can' (*Onafhankelijkheid: moet en kan*). There the party argued that the Walloons had historically claimed tutelage over Belgium and violently repressed those Flemings who resisted francophone homogenisation. These latter had thus become legitimately anti-Belgian (Van Hauthem and Verreycken 1990, pp. 80–90). The humiliation and sacrifice experienced by Flemish soldiers under francophone command during the Great War, the two post-war repressions of the Flemish movement and the 'Frenchification'[8] of large swathes of originally Flemish territory were mentioned as examples of the many injustices suffered by the Flemings.

The claim of linguistic oppression – a mainstay of the Flemish movement – has for decades reflected a feeling of political subordination shared among the Flemish majority due to the lower social status of Dutch as compared to French for most of Belgian history (see below for further detail). Therefore, it is not surprising that it has held a central role in the VB's propaganda, not only during the late 1970s and early 1980s, when the linguistic conflict was at its peak, (see JVS 1979, Wouters 1982, VB 1984), but even in the last decade, when the party has consistently demanded the cancellation of the linguistic facilities – special derogations to the otherwise strictly monolingual character of Flanders granted to some border municipalities with sizable francophone minorities – in the area around Brussels and accused the Francophones[9] living there to deliberately sabotage the language laws (Van Overmeire 2002, p. 21, De Man *et al.* 2005, pp. 11–17, Michiels 2007, Hiers 2015).

However, the most important political argument made by the VB with regard to the relationship between Flemings and Francophones within the Belgian state has concerned the use of the constitutional safeguards introduced in the 1960s (see below for further detail). Through these, the Francophones are considered by the party to have forced upon the Flemings an undemocratic structure that provides a minority with unlimited resources to block the decisions adopted by the majority of the country. Therefore, Belgium is deemed not to be a democracy, since the Flemish majority is turned into a de facto minority (Dillen 1983, VB 1988, Leen and Van den Troost 2005, p. 31, Valkeniers 2012). As asserted in 1996: 'the Vlaams Blok rejects the Belgian federalism as a government system that is used to prevent Flanders from ever being able to assert its rights of majority in Belgium. It has as its only purpose the continuous minoritisation of the Flemish majority and the maintenance of Wallonia's privileged position at the political, financial and social levels' (Arckens 1996). This minoritisation is deemed by the party to be all the more frustrating because Flanders and Wallonia represent two different worlds that cannot agree on almost anything and where 'Wallonia thinks and votes left' while 'Flanders thinks and votes right' (Leen and Van den Troost 2005, p. 29). Hence – the VB has argued – Belgium is a blocked country, where democracy does not work, governance is highly inefficient and the Walloons can ultimately afford not to worry about these problems because Flanders foots the bill (Annemans 1993, p. 14, Van Overmeirc 2002, p. 16, VB 2007, p. 3, VB 2009a, pp. 5–6, VB 2013b, Pas 2013). The conclusion drawn by the party from the state of affairs portrayed above is that, while Flanders deserves more democracy and needs better governance to compete in the global economy, Belgium cannot provide that. In this framework, independence is considered as the only way to ensure the necessary good governance because Belgium is deemed to be unreformable (VB 2010b, p. 30).

But how to set about achieving independence? In the early 1990s, the VB began providing some answers to this question. First of all, it argued that a peaceful secession, with minor economic and social disruptions, could be achieved, as Norway and Sweden, as well as the Czech and Slovak Republics, had previously demonstrated (Annemans and Builtinck 1997, p. 15, see also VB 2001, p. 22). In the mid-2000s, the party suggested that Belgium was already irremediably divided and 'one day, the system will simply get stuck by itself' (Leen and Van den Troost, 2005, p. 3). Finally, in 2011, VB members Gerolf Annemans and Steven Utsi drafted a comprehensive roadmap. This entailed the presentation of the Flemish case on the international stage stressing the long-lasting injustices experienced by the Flemings and the impossibility of changing Belgium. Independence – they argued – would also need to be presented as a case of dissolution of an artificial federation rather than as one of secession, while a unilateral declaration should only be considered as a last resort. The text expressed scepticism of an independence referendum, claiming that it would make things excessively complicated.[10] The process will rather be triggered when a majority of Flemish MPs supports independence (Annemans and Utsi 2011, pp. 167–213).

The sum of two democracies

As for the economic dimension explored above, the arguments of political marginalisation made by the N-VA have been similar to those of the VB. Yet, the N-VA has been much less concerned with linguistic and historical issues, and focused on the socio-economic and governance consequences of the cultural differences between the two communities.

Two considerations have been key in the party's discourse. On the one hand, the N-VA has argued that Belgium is an irremediably divided country whose communities should simply accept their separation and get a consensual divorce. As the party suggested in its early years, 'Belgium is a brake on the development of the prosperity and welfare of both Flanders and Wallonia. Both live in their own socio-economic reality, they have their own public opinion and parties and media that express this attitude. The separation of the souls has been there for long, people only do not dare extend it to the facts' (N-VA 2003, p. 10, see also N-VA 2002a, p. 3, 2010, p. 70). On the other, the party has claimed that Belgium is not a democracy, but the 'sum of two democracies' that are constantly forced to find a compromise (N-VA 2005, 2016). Yet, because of their fundamentally opposed mentalities, reaching such a consensus is impossible. As a result: 'in almost every issue that is regulated at the Belgian level, Flemings and Walloons are at loggerheads [...] due to these unworkable conditions a great many things get endlessly stuck or, too often, half-hearted steps are the result. All Flemings may well agree on something, it is sufficient that the PS [*Parti socialiste*] says "non" for the issue to get jammed' (N-VA 2002a, see also N-VA 2007c).

This situation is all the more detrimental to the Flemings, because they are a demographic majority and would thus profit most from abandoning Belgium's consociational style of politics. As claimed in the 2009 manifesto, 'whenever a minority has at its disposal endless resources to block a majority, we call it a democratic crisis' (N-VA 2009a, p. 4). The party has recognised to some extent the legitimacy of the constitutional safeguards introduced in the 1960s to defend the rights of the Francophones, but it has also concluded that these guarantees have been abused by French-speakers (N-VA 2011). The N-VA has thus depicted the Francophones as the real conservatives in Belgium, who always block any Flemish attempt to reform the 'moribund' Belgian system (N-VA 2004d, De Wever 2013), and itself as a party of change (De Wever 2010, 2014). Furthermore, the N-VA has suggested that the francophone defence of the Belgian status quo is inherently contradictory since either French-speakers think that Belgium is divided into two different communities, whereby, a consensual divorce would make much more sense; or they believe in the existence of a unitary Belgian constituency, but in that case they should scrap the safeguards and accept the rule of the majority (N-VA 2010, p. 69).

Contrary to the VB, despite being willing to bring about the break-up of Belgium, the party has adopted a gradualist policy, whereby independence is not necessarily conceived of as an event, but rather as a process of ever increasing transition of powers from the federal to the regional and European levels. This has gone along with the idea, seen in the previous section, that small communities fare better in the contemporary world: 'our party believes that the challenges of the twenty-first century can best be answered by the establishment of strong communities on the one hand and by means of a well developed international cooperation on the other hand. In between these two levels, the level of the Belgian Government will evaporate, while already now good governance seems out of reach at the Belgian level' (N-VA 2013a,[11] see also N-VA 2010, p. 8). At the same time, the party has shown a flexible strategy, whereby it has held government positions in partnership with other parties at the local and regional levels, while it has assumed a more uncompromising stand concerning state reform at the federal level (see Chapter 9 for further detail). Thus, in the short term, the N-VA has advocated a move to a confederation with all the competences for economic and social policy, as well as the collection of the relevant taxes, devolved to the confederated states. In the long term, however, the Alliance believes independence to be the only solution to overcome the irremediably compromised Belgian system. In this connection, the 2007–08 and 2010–12 deadlocks in the formation of the government were deemed by the party to epitomise Belgium's impasse (N-VA 2009a, p. 4, Peumans 2012).

At the roots of the VB's and the N-VA's discourse

The rise of Flemish nationalism in the second half of the twentieth century is often explained with reference to the increased self-awareness of new Flemish elites that originated in the region's formidable economic performance after the Second World War, their dissatisfaction with persisting linguistic inequality and the opposing demands of Walloon elites coming to terms with the economic decline of their region (Wils 1992, pp. 31–33, Vos 1993, pp. 139–143, Buyst 2000, Meynen 2009, 276–277, De Wever *et al.* 2015, 242–247). As the reversal of the economic fortunes of the two areas played a key role in this process it is necessary to briefly describe Belgium's economic development.

From poor to rich Flanders

As of 1846, the Northern Belgian provinces recorded a higher industrial employment than the southern part of the country. By 1880, however, the relative positions of the two territories had been reversed, with Wallonia accounting for 56.3 per cent of it against only 36.3 per cent in the North (Nagels 2002, p. 98). Thanks to its large coal deposits, Wallonia profited from the first wave of industrialisation and established itself as a leading manufacturing region. By contrast, Flanders' textile and agricultural sectors were outcompeted by cheaper foreign products and suffered from structural unemployment for several decades. The Northern region started showing some signs of improvement around the beginning of the twentieth century. The port of Antwerp benefited from its connection with the surrounding industrial areas of Wallonia, Northern France and Western Germany, as well as from an incipient process of trade globalisation. Moreover, the incipient exhaustion of coal deposits in Wallonia increased ore imports that favoured the rise of chemical and steel plants near the ports of Antwerp, Ghent and Zeebrugge. Thus, although Wallonia was still more prosperous on average, by 1947, the geographical distribution of GDP in the country had changed substantially (Buyst 2011, pp. 331–333) (Figure 3.2).

In the immediate post-Second World War period, Belgium experienced a short 'economic miracle', followed by a decade of stagnation. At the same time, the economic catch-up of Flanders slowed down, as Wallonia profited from the high demand of heavy-industry products needed for European reconstruction (Van der Wee 1997, pp. 58–60, Savage 2005, p. 86). Things began to change radically at the end of the 1950s. The coming of the oil-age accelerated the decline of Wallonia, while increasing European integration favoured the relative rise of Flanders. Furthermore, during the 1950s political parties in Flanders called for state intervention to boost the Flemish economy. Although they were not primarily conceived as a regional measure, the 1959 laws of economic expansion addressed such requests by increasing state intervention through the provision of subsidies to domestic and foreign investments. All this led to sustained growth – at around 5 per cent a year – throughout the decade, but with striking regional differences: while Flanders attracted many foreign companies, state subsidies to Wallonia only prolonged the agony of its declining manufacturing sector (Meynen 2009, pp. 279–281). In this process, the North was certainly advantaged by its strategic location along the coast, its good infrastructure and its cheap and abundant workforce. As a result, two-thirds of foreign investment entering Belgium in the 1960s targeted Flanders, strongly contributing to the reduction of its structural unemployment and to the modernisation of its industrial base (Van der Wee 1997, p. 62). Next to this 'Fordist' model of development, the region experienced the emergence of a robust array of SMEs in the province of West Flanders (Vandermotten 1997, pp. 156–164). In 1965,

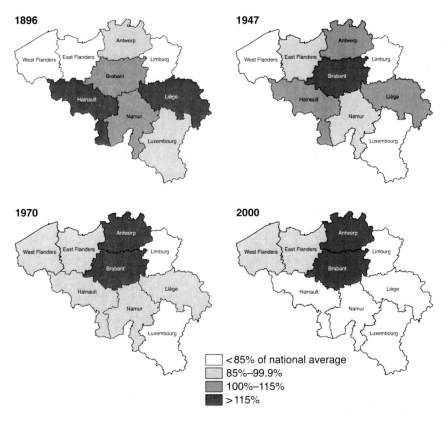

Figure 3.2 Belgium's GDP per capita by province, 1896–2000 (national average = 100).
Source: my elaboration on Buyst 2011, p. 337.

the Flemish economy overtook the Walloon one and the gulf widened in the second half of the 1970s.

Then, in the mid-1970s, the country was hit by a sudden fall in productivity not followed by wage restraint, which caused rising unemployment (from 3.1 per cent in 1971 to 10 per cent in 1981) and fast-growing public expenses (from 34 per cent to 50 per cent of GDP in 1960–76). The two oil shocks contributed to exposing the weaknesses of the Belgian economy. The rigidity of the Belgian system of wage indexation plunged the country into a vicious cycle of increasing inflation, labour costs, unemployment, and social spending that crippled firms' productivity, slowed growth and reduced government revenues. Successive governments cumulated budget deficits year after year reaching 16 per cent of GDP in 1981, despite attempts to increase tax revenue (which went from 38 per cent of GDP in 1970 to 48 per cent in 1985). Things began improving after the devaluation of the franc in February 1982, but in 1986 the deficit was still equal to 8 per cent of GDP, unemployment never went back to pre-oil crises levels and public debt kept creeping up until it hit 134 per cent of GDP in 1993 (Figure 3.3) (Mommen 1994, p. 158, Meyen 2009, pp. 295–296, Callatay and Thys-Clement 2012, p. 314, Smeyers and Buyst 2016, pp. 317–410).

The impact of these crisis years was not the same in the two halves of the country. While Wallonia's most important industrial sectors – coal and steel – disappeared or went through a phase of painful restructuring, Flanders could more easily take advantage of structural change. Although the Flemish textile and shipbuilding industry also suffered considerably, 'the Flemish provinces benefited strongly from the franc's devaluation and the accompanying austerity measures because of their export-oriented structure, so they could take full advantage of the international economic upswing of the mid- and late-1980s' (Buyst 2011, p. 335). The end result was a period of prolonged economic divergence in per-capita income (lasting until the mid-2000s) and, while unemployment in Wallonia stagnated in the second half of the 1980s, it remained consistently higher than in the North – 22 per cent in 1987 vs. 14 per cent in Flanders.

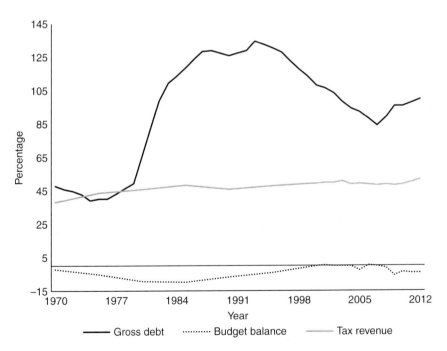

Figure 3.3 Belgium's public debt, budget balance and tax revenue, 1970–2012 (percentage of GDP).

Sources: my elaboration on Callatay and Thys-Clement 2012, pp. 306–307, IMF-FAD 2012, NBB 2017a.

It is in coincidence with the climaxing of this economic crisis that systematic studies on inter-regional transfers began being produced at the Catholic University of Leuven, in Flanders. In 1979, Paul Van Rompuy and Albert Verheirstraeten were the first to rigorously calculate them. They found that, in 1970 and 1974, Flanders contributed 6 and 15 billion francs more to the central government respectively in taxes and social security charges than it received, mostly to the advantage of Wallonia (Van Rompuy and Verheirstraten 1979). The Flemish newspaper *De Standaard* (1979) reported this data even before the publication of the paper and defined the study as 'politically explosive'. In later years, Van Rompuy and colleagues carried out further studies culminating in the 1988 'Ten Years of Financial Transfers between the Regions in Belgium' that highlighted a consistently growing transfer from Flanders to Wallonia throughout the 1975–85 period, going from 2.4 per cent to 10.4 per cent of Flemish GDP (Van Rompuy and Bilsen 1988, p. 24). The steepness of the hike, however, was largely due to the introduction of a methodological change in the regional distribution of the interests on the debt (from the benefit principle to the accrual principle),[12] since on the basis of the benefit method the evaluation of the deficit stopped at 5.9 per cent of Flanders' GDP. The validity of the accrual principle was later contested by other scholars (Jurion *et al.* 1994, De Boeck and Van Gompel 1998, p. 217) and the interest on the debt was not included in most following studies – see Van Rompuy's (2010, p. 119) own reflections on this. But this did not prevent the VB, and later the N-VA, from adopting figures based on it in their own calculations.

Most other analyses carried out in the 1980s focused on transfers within the social security system. They all confirmed the picture seen above of increasingly larger positive social security balances in Flanders against ever-larger deficits in Wallonia (see GERV 1983, Dethée 1984, 1990). While these studies, as well as those of Van Rompuy and colleagues, aimed at gauging the size of the transfers, in 1989, researchers at the University of Antwerp tried to identify the reasons behind them. They concluded that these mainly lay in regional structural differences at the economic, demographic and labour market levels resulting from historical processes that could not be easily reversed. Yet, they also warned that 'the existence of a historical border between the two federal regions lent a political meaning to these solidarity transfers; similar transfers can (and probably will) occur within one political sphere' (Deleeck *et al.* 1989, p. 268).

The appearance of such academic interest in the solidarity between Flanders and Wallonia at the end of the 1970s reflected a wider societal concern with the way in which resources were distributed between the two halves of the country and whose salience was increased by three inter-related factors: the process of federalisation initiated in 1970, the economic crisis that hit the country after the first oil shock (as seen above) and the different economic structures of Flanders and Wallonia.

On the Flemish side, the federalisation of the country had mainly been sought for cultural reasons pertaining to the protection of the Dutch language and culture. Yet, from the mid-1970s on, despite the lingering of problematic exceptions in border areas, the linguistic issue progressively gave way to economic disputes. For instance, in 1976, the *Vlaams Economisch Verbond* (Flemish business organisation – VEV) considered the 'Dutchification' of enterprises as an achieved goal and in 1983 the leader of the *Volksunie*, Hugo Schiltz, argued that, apart from some exceptions, 'the language issue is over in Flanders' (quoted in Govaert 1983, p. 43). In a longer historical perspective, Flemish economic demands built upon an older tradition within the Flemish movement, involving accusations of Flanders' colonisation on the part of the francophone elite, that could be easily adapted, in the context of the 1970s, to Flanders' 'fiscal victimisation' (Boehme 2008a, p. 558, 2008b, pp. 148, Luyten 2010, pp. 5–46). Furthermore, increasing Flemish socio-economic demands were a reaction to similar calls for economic autonomy formulated since the early 1960s by Walloon parties believing that their region's decline depended on the dominance of Flemish pressure groups within the Belgian state (Mommen 1994, p. 129).

The establishment of the regions also coincided with the shift from Fordism to post-Fordism. In the face of this challenge, the very different structures of Flanders and Wallonia favoured the adoption of diverging tactics. Since the five national sectors mostly hit by this economic transition were more heavily concentrated in Wallonia – especially coal and steel – local actors pushed for renewed state support. The adoption of alternative strategies was discouraged by the fact that the consequences of adjustment could less easily be absorbed by other economic sectors. By contrast, as argued by Osterlynck (2009, p. 89), 'because of the sector and job diversity of its industrial structure, the Flemish economy was more open to alternative economic imaginaries'. These alternatives were provided by theories of economic regionalism, neoliberalism and the transition to new technological sectors, then in vogue at the international level. The first suggested that the key to economic growth resided in factors such as innovation, entrepreneurialism and craft-based industrial districts that were 'territorially embedded', a notion in line with the kind of culturally-determinist argument about economic success made by the VB at the time; the second prescribed the rejection of direct state intervention, especially through subsidies, and confined government to the role of regulator and 'facilitator' of market processes, which contrasted with the lingering support for Keynesianism within Walloon institutions; the third offered the opportunity to project the image of a prosperous, technically advanced and highly skilled Flanders opposed to that of an old and declining Wallonia, but also lent legitimacy to the denunciation of unjust transfers, as the development of new technological sectors required heavy capital investments (Govaert 1983, pp. 40–43, Osterlynck 2009, p. 90).

The 'territorial embeddedness' of the factors for economic growth and the focus on individual entrepreneurship emphasised by theories of economic regionalism, along with increasing attention on the transfers, the dire state of national accounts, the asymmetric impact of the crisis and the lingering support for Keynesian policies in Wallonia, favoured the creation of a discourse in which the Walloons were portrayed as lazy profiteers living off subsidies coming from Flanders. The VB has not been the only actor nourishing such a narrative. In 1977, the *Volksunie* had already used the slogan *Vlaams Centen in Vlaamse Handen* (Flemish Money in Flemish Hands) that was later adopted by the VB, complaining that Flemish money was used to pay for Walloon 'capriciousness' and to prop up dead firms in the steel sector (VU 1977, see also VU 1978). In the early 1980s, similar arguments spread to propaganda pieces of the *Christelijke Volkspartij* (Christian Social Party, CVP), the dominant party in the region. For instance, in an electoral flyer for the 1981 election, the soon-to-be first Minister-President of Flanders, Gaston Geens (1981), defined Flanders as a beehive, 'where work is still taken seriously'. The flyer also reported words from the francophone Belgian newspaper *L'Avenir* – thus showing the widespread nature of such representations – lamenting that 'we Walloons, we organise meetings, we argue and we endlessly complain. And the Flemings, they work. They roll up their sleeves, while we keep them in our lap'. Such an image of Flemish and Walloon divergent attitudes to work echoed among the wider population. According to a poll published in 1981 on *De Standaard* and *Le Soir*, the first adjective used by both linguistic communities to represent the Flemings was 'hard-working'; in Flanders, on the contrary, the three adjectives most frequently used to described the Wallons were 'fanatic', 'rebellious' and 'lazy' (De Standaard 1981).

The nationalism of the rich formulated by the VB, and later the N-VA, could thus profit from cultural resonance (Gamson and Modigliani 1989). Nevertheless, until the formation of the N-VA, the VB was the most radical political actor denouncing the transfers, furthering a cultural-deterministic interpretation of the economic imbalances between Flanders and Wallonia, and proposing a simple and extreme solution to this problem, i.e. independence. Through its electoral success, it has played a key role in hardening the positions of the other Flemish parties, as shown by the debate over the 'communitarisation' of social security. While the VB demanded its complete devolution to the regions all along, in the late 1970s there was broad agreement that social security should remain a federal competence. Since the late 1980s, however, ever more actors have come to support a partial 'communitarisation', which found its final expression in the five resolutions on state reform approved by the Flemish Parliament in 1999 (Poirier and Vansteenkiste 2000, pp. 347–352). The influence of the VB's growth was especially strong on the VU, which in the early 1990s tried to abandon the strategy of *'détente'* towards the Walloons adopted in the previous decade. While in 1989 Schiltz had argued that the reform just implemented had put an end to the unjust transfers and there was no mention of the matter in the 1990 Congress, Bert Anciaux, elected party chairman in 1992 – right after the VB's electoral overtaking of the VU – imposed the suppression of the transfers as an over-riding condition for approving the 1993 federalisation (Govaert 1993, pp. 54–68). The reform left social security unchanged, but the VU obtained the creation of the Flemish Research Group on Social Security 2002. This drafted a plan for a redistribution of competences that constituted the basis for the 1999 Resolutions. The plea for homogenous competences and for an end to 'subjective' transfers became the new mantra. The latter element is particularly interesting in light of the discourse highlighted above because these 'subjective transfers' depend on 'cultural differences' between Flemings and Walloons in the way they consume social services, whereby the 'Walloons are said to "cost" more to the health insurance system as a result of bad life habits' (Beland and Lecours 2005, p. 273).

The persistence of the transfers

In the last two decades further evaluations of the transfers have been conducted. Using a mix of the benefit and monetary flow methods, and excluding the interest on the debt, De Boeck and Van Gompel (1998, p. 229) found a steady transfer equal to 3.5–3.7 per cent the Flemish GDP for the period 1990–96, with social security accounting for 63 per cent of the total imbalance (see also De Boeck and Van Gompel 2002). In 2004, the Flemish Community commissioned a study to its finance administration with a view to estimate the transfers for the period 1990–2003. Using largely the same methodology of the above authors, the body concluded that, on average, Flanders contributed a constant flow of 4.2 per cent of its GDP throughout the years analysed (Van Rompuy 2010, pp. 117–121). Similar, although somewhat lower, figures have recently been calculated by the Belgian National Bank for the 1995–2005 period, with Flanders' contribution around 3–3.5 per cent of its GDP. This study also argued that inter-regional transfers were accompanied by considerable intraregional transfers at the level of the provinces (Dury *et al.* 2008).

Similar to the Catalan case, the existence and persistence over time of sizable transfers between Flanders and Wallonia is an undisputable fact. Compared to the Spanish region, however, the size of the transfers seems to be more modest and more stable. As argued in Chapter 2, such stability suggests that, despite being fundamental to explain the formation of the nationalism of the rich in the region, the transfers are not, by themselves, a powerful factor in explaining the successive electoral evolution of the VB and the rise and trajectory of the N-VA. At the same time, the constancy of the transfers has certainly enabled these parties to criticise Belgian solidarity on account of the lack of convergence between Flanders and Wallonia, as well as to support the claim that the reforms undertaken did not bring any fundamental improvement. In light of these conclusions, it is necessary to briefly look at the efficiency of the Belgian social security system, its possible overcompensation effects, its reversibility over time, patterns of convergence, and overall growth.

Comparative studies show that Belgium is one of the most effective countries in the EU in reducing inter-regional inequality (Cantillon *et al.* 2006, p. 1044). In the past, this also led to overcompensation of income. In 1989, Deleeck *et al.* estimated that, on average, despite recording a lower primary income, after taxes and social benefits the Walloons enjoyed a higher disposable income than the Flemings. This, however, was a temporary effect mostly due to Wallonia's demographic structure and lingering higher wages – translating into higher pensions and benefits – which disappeared a few years later (Poirier and Vansteenkiste 2000, pp. 347–348). Since then, Flanders' disposable income has remained higher than the Walloon one (Dury *et al.* 2008, p. 101). However, some overcompensation persists at the level of regional funding, as despite having a higher per capita fiscal capacity than the Walloon region (103 per cent of the national average against 88.5 per cent in the south), the Flemish Community has received lower per capita revenues (96 per cent against 99.5 per cent in Wallonia) (Van Rompuy 2010, pp. 120–121; see also Heremans *et al.* 2010, p. 22).

Although the scarcity of regional data for the 1950s and 1960s invites us to take any results cautiously, the argument whereby Flanders did not profit from social security in the past seems to lie on shaky ground. Dottermans (1997, p. 145) found that Flanders did profit from inter-regional solidarity between 1955 and 1962, although the transfers came from Brussels. Similarly Meunier *et al.* (2007, pp. 47–69) calculated that Flanders received a net transfer of about 3 per cent of its GDP in the years from 1955–68, once again, mainly financed by Brussels. This data thus seems to suggest that Flanders did benefit from redistribution mechanisms similar to those that the VB and the N-VA have questioned – although probably of lower magnitude and mainly coming from the capital – which would confirm their historical reversibility. This would also be in line with the history of social security in the country, whose bases were already laid down in the interwar years and then considerably extended in 1944 – with the introduction of obligatory insurance for unemployment and sickness-disability for employees (Vanthemsche 1994, pp. 10–80, Poirier and Vansteenkiste 2000, pp. 335–337).

The most important criticism made by the VB and N-VA, however, pertains to the lack of regional fiscal responsibility and the ensuing disincentives to endogenous growth that are deemed to stem from the transfers. This view finds echo in academic circles. More specifically, the financing system of the federal entities and the social security is deemed to be inefficient for two reasons: it lacks a clear link between policy and financial accounts that can act as a feedback mechanism; it causes a 'development trap' whereby any attempt of the lower income regions to increase their tax revenue is outpaced by the loss in the solidarity grant that they receive (Deschamps 2010, p. 9, Heremans *et al.* 2010, pp. 24–25). The lack of any feedback mechanism, especially because of the unclear division of competences between the federal and community levels, is deemed to make citizens unable to easily attribute responsibility for the taxes they pay and the services they receive. Yet, while the solution often envisaged is further decentralisation, a re-centralisation of competences already devolved would work as well. The 'development trap' argument, on the other hand, is often considered as explaining the lack of convergence between Flanders and Wallonia (Heremans *et al.* 2010, p. 25). While it is beyond the scope of this work to determine whether inter-regional redistribution is detrimental to regional convergence (see Checherita *et al.* 2009, Persyn and Algoed 2009, Kessler and Lessmann 2010 for a wider discussion), two relevant considerations can be made: first, divergence rather than convergence has occurred – except for a slight reversal since 2006 (De Grauwe quoted in Thomas 2014); second, there is evidence that the funding system of regions and communities overcompensates increases in their tax base, thus acting as a disincentive for regional governments to boost endogenous growth (Cattoir and Verdonck 2002, Algoed 2009). Although these considerations do not allow to conclude that lack of convergence has depended solely, or even mainly, on such a 'development trap', both points clearly contribute to lending legitimacy to some of the VB's and N-VA's arguments.

Finally, in terms of overall growth, between 1986 and 2007, the Flemish economy has recorded stable GDP and gross disposable household income (GDHI) per capita real growth at 2.4 per cent and 1.4 per cent per year on average, with only a few years of recession.[13] During the 1980s and 1990s, the region took advantage of its relatively high – by international standards – labour productivity and managed to remain at the top of the technological frontier, especially in the sectors of micro-electronics and biotechnology, although in the last decade it has lamented a loss in investments in research and development and market share in high-tech sectors as compared to its direct competitors, which led the Flemish Government to devise new approaches to industrial innovation (Capron 2000, Larosse 2012). The recent economic crisis did eat into people's standards of living, but it did not have as devastating an impact as in Catalonia. Regional GDP per capita real growth de facto stagnated at 0.3 per cent on average between 2008 and 2015 and GDHI shrank, but only by 1.2 per cent on average from 2008–2014. At the same time, unemployment grew only from 3.9 per cent to 5.1 per cent over the same period, which remains low by European standards (my calculations on DGSIE 2017, Eurostat 2017b, NBB 2017b, Statistics Belgium 2017, World Bank 2017). As we will see in Chapter 9, this generally stable outlook might well account for the lack of any radicalisation of support for independence in the region.

The 'minoritised' majority

The VB's and N-VA's claim of Flemish political marginalisation tap into a much longer history of linguistic discrimination suffered by the Dutch-speaking majority of the country that mainly relates to the peculiar features of Belgian nation-building in the nineteenth and early twentieth centuries. Before addressing the current sources of the political marginalisation perceived by part of Flemish society, it is therefore necessary to briefly look at Flemish-francophone relations in Belgium in a longer historical perspective.

As argued by Louis Vos (1993, p. 128), at the time of independence 'there was no question of a Flemish and Walloon nation respectively. Consideration was given only to the establishment of a Belgian nation'. The creation of Belgium reflected the interests and identity of the United Provinces' upper classes – some of which of Flemish origins – that had decided to use French as the national language because it was deemed intrinsically superior to Dutch. Yet, early on, part of this elite began contesting the dominance of French (Beyen 2009). The later swelling of state bureaucracy and the advances of democracy made language discrimination more salient to Dutch-speakers, thus increasing the popularity of the Flemish movement (Zolberg 1974, pp. 204–205). The electoral reforms of 1893 and 1919 contributed to this process by integrating the Flemish masses into the political system. Furthermore, the first achievements of the Flemish movement, such as the introduction of primary, and later secondary, education in Dutch, which ensured the formation of a Flemish petty-bourgeoisie, further consolidated the Flemish identity (Stengers 2004, p. 253, Van Goethem 2010, pp. 15–16, De Wever *et al.* 2015, pp. 233–242).

The reaction of the Belgian state to the demands for linguistic parity probably had an even greater impact on the radicalisation of Flemish claims. Since independence, language policy was based on a laissez faire approach, which clearly favoured French because the linguistic divide also had a social connotation: 'the area in which the lower-status language was spoken was also economically and socio-politically subordinate' (Witte 1993, p. 221). Dutch was therefore associated with Flanders' economic backwardness. The first laws recognising the use of Dutch in the courts and the administration were adopted only near the last quarter of the nineteenth century (1873) and culminated in the official linguistic parity in the promulgation of laws established in 1898. Yet, this was far from the official bilingualism advocated in Flanders.

During the Great War clear anti-Belgian sentiments appeared within the Flemish movement (Wils 1992). The so-called activists took advantage of the Flemish policy enacted by the German occupants to obtain many of the demands until then ignored by Belgian authorities. Although the collaboration remained limited, the occupation showed that long-standing Flemish goals could be achieved. When, in the early 1920s, some of these claims were ignored by the Belgian elite, the activists could be turned into martyrs of the newborn anti-Belgian cause (Van Goethem 2010, p. 107).

Yet, as argued by Marnix Beyen (2009: 22–23), active state-supported linguistic oppression never occurred in Belgium: 'in their attempt to Frenchify Flanders, the Belgian élites were never backed by an official state policy [...] repressive language policy certainly was a reality, but it was carried out at an intermediate level (school boards, enterprises, ...) rather than at state level'. The Belgian state thus remained stuck between a formal laissez faire that naturally, but not actively, favoured French and a unitarist conception of the state that prevented any adaptations to a federal or confederal structure until the 1970s. 'Hence – Beyen concludes – Frenchification, as a social process, was strong enough to foster frustration among Flemish speakers [...] but not strong enough really to create a unilingually French state, based on a homogeneous nation'.

Monolingualism in Flanders was practically obtained during the interwar years. After the Second World War, however, the 1947 census revealed that the linguistic border was moving up, further extending the francophone area. While each municipality had been granted monolingual status, except for Brussels, such status could change according to the results of the censuses. Seeing their cultural perimeter shrinking, Flemish parties began campaigning to fix the border, although the issue only really flared up in the early 1960s (Sinardet 2008b). This unsurprisingly coincided with the reversal of economic fortunes between the two halves of the country. Wallonia's decline undermined the legitimacy of the political primacy and higher social status of the francophone minority (Buyst 2000). While the dominance of French lingered on, ever fewer Flemings were ready to stand it. As argued by De Wever *et al.* (2015, p. 245), 'the rising Dutch-speaking middle-groups saw in the relics of the superiority of French an obstruction to their social ascent'. Reflecting a change in the balance of power between the two communities, the breakout of the community conflict in the 1960s and early 1970s can therefore be read as a sign of the progressive end of Flanders' political subordination. Yet, despite their ascent, in 1981, 45.1 per cent of the Flemish population – in fact a relative majority, since only 17 per cent disagreed and 20 per cent did not know – perceived themselves to be disadvantaged, as compared to the inhabitants of the other two regions, with regard to their influence on the important political decisions taken in the country, thus suggesting the lingering of a sentiment of political marginalisation (Delruelle-Vosswinkel and Froignier 1981, p. 13).

Past memories of Flemish socio-political subordination however cannot explain the persistence of such a feeling. In the 1960s, francophone parties managed to negotiate a series of consociational guarantees with far-reaching consequences. As a counterpart to the division of the country into rigid linguistic territories and the adaptation of seats to make Parliament more representative of the true demographic weight of each community (putting an end to Flanders' underrepresentation), they obtained the introduction of a set of safeguards including: the requirement of a two-thirds majority in the Chamber of Representatives, and an absolute one in each linguistic group, to modify special laws; an 'alarm bell procedure' whereby 75 per cent of the MPs of a linguistic group can defer the adoption of a bill for 30 days, if they deem it harmful to their interests; and linguistic parity in government, Prime Minister excluded. It is precisely these kinds of consociational mechanisms that the VB and N-VA deem responsible for the persistent minoritisation of Flanders, regardless of the fact that similar measures were later extended to the Flemish minority in Brussels.

Centrifugal tendencies

Before the 1960s, the linguistic fracture was not the main social cleavage cutting across Belgian society. By way of generalisation, the history of Belgium can indeed be divided into three major periods: from 1830–1900 the religious/free-thinkers divide was prevalent; between 1900 and 1960 class struggle swept the country; and after 1960 the linguistic confrontation took over. These corresponded to three different party systems: a two-party one (Catholic vs. Liberals) in the first; a 'two and a half' one (Catholic, socialists, liberals) in the second; and extreme fragmentation, mainly due to the rise of regional parties and the split of traditional ones along the linguistic line, in the third (De Winter *et al.* 2006, p. 934). Furthermore, Belgium had early on developed consociational conflict-management mechanisms (Huyse 1971, see also Deschouwer 2006) that in the 1960s were adapted to the new circumstances of federalisation. The country thus moved from non-territorial to territorial (federal) consociationalism[14] (Dalle Mulle 2016a, p. 106) and the adjustment was made easier by the partial overlapping of cleavages, since Flanders had historically been more Catholic and less socialist than Wallonia (Deschouwer 2006, pp. 895–904, De Smaele 2009). Federalism was introduced to reduce conflict between the linguistic communities of the country and to improve governance. The continuing existence of the country and the absence of violence among the territorial segments suggest that such a goal has been achieved. Yet, at the same time, some of the peculiar features of the Belgian federation might have ended up fuelling tensions, notably: its bipolarity and the scarcity of actors capable of and/or with an interest in bridging the segments (Peters 2006, p. 1082, Deschouwer 2012, p. 73).

In the 1960s, the differing priorities of Flemish and Walloon parties – the former interested more in cultural autonomy, the latter in economic competences – ended up producing a double structure with three communities (the Flemish, the French and the German-speaking) catering for individual matters in the realm of culture, education, language-use and welfare; and three regions (Flanders, Wallonia and Brussels-Capital) in charge of territorial competences relating to, among others, regional economy, agriculture, infrastructure and the environment (Hooghe 2004, pp. 21–22). The seemingly triadic architecture of the communities in reality hides a mostly bipolar structure in which Dutch- and French-speakers often confront each other, while German-speakers – representing only 0.75 per cent of the Belgian population – do not play a meaningful role. Such dyadic structure is partly confirmed at the regional level, where Brussels frequently sides with Wallonia. The bipolarity of the Belgian federation is then reinforced by the partial overlapping of cleavages mentioned above, which contributes to the perception that the country is divided into two homogenous blocs and reduces the possibility of finding alternative alliances across different lines of fracture (Peters 2006, pp. 1082–1083). Furthermore, Belgium's federalisation has gone along with a consistent hollowing of the centre (Hooghe 2004, pp. 34–35). One source of such process has been the package of reforms agreed in the second half of the 1960s. This entailed, among others, the division of all MPs into two linguistic groups (Flemish and French-speaking) whose 'end result is a parliament in which the representatives are supposed to represent their own language group' (Sinardet 2010, p. 352) rather than the entire country. Another, and related, source was the splitting of national parties along linguistic lines, leading to the unique situation whereby there are no longer federal parties bridging the linguistic frontier in Belgium (Deschouwer 1997). It is important to note that in Flanders and Wallonia people cannot vote for parties registered in the other region. Only, in Brussels, both sets of parties compete for the same votes.

All this favours the development of centrifugal tendencies and makes the system 'tilt towards confederalism' (Hooghe 2004, p. 28). Parity in the decision-making process, whereby each time that a community has a problem it cannot act unilaterally, has probably avoided the break-up of the country, but it has also become increasingly expensive for the federal budget – since resources and competences were transferred without an adequate devolution of fiscal responsibilities – and has furthered claims of political marginalisation (Deschouwer 1997). Consensus has been forced upon the two big communities, provoking frustration when the system falls into joint-decision traps producing non-decision. This has especially been the case in Flanders because Flemish parties have more vocally called for reform – although such calls do not seem to coincide strictly with wider popular attitudes (see Chapter 9) – and because they represent the majority that would profit from a different style of democracy, thus generating some fatigue with non-majoritarian politics (Deschouwer 1999, p. 6).

In this connection, financial issues have progressively taken centre-stage in driving Flemish demands for further devolution of powers. Although by 1989 the portion of the federal budget transferred to regions had reached 32 per cent – it was only 9 per cent in 1980 – the fiscal responsibility of the regions was basically nil. The 2001 Lambermont agreement increased federal transfers to the communities and made the ensuing apportioning of their budget more proportional to their tax-raising capacity. Regions were also granted the power to reduce or increase the federal personal income tax levied on their territory by 3.25 per cent until 2003 and by 6.75 per cent thereafter. Yet, until the most recent reform, in 2011 – whereby the regions can vary personal income tax by a margin of 25 per cent, ending up financing 70 per cent of their budget with their own taxes – regional fiscal autonomy has remained quite low (Verdonck and Deschouwer 2003, pp. 95–108, Deschouwer 2012, pp. 69–72). More importantly, looking at the entire process of fiscal federalisation, Verdonck and Deschouwer (2003, p. 97) concluded that 'the present financing system is fashioned less by economic rationality than by the very specific characteristics of the Belgian federation: bipolar and centrifugal, double and asymmetrical'. Belgium's federalisation has thus been conducted in a chaotic fashion, without a clear plan in mind or a consensus on the final outcome of the process.

Political vs. societal divisions

The VB and the N-VA have also framed the division between Flemings and Walloons/Francophones as resulting from differences in individual values. This argument is very important because it is precisely such divergence in preferences that is deemed to make the Flemish political marginalisation so detrimental and to warrant a 'consensual divorce'. Yet, Billiet (2011) has shown that, although there are differences in attitudes between the residents of the two regions, these are much smaller than the political debate would suggest and sometimes vary in unexpected ways. If one focuses on attitudes usually associated with the left-right divide such as income inequality, the responsibilities of the government, and the 'side-effects' of social benefits, only some of them are significantly different across the linguistic border and, still, less than expected. Between 1991 and 2007 for instance, while 76 per cent of Wallonia's population on average thought that the government should reduce income inequality and 28 per cent found large disparities in revenues to compensate merit unacceptable, the relative figures in Flanders were 66 per cent and 21 per cent. More surprisingly, people south of the border were significantly more prone (53 per cent) than north of it (31 per cent) to condemn the bad moral consequences of social benefits (i.e. that they would make people less willing to work and to take care of each other). Obtaining similar findings in a previous study, Billiet et al. (2006, p. 930) had concluded that, although being a consequence rather than a cause of the social fracture between the linguistic segments, the division of the country into two separated 'circuits of communication' and political spheres had reinforced such divergence. Survey data from the late 1970s seems to suggest that this is a long-standing process. In 1979, both in Flanders and Wallonia about 48 per cent of the population thought that there were big differences in mentality and life style between the two regions, a figure that had increased to 60 per cent and 56 per cent respectively by 1982 (Delruelle-Vosswinkel *et al.* 1983, pp. 32–34).

Another surprising finding relates to the evolution of national identity in Flanders (on support for independence see Chapter 9). When considering the electoral success of the VB and the N-VA, as well as the rising demands for autonomy of the other Flemish parties, one would expect a progressively stronger Flemish identity. This is only partially true. Despite remaining higher in Flanders than in Wallonia, since 1979 the Flemish region/community consistently dropped as the first site of territorial identification of the local population and from 1986 onwards more people identified with Belgium than with the Flemish region/community (De Winter 2007, pp. 579–580). This suggests that the nation-building purpose of federalisation has worked in Belgium, at least to some extent. This would be even more reasonable in the Belgian context, where, despite having for decades been considered a 'sociological minority' (Van Velthoven 1987), the Flemish population is in fact a majority. Therefore, one might argue that as Belgium became 'more Flemish' a progressively bigger share of the region's population came to identify with the state. At the same time, other figures – relating to national identity, rather than territorial identification – partly contradict the above-mentioned data, showing an overall strengthening of the Flemish identity since 1995, but especially between 2003 and 2010 (Table 3.1).

Finally, the theme of political marginalisation has not been limited to the wider conflict between linguistic communities, but it has also pertained to the particratic character of the Belgian democracy. Belgian politics was based on an oligopolistic system of pillars (Catholic, liberal and socialist), that is, a network of organisations linked to political parties roughly coinciding with the two cleavages prevalent before federalisation (clerical/anti-clerical and labour/capital). Particracy helped stabilise the system, but in periods of stagnation or recession it was hardly tenable, because inefficient and expensive. Furthermore, while the saliency of the traditional fractures progressively decreased (de-pillarisation), the old structures have remained in place, offering an opportunity for contestation to political parties on the fringe (Witte 2009c). Such a de-legitimation has been

Table 3.1 National identity in Flanders, 1995–2014 (percentage of regional population)

	1995	1999	2003	2007	2010	2014
Predominantly Flemish	26.5	28.5	29.7	34.7	35.4	31.1
As Flemish as Belgian	45.5	42.8	43.4	35.5	41.3	38.7
Predominantly Belgian	28	28.7	27.0	29.7	23.3	29.8

Source: Swyngedouw *et al.* 2015.

intensified by the corruption and policy failures scandals of the 1990s (Maesschalck and Van de Walle 2006, pp. 1012–1014, Delwit 2009, pp. 232–316). Several Eurobarometer polls showed that between 1989 and the mid-1990s, the Belgians' satisfaction with the functioning of their democracy decreased from beyond 60 per cent to below 30 per cent (Deschouwer 2012, p. 244). Other surveys confirm an increased perception of corruption as a major problem in the country peaking around 1997–98 (Maesschalck and Van de Valle 2006). At the political level, the break-through of the VB in the early 1990s was interpreted as a sign of a 'confi-dence gap' between the citizens and the political elite. As seen above, the VB not only profited from such deligitimation, but also actively shaped the debate framing the scandals in terms of the opposition between a clean Flanders and a corrupt Belgian-francophone state.

Conclusion

The VB and the N-VA have both consistently lamented the fiscal exploita-tion and political marginalisation of Flanders as central themes in their propaganda. Although the VB produced its most complete brochure on the transfers going from Flanders to Wallonia only in 1992, the issue featured in the party's propaganda since its foundation. The estimates provided by the VB have varied from 50 billion Belgian francs in the early 1980s to 16 billion euros per years (about 7 per cent of regional GDP) in 2015. While in its early years the VB referred extensively to the subsidies given to dying Walloon steel enterprises, the main concern progressively became Belgian public finances – a theme that has resurfaced in the context of the euro crisis – and the social security system. What has remained constant is the idea that the economic difference between the two regions is culturally driven. According to this narrative, Flanders has been the engine of the country's economy thanks to the hard-working ethos of its population, while Wallonia has remained stuck in a statist conception of the economy and has lived off the Flemings' back through the profligate Belgian solid-arity system. In this framework, independence is deemed to be a necessary prerequisite for any social policy in Flanders, since it would make substan-tial resources available to invest in welfare for the Flemings without harming the economic dynamism of the region.

According to the VB, the fiscal exploitation of Flanders has mainly resulted from its political marginalisation within the Belgian state. Histori-cally – it has argued – this condition took the form of a social and political domination on the part of the francophone elite that founded the country. Accordingly, the party has vocally denounced linguistic oppression espe-cially in municipalities along the linguistic frontier and in the Brussels peri-phery. In the 1990s, it played heavily on the corruption scandals that hit the traditional establishment to highlight the rotten character of the Belgian (francophone) democracy pitting it against cleaner Flanders.

However, the most important argument has concerned the persistent privileged position enjoyed by the Francophones thanks to the consociational safeguards introduced in the 1960s, which are deemed to cause the 'minoritisation' of the Flemings due to the continuous vetoes posed by the Francophones at the federal level. As Flanders pays the price of the 'status quo' through the transfers, the Walloons have no interest in reforming the country. Hence, splitting Belgium is considered the only solution to the malfunctioning of the system.

The N-VA has made very similar arguments, although it has been much less concerned with linguistic issues. In economic terms, it has been open to a smoother transition envisaging the maintenance of the transfers for a while after independence. More generally, the N-VA has proposed a less 'principled' nationalism, focusing more on an instrumental idea of independence as a means to achieve better democracy, more effective governance and improved welfare for the Flemings. It has also adopted a gradualist strategy envisaging an intermediate step with the formation of a confederation, which has instead been generally rejected by the VB. Despite underlining the 'cultural content' of the Flemish identity, as compared to the ethnopluralism of the VB, the N-VA has espoused a more flexible definition of it. The criterion of identity has thus been less relevant in the N-VA's rejection of solidarity with Wallonia, as compared to the VB's propaganda, while those of control, attitude and reciprocity have been more highlighted. Both parties have however articulated a culturalised welfare producerism in which the entire Flemish nation discursively coincides with the 'community of welfare producers' and Wallonia (or francophone Belgium) with the 'community of welfare recipients'.

To trace the origin of the formation of the nationalism of the rich in Flanders one has to look at the crucial decade of deep economic crisis experienced by Belgium between 1975 and 1985. The slump following the oil shock, the appalling situation of state finances and the divergent performances of Flanders and Wallonia increased the salience of the – just discovered – inter-territorial transfers, as well as the urgency of economic federalism. Theories of economic regionalism offered a valuable intellectual framework to answer the transition to post-Fordism in Flanders. Their emphasis on 'territorial embeddedness', skills and free enterprise favoured the development of cultural-determinist arguments about socio-economic development that laid favourable ground for the emergence of the nationalism of the rich articulated by the VB, and later the N-VA. While the two parties have represented the most radical embodiments of such a discourse, this has been shared to varying extent by other regional actors that have however been pushed to progressively harden their positions by the VB's and N-VA's electoral success.

All studies on the transfers confirm their existence and stability over time – at a rate of about 4 per cent of the Flemish GDP for the period 1990–2004 at least – although they substantially moderate the VB's and

N-VA's estimates. About two-thirds of such flows are due to the social security system. Hence, the transfers mainly result from the establishment of mechanisms of automatic redistribution (chiefly since 1944) and the reversal of economic fortunes between Flanders and Wallonia occurred during the 1960s. The current system has gone along with lack of economic convergence and incentives to regional growth, as well as with some overcompensation effects. Although the identification of the reasons for the lack of regional convergence, and whether the disincentives to increase the regional tax base are among them, are beyond the scope of this work, it is reasonable to think that these elements have contributed to reinforcing the legitimacy of the VB's and N-VA's claims.

Experiences of both linguistic and social discrimination in a francophone-led country were a fact among the Flemish population at least until the interwar years, whereby the Flemish majority could be considered as a 'sociological minority'. However, linguistic oppression was never actively implemented by the state, but rather resulted from spontaneous social dynamics long neglected by state authorities. This social process frustrated the Flemish majority without homogenising it completely. Yet, the current major source of perceived political marginalisation of the Flemish majority lies in the constitutional safeguards for the francophone minority adopted in the 1960s with the adaptation of the former consociational mechanisms to the linguistic-territorial conflict. As the differing economic structures of the two halves of the country have for a long time entailed divergent interests and agendas, joint-decision traps between the two segments have fuelled frustration among the federated entities. All this has been exacerbated by some peculiar characteristics of the Belgian federation: its bipolarity and the partial overlapping of cleavages indeed make that tensions are often framed as a direct confrontation between Flemings and Francophones/ Walloons; the division of the MPs into two (nearly completely territorially divided) linguistic groups and the ensuing split of traditional parties along linguistic lines has reduced the number of actors capable of, and with an interest in, bridging the gap between the two groups.

Notes

1 For reasons explained later in the text, the acronym VB will be henceforth used to refer to both the *Vlaams Blok* and the *Vlaams Belang*.
2 The N-VA also joined the CD&V and the *OpenVLD* in a government coalition at the regional level.
3 Conversion in 2010 euros based on Eurostat 2017a and World Bank 2017.
4 See supra note.
5 From other quotes one can deduce that solidarity's limitation to the ethnic community is not only a moral imperative, but also a prerequisite for its sustainability, since – the party seems to believe – ethnic commitment reduces free-riding and improves the efficiency of redistribution (see Van Hauthem and Verreycken, 1990, p. 81).

6 On the social dimension of the VB's discourse see also Derks 2004, pp. 183–187, Swyngedouw and Ivaldi 2011, pp. 7–12.
7 The party tends to accuse francophone political parties – the PS above all – of keeping their electorate dependent on public subsidies and employment for clientelistic reasons. Yet, what is implicit in this account is the, at least passive, connivance of the Walloons who vote for them.
8 With this term, it is meant the more or less deliberate transformation of Dutch-speaking areas into French-speaking ones, either through the linguistic assimilation to French of the local Dutch-speaking population, or through the migration of French-speakers in the area.
9 The term 'francophone' is not to be understood as synonymous of Walloon. The former includes also the French-speaking community in Brussels that is neither geographically located in Wallonia, nor shows to feel Walloon.
10 In an interview for this study Annemans confirmed this point.
11 This source is no longer available online. Please contact the author to obtain a copy.
12 See Van Hecke 2010, pp. 20–33, for an overview of the Belgian debate on how to regionalise public debt and the interests on it.
13 My calculation on data from the HermReg Databank, provided directly by the Research Centre of the Flemish Government.
14 Consociationalism is government by elite bargaining where elites represent societal segments. It is founded on four main features: each segment governs itself as much as possible; each obtains a proportional share of public resources; group leaders bridge segments, the state and citizens; citizens are passive (Hooghe 2004).

4 Northern Italy

Thieving Rome and the Southern-dominated Italian state

Origins and evolution of the *Lega Nord*

The *Lega Nord* (Northern League, LN) arose at the turn of the 1990s from the merger of a series of autonomist movements that had appeared across the North of Italy a decade earlier. The most important among these were the *Łiga Veneta* (Venetian League) and the *Lega Lombarda* (Lombard League) – founded in 1980 in Veneto and 1984 in Lombardy respectively. Both demanded a special Statute of Autonomy for their regions (along the lines of those already enjoyed by a few other Italian areas such as Aosta Valley and Trentino-Sudtiröl), questioned the existence of the Italian nation and claimed that regional identities were, in fact, truly national identities. Although the Venetian League initially had more success, the Lombard League later replaced it as the leading regionalist movement in the North. After having obtained a seat in Parliament and one in the Senate at the 1987 elections, the latter began promoting the unification of all regionalist leagues under a common umbrella. The Lombard League made its breakthrough at the 1989 European election, obtaining 8.1 per cent of the overall vote in the region of Lombardy (Moioli 1990, pp. 1–19, Jori 2009, pp. 36–71, Cavallin 2010, pp. 20–65). In December that year the Statute of the Northern League was signed. The process of unification ended in February 1991, when the party's first Congress was organised and the idea of a federal division of Italy into three macro-regions (North, Centre and South) was approved as its main objective (Tambini 2001, pp. 39–65).

At the 1992 general elections the LN scored an impressive 8.6 per cent of the national vote (16.2 per cent in the North) and obtained 80 seats in Parliament. The League's victory contributed to weakening traditional parties such as the Christian Democratic and the Socialist Party, triggering a process that led to their dissolution and the so-called fall of the First Republic (Diamanti 1994, p. 88, Biorcio 1997, pp. 79–82). After the 1994 election, in which the party consolidated its strength, the LN entered a government in a coalition with *Forza Italia* (Go Italy, FI), a party founded only three months earlier by the media tycoon Silvio Berlusconi, but called it off after just eight months (Diamanti 1996). In June 1995, the *Lega* founded a Northern Parliament in Mantua and launched a secessionist project aiming at the independence of Padania – as it named the Northern Italian nation. At the following general election, in April 1996, it recorded its best performance until then (10.1 per cent nationally, 19.3 per cent in the North) and on September 15, after a three-day procession along the river Po, it declared the independence of Padania (Cento Bull and Gilbert 2001, pp. 106–112). This 'march for independence', however, attracted little popular support and by 1998 the separatist thrust seemed to have come to a halt. Despite remaining the official goal of the party, secession was sidelined and regional devolution of powers became the new immediate goal. At the same time, the party assumed a tougher stance on issues like immigration and globalisation, but lost half of its support at the 1999 European elections (Biorcio 2010, pp. 20–30). Considerably weakened, the LN entered a new alliance with Berlusconi's party for the 2001 general election, in which it polled only 3.9 per cent of votes (7.8 per cent regionally). Yet, thanks to the alliance's victory, it entered government again, managing to push through a proposal for constitutional reform that would devolve exclusive legislative powers regarding healthcare, education and the police to the regions. The Italian population however rejected the bill in a referendum held in 2006, although the League's strongholds – Lombardy and Veneto – supported the proposed change (Passalacqua 2009, pp. 122–160).

After another weak result at the 2006 general election (8.3 per cent in the North) and two years in the opposition, from 2008 on, the LN began to grow stronger, winning 16.7 per cent of the northern electorate in the general election that year and coming into office again in an alliance with Berlusconi's new party, *Il Popolo della Libertà* (the People of Freedom – PdL). At the following regional elections, in 2010, it achieved an all-time high, with 19.7 per cent of the northern vote. In the meantime, it tried to push through a new federal reform devolving fiscal powers to regions and municipalities, but it could not because of the government's fall in November 2011 (Passarelli and Tuorto 2012, chapter 1). With the euro crisis ravaging the country and a new government of technicians imposing painful austerity measures, 2012 seemed to reintroduce some of the conditions that had contributed to the League's strength in the 1990s. Yet, internal divisions and the outbreak of a scandal involving the party's mismanagement of public funding jeopardised its reputation. After two years of infighting and reform, during which the party nevertheless secured the Presidency of the region of Lombardy, in February 2013, a new young leader, Matteo Salvini, steered the movement further towards a populist right-wing position focusing on a bid to withdraw Italy from the common currency and an even tougher approach to illegal immigration. Profiting from the collapse of the PdL, the LN bounced back after about two years of steady decline and, in 2015, it secured the re-election of its member Luca Zaia

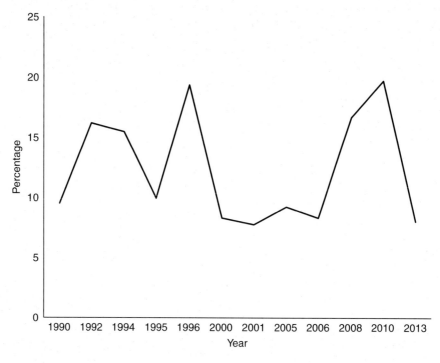

Figure 4.1 LN's electoral results, regional and general elections, 1990–2013 (percentage of regional vote).*

Source: my elaboration on Ministero dell'Interno 2017.

Note
* The results concern the regions of Piedmont, Lombardy, Veneto, Liguria, Emilia-Romagna, Trentino-Südtirol (not for regional elections) and Friuli-Venezia Giulia (not for regional elections).

as President of the region of Veneto. Salvini has also tried to widen the League's popularity throughout Italy as a whole, which has inevitably entailed a silencing of the party's northern ethos. However, it is too early to say whether this change will have a lasting impact on the movement's identity (Cremonesi 2013, Diamanti 2014, 2015a).

The LN's nationalism of the rich

The protest against the economic exploitation of the North has probably been the most innovative and successful argument made by the LN. This claim, already present in the propaganda of the Lombard and Venetian leagues, represented a major change in discourses about Italy's socio-economic development since one of the standard arguments until then had been that the North-South economic relation had historically advantaged the North rather than the South.

Thieving Rome

The LN's arguments of fiscal protest boil down to an accusation of misuse of public funds, mostly provided by the Northern regions, on the part of the inefficient and centralist state bureaucracy as well as by the corrupt Italian political class, which is deemed to have used such resources to fund clientelist networks in Southern regions. As we will see in the next section, both the state administration and the traditional parties have been portrayed as being dominated by southerners and promoting a use of public services and jobs, labelled *assistenzialismo* ('welfare dependency'), that led to unmanageable levels of public debt and deficit without solving the country's territorial imbalances (Vallanz 1990, LN 1996a, p. 21, Montero 2000, Carcano 2006, LN 2013a). The list of outcries has included, among others: the dilapidation of resources caused by the *Cassa per il Mezzogiorno* (Special Fund for the South) and other forms of preferential treatment targeting the South (LN 1992, Bonometti 1998, Ruspoli 2002, LN 2012a); an unbearable and absurd fiscal imposition (Della Torre 1990, Delfi 1997, Pagliarini 2006, Petra 2012); the mismanagement of funds in the healthcare sector (Gubetti, 1992, LN 1996a, Pellai, 2008, Girardin, 2013); and the frauds involving fake disability pensions (LN 1992, Piazzo 1996, Mariani 2008).

Throughout the 1990s, such waste of public resources was deemed to have become more salient because of the dire state of Italy's public finances. As argued in the manifesto for the 1996 elections: 'the public debt is a bottomless pit that currently averages 2,000 billion [liras], for which we have to thank the irresponsible policies of welfare dependency that the Bourbon-like centralist state has pursued until today. The innocent casualties of this "tragedy" are above all the populations of the North, who are always called upon to try to satisfy a monster [the state] that cannot be controlled any longer' (LN 1996a, p. 20). This state of affairs was considered to be even more detrimental to the North because it risked leaving the area out of the coming monetary union, which would have been a tragedy for the region's economy (Bossi 1991a, Staglieno 1994). At the same time, the party feared that, even in the event of Italy joining the euro, the country's persisting structural inefficiencies – mainly due to Southern backwardness – could stifle northern firms, killed by the competition of companies located in the more advanced states of Northern and Central Europe. It was in this context, that the LN launched the idea of the independence of Padania as a way to protect the economic future of the area (Paini 1996, Bossi 1996). As argued in the party journal *Lega Nord* in mid-1996: 'two different monetary systems for two different productive systems [...] that would allow Padania to enter the European common currency avoiding the destruction of its productive system, and the *Meriodione* [another name commonly used to indicate the South] to decrease labour costs, which would attract investment and enterprises. This is the only democratic solution to the Italian crisis' (LN 1996c).

Italy eventually managed to enter the common currency and, although successive governments in the second half of the 1990s had to push painful austerity measures through, the doomsday scenario portrayed by the League never came about. The party thus sidelined independence in favour of a more gradualist policy focused on devolution of powers to the regions in the short term. Its electoral weakness forced it to find agreement with more centrist forces – some of which also enjoyed strong electoral support in the South – with which it participated in government between 2001 and 2006. For these reasons, and despite maintaining the territorial fiscal protest as one of its mainstays, in those years, the party toned down its rhetoric against the South and switched its attention to issues relating to immigration, globalisation, unfair Chinese competition, law and order, and a growing anti-EU rhetoric (on these aspects see Albertazzi and McDonnel 2005, Biorcio 2010, pp. 15–37, Zaslove 2011, pp. 193–205).

By 2008, however, the territorial conflict began to assume, once again, central place in the party's propaganda. The 2008 election campaign was centred around the idea of fiscal federalism, with the party strongly condemning resource mismanagement in the South, without however neglecting the other themes mentioned above. Thus, for instance, the party denounced the fact that 'our workers in Padania have realised that they are squeezed to the bone in order to allow Italian parties [...] to maintain their electoral reservoirs in the *Meridione*, to the extent that a small family of four people resident in the North is deprived of 12 thousand euros a year' (Dussin 2008a). Similarly, the peak of the debt crisis, around the end of 2011 and the beginning of 2012, coincided with a revival of the League's secessionist stand in its internal propaganda. In August, an article on *la Padania* compared Italy to a family, which 'has four brothers who work – their names are Piedmont, Emilia-Romagna, Veneto and Lombardy – and at least thirteen who live off the others because the cash machine is in common and they are a majority' (Dussin 2011a, see also Dussin 2011b, 2011c). Unilaterally leaving the family – the piece suggested – was the only way for the four to survive in the context of the crisis. The movement seemed more than ever torn between its militants, willing to revive the independence agenda, and the more pragmatic leadership, when a financial scandal broke out jeopardising the party's reputation.

Despite all its accusations of fiscal exploitation, however, the LN has tended to rely on anecdotal evidence of the size of inter-regional fiscal flows, rather than providing detailed evidence of their nature and amounts based on existing academic studies. In the early 1990s, it claimed that Lombardy was transferring 30,000 billion liras (about 27 billion constant 2011 euros)[1] per year to the South (Moltifiori 1990). Again, in the 1996 manifesto, the party claimed that: 'four regions of the North (Lombardy, Veneto, Piedmont and Emilia-Romagna) alone send to Rome about 50% of the taxes that the State cashes in and they receive in return a derisory share of the spending managed by the central State' (LN 1996a, p. 3, see also LN 1996b, Piazzo and Malaguti 1996). In the context of the recent economic and financial crisis, in several articles, the party tossed off figures indicating that between 60 and 100 billion euros a year went from North to South (Castelli 2011, Ballarin 2012a, LN 2012b), which would amount to about 6.7–11 per cent of regional GDP.[2]

To counter the accusations of selfishness that it received, the LN has stressed that the resources transferred from North to South have not been used to ensure wealth redistribution, through services and social benefits, or to finance investments for southern development, but to nourish an elephant-like inefficient state administration and clientelistic networks. More importantly, the *Lega* has made a cultural-determinist argument about the socio-economic development of the North according to which the economic difference between the two halves of the country stems from the different cultures of the peoples inhabiting the Italian peninsula: while northerners are deemed to be hard-working and entrepreneurial, Southerners are characterised as lazier, more prone to passively rely on welfare and public jobs, and even to resort to organised crime. As one could read in the party's paper *Lega Nord* in 1990: 'we have been poor here in Lombardy too. But in Brianza's wasteland, in the foggy Padanian flatland, in old working-class Milan, in the beautiful and harsh mountains of Lombardy, the Lombard people have made their way without resorting to kidnapping, mafia, 'ndrangheta or camorra,[3] but working hard, day by day, with honesty and profound dignity' (Castellazzi 1990, see also Arcucci 1992, LN 1996d, Dussin 2008b, Neri 2013). In such a representation, the association between the North and its widespread network of SMEs has played a key role since these have not only been portrayed as responsible for the area's economic performance, but also as embodying the values of hard-work and entrepreneurship defining the northern identity (on this see also Huysseune and Dalle Mulle 2015, Dalle Mulle 2016b).

Hence, the LN has subscribed to a strong form of welfare producerism (Abts and Kochuyt 2013, 2014), whereby not only solidarity with the South has been rejected on account of the principles of control (Southerners are deemed to be responsible for their own state of need because of their lack of entrepreneurship and work ethic), attitude (they do not make a sincere effort to get out of their needy condition) and reciprocity (the North does not receive enough as compared to its effort), but it has also culturalised such welfare producerism, i.e. it has made a discursive equivalence between the northern 'Padanian' nation and the 'imagined community of welfare producers'. In this way, the party has proposed institutional reform – be it independence in the long term or federalism in the short one – as a means to improve the welfare of the Northern Italians. As lamented by the party in 2008, 'we pay taxes as in a civilised country in return for Third World [public] services' (Pellai 2008, see also LN 1996a, p. 47, 2013a).[4]

The Southern majority

As with the other case-study parties, the LN has directly linked the economic victimisation of the North to the region's political marginalisation. The Lombard and Venetian leagues even used colonial metaphors to describe the policies of the Italian state in the area (Bossi 1982, 1986, Cestonaro 1987). In the following years, such claims of cultural colonisation became marginal. What persisted, however, as a mainstay in the party's rhetoric was the idea that centralism had remained a fundamental trait of the Italian state and the traditional parties, both of which had been taken over by Southerners.

In the League's discourse the South is the 'relevant other' enabling the North to define its own identity, but the opposition between these two has also been nuanced according to the need of the time. The LN has indeed often argued that Rome – as the embodiment of the state bureaucracy and the traditional parties – is the main entity responsible for Italy's inefficiencies as well as for the South's backwardness, as it is deemed to have deliberately kept the South dependent on state allocations (Magri 1992, LN 1994, pp. 19–24, 2001, pp. 3–4, Carcano 2006, LN 2013b). Accordingly, in the early 1990s, the party's most famous slogan was *Roma ladrona, la Lega non perdona* (thieving Rome, the League doesn't pardon). At other times, however, the Southerners' seizure of parties and institutions has been openly denounced. In 1990, for instance, the LN wrote: 'if in South Africa the white people exercise their political control through weapons, in Italy, the southern ethnic majority need not use physical coercion: its political representatives only need to get most of the votes in the elections to be legitimated "by the people" to exercise political control over minorities' (Vallanz 1990).[5] Southerners have thus been accused of acting as a self-conscious ethnic group for the pursuit of their own interests by taking over parties and state institutions and 'over-profiting' from the public purse (Orestilli 1991, LN 1995, Cornali 1998, Montero 2000, Dussin 2008b, Neri 2013). Even when putting the blame on institutional actors such as 'Rome', rather than directly on Southerners, the *Lega* has portrayed Southerners as, at best, passively accepting the clientelist tactics used by traditional parties and the state administration.

Apart from a short eight months of experience in government, the LN was continuously in the opposition throughout the 1990s. In the 2000s, by contrast, it took part in two government coalitions accounting for about eight of the ten years between 2001 and 2011. Quite obviously, during these two periods in government the party's claim that the North was marginalised was more difficult to make. As mentioned in the previous section, in this period, the *Lega* focused its attention on other themes. At the same time, it also managed – in accordance with the slogan *Lega di lotta e Lega di governo* (ruling and fighting League) – to keep the appearance of being a territorial movement representing the interests of the North without becoming an established 'Roman' party, while at the same time being in office in Rome (Albertazzi and McDonnel 2005, p. 953). This is an issue that has regularly generated tensions between the more pragmatic leadership, aware of the need to compromise with other forces to have policy impact, and the militants, keener on maintaining a more pure, less compromising stand. In June 2002, for instance, a year into the second Berlusconi cabinet, and in the wake of the yearly meeting of the League's militants in the Lombard village of Pontida, in the party magazine *Il Sole delle Alpi* one could read:

> The League's basis, which keeps the movement running [...] is by now an inseparable mix of federalists and secessionists who feel awkward sharing spaces and perspectives with others for whom the freedom of the North is blasphemy. I know for sure that those people [...] continue to perceive the Italian state as an incomprehensible and uncontrollable mechanism that has little to do with the daily existence of each of us. A State that, since a year now, also features many ministers from the North and from the League, without this meaning that the people of Pontida perceive it as less surly.
>
> (Reina 2002)

To assuage such tensions and pursue its double strategy of compromise and protest, the leadership represented the party as the only force within the government capable of driving change – notably devolution of powers to the regions (Salvini 2001, Ambrosetti 2002) – and often harshly criticised other members of the governing coalition, accusing them of being centralist and slowing down the pace of reform (Parisi 2002, Eisen 2003, Bassi 2005). Similarly, two years into the third Berlusconi cabinet (2008–11), with progress on the federal reform promised during the electoral campaign faltering, the movement blamed the slowness of the process on the centralist state and the Roman bureaucrats, but also on unspecified financial interests and obscure major powers (*poteri forti*) purportedly interested in keeping the North politically and economically subordinated (Stucchi 2010, Zaia 2010, Franco 2011).

Back in the opposition, the party stressed once again its protest profile and strongly criticised the government of technocrats led by former EU Commissioner Mario Monti for systematically favouring the South to the disadvantage of the Northern economy and defining it as centralist and unaccountable (Castelli 2011, Ballarin 2012b, Carcano 2012). The 'all-Italian turn' imposed by Matteo Salvini since early 2014 has changed much of that. This does not mean that the party has completely abandoned the territorial struggle, or that it does not complain about the centralising tendencies of the state and the mismanagement of public funds in the South (see for instance Garibaldi 2014, LN 2014), but these themes have become more marginal.

In order to end the political marginalisation of the North, the LN has envisaged two strategies over the course of its history. Federalism was the *Lega*'s original goal. This came first to be embodied in the idea of the creation of a Northern Republic within a larger Italian confederation (Bossi 1991b, Speroni 1991). This idea later evolved into the project of the independence of Padania. Due to low popular support, however, the party backed down and adopted a more gradualist policy. As Bossi argued in 1999, Padania will come 'not anymore through the Big Bang of secession [...] Padania will come by Darwinian evolution, step by step' (quoted in Savoini 2000). Yet, the independence of Padania has remained as the official goal of the party, the dream of many of its militants and a constant reference in its internal, especially visual, propaganda, as well as at the party's official events, such as Pontida.[6]

At the roots of the LN's discourse

When the *Lega Nord* began lamenting the fiscal exploitation of the North, it completely reversed the terms according to which Italian socio-economic history had been interpreted until then. Yet, the party was not inventing everything from scratch. The movement was at least partially giving voice to concerns arising in areas of late industrialisation in the non-metropolitan North (especially in Veneto and Lombardy) that had recently experienced a process of very rapid and formidable economic growth, the so-called Third Italy.

The rise of the Third Italy

The birth of the geo-economic concept of the Third Italy can be attributed to the works of Arnaldo Bagnasco in the mid-1970s. In *Tre Italie* (Three Italies), he interpreted the evolution of the Italian economy as the interrelation of three different socio-economic systems endowed with a specific function and a precise territorial delimitation: the South, as an underdeveloped area dependent on the industrialisation of the North-west; the North-west – especially the metropolitan triangle between Turin, Milan and Genoa – as the site of big industry and the chosen recipient of state investments towards technological excellence; and the Centre-north-east, as the region of late industrialisation where SMEs proliferated. The Third Italy was essentially made up of the regions of Veneto, Tuscany and Emilia-Romagna, where, in 1971, SMEs accounted for more than 75 per cent of total manufacturing firms in each of them. Yet, SMEs represented an important part of the north-western economic fabric as well. In Piedmont, in the first half of the 1970s, about 50 per cent of the car industry production was in fact carried out within SMEs, and in Lombardy, although SMEs represented a smaller share of the total number of firms than in Veneto, Emilia-Romagna and Tuscany, in absolute terms they employed more than 1 million people, equal to the total amount of SME employees of those three regions (Bagnasco 1977, pp. 153–219).

SMEs were territorially diffused, often organised in industrial districts, specialised in traditional labour-intensive sectors – such as furniture, footwear and leather, textiles and garments – and mainly employed cheap labour on flexible contracts. The small size stemmed from both practical reasons (mostly linked to the need for higher flexibility) and distortions induced by domestic inefficiencies (especially in the public and financial sectors). Thus, the Third Italy represented a section of the Italian economy that filled specific niches in traditional sectors, often coinciding with previously existing craft traditions, and targeted either the supply of semi-processed products to big domestic firms or international markets – exports made up 20 per cent of total production (Bagnasco 1977, p. 219). It also constituted an answer to the problems experienced by the model of big – and often state-aided – industrialisation characterising the Turin-Milan-Genoa triangle, which, in the 1970s, struggled to compete internationally. These smaller units often provided lower costs and higher flexibility, although later some of them also developed technological excellences and became world leaders in specific productions. Such a process was hardly the result of a conscious government choice, since, even if SMEs certainly profited from the devaluation of the lira in the 1970s, they also suffered from the anti-inflationary measures adopted in the following decade and were not the main target of state subsidies (Bagnasco and Trigilia 1993, pp. 39–49).

The rise of the Third Italy did not only contribute to propelling Italy into the league of the top ten industrial countries in the world. It also had non-economic consequences. The first was that it challenged the then dominant interpretive framework whereby Southern backwardness resulted from a relation of 'unequal exchange' between the North and the South. The 'spontaneous' rise of the 'peripheral North' to a position in which it could challenge the leading North-west inevitably cast a new light on Southern underdevelopment (Bartolini 2015, p. 31). The second was a 'rediscovery' of culture – much similar to that highlighted in Chapter 3. The study of the Third Italy, which flourished in the late 1970s, brought with it the resurrection of the concept of 'industrial district' proposed by Alfred Marshall a century before in his analysis of the British Midlands. Marshall laid great emphasis on the socio-cultural factors driving economic development in specific locations. Building on these ideas, Italian economists and economic sociologists interpreted the development of Northern Italian districts as linked not only to structural and organisational variables, but also to a specific 'environment' meant as 'a set of shared values and practices for the achievement of common wellbeing' (Bartolini 2015, p. 41). The districts were portrayed as communities of 'small producers' whose economic success depended on the values of hard-work, creativity, entrepreneurship and flexibility shared by their members, thus offering a key precedent for the LN's representation of the North (which the party essentially depicted as an industrial district writ large), especially given that this productive local context was unavoidably pitted against the inefficient national one (Bartolini 2015, p. 56).

As Figure 4.2 shows, between 1951 and 1991, the Centre-north-east, along with some rural provinces of the North-west, experienced a general convergence towards the living standards of the industrial areas of the Turin-Milan-Genoa triangle. The region of Veneto is an exemplary case in this respect. While in 1951 its per capita value added was equal only to 81 per cent of the national average, by 1981 it hit 109 per cent, displaying the quickest growth rate among northern regions (my calculations on Istituto Tagliacarne 2011).

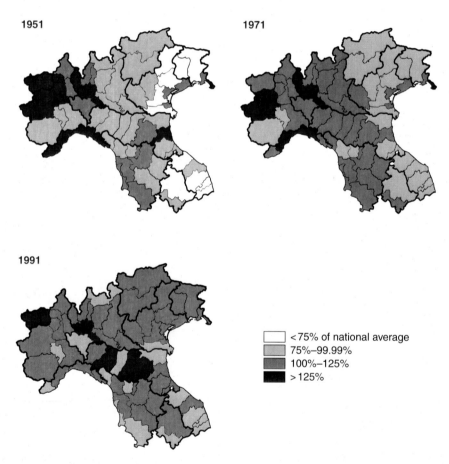

Figure 4.2 Northern Italy's value added per capita by province, 1951–91 (percentage of national average).

Source: my elaboration on Istituto Tagliacarne 2011.

Electoral studies have shown a striking correlation between support for the LN and employment in areas of SMEs industrialisation. Analysing the Lombard League, Moioli (1990) stressed that among its voters there was a high proportion of private sector workers and self-employed living in small centres with higher than average employment but lower than average levels of education, salaries and ratios of civil servants to the total population. Diamanti (1994) confirmed a similar profile for the electors of the new Northern League at large. According to his findings, most lived in small centres of diffused industrialisation enjoying lower than average levels of state transfers (see also Bonomi 1997). The correlation between SMEs and the electoral success of the League, however, did not hold for the region of Emilia-Romagna. The explanation is probably to be found in the communist subculture that prevailed in the region since the post-War period, which, being ideologically too distant from the LN's right-wing message, probably limited massive voters' defection to the *Lega*. Furthermore, the *Partito Comunista Italiano* (Italian Communist Party, PCI) did not melt away as the *Democrazia Cristiana* (Christian Democray, DC) and the *Partito Socialista Italiano* (Italian Socialist Party, PSI), but rather reformed itself into a social-democratic movement, the *Partito Democratico della Sinistra* (Democratic Party of the Left, PDS), that managed to maintain its territorial hold on the region (Hine 1996, Levy 1996).[7]

Between the late 1980s and the early 1990s, the League did voice some of the concerns of the Third Italy by introducing the 'Northern Question' into Italian politics. Yet, traditional parties had not completely ignored these demands in the previous years. Between the late 1970s and early 1980s, all three traditional parties – DC, PCI and PSI – tried to address the claims of these new constituencies within the general framework of the so-called *nuovi ceti medi produttivi* (new productive middle strata), although they also generally avoided territorialising their requests. The PSI was especially active in this respect and it frequently extolled the 'archipelago of local economic systems that [...] has made a different Italy built on fantasy, attitude to work and disposition to risk, on the will to innovate, and also of profit, of thousands and thousands of workers and entrepreneurs'. Similarly, the DC took an interest in the 'new productive middle strata' by creating a department devoted to studying them in the early 1980s. Surprisingly, it was the PCI that at times did play on territorial differences. This is the case with communist President of Emilia-Romagna Guido Fanti who, in 1975, proposed the creation of a kind of 'League of the Po' (which is the river crossing the Padanian flatland) to find coordinated solutions to the unresolved problems of an area that – he argued – was the engine of Italy's growth. His proposal did not lead anywhere, but it constitutes an important precedent and even contained some fiscal complaints in line with future LN arguments (quoted in Bartolini 2015, p. 125).

More generally, however, between the late 1970s and mid-1980s, these parties tended to praise the work ethic and entrepreneurship of the new middle strata and to suggest the existence of a rising social conflict – in part reformulating more traditional class references – between 'producers' and 'parasites', with the former being identified with the new class of small entrepreneurs and professionals and the latter variably, according to each party, with big capital (as opposed to SMEs) and/or white-collar workers (executive or clerical) exploiting rent-seeking positions (Bartolini 2015, pp. 90–126). In this way, they involuntarily paved the way for the territorialisation of such an incipient conflict that the League would bring about towards the end of the 1980s.

The inter-territorial transfers

Contrary to other cases analysed in this study, the LN did not profit from academic calculations of inter-territorial transfers, since the first studies were only carried out in the early 1990s. By contrast, successive governments throughout the 1970s and 1980s, along with much of the Southern political class, widely publicised the extraordinary state intervention in the South to ensure consensus there, especially the industrial and infrastructural projects linked to the *Cassa per il Mezzogiorno* – a special investment fund established in 1950 to promote the development of the area (Viesti 2003, p. 51).

In 1992, Carlo Trigilia (1992, pp. 37–73) showed that per capita state expenses were roughly proportional to the population both in the North and the South, but the latter contributed 50 per cent less than what it received and therefore profited from inter-regional redistribution, although mainly from ordinary rather than extraordinary spending, which had been the focus of northern criticism. His data refuted some evaluations carried out at about the same time by Giuseppe de Meo (1992) and other researchers who, in fact, tried to provide evidence that taxation in Italy was regressive and the South was in fact subsidising the North. More in-depth analyses came from the late 1990s onwards. As can be seen from Table 4.1, despite showing sometimes large differences, these studies confirm the existence of substantial transfers from the North to the South (in the 4.7–11.5 per cent range of the region's GDP) that, when considering the regions that contribute most, such as Lombardy and Veneto, are generally higher than those reviewed in the previous chapters (13 per cent of Lombardy's GDP and 8.9 per cent of Veneto's on average). All southern regions are net recipients, but so are those northern regions that enjoy a special Statute, especially Aosta Valley and Trentino-Süd Tirol, even if they enjoy high levels of income per capita (131 per cent and 125 per cent of the Italian average respectively).

Commenting on the results, Staderini and Vadalà (2009) argued that the flows were quite proportional to the distribution of income across the peninsula and largely justified on account of interpersonal redistribution, only magnified by the big gap between northern and southern regions (see also

Table 4.1 Northern Italian regions' fiscal balances, various estimates (percentage of regional GDP)

	Ambrosiano et al. (2005, bf)	Arachi et al. (1996–2002, bf)	Brosio et al. (1997, mf)	Maggi and Piperno (1995, bf)	Staderini and Vadalà (2004–05, bf)
Abruzzo	6.9	4.2	-0.6	6.0	5.9
Aosta Valley*	2.8	11.7	10.3	13.9	11.2
Basilicata	13.7	19.6	9.8	22.0	23.1
Calabria	17.8	26.9	7.7	31.2	25.6
Campania	14.6	14.3	2.0	13.1	14.9
Emilia Romagna	-5.9	-11.6	-5.4	-9.4	-8.4
Friuli-VG*	-0.8	-3.0	7.2	0.9	-0.4
Lazio	2.5	-9.7	7.4	-1.3	-8.5
Liguria	5.6	1.0	-0.1	1.7	3.7
Lombardy	-11.6	-17.9	-6.0	-14.4	-14.6
Marches	0.6	-2.4	-4.4	-1.7	-1.5
Molise	14.1	15.2	2.8	17.9	20.3
Piedmont	-1.8	-8.6	-4.5	-7.2	-5.1
Puglia	12.9	12.2	1.5	10.4	14.3
Sardinia*	12.4	16.6	12.9	19.5	15.4
Sicily*	16.5	20.4	8.8	20.4	18.7
Trentino-ST*	-1.3	2.2	11.0	12.2	4.7
Tuscany	0.6	-4.5	-5.7	-4.3	-4.1
Umbria	7.8	3.8	-0.3	4.7	6.6
Veneto	-6.4	-11.1	-9.8	-9.4	-7.6
North**	-6.5	-11.5	-4.7	–	-9.6

Sources: Ambrosiano et al. 2010, Arachi et al. 2006, Brosio and Revelli 2003, Maggi and Piperno 1998, Staderini and Vadalà 2009.

Notes

bf = benefit-flow; mf = monetary-flow.

* Region with special statute of autonomy.

** My calculation on data provided by the authors cited.

Maggi and Piperno 1998, p. 42). Likewise, Ambrosiano *et al.* (2010) found tax revenue to be substantially proportional to income and only slightly higher in richer Lombardy (24 per cent) compared to poorer Calabria (22.4 per cent). These conclusions would therefore confirm that social redistribution – in principle an interpersonal matter – lies at the core of the inter-territorial transfers so central to the LN's arguments. However, both studies also pointed to some problems. Staderini and Vadalà made room for the possibility that part of the transfers was generated by lower efficiency in the public sector in southern regions, while Ambrosiano *et al.* focused on the lack of convergence between the South and the rest of the country and wondered whether, in the context of the recent economic and financial crisis, such generous flows could still be sustainable.

Unfortunately, no study provides a longitudinal analysis of the evolution of the transfers over an extended period of time. Maggi and Piperno (1998) did compare data from 1989 and 1995, showing a clear deterioration of fiscal deficits for the 'Padanian regions' of Piedmont, Lombardy, Emilia-Romagna and Veneto (their aggregate contribution went from 2.8 per cent to 5.2 per cent of Italian gross value added (GVA)), which they mostly explained with reference to the massive fiscal consolidation carried out by successive Italian governments in those years. While this can explain the formation of the League's nationalism of the rich and its breakthrough in the early 1990s, it cannot account for later trends. A look at the evolution of the relationship between primary and disposable income per capita in the three northern regions where the League has been most successful – Lombardy, Veneto and Piedmont – can help complete the picture. As shown by Figure 4.3, obtained through a revised version of a formula by Lago-Peñas *et al.* (2013, see figure caption), the redistributive effort of Lombardy and Veneto has remained quite stable in the period 1995–2011 – although it slightly worsened – while Piedmont's has almost completely reversed. This data suggests that, from the mid-1990s, Veneto and Lombardy's fiscal deficit has remained quite stable and cannot therefore account for major variations in the salience of the transfers. As in the other cases, however, they can account for the persistence of the Northern Question. In order to explain variability one has to look at other – economic and non-economic – factors. Among the former, over-compensation effects and economic convergence must be taken into account, as well as the efficiency of the public administration, patterns of public spending and growth trends.

Leaving the last three for the next section, let us focus here on the first two factors. By integrating estimates of public sector efficiency and fiscal evasion into calculations of inter-regional fiscal transfers, Ricolfi (2010, pp. 82–112) recently concluded that northern residents have not only paid more on average, but also received less in both relative and absolute terms (about 500 euros less yearly per capita). Other studies suggest that this has been accompanied by lack of economic convergence. By the early 1990s,

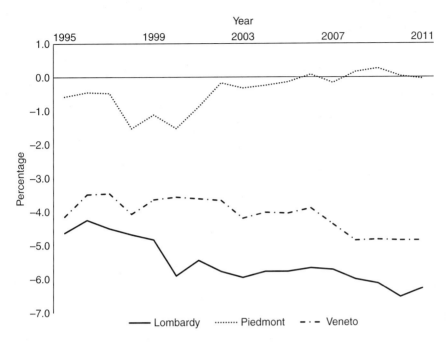

Figure 4.3 Northern Italy's redistributive effort per capita, 1995–2011 (percentage of standardised primary income).*

Source: my elaboration on ISTAT 2013.

Notes
* Redistributive Effort = ((Di/Dn) – (Pi/Pn))/(Pi/Pn);
Di = regional disposable income per capita;
Dn = national disposable income per capita;
Pi = regional primary income per capita;
Pn = national primary income per capita.
(see Lago-Peñas *et al.* 2013, p. 13).

the South's GDP was 60 per cent of that of the North, i.e. about the same as in 1945. Considering that in the meantime northern regions had made an impressive leap forward, in absolute terms this was a positive result. Yet, southern development resulted more from public employment (public sector jobs accounted for about 50 per cent of its GDP against 30 per cent in the North in the early 1990s) and top-down industrialisation than from the creation of endogenous factors of growth (Trigilia 1992, pp. 37–73, Viesti 2003, pp. 51–53). Furthermore, analysing convergence from the 1950s up to the 2000s, Padovano (2007, p. 90) found that, when redistribution was geographically regressive – i.e. the average tax rate decreased as income increased – southern economies converged towards the northern ones, while when it was progressive the gap widened. This change from regressive to progressive taxation mainly occurred in the 1970s, when the Italian

Government began to redistribute through cash transfers instead of capital expenditure, thus propping up consumption. While such a change might have had a positive impact in improving living standards in the *Meridione*, from a production-side perspective, it arguably advantaged firms in the North, which could sell their products to a wider market in the South, and did not go along with convergence. Padovano (2007, p. 12) thus concluded that this finding would 'run counter to the notion that government policy in favor of *Mezzogiorno* was [...] in favor of *Mezzogiorno*'.

The fiscal crisis of the state

Between 1970 and 1990, Italy's public spending rose dramatically. At first, this happened without a substantial increase in taxes, as budget deficits were mainly financed through debt and inflation. Yet, by the early 1980s this strategy became unsustainable (Viesti 2003, pp. 41–51). A sudden tax hike occurred between 1981 and 1983 and, although at a lower pace, it continued edging up between 1985 and 1993, from 35 per cent to 43 per cent of GDP. Spending was very much affected by the stock of debt accumulated and the interest paid on it. In the early 1990s, public expenditure net of interest payments on debt was equal to 39.2 per cent of GDP, slightly lower than the European Economic Community (EEC) average. Yet, the draconian interest rates (10–12 per cent a year) and the size of public debt pushed spending up to 53.2 per cent of GDP (Padoa Schioppa Kostoris 1996, pp. 273–276). This was the result of policies adopted throughout the 1980s, when the country recorded the second-highest rate of increase in public spending in the Organisation for Economic Co-operation and Development (OECD) behind Spain (my calculations on Tanzi and Schuknecht 2000, pp. 6–7). Accordingly, public debt increased from 60.4 per cent of GDP in 1975 to a 121.8 per cent in 1994 (Figure 4.4).

All this was made worse by an inefficient administration and by one of the most unbalanced welfare states among advanced economies. Although it is hard to comparatively gauge the former, there is a general consensus in the literature that the standards of the Italian bureaucratic service – although with geographic variations – have not been up to those of other countries with similar, or even lower, levels of spending (Cassese 1998, pp. 60–76, Ginsborg 1996, p. 23). Similarly, Italian welfare was among the most distorted in Europe. By 1980, pensions accounted for 80 per cent of total social spending. Given the huge differences in income from work and employment between the two halves of the country, 69 per cent of it went to the North, although only 45 per cent of the elderly population lived there. This not only advantaged the North over the South, but it also mainly catered for workers with standard long-term careers, who could be found more often in big firms than in SMEs. Along the same lines, the progressive extension of the *cassa integrazione* (redundancy fund) chiefly targeted employees in big industrial plants and was consistently preferred

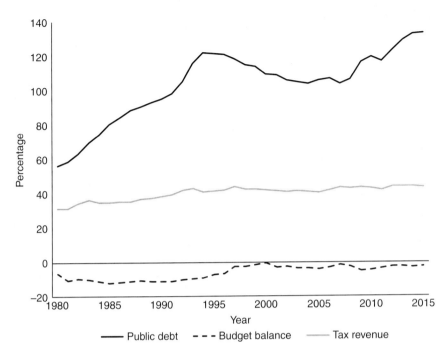

Figure 4.4 Italy's public debt, budget balance and tax revenue, 1980–2015 (percentage of GDP).

Sources: my elaboration on ISTAT 2017b, 2017c, IMF-IFAD 2012.

over the establishment of a universal unemployment benefit scheme (Ferrera *et al.* 2012, pp. 330–331). As a compensation to the South, public employment and disability pensions were used there as a kind of 'permanent unemployment benefit', albeit a very unfair and ineffective one from a social welfare perspective, because highly selective and often linked to clientelistic relations (Ferrera 1993, pp. 25–29, Alesina *et al.* 1999, Fargion 2005, pp. 127–134). The flexible labour force on short-term contracts and the small entrepreneurs prevalent in the Third Italy were often left without welfare coverage.

In the early 1990s, the dire situation of Italian public finances cast a long shadow over the chances that the country would be able to respect the criteria for membership in the coming European monetary union. Concerns for the state of national accounts evolved into a true emergency in summer 1992, when a speculative attack on the lira pushed its value down by 15 per cent, forcing it out of the European Monetary System (Gundle and Parker 1996, pp. 1–15). The government, led by Giuliano Amato, responded with a bill that cut the budget deficit by 90 thousand billion liras in just 1 year (about 74 billion constant 2011 euros).[8] Still in 1992, a judicial inquiry called *mani pulite* (Clean Hands) exposed a systematic system of clientelism and corruption with ramifications throughout the country. The ensuing scandal – named *Tangentopoli* (Bribesville) – led to the dissolution of both the DC and the PSI and the end of the so-called First Republic. In the face of these events, the idea that Italy had been brought to the verge of collapse by a corrupt and incompetent political class inevitably struck a chord. Furthermore, in light of the opportunities and threats posed by the coming European Single Market, a substantial part of Northern Italian society began to realise that clientelism 'had become increasingly uneconomic and was placing burdens on local business' (Cento Bull and Gilbert 2001, p. 82). Out-sourcing of production had already begun in the late 1980s causing unemployment and workers' anxiety. Enterprises also began to need more resources in terms of information and marketing and realised that local, and especially regional, institutions could play a critical role in providing firms with such services. For these reasons, industrial districts started asking for liberal measures, local autonomy and a bigger say in state politics, all demands that – between the late 1980s and the early 1990s – were captured by the League (Cento Bull and Gilbert 2001, pp. 79–98).

Towards the end of the 1990s, fiscal reforms began delivering results and the country managed to enter the monetary union. Yet, success was mixed. While public finances were brought under control, debt began decreasing and unemployment was very low (4.1 per cent on average in the North between 2000 and 2007), the 2000s were also years of sluggish real GDP growth (1 per cent in 2000–07) (my calculations on ISTAT 2017d, 2017e). Furthermore, during these years Italy lost the opportunity to use the resources freed by the reduced interest on debt – which had shrunk from 12.6 per cent of GDP to less than 5 per cent in about a decade – to invest in innovation and reduce inefficiencies in the public sector. Between 2000 and 2007, northern enterprises became very good at internationalising their production, but remained generally undersized as compared to their rivals abroad, did not manage to expand into high-tech sectors and suffered heavily from Chinese competition (Fortis and Quadro Curzio 2003, Grandinetti 2010, Picchieri and Perulli 2010, Cannari and Franco 2012, pp. 103–127).

For the Northern economy, the recent economic crisis has had a worse impact than that of the early 1990s. While two decades earlier the fiscal crisis of the state had been accompanied by good growth rates, this time the 'real' economy was hit quite harshly. Real GDP decreased by 7.1 per cent in 2009 and again by 5.4 per cent in 2012–13 (my calculations on ISTAT 2017d). Although it remained low by international standards, unemployment increased from 3.9 per cent in 2008 to 8.6 per cent in 2014 (ISTAT 2017e). But the highest price was paid by industrial production that in 2014 was 76 per cent of its 2007 level, or about the same as in 1985–86 (OECD 2017).[9] As we will see more in detail in Chapter 9, between 2010 and 2011, opinion polls suggested a revival of demands for more autonomy in the North coinciding with the peak of the crisis, but that discontent was later channelled in different directions.

Italy, a 90-minute nation?

Although the *Lega* invented a completely new identity for the North, its controversial territorial claims built on an entrenched perception of a cultural difference between the two halves of the country. Yet, despite being a central theme of Italian politics, the North-South fracture never was a threat to Italian unity. On the contrary, it was seen as a goal of the entire polity to overcome on the path towards modernisation.

Before unification the major concern of those Italian intellectuals who engaged with the subject of national unity regarded the need to regenerate the Italian people in order to bring them up to the standard of the other great European nations. In this context, idiosyncratic flaws such as idleness were attributed to the inhabitants of the whole country. Yet, in the early post-unification years, mainly as a consequence of the war against *brigantaggio*,[10] the South became the internal 'other' representing all what was not modern about Italy (Huysseune 2006, pp. 39–79, Patriarca 2011, pp. 74–108). Later on, southern underdevelopment was mainly explained through the interpretation of the so-called 'meridionalist school', which read the 'Southern Question' as the consequence of the Piedmontese 'invasion' that imposed northern economic dominance over the South through a pact between southern big landowners and the northern rising industrial bourgeoisie – the so-called *Blocco storico* (historical block). Although this explanation underlined the existence of 'two Italies', it did not question Italian unity and the existence of an Italian nation (Teti 2011).

Italian unification had been a top-down affair triggering little popular enthusiasm. Despite being limited to 6 per cent of the population – extended to about 20 per cent in 1882 – elections showed a remarkably low turnout suggesting that 'the liberal and moderate elites that were in power ruled, but were not hegemonic' (Patriarca 2011, p. 41). Furthermore, Italy was divided among dozens of languages, identities and local cultures that seriously threatened the unity and legitimacy of the state. Fearing for the survival of the Kingdom, the Piedmontese extended their legislation to the entire country and imposed a very high level of uniformity (Lepschy *et al.* 1996, Vandelli 2011, p. 421). Regional elites did complain about excessive centralisation, yet they never dared openly challenge state authority, nor did they develop any forms of political regionalism, because they felt their power was precarious and thus accepted state protection, seeking to maximise the benefits derived from their position as intermediaries between the state and civil society. Hence, state legitimacy came to be based on the mediation of the political class (Lyttelton 1996, p. 43, Cammarano 2011, pp. 72–78). Such weak legitimacy coupled with a centralised architecture hampered the definition of a general interest and is often deemed to be the main cause of the development of a peculiarly Italian feature, *trasformismo* (transformism), i.e. a 'form of political action that is designed to cater to multiple interests and that, instead of achieving a general synthesis, seeks short-term and partial syntheses' (Graziano 2010, p. 5). Clientelism would be a corollary of transformism and, although today discredited, in the early phases of consolidation of the new Italian state, it served the need to weave together the very different societies making up the country (Lyttelton 1996, p. 45).

The First World War and the ensuing fascist age tried to provide founding myths and a 'grand design' for the nation. Yet, fascism and the tragedy of the Second World War constituted a major collective trauma, seriously hampering any nation-building effort for the following half a century (Rusconi 1993, p. 13, Patriarca 2001, pp. 21–22). Two further issues contributed to preventing any serious discourse about the nation in public debates. First, the Resistance had become the most immediate myth of national unity, but, this had in fact been a civil war between anti-fascists and collaborationists that stretched well into the first years of the Republic (1945–48). Second, as Norberto Bobbio (in Bobbio and Rusconi 1992, p. 1023) argued, after the War, the leitmotif of national unity moved from being the anti-fascist struggle, in which the communists had played a key role, to anti-communism, therefore laying the foundation for the post-war national identity on even more shifting sands. Paradoxically, the rise of the LN at the beginning of the 1990s unleashed an unprecedented level of discussion on and attention to Italian national identity. Hence, not only did the *Lega* expose once again the problematic features of this identity, but it also reignited a conversation that had been dormant for about half a century.

Opinion polls generally confirm the 'weakness' of the Italian identity, which is often blamed on the 'failure' of Italian nation-building. Graziano (2010, pp. 61–64), for instance, stresses how, at unification, Italian was spoken only by 2.5 per cent of the population and often as a dead written language. In 1910, 50 years later, the Ministry of Education still complained that two-thirds of school classes were of inadequate quality. In many places, illiterate teachers were hired because of lack of literate ones and even those who spoke Italian often had to use dialects to be understood by pupils. The most intense phase of cultural and linguistic homogenisation occurred after 1945, with the expansion of education, the increase of wellbeing and, above all, the spread of radio and television, which brought standard Italian to virtually all households in the country (Lupo 1996, p. 258). However, at the same time, an important nuance should be stressed. Several studies have shown that about 80 per cent of Italians declare themselves proud of their national identity, a percentage in line with wider European trends. Nevertheless, Italians stand out by virtue of a substantially lower attachment to political institutions. Thus, the 'weakness' would lie in the political rather than the cultural dimension of Italian identity (Segatti 1999, 15–23, see also Huysseune 2002, p. 220).

Although the idea of the existence of a northern (or Padanian) nation did play on the cultural fracture between the North and the South and could exploit some 'weaknesses' of Italian nation-building, it did not have any real historical precedent. This absence of past instances of northern political unity, from which the positive characters of northern identity could be derived, has led the party to mainly create them by opposition to the well-defined – because available in the rich literature on the 'Italian national character' and the Southern Question – profile of Southerners (see Huysseune 2006, Patriarca 2011). Furthermore, despite attempts to 'homogenise' the Padanian self-understanding, pre-existing cultural differences between Venetians, Lombards and other northern groups have lingered on, making the Padanian identity a light overarching feature of the fragmented northern community. Yet, the League's nation-building effort has not been totally unsuccessful. According to figures reported by Biorcio (2010, pp. 40–41), in 1996, only 5.3 per cent of Northern Italians declared belonging to Northern Italy as their primary territorial identity. By 2008 the figure had reached 22.7 per cent (see also Diamanti 2008).

A Southern-dominated state?

The LN's main argument of political marginalisation has concerned Southerners' domination of state bureaucracy and political parties. Even here, the *Lega* was not building totally from scratch, since the idea that northern and southern elites had followed complementary paths of specialisation, the former taking care of the economy and the latter focusing on the management of the state, had roots reaching back to the interwar years and even further (see Cassese 1977, pp. 87–106).

With regard to the bureaucracy, there is evidence of a process of 'southernisation' at least up to the early 1960s. After an early domination by Piedmontese civil servants, from the last quarter of the nineteenth century, there was a steady flow of officials from the South. By 1954, Southern bureaucrats were overwhelmingly represented among the higher ranks (56 per cent against 13 per cent from the North), while in 1961 the ratio of civil servants in the central administration on the total population of their circumscription of origin was 15.4 for 100,000 inhabitants in the Northwest, 48.4 in the North-east and the Centre, 102.9 in the South and 127.5 in Sicily and Sardinia. According to Cassese (1977, pp. 70–117), this was the result of a set of historical reasons, whereby public employment became the best chance of social mobility for the southern middle-class and this condition was deliberately tolerated, even encouraged, by successive governments for reasons of consensus.

With regard to political parties, there is some evidence of Southern over-representation among the traditional ones in the last decades of the First

Republic, although mostly in an indirect way. Since the end of 1970s, the DC, the PSI and the PCI began a long-lasting electoral decline that was, however, more pronounced in the North than in the South – especially concerning the DC and the PSI. An important consequence of these developments was that 'the political class of the DC and the PSI elected at the national level inevitably became more southernised' (Trigilia 1992, p. 70).

But the League's argument of political marginalisation did not only pertain to the North-South fracture. It also referred to a divide between two types of Norths. The historical thesis of the *Blocco storico*, for instance, stressed how the North-west had remained the over-riding target of investments for the development of big industries since the late nineteenth century. As shown by Silvio Lanaro (1988, p. 81, 1993, pp. 31–32), since unification, such northern, especially Milanese, elites had remained content with their economic prosperity and rather uninterested in political positions, sending few representatives to participate in central governments. Yet, with regard to the non-metropolitan northern areas, the 1980s brought about a perception of marginalisation, rather than of deliberate indifference to national politics. Such feelings were openly expressed at the end of the 1980s by the Venetian Senator of the Christian Democrats Antonio Bisaglia, when he declared that 'the state has very often considered my region as an isolated area, alien to the strategic choices of the country. It has focused its attention on the big metropolitan areas, that fortunately we do not have, or on the South. Hence, the area in between, that has neither Naples, nor Turin, nor Milan, has been sacrificed' (quoted in Diamanti 1988, see also Bartolini 2015, p. 124). Non-academic accounts provided some statistical evidence, although the calculation was limited to the North-east and covered a very short time period. Gian Antonio Stella (2000), editor of *Il Corriere della Sera*, showed that at the beginning of the 1990s the area accounted for 14 per cent of the national wealth and 20 per cent of exports, but only 4 per cent of government members belonged to it.

The corruption scandals that broke out at the beginning of the 1990s, along with the dire conditions of state accounts, exposed the inefficiency of the centralist political system. Also thanks to the rise of the LN, a consensus arose around the idea that decentralisation could bring about more accountability and efficiency in public spending as well as provide a solution to northern perceptions of political marginalisation (Fabbrini and Brunazzo 2008, p. 105). Hence, ordinary regions, which were originally established in 1970 but endowed with very few powers, were progressively granted more autonomy. The ratio of own taxes on regional spending increased from 15 per cent in 1992 to over 50 per cent by 2000 (Ambrosiano *et al.* 2010, pp. 84–85). The most important institutional modification, however, came in 2001. This introduced a list of competences reserved to the state, leaving all the residual ones to the regions except for some concurrent legislation, and it allowed regions, at least in principle, to claim more competences than those initially attributed to them, thus opening up the possibility of asymmetric federalism as in Spain (Giarda 2004, pp. 1–15). Nevertheless, the latter provision was never implemented. This was the case as well with the modification of article 119 of the Constitution, which in its new form could allow regions to be totally financed by their own revenues and tax shares, ruling out earmarked central transfers as standard practice, and would set up a new inter-regional equalisation fund aimed at reducing differences in fiscal capacity, but with no consideration of regional needs or historical expenditure (Ambrosiano *et al.* 2010, pp. 80–81).

Overall, thus, the Italian process of federalisation has been limited and contradictory (Bull and Pasquino 2007, pp. 671–672, Fabbrini and Brunazzo 2008, p. 117, Roux 2008, p. 334). From data concerning fiscal autonomy, one could be led to conclude that Italian regions have greatly improved their powers. Yet, specific provisions in the 2001 constitutional reform constrained the scope for differentiation. Some clauses have ensured the primacy of uniformity over autonomy, both in the levels of spending and the quality of services (Giarda 2004, pp. 21–22). In addition, many of the modifications have not been implemented (most strikingly not even by the League once in government), leaving their autonomist potential largely unexploited. As in all the other case studies, the process has lacked vision and has mainly been guided by short-term political compromises (Fabbrini and Brunazzo 2008, p. 114).

Finally, the role played by regional institutions in the other case studies suggests that the fragmentation into different regions of the northern constituencies targeted by the *Lega* has disadvantaged the party, although such fragmentation clearly reflects the indeterminacy and weakness of the overarching northern identity. In other words, the centre-periphery cleavage in Italy has not been as clear-cut as in other countries. Also, there has not been a substantial overlap between territorial and ideological cleavages with a clear domination of the Right in the North and of the Left in the South. Some southern regions have indeed consistently voted for FI – Sicily for instance – and the Left has been successful in some northern regions, notably Emilia-Romagna. Yet, when considering the three key regions of Lombardy, Piedmont and Veneto, the Centre-Left has won only two regional elections of the 15 held between 1995 and 2015. All the others have been won by centre-right candidates, mostly resulting from alliances between the LN and FI (PdL from 2008–13). The centre-right domination of these three regions has upheld the idea of a more entrepreneurial North out of tune with the rest of the country, which largely reflects the LN's propaganda. Such concerns have also been openly expressed by some northern leaders of the Centre-Left. After the 2000 election, for instance, Piero Fassino, senior member of the then *Democratici di Sinistra* (Leftist Democrats), publicly argued that the party's defeat 'expressed the difficulty in the relationship between the Centre-Left and the northern society. Where society is more dynamic – he continued – the Centre-Left has a greater difficulty to understand and represent this reality' (quoted in Roux 2008, p. 331).

Conclusion

The 'Northern Question' has undeniably been the most important novelty introduced by the LN in Italian politics. This has consisted in a reversal of traditional interpretations of Italian economic development according to which it was necessary to develop the South in order to make Italy modern. In this framework redistribution had often been justified on the grounds that state policies had favoured industrialisation in the North while keeping the South backward. The League has consistently suggested that the money transferred from the North to the South has been wasted and used to finance clientelism and corruption. The party has however rarely provided detailed accounts of the transfers and mainly relied on anecdotal evidence. Most importantly, the *Lega* has formulated a culturalised welfare producerism, whereby not only solidarity with the South has been rejected on account of the deservingness criteria of control, attitude and reciprocity, but it has also discursively identified the entire northern nation with the 'imagined community of welfare producers'. This has allowed the party to propose independence, and/or more autonomy, as a means to improve the welfare of northern Italians without harming the region's competitiveness.

The other pillar of the *Lega*'s nationalism of the rich stems from the accusations against the centralist tendencies of the Italian administration and the traditional parties, both of which have supposedly been controlled by Southerners. The *Lega* has often changed tone strategically, at times emphasising the responsibility of Rome in making the South dependent, at others, depicting Southerners as a cohesive ethnic group deliberately plotting against northerners. In any case, the North, and, in particular, the non-metropolitan areas of so-called Third Italy have been portrayed as not having power in line with their economic weight. Their economic victimisation is thus deemed to derive from this political subordination.

While in the 1990s the party was in the opposition for nearly the entire decade, it held government responsibilities in Rome for most of the 2000s. Despite this privileged position, the *Lega* has not been able to solve the 'Northern Question', nor to substantially increase the autonomy of the northern regions. In such a context, the marginalisation of the North has been a much harder claim to make. Yet, the League has been at least in part able to continue to shift the blame for the lack of success of its reform agenda onto other government partners, described as defending the interests of Rome and the South.

In historical perspective, the nationalism of the rich in Northern Italy did not arise in those areas that had enjoyed unchallenged primacy in the national economy since the beginning of the century, that is, the metropolitan areas included in the Turin-Milan-Genoa triangle. It rather originated in semi-rural areas, especially those of Veneto and Lombardy, that between roughly 1960 and 1980 experienced a spread of industrial districts of SMEs combining high flexibility and specialisation leading to the so-called 'second Italian economic miracle'. Although having been richer than most of the South since the end of the Second World War, many of these provinces went from enjoying a GDP per capita closer to that of the *Meriodione* than to that of the richest industrial areas of the North, to joining the group of the most prosperous regions of the country. They thus went through a situation of economic reversal similar to that realised in Flanders and, if one counts the potential wealth deriving from oil, Scotland.

As compared to the other case studies, rigorous assessments of interterritorial transfers between the North and the South came well after the LN had openly questioned their legitimacy. This delayed interest on the part of Italian economists might have been due to the initial scepticism, and often scorn, with which the League was hailed in mainstream Italian politics. Despite varying widely, the available estimates show sizable transfers between the North and the South, although especially coming from the regions of Lombardy, Veneto and Emilia-Romagna, and usually of greater magnitude than those registered in the other case studies (8–15 per cent of regional GDP). Their magnitude mainly depends on the wide income gap between northern and southern regions, yet some authors have also pointed out problems linked to overcompensation, lack of convergence and lower administrative efficiency in the South, which in turn would also depend on the wider use of some welfare provisions – notably disability pensions – and public employment for clientelist purposes. Yet, probably the most important factor explaining the questioning of North-South solidarity since the mid-1980s has been the progressive worsening of state finances with the parallel increase of deficit, debt and taxation throughout the following decade.

Both the arguments of economic victimisation and political marginalisation require a claim of difference based on the belief in the existence of a distinct political community. Although new and surprising, the assertion that the North constituted a different nation could rely upon the well-entrenched perception of a cultural difference between the two halves of the country. It probably also profited from some weaknesses of the process of Italian nation-building. Enjoying little grassroots legitimacy, the Savoy monarchy had indeed imposed a strongly centralised administrative system that, at the same time, had few resources to bring about a thorough process of nation-formation. Paradoxically, however, the rise of the regionalist leagues, in the 1980s, came after that the first period of true cultural homogenisation, with the spread of mass education, cinema, radio and TV in the post-Second World War period, had come about.

Finally, the LN has accused Southerners of having taken over the administration and the political parties. While there is evidence concerning the over-representation of civil servants coming from Southern regions within the central administration at least up to the early 1960s, figures regarding political parties are more fragmentary. There would however be some ground to confirm an at least partial 'southernisation' of the DC and the PSI throughout the 1980s. All this arguably contributed to the perception of a political marginalisation in the non-metropolitan areas of diffused industrialisation, a perception greatly enhanced by the *Tangentopoli* corruption scandal, which, although having ramifications throughout the country, was mostly depicted by the League as being due to a southernised partitocratic system.

Notes

1 Figures in constant euros are my calculations on ISTAT (2011).
2 Figures in share of regional GDP are my calculations on ISTAT (2017a).
3 *'ndrangheta* and *camorra* are the names used to indicate mafia-style organised crime in the region of Calabria and Campania.
4 Here, welfare producerism concerns not only social provisions, but also public employment more generally, since, according to the party, (useless) public jobs were distributed in the South as a form of social support (see LN 1992, 2013a).
5 The claim that the North constitutes a minority is of course disputable (see next section and Chapter 6 for further detail).
6 On the internal function of the idea of Padanian independence see Avanza 2009.
7 In the late 2000s, however, the League consolidated its support in Emilia-Romagna as well, especially playing on its arguments against foreign immigration (Anderlini 2009, Passarelli and Tuorto 2009).
8 My calculations on ISTAT 2011.
9 Data are for Italy as a whole, but given the concentration of industrial production in the North it is reasonable to assume that it reflects general trends there.
10 The term refers to the illegal activities of bands of brigands in the South in the first years of the new Kingdom.

5 Scotland

The economics of independence and the democratic deficit

Origins and evolution of the SNP

Born in April 1934 of the merger between the National Party of Scotland and the Scottish Party, the SNP's main objective at its founding was to establish a Scottish Parliament dealing with Scottish affairs. Until the end of the 1960s, however, the SNP mostly remained a marginal organisation. At the beginning of that decade, a group of new young members ameliorated its structure and policy-making, enabling the party to contest an increasing number of seats and to considerably enlarge its membership. The victory at the Hamilton by-election, in Lanarkshire, in 1967, where Winifred Ewing gained one of Labour's safest seats in Scotland, served as a precipitating event propelling the SNP to the centre of Scottish politics (Brand 1978, pp. 257–264, Finlay 1994a, Mitchell 1996, p. 193).

Nevertheless, after 1968 the party was already showing signs of exhaustion (Lynch 2002, p. 120). It is in this context that the first oil fields in the North Sea were discovered in 1970. The SNP had already claimed that Scotland was subsidising the Union by some million pounds a year, but before the discovery of oil, such arguments were easily dismissed by the British Treasury (Harvie 1995, p. 122). Oil thus blew 'away the central anti-Nationalist argument [...] that Scotland was simply too poor to go it alone' (Marr 1992, p. 132). Thanks to the impressive results achieved at the general elections of February and October 1974, when it obtained 22 per cent and 30 per cent of Scottish votes (see Figure 5.1), the SNP was able to impose the question of the establishment of a Scottish Assembly on the British political agenda (Mitchell 1996, p. 205). Yet, the 1974–79 years largely ended in disappointment. Lack of leadership and internal discord prevented the party from sending out a consistent message, especially regarding devolution (Levy 1986). In March 1979, 52 per cent of Scots voted in favour of a Scottish Assembly, but they represented only 33 per cent of persons registered on electoral rolls, thus the controversial 40 per cent threshold that had been introduced in 1978 was not met. At the general election that immediately followed, the party lost nine seats and entered a phase of internal factionalism and crisis (Hutchison 2001, pp. 145–147, Mitchell 2009, p. 38).

In 1983, a very divided SNP recorded one of its worst recent performances (11.8 per cent of votes) (Torrance 2009, pp. 162–172). From that year on, however, the party slowly recovered. It positioned itself more comfortably on the Centre-Left and revised its European policy, officially embracing 'Independence in Europe' in 1988 (Mitchell 1988). The SNP also began campaigning heavily on the issue of the 'democratic deficit', whereby an English-based Conservative government ruled an increasingly anti-Conservative Scotland (Curtice 2012, p. 117). The party polled well at the turn of the decade, especially after Alex Salmond took over leadership in 1990 and improved its structure and financial resources (Lynch 2002, pp. 203–204). But, as oftentimes in its history, the 21.5 per cent obtained in the 1992 elections translated into only three seats at Westminster (Bennie *et al.*, 1997, pp. 76–78).

In 1997, 74.3 per cent of Scotland's population voted in favour of the establishment of a Scottish Parliament in a referendum organised by the new Labour government of Tony Blair. Two years later, Labour won the first Scottish election, while the SNP became the main opposition party (Devine 2012). The first few years of the Scottish Parliament were not easy for the SNP. Weakened by the change in leadership – Salmond stepped down in 2000 – and divided by new fights between gradualists and fundamentalists,[1] until 2004 'the SNP was uneasy with itself and unsure of its direction' (Mackay 2009, p. 83). Despite disappointing electoral results, however, party chairman John Swinney managed to complete the SNP's transformation into a fully professional organisation. Salmond took over again in 2004 and the party went on to obtain a narrow victory in the 2007 Scottish election, followed by a four-year minority government. In 2011, the SNP was reconfirmed in power after obtaining 69 seats out of 129, i.e. an absolute majority (Hassan 2011).

The new Scottish Executive immediately started negotiations with the British Government for a referendum on independence, which was held on 18 September 2014. Scottish residents aged 16 or more with British, EU or Commonwealth nationality voted by 55 per cent to remain part of the UK – turnout was 85 per cent. While many expected the SNP to be negatively affected by the defeat, the ensuing British election, in May 2015, saw a 'seismic change', since the SNP obtained 50 per cent of votes and all but three of the 59 Scottish seats at Westminster (Mitchell 2015). The SNP's dominance was in evidence once more at the next Scottish elections a year later, in which the party slightly improved its share of votes, as compared to 2011, although it lost six seats and its absolute majority (Anderson 2016). After the 2015 landslide, its new chairman, Nicola Sturgeon, ruled out the organisation of another independence vote in the near future. The victory of the Leave camp in the referendum on UK's membership of the European Union, held in June 2016, temporarily reopened the question. Stressing that a majority of Scotland's population had opted to Remain, and would therefore be taken out of the EU against its will, Sturgeon called for a new independence referendum to let people choose between this and remaining in the UK despite the 'hard Brexit' looming on the horizon (Carrell 2017).

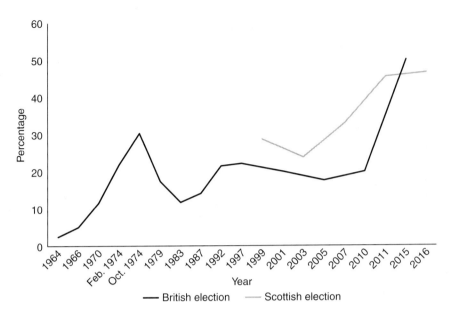

Figure 5.1 SNP's electoral results, UK and Scottish elections,* 1964–2016 (percentage of Scottish vote).

Sources: my elaboration on Audickas *et al.* 2016.

Note
* For the Scottish elections the constituency vote has been taken into account.

Nevertheless, the disappointing performance at the 2017 early general election urged Sturgeon to change her mind. After losing 13 per cent of votes and 21 seats, the SNP put the organisation of another vote on self-determination on hold – pending the results of the Brexit negotiations – and focused on a package of pragmatic policies (*The Economist* 2017b).

The SNP's nationalism of the rich

Although the rise of Scottish nationalism is often associated with the discovery of oil, both the SNP's revival and the argument of economic victimisation appeared before the successful strikes in the North Sea. In 1961, for instance, the party complained that Scotland handed over £100 million every year to subsidise England (SNP 1961, see also Halliday 1959, Macintosh 1966, p. 11) and similar claims were voiced in the 1968 policy statement *SNP&You* (SNP 1968). The party however lacked enough evidence to make a compelling argument, thus exposing itself to criticism from the central government. Oil fundamentally changed all that.

It's Scotland's oil

Whatever claims the SNP may have made before the discovery of the North Sea fields, it is widely recognised that, as SNP chairman William Wolfe declared at the 1972 party conference, oil 'added a whole new dimension to the cause of freedom' since with control over its own affairs Scotland could now 'be among the most prosperous countries in Europe' (Wolfe 1972; see also McIntyre, quoted in Miller 1981, p. 59). In September of the same year, the party organised what has probably become its most famous electoral campaign – entitled 'It's Scotland's Oil' – with the precise goal of making people understand the formidable potential represented by an independent oil-rich Scotland. Its best compendium is to be found in Nicholas Dekker's booklet 'The Rea£ilty of Scotland's Oil'. Dekker argued that, while at the beginning of the twentieth century the Scots enjoyed the highest per capita income in the world, in the following decades they had been overtaken by several other countries. Hence, oil constituted a once-in-a-lifetime opportunity to reverse this 'relative decline', but, 'without independence for the Scottish Nation, the bulk of oil-based benefits [would] pass Scotland by' (Dekker 1972, p. 2). Dekker further pointed out that the government in London was desperate to get oil to redress its bottomless balance-of-payments deficit and, therefore, had granted extremely generous conditions to the oil companies. That notwithstanding, according to his calculations, the estimated reserves would generate at least £1 billion a year in revenue or 50 per cent of Scotland's total public spending (Dekker 1972, pp. 4–7). The SNP pledged to use this money to improve services for the Scottish people, building schools and hospitals, with the aim of making Scotland a more just society (SNP 1972a), but also to invest the revenue in capital assets, thus boosting long-term growth (SNP 1974, SNP Research Department 1975). Norway was the SNP's model in this regard (Dekker 1972, pp. 7–9, SNP 1972a, 1974).

In its first phase, the 'It's Scotland's Oil' campaign stressed the amazing economic opportunities offered by North Sea fields. As asserted by some evocative campaign flyers, the choice was one between 'Poor British or Rich Scots' (SNP 1972b) and it required a radical step because 'England was expecting Scotland's oil' (SNP 1972c). Nevertheless, this approach exposed the SNP to accusations of selfishness. The second phase of the campaign, launched about a year later, thus underlined the extent of Scotland's deprivation and pleaded the case for independence on the basis of social justice. The images used in a series of posters published that year – showing a poor child, an unemployed man, a young woman living in bad housing conditions and an old lady suffering due to lack of proper heating under the banner 'it's her/his oil' – deliberately set the tone in strongly emotional terms (SNP 1973, see also Bain 1975).

In the second half of the 1970s, as the political debate focused on the establishment of a Scottish Parliament, oil became a secondary item (Wilson 2009, pp. 89–90). Yet, it remained a mainstay of the SNP's discourse and was played upon in different moments, according to the need of the time. In the latter part of that decade, the party complained that 'Scotland might be the first country in history to discover oil and yet be no better off than before as a result' (Murray 1977, p. 7). Similarly, in 1984, in the midst of Margaret Thatcher's austerity agenda, the SNP pointed out that 'oil revenues have soared over the last decade to stand this year at £11,500 million', while regional aid had been 'cut dramatically over the same period to stand, in real terms, at only 40 per cent of the 1975 level' (SNP 1984). Hence – the party claimed – oil revenues going to the UK were equal to almost 50 times total regional aid to Scotland. Unsurprisingly, in party posters, Margaret Thatcher was portrayed as a vampire sucking away Scotland's oil (SNP c.1980s).

Even more recently, the oil issue has continued to inform the SNP's discourse. In the early 2000s, the party revived, and partially modified, its proposal, first made in the late 1970s, to create a national investment fund where part of oil revenues would be channelled every year, following the Norwegian model (SNP 2001, p. 9; for the older proposal see SNP 1978, p. 7). In 2003, it revealed that, since the beginning of extraction, the UK Treasury had taken £160 billion in taxes from the North Sea, i.e. about £32,000 per Scot (SNP 2003) and two years later it announced that new discoveries had brought the estimates of reserves to 28 billion barrels, equal to £600 billion, or £100,000 per Scot (SNP 2005). The 2011 manifesto illustrates quite well how oil has remained a fundamental pillar in the party's argument for independence without being excessively emphasised. Until the penultimate page the document barely mentions the word 'oil' and never in direct connection with independence. Yet, at the end, in a section tracing the history of the party, one can read that:

> in 1970 North Sea Oil was discovered, with 90% of it lying in Scottish waters. This led to one of our most successful campaigns – It's Scotland's Oil. With new oil fields still being found to this day, there is no doubt that Scotland should be responsible for its own natural resources. During 2008–09, in the middle of the recent severe recession, Scotland was in surplus to the tune of £1.3 billion, compared to a UK deficit of £48.9 billion – just think what we could do to tackle poverty and create jobs in Scotland with responsibility for these resources.
>
> (SNP 2011, p. 40)

Similarly during the independence referendum campaign the party described oil as a 'financial safety net' – 'one of the best of any country in the world' – rather than as the cornerstone of Scottish success and prosperity (Scottish Government 2013a, p. 57; see also SNP 2012, p. 4).

The economics of independence

The SNP's 'economic case for independence' has gone beyond oil, especially from the late 1980s onwards. The gist of such case consists in the party's acknowledgement that Scotland and England have different economic structures and, for this reason, need different policies. Successive UK governments, however, have applied policies tailored to the South-east of England to the entire country. Similar ideas were already aired between the end of the 1960s and the mid-1970s, when party leaflets complained about the government's restrictive credit policy at a time when Scotland's economy was stagnating (SNP 1967; see also SNP 1974, p. 16, Crawford 1975). The best early elaboration of the economic case for independence, however, came at the end of the 1970s, incidentally from the young Alex Salmond. In an article entitled 'The Economics of Independence' – a headline that he reused 20 years later – he argued that, contrary to the Tory and Labour belief that Scotland was structurally poor, the region only suffered from an over-reliance on traditional sectors and a chronic lack of investment. It therefore needed expansionary reconversion measures that could be easily financed by oil revenues. By contrast, the government clung consistently to deflation, which was tantamount to 'putting a starving man on a diet of bread and water to cure his neighbour's obesity' (Salmond 1977).

In the early 1980s, mainly because of internal factionalism, the party had trouble producing clear policy proposals on the economic relationship with the rest of Britain. Things began changing in the latter part of the decade. In 1989, Jim Sillars (p. 8) pointed out that UK regional policy had failed because 'it was never formulated in the nation or region which suffered, but in the Centre whose growth and increased power created the disparity'. Some years later, Salmond went further and argued that the United Kingdom was not a 'level playing field' for Scottish companies. With so much power and first-class infrastructure concentrated around London, Scotland could only compete in attracting business by creating a new centre of power in Edinburgh (Salmond 1993a, p. 17).

At the same time, from the late 1980s, the SNP committed to shattering the myth that the Scots were 'subsidy junkies'. In this way, it implicitly reacted to statements, made by the Conservative Chancellor Nigel Lawson in the aftermath of the 1987 election, complaining about the existence of a 'subsidy culture' in the region (Finlay 2005, p. 369). That same year, as the party's vice-chairman for publicity, Salmond helped establish the Scottish Centre for Economic and Social Research, a think tank that released papers on the economic prospects of independence aimed at showing that Scotland was not subsidised by the rest of the UK (Lynch 2002, pp. 206–211). Later, he even straightforwardly declared that: 'the subsidy junkies of the UK live in the South-east where even the cosseting of transport subsidies, Docklands development, civil service concentration and mortgage tax relief has proved inadequate to support an economy totally vulnerable to consumer demand and the decline of the defence budget' (Salmond 1993a, p. 18).

In the first half of the 1990s, the party set up a research team in charge of working out in detail the economic case for independence.[2] The results were presented in a series of three papers published in 1995 under the title 'For the

Good of Scotland'. The first aimed at demonstrating that Scotland already was recording a surplus siphoned off by the rest of Britain; the second was a study from a consultancy firm calculating the advantages that the process of independence itself would bring about – mainly by creating a new centre of power in Edinburgh; the third presented the first four-year budget of a future independent Scotland and boldly asserted that: 'Scotland is a wealthy country with a large and varied resource base, a traditionally good education system, and an export performance 30 per cent ahead of the rest of the UK [...] Independence will enable us to advance from our subordinate position within the UK and generate a new prosperity for Scotland' (SNP 1995a, p. i; see also SNP 1995b, 1995c). As compared to the more inconsistent and less sophisticated economic case made in the 1970s, here – as well as in subsequent texts – oil was only one of a number of assets that Scotland could use to improve its standard of living.[3] Yet, Scotland's fiscal position within the UK – i.e. whether it is a net contributor or recipient region – has historically been ambiguous, with obvious consequences on the credibility of the SNP's economic arguments. For instance, when, in autumn 1995, the Scottish Office promptly released figures showing that the region received from the Exchequer an £8 billion transfer, the party published a detailed rebuttal, accusing the Conservatives of using a biased report to talk the nationalists down. But, while the reply did provide evidence that Scotland 'paid her way', even including oil and gas revenues, the claimed fiscal deficit amounted only to 0.2 per cent of the region's GDP, much lower than that recorded in the other cases studied here, thus considerably weakening the argument that the region would certainly be better off if independent (SNP 1996, p. 2).

Precisely because of this ambiguous fiscal position, throughout the 1990s, Salmond also tried to dismiss the relevance of the region's finances, arguing that fiscal and economic policies were contingent issues. What really mattered – according to him – was growth and whether Scotland had the necessary comparative advantages to realise it. Scotland did have them – he asserted – in oil and gas, engineering and textiles, food and fish, electronics and finance. Thus, since in terms of economic factors Scotland was not fundamentally worse off than other small European nations that had grown at a substantially quicker pace, the problem – he concluded – had to lie with management. What Scotland really needed was control of 'the economic forces which can make or destroy communities' and 'the empowerment which only independence in Europe can offer' (Salmond 1993b, p. 7). This was deemed by him to be even more important in a globalised economy, where businesses tended to concentrate in few areas to exploit economies of scale. Peripheral territories must therefore offer something else to attract companies, for instance a lower corporation tax (Salmond 1998, p. 5, 2003; see also SNP 1997, p. 8, 1999a, p. 9). The underlying assumption also was that small countries, like small businesses, are better able to adapt quickly to the shocks of the global economy, while bigger countries are not, because they often lack the cohesion required to make radical changes. After all – as the SNP was keen to recall – 25 out of 35 of the richest countries in the world had no more than 10 million inhabitants and, on a per-capita basis, Scotland was deemed by the OECD to be the eighth in the developed world (SNP 1997, p. 4).

In the last decade, there has been no major change to this economic case (see SNP 2002a, Salmond 2003). Albeit aimed at presenting the economic strategy of an SNP-led Scottish Government rather than any post-independence scenarios, the 2007 economic strategy *Let Scotland Flourish* played on the usual themes of a Scotland rich in natural and human resources that has been penalised by London mismanagement and only needs the right policies to increase its prosperity (SNP 2007a; on London's mismanagement see also Sturgeon 2013). The onset of the crisis allowed the party to resume the old theme of austerity policies imposed by an illegitimate Conservative government over a Scotland that instead needed economic stimulus to lead to recovery – and that would favour a more egalitarian and inclusive economic model. The slogan for the 2010 British election – 'More Nats, Less Cuts' – illustrates this position nicely (SNP 2010) as well as the commitment, at the core of the 2015 manifesto, to 'move away from the damaging austerity agenda of the current UK government, so that we can protect Scotland's public services from future Tory cuts' (SNP 2015, p. 24). At the same time, the financial crisis also imposed some changes in the foreign models proposed by the party. As the 'arch of prosperity' made up of, among others, Ireland and Iceland was renamed the 'arch of insolvency' – because of the financial problems faced by these countries, as well as by Scotland, notably the bail-out of Royal Bank of Scotland – those countries were removed from the list of examples to emulate (compare SNP 2007b, 2010, 2011).

The democratic deficit

In the SNP's discourse, the economic victimisation examined in the previous sections is the result of Scotland's supposed political marginalisation. This argument became preponderant in the 1980s, but similar, although less sophisticated claims had already been made before. The most important issue in the 1960s and the 1970s had to do with the equality of England and Scotland within the Union. As asserted in the 1978 electoral brochure *Return to Nationhood*, 'Scotland has never been regarded by British governments as a free and equal partner in the Union with England but as a lesser province with reservoirs of manpower, ability, space and wealth which could be tapped as required' (SNP 1978, pp. 11–12). England's preponderance was deemed to be reflected in the state's presence in Scotland, which took the form of 'government by dinosaur' (Reid 1975, see also SNP 1972d), whereby the bureaucracy overwhelmed politicians. Only the establishment of a sovereign Scottish Parliament – it was argued in the 1970s – could rebalance the relations between administration and politics (SNP 1974, p. 3).

After the 1974 elections, the SNP was confronted with the possibility of partially reversing Scotland's marginalisation. Yet, those years ended in disappointment plunging the party into nearly a decade of crisis and political irrelevance. At the same time, the 1980s prepared the ground for the SNP's subsequent take off. The 'Thatcher years' gave birth to the claim of a true 'democratic deficit', since Scotland's and England's voting patterns increasingly diverged, whereas the Tories' austerity policy sharpened the region's economic and social crisis. The SNP portrayed the issue as a clash of civilisations: 'we have had bad governments in the past [...] but we have never [...] until now had a government whose basic principles were so utterly against the most essential traditions and aspirations of Scottish life' (McIlvanney 1987, p. 8). Scotland's identity was at risk more than ever before because Thatcher had set out to change the Scots' mindset from their higher belief in compassion and humanity to cold individualism. This was all the more unacceptable as the Scots – the SNP argued – 'had consistently rejected the ethical, social and political values entailed in Thatcherism which Britain as a whole has endorsed' (Wilson 1988, p. 11).[4] The poll tax, replacing the system of domestic rates previously in force, and introduced a year earlier in Scotland than in England, was regarded as the best embodiment of Thatcher's merciless assault on the Scots. To counter it, the SNP mounted a civil disobedience campaign (entitled 'Can Pay – No Pay') (see SNP 1989) that although leading to mixed results contributed to framing the tax as a powerful symbol of English hostility towards Scotland (Lynch 2002, pp. 161–190).

The end of Tory rule in 1997 opened up the possibility for constitutional change. In the party's discourse, the new Parliament was inspired by a different conception of democracy. Scotland's democratic tradition was deemed to rest on the principle of popular sovereignty, rather than Britain's Crown-in-Parliament, entailing proportional representation, a single elected chamber – no place for the hereditary rights of the House of Lords – and popular input in the legislative process through public committee hearings and referenda (Salmond 1993c). Yet, the new Parliament – established in 1999 – was quickly judged to be insufficient. In 2003, for instance, the SNP claimed that it had 'less power than practically any other legislative Parliament in Europe – devolved or independent – to decide how it raises its own income' (SNP 2003). By contrast, an independent Scotland would have complete control of its own taxes – 'leaving out the London middleman who takes his slice off first' (SNP 2002b) – and, contrary to the UK, a written constitution defending basic human rights, whereby the Scots would be citizens, not subjects. In an independent Scotland – the SNP concluded – there will not be any democratic deficit as there was under Margaret Thatcher (SNP 2003).

Both the argument on the democratic deficit and that whereby Scotland would be a more egalitarian society have played a momentous role in the campaign for the 2014 independence referendum. The former lay at the core of the White Paper for independence prepared by the SNP-led Scottish Government (2013a, p. xi). This asserted that the fundamental point about independence was that 'the people of Scotland are in charge' and that 'it will no longer be possible for governments to be elected and pursue policies against the wishes of the Scottish people'. As a result (and implicitly because of its supposedly more social-democratic outlook), Scotland would be free to follow a different economic model from the unequal one pursued by the UK, 'a model focused on delivering long-term sustainability and economic opportunity for all and not a targeted few' (Scottish Government 2013b, p. v).

But how to bring this about? Despite all the talk about independence since the 1960s, it is hard to find a clear blueprint for transition in the party's publications until the manifesto for the 1992 general election, which detailed a six-step procedure involving negotiations with the British Government after the election of a SNP majority at Westminster, the drafting of a constitution to be approved in a referendum and automatic EEC membership (SNP 1992, pp. 2–3). This policy was revised in 1999, when the party recognised the historic change brought about by the establishment of the Scottish Parliament and pledged to hold a referendum on the matter within the first four years in government (SNP 1999b). This promise could not be kept during the first SNP mandate at Holyrood because the party did not have an absolute majority, but it was duly honoured after the 2011 election.

At the root's of the SNP's nationalism of the rich

As Alex Salmond (2003, p. 15) once noticed, 15 out of 25 of the articles of the 1707 Treaty of Union concerned economic matters, which underlines the fundamentally economic rationale behind the establishment of the United Kingdom, at least on the Scottish side. One of the SNP's major arguments, in contrast, has been that Scotland has been held back by the rest of the UK and would be economically better off as an independent country. Hence, this amounts to a fundamental questioning of the British-Scottish relationship. We therefore need to look briefly at Scotland's position within the UK until the early 1970s.

From empire and industrialisation to welfare and structural change

In the historical literature, there is a consensus that, at least until the Great War, Scotland did profit from the marriage with its southern neighbour. From at least 1750 until the end of the nineteenth century, access to the British domestic market and the colonies gave Scotland a decisive edge over its competitors that would have not been available had the country preserved its independence, since most European markets were protected by tariff barriers (Lee 1995, p. 50, Devine 2008b). David McCrone (2001, p. 62) has proposed the concept of 'development by invitation' when referring to Scotland's impressive growth during the eighteenth and nineteenth centuries, whereby, out of security concerns, the English elites let their Scottish counterparts take advantage of participation in the British Empire. Hence, Scotland was 'able to move from peripheral to semi-peripheral to core status because of its early "dependency"', where dependency is not to be understood as establishing a colonial relationship between Scotland and England (see also Kendrick *et al.* 1985, Marr 1992, p. 22).

Although the Victorian era marked the peak of Scotland's development, it also set the stage for the massive structural adjustment experienced after the Second World War. An overdependence on heavy industry and the capital goods sector along with chronically low wages were the negative legacies of this golden age. The former stemmed from Scotland's comparative advantage in coal and iron-ore deposits and the cheap transport costs offered by the river Clyde, which favoured the creation of shipbuilding, steel and locomotive industries – with the latter two mainly dependent on the yards. Despite slowing competitiveness, and after having been hit hard by the Great Depression, Scottish shipbuilding performed well until the mid-1950s thanks to military tenders relating to the Second World War and the Korean War (Brand 1978, pp. 68–88). Yet, by 1968, the region's market share in global shipbuilding had shrunk from 12 per cent in the early 1950s to 1.3 per cent (Harvie 1998, p. 122). Adjustment would have required huge investments for conversion and modernisation already at the end of the nineteenth century. These did not come because local shipbuilders were reluctant to accept change and pool resources for modernisation and rationalisation. Furthermore, government war requirements slowed down reconversion in the first half of the century, while later regional policy prolonged the life of uncompetitive firms (Payne 2003). Low Scottish wages worsened the situation, as they translated into lower spending and, therefore, hampered the development of a thriving consumer goods industry (Harvie 1998, p. 45). They also entailed bad housing and health conditions, which translated into a demand for more government intervention.

Before the Great War, Scotland's economy had been based on the dominance of private local capital, while in the interwar years and, especially, in the post-Second World War decades, the state became the major economic actor in the region (McCrone 2001, pp. 5–29). The establishment of the welfare state brought an unprecedented level of wellbeing to Scotland. People were now assured decent housing, healthcare and unemployment benefits, that, when confronted with downward economic cycles, would protect them against severe conditions of relative deprivation. Between 1950 and 1960, total earnings doubled and wealth became better spread, favouring the expansion of the middle-class. Unsurprisingly, unionism remained a hegemonic force in the region throughout this period (Finlay 2005, pp. 237–238).

However, things started to change in 1957. Between then and 1961, Scottish per capita GDP shrank from 91.7 per cent of the British average to 86.1 per cent (McCrone 1965, p. 32, Finlay 2005, pp. 255–261). This was mainly due to a slower rate of growth than the rest of the UK. Furthermore, although at historically low levels – 2–3 per cent since 1945 – unemployment had remained about twice as high as in the rest of the UK and increased to 4–4.5 per cent from 1958–60. Migration also remained quite constant, with an average yearly outflow of about 25,000 people in the 1950s, which increased to about 35,000 in the first half of the 1960s (Secretary of State for Scotland 1966, p. 154). To address these issues, from 1960 on, regional policy, which had in fact existed since the 1930s, was transformed. Public expenditure rose by 900 per cent between 1964 and 1973, 20 per cent more than the British average. The entire region, except for Edinburgh, obtained special development status, the number of universities doubled, jobs in teaching increased by a fifth, and the Scottish Development Department was created along with the Highland Development Board and the Scottish Development Agency. Between 1965 and 1975, Scottish per capita GDP caught up relatively to the rest of the UK (McCrone 1969, Buxton 1985, Devine 2008a, pp. 148–150).

In light of the above figures, it might seem puzzling that Scottish nationalism arose precisely at this time and even more so that it voiced claims about an unequal redistribution of resources between Scotland and the rest of the UK. Two considerations might help understand why this occurred. First, the British Government's lavish expenditure also had downsides. On the one hand, planning was perceived as an imposition from above – the *Scotsman* described the Highland Development Board as 'an almost perfect example of Voltairean enlightened despotism' (quoted in Harvie 1998, p. 131). Similarly, the central government strategy to attract foreign investment by contributing 10 per cent to the construction of new productive plants fuelled accusations that it was seeking to turn Scotland into a low-wage branch-plant economy (Harvie 1998, p. 124). On the other, the planners' promises were simply too large to be realised. Structural change was under way, but it was a slow process requiring decades and, while regional policy could mitigate it, it could not avoid it entirely. Moreover, while regional policy provided Scotland with disproportionate resources, other government policies did not suit its economy at all. This was especially the case with the stop-go strategy adopted by successive governments for electoral purposes between 1951 and 1964, whereby taxes were decreased before a general vote and then a squeeze came after re-election had been secured. The policy deterred new business formation and had a stronger impact in Scotland because the region was more dependent on public spending (Finlay 2005, pp. 267–269). It favoured a perception of government policy failure and a general sense of British decline. For instance, in 1964, Labour won an election promising an end to deflationary policy. By July 1966, the promise had to be broken and the government passed a series of cuts to public spending and a wage freeze that *The Economist* defined as 'the biggest deflationary package that any advanced industrial nation has imposed on itself since Keynesian economics began' (quoted in Marquand 2008, loc. 4383). The following year – two weeks after the victory of the SNP in Hamilton – confronted with another balance of payment crisis, the government had to accept the humiliation of sterling devaluation that it had sought to avoid since it came into office. It is in this context that nationalism arose as an alternative to the traditional parties, not just in Scotland, but also in Wales, where Plaid Cymru won a by-election in July 1966 (Hassan 2007, pp. 75–93).

Oil and the 'revolt of rising expectations'

The importance of the discovery of oil fields in the North Sea for Scottish nationalism could hardly be overestimated, although it has probably been more psychological than material. The discovery played a role similar to the extraordinary economic growth experienced by Flanders relatively to Wallonia in the post-war period, in the sense that it set the stage for the transformation of Scotland's dream of independence from an idea cherished by a few hard-core nationalists to a constitutional option with potential mass appeal.

The rise of the SNP to prominence – which, as seen above, was initially unrelated to oil – forced a debate over the fiscal position of Scotland within the UK. Enticed by the nationalists' breakthrough, in October 1969, her Majesty's Treasury and the Scottish Office published figures showing that Scotland's deficit towards the Exchequer was equal to £466 million for the fiscal year 1967–68, or 42 per cent of the region's revenues (Begg and Stewart 1971, pp. 149–150).[5] It is at that moment that oil came to the rescue of the SNP. Surprisingly, there was initial reluctance among the party's members to take up the issue. Gordon Wilson's proposal to organise a campaign on the theme was accepted by only 93 to 76 votes at the SNP conference (Miller 1981, p. 60). Yet, a year later oil prices soared, plunging Britain into its worst balance of trade deficit ever. The nationalist argument that resources were being drained away from Scotland and that independence would afford the Scots a higher standard of living now seemed beyond doubt. On the micro-level, the peculiar situation of the 1973 winter – with a miner's strike made worse by the increased reliance on coal after the oil hike, a 3-day working week and inflation at 18 per cent – most likely contributed to the impressive result achieved by the SNP in February 1974 (Devine 2008a, p. 149). More generally, as Milton Esman commented in 1975 (pp. 40–41), 'economic prospects in Scotland, for the first time since the turn of the century, had become far more promising than in England, where the economic outlook was gloomy [...] attitudes were shifting dramatically from relative deprivation to rising expectations' (see also Brown 1975, p. 7).

The argument that it was 'Scotland's oil' depended on and, at the same time, reinforced the claims of the existence of a sovereign Scottish nation. It depended on them because only the recognition of Scotland as a constitutive unit of the UK endowed with the right to self-determination could justify the assertion of Scottish sovereignty over this resource. It reinforced them because the issue of ownership and use of oil resources increased the salience of Scottish statehood. More fundamentally, as seen above, North Sea oil did away with the main unionist argument that an independent Scotland would go bankrupt in a fortnight because of its substantially higher levels of per capita government expenditure. Yet, at the same time, Scotland's fiscal position within the UK remained – and still is – ambiguous, especially if compared to that of other regions analysed in this study.

From the early 1990s, a war of numbers began between the SNP and successive British governments. The debate is probably insoluble because, while 70 per cent of spending can easily be regionalised, the other 30 per cent is hard to disentangle.[6] In 1992, Midwinter *et al.* (pp. 98–114) argued that the then existing studies on the subject confirmed a per capita spending 20 per cent above the UK average for the period 1967–89. Nevertheless, they pointed out some flaws and wondered whether such higher spending reflected need rather than preferential treatment. Also, the studies reviewed by the authors only included what the British Government labelled as 'identifiable public expenditure' – i.e. all those expenses clearly incurred in a specific territory. Hence, expenses such as defence and mortgage tax relief, which were higher south of the border, were not taken into consideration. Gavin McCrone has recently drawn similar conclusions (2013, loc. 188–284). According to his calculations, Scotland's spending has been higher than the British average since the 1960s, and probably even before, although it has progressively narrowed, from about 20 per cent until the 1990s, to 15 per cent in the 2000s and 10 per cent in more recent years. On the revenue side, the SNP claim that oil has largely compensated for higher spending depends on the periods considered. For most of the 1970s, oil did not bring in revenue, thus an independent Scotland would have recorded budget deficits between 7 and 10 per cent of its GDP. In the following decade, with oil production in full swing, the region would have recorded a massive surplus, equal to more than 40 per cent of its GDP on average. Therefore, on a purely arithmetical basis, Scotland would have probably been better off in the Union in the 1970s, and out of it in the following years, although falling oil prices in the second half of the 1980s would have exposed the country to wide deficits from the beginning of the 1990s (Lee 1995, pp. 150–151) (Figure 5.2). This is, however, pure speculation, as it is impossible to gauge the effect of oil revenues on endogenous growth in an independent Scotland.

McCrone (2013, loc. 188–284) has also calculated that, in 2011–12, Scotland's public expenditure per capita was still £1,197 higher than the British average and that an independent Scotland would have recorded a

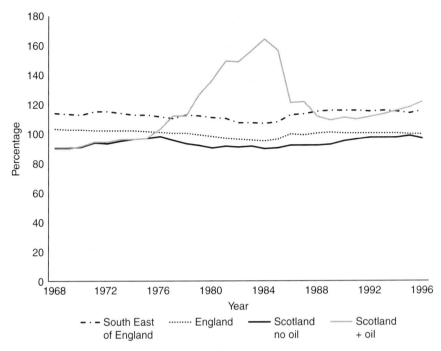

Figure 5.2 UK's GDP per capita by selected regions, 1968–96 (UK = 100).*

Source: my elaboration on figures provided by the UK Office of National Statistics.

Note

* I obtained the 'Scotland + oil' series by adding 90 per cent of continental shelf GDP data to Scottish GDP data.

fiscal deficit of 14.6 per cent of its GDP. If 90 per cent of oil and gas tax revenues were included in these calculations, the deficit would have shrunk to 5 per cent, still high, but lower than the UK's (7.9 per cent) (see also Crawford and Tetlow 2014, p. 44).[7] In other words, despite having a sizable deficit, Scotland would still be in a better financial position as compared to the rest of the country. Similarly, and still with reference to the fiscal year 2011–12, McCrone has confirmed the SNP's claim that an independent Scotland would be one of the richest countries in Europe. Oil and gas would indeed increase Scottish GDP by 21 per cent. Yet, this depends on the assumption that 90 per cent of North Sea oil revenues will be allocated to Scotland. Although it is the most credible estimate, in the event of Scottish secession this would still be a matter for negotiation and, given the weight of oil revenues on Scottish GDP, even a marginal difference might have a large impact (Kemp 2011, pp. 62–85). Furthermore, oil prices are by nature highly volatile thus making tax revenues quite unpredictable, as clearly shown by the 2016 plunge: while revenues amounted to

£12.4 billion in 2008–09, they were even slightly negative (–£24 million) because of decommissioning costs in 2015–16 (HM Revenue & Customs 2017). Thus, although in 2013 reserves were estimated to run for another 30–40 years, oil's real impact on the Scottish economy is hard to estimate. All this confirms the more ambiguous fiscal position of Scotland within the UK as compared to the other cases analysed here, which makes its fiscal future more indeterminate. Such indeterminacy is key to explaining the persistence of the discussion of whether Scotland 'pays her way' or not and is evidenced by the fact that ahead of the 2014 referendum 70 per cent of the Scottish population believed that 'neither campaign can accurately estimate the consequences of independence' (Henderson *et al.* 2014, p. 8).

Beyond oil

Structural change eventually came in full swing in the 1980s. In the second half of the decade, the rise of services allowed the partial absorption of unemployment and by the mid-1990s Scotland had almost totally closed the gap with the UK in terms of GDP per head (Payne 2003). When looking at per capita statistics, the argument that Scotland has not grown at the same pace as the rest of the country is not supported by evidence (Table 5.1). Yet, such convergence was mostly achieved through emigration (Peden 1993). Similarly, the unemployment rate tended to be higher than in the UK as a whole, increasing substantially in the 1980s (from the 6.4 per cent of the 1973–79 years to 11.6 per cent in 1979–88 – the British averages were 4.8 per cent and 9.8 per cent respectively) (Lee 1995, p. 67, McCrone 2013, loc. 142, ONS 2013). Hence, as Richard Finlay (2008, p. 163) pointed out, 'whatever the success of government policy in restructuring the Scottish economy [...] the fact remains that it was not done without pains'.

Interestingly, Bennie *et al.* (1997, p. 130) found that, in the early 1990s, about half of the Scottish population thought England profited most from the Union with Scotland, while only 14 per cent reckoned the opposite to

Table 5.1 UK's real GDP growth per capita by selected regions, 1970–95 (average by decade) (percentage of regional GDP)

Period	England	South East of England	Northern Ireland	Scotland	Wales	UK
1970–79	1.8	2.1	2.9	2.4	1.9	2.2
1980–89	1.9	2.1	1.6	1.8	2.1	1.7
1990–96	1.0	1.2	1.9	1.9	0.5	1.2
1970–96	1.6	1.8	2.2	2.0	1.6	1.8

Source: my calculations on GDP data provided by the Office of National Statistics. ONS (2016c) for GDP deflator data (2015 = 100).

be true. Between 2000 and 2013, that figure decreased to 32 per cent on average, while 22 per cent believed Scotland profited more than England (for 40 per cent both profited equally). Over the same period, 44 per cent on average deemed Scotland to be getting less than its fair share of government spending, 12 per cent more and 37 per cent its fair share (SSAS 2017a, 2017b). These figures suggest that the SNP's arguments have made inroads into a sizable part of the Scottish population. What is surprising, however, especially in light of the recent events leading up to the independence referendum, is that the number of those deeming Scotland to be at a disadvantage has decreased over time, which is also consistent with a lack of radicalisation in grassroots support for independence before the 2014 referendum (see Chapter 9). Such lack of radicalisation before 2015 can in part be explained with the moderate impact of the economic and financial crisis. Although the region was hit badly in 2009–10, real GVA and GDHI per capita decreased only by 0.5 per cent on average between 2008 and 2014 (my calculations on ONS 2016a, 2016b, 2017). Unemployment increased (from 4.7 per cent in 2008 to 8.2 per cent in 2011) but remained low by European standards and later shrank (5.8 per cent in 2015) (ONS and Scottish Government 2016), which probably contributed to the fact that a scenario such as that occurred in Catalonia was avoided.

A nation without nationalism?

Why the nineteenth century did not see nationalism explode in a region with one of the longest sovereign traditions in Europe at a time when similar ideologies were sweeping the continent has been a recurrent question among scholars (Kidd 1993, Harvie 1998, Nairn 2003). It is tempting to conclude that Scotland was a nation without nationalism, but this would be an incorrect assertion. Scotland's nationalism was unionist-nationalism and the Scots' self-understanding was grounded in the parallel recognition of their distinctiveness as Scots and their participation in the union state of Great Britain (McCrone 2012). The true novelty of the SNP's nationalism lay in its anti-unionist character: it was not the awakening of a dormant identity, but the reinterpretation and questioning of part of it, i.e. Britishness.

As argued by Linda Colley (1992, p. 130), the British identity was forged out of the Union between England and Scotland – in which also Wales and, later, Ireland participated – and was based on the pillars of Protestantism, the rivalry with France, and the empire. The last element was especially important to the Scots, not only for its obvious economic advantages, but also because it was one of the few realms in which they could truly feel they were equal partners, on a par with the English. Despite Scotland representing about 10–13 per cent of the British population, between 1850 and 1939, a third of governors-general in the empire came from the region (Finlay 1994b, p. 29). By the early twentieth century,

English political propaganda could even satirically decry the Celtic 'take over' of British institutions, with the Scots playing a leading role (Colley 1992, p. 163).

Nevertheless, the British self-understanding never truly replaced the identities of the constituent units of the United Kingdom that pre-existed it. Colin Kidd has argued that, at the time of the Acts of Union, the population of Scotland had already achieved a fully-formed national consciousness, mainly based on ideas of contractualism between the King and the 'community of the realm' and a specific Scottish Whig tradition distinct from the English one (Kidd 1993, p. 7). Yet, during the crucial decades of the Scottish Enlightenment, the ideas of freedom and nationhood that had gone hand in hand in the Scottish Whig tradition came to be dissociated. Liberty was now identified with the advantages offered by the Union and entailed a rejection of Scottish feudal institutions, seen as backward and uncivilised (Kidd 1993, p. 272). In these conditions, the Scottish past could not sustain a solid ideology of nationhood. Yet, at the same time, the Scottish and English Whigs did not manage to forge a genuine British identity. The results were 'the dismal failure to construct a wholeheartedly "national" British identity different from loyalty to Crown or to Empire; and a continuing Scottish national identity weakened by a loss of ideological coherence' (Kidd 1993, p. 272).

This 'unaccomplished work' was reflected in Britain's institutional architecture, as the Kingdom became a union, not a unitary state (Mitchell 1996, p. 38, McCrone 2003, pp. 141–142). Its constituent parts enjoyed considerable autonomy and policies of complete homogenisation were never pursued. On the contrary, while the old landed Scottish aristocracy affected English manners, despite being strongly unionist, the commercial bourgeoisie that arose from the buoyant exploitation of imperial markets was also proudly Scottish: 'not only did it speak with a Scottish accent, it immersed itself in the folklore and literature of its native land' and 'it celebrated its distinctive values of thrift, hard work and personal achievement' (McCrone 1992, p. 182). Largely diffused by the popular literary tradition of the Kailyard, which arose at the end of the nineteenth century, the myth of the 'lad o' pairts', a poor but talented individual, was a widespread stereotype of Scottish society, which was deemed naturally more egalitarian than the English one. Scotland could also retain its own legal and education systems, the national Church maintained its autonomy and, until the interwar years, local boards governed daily affairs. Hence, since the Scottish middle-classes already possessed 'liberty, economic prosperity and cultural integrity, the very advantages for which European nationalism had yearned for so long', it had 'no reason to seek parliamentary independence' (Devine 2008b, pp. 13–14).

The interwar years brought about a much stronger centralisation. Along with the demise of empire, such a shift of powers to London did bring about a feeling of marginalisation among the Scottish population (Esman

1975, p. 15). Yet, the SNP had to wait about 30 years before having a decisive impact on British politics. Among the reasons for this, the creation of a new British consensus based on the welfare state probably best explains the persisting strength of unionism. Furthermore, some authors argue that the 'welfare years' were characterised by a truly Scottish welfare in the form of a kind of administrative devolution that reinforced the idea of Scotland as a territorial and administrative unit of development with its own peculiar interests and agenda separate from the rest of the United Kingdom (McCrone 2001, pp. 114–118). As Lindsay Paterson (1994, pp. 130–131) has argued, a Scottish technocracy, enjoying great autonomy through the interpretation and implementation of laws, progressively developed. This institutional architecture also granted privileged contact with the centre, which until the 1970s was considered more valuable than political autonomy because it secured access to the wider pool of British resources.

Consciously or not, Labour and the Tories actively exploited such a 'Scottish dimension'. Winston Churchill, for instance, played the Scottish card against socialism and centralisation in a way that, to some extent, anticipated elements of the rhetoric of the democratic deficit when, attacking Labour's centralisation goals at a meeting in Edinburgh, he concluded that 'I would never adopt the view that Scotland should be forced into the serfdom of socialism as a result of a vote in the House of Commons' (quoted in Miller 1981, p. 21). Similarly, Labour's main propaganda document in the early 1960s – *Signposts for the Sixties* – displayed arguments surprisingly close to those that the SNP would make some years later. It declared for instance that: 'the truth is that the prosperity so often claimed for Britain has been more or less confined to the range of new and expanding industries that have settled overwhelmingly in the area running from Birmingham to London' (quoted in Miller 1981, p. 35).

One should refrain from purely instrumentalist understandings of the welfare consensus, as the British identity still had strong emotional currency in the 1970s (Finlay 2005, p. 330; see also McEwen 2002, p. 71). Nevertheless, the technocratic character of government in Scotland stemmed from a fundamental tenet of the social agreement at the basis of post-Second World War Britain, i.e. the bipartisan paternalist idea that democracy was not so much about participation, as about improving people's material conditions. In this framework, efficiency warranted large powers being devolved to unaccountable bureaucracies, but the system could enjoy solid legitimacy provided that welfare institutions delivered the goods. From the late 1950s on, however, the technocrats had troubles living up to their promises; hence, people looked for other ways of organising the state. The SNP's radical claim of self-determination was one such way, although helped by fortune, as the discovery of oil occurred at a time when it could make a formidable difference in the party's rhetorical arsenal (Finlay 2005, p. 255).

Conservative England vs. social-democratic Scotland

Although there are different opinions about the precise beginning of the process of political divergence between Scotland and England (see Miller 1981, pp. 27–30, Finlay 1994b, pp. 138–140, Hutchison 2001, p. 98), it became evident in the 1983–97 years: while in England the Tories won a majority of seats in three out of the four elections contested in this period, in Scotland they went from gaining 21 seats out of 72 in 1983 to none in 1997.

Margaret Thatcher is widely believed to have dealt the mortal blow to the Conservative party in Scotland, although this process should not retrospectively be extended to the entire 1980s, but rather set in from the second half of the decade. In a way, the SNP's argument that Thatcher was utterly against the values of the Scots makes sense, as she directly attacked the main source of the Union's legitimacy in Scotland since the interwar years, i.e. the welfare state (Marr 1992, p. 168). Although the impact of her policies was often more rhetorical than effective, it nonetheless had real consequences for the self-understanding of the Scottish population: 'national identity, social democracy and the demand for constitutional change represented mutually reinforcing factors that combined to emphasize a sense that "Scotland is different"' (McEwen 2002, p. 79, see also Hearn 2000). But the process went beyond that. On the one hand, Thatcher openly identified the Scottish autonomous institutions as a cause of British decline and, thus, as an obstacle on her revolutionary march (Mitchell and Convery 2012, pp. 178–179). Although, strictly speaking, she did not do anything undemocratic, she showed a poor understanding of unionism and tended to confuse it with unitarianism (Finlay 2012, p. 168). On the other, Thatcherism provided Scottish anti-unionists with material to craft the narrative of victimisation that had been lacking, or was weak, until then, a narrative that enabled them to clearly identify a force responsible for all that was wrong with Scotland (Hassan 2012, p. 85). As a result, in 1989, 77 per cent of Scots felt treated as second-class citizens by Thatcher (Bennie *et al.* 1997, p. 146; for the persistence of the Conservatives' de-legitimation in Scotland see Curtice 2012, pp. 119–123).

The Scottish defence of welfare largely stemmed from the higher dependency on it by the Scottish middle-class as both providers and users – itself a legacy of Scotland's relatively larger share of civil servants and social housing.[8] Also, the technocratic elite that – as seen above – developed during the welfare years set a more corporatist than market-driven agenda for addressing the need for economic adjustment (McCrone 1992, pp. 190–191). As a result, Scotland's population has tended to hold more left-wing attitudes than England's, although this was probably more the case in the past than today. Reporting figures from 1974, Miller showed that there were differences between Scotland and England, although some could be linked to more general North-South and centre-periphery patterns.

People in Scotland were more critical of the government's performance than in England (10 per cent fewer people judging it positive); more opposed to cuts in social spending (66 per cent vs. 61 per cent) and supported redistribution to a larger extent (64 per cent vs. 55 per cent). Also, they were much more likely to define themselves as belonging to the working-class (Miller 1981, pp. 81–89). Using data from the beginning of the 1990s, Bennie *et al.* (1997) obtained similar, albeit more divergent, results. On average, more Scots than English perceived themselves as working-class (74 per cent vs. 57 per cent), held the government accountable for the state of the economy (68 per cent vs. 53 per cent) and believed in redistribution (60 per cent vs. 45 per cent) (Bennie *et al.* 1997, pp. 102–124). Since then, however, and especially after devolution, while political divergence has increased, social differences have shrunk (Curtice and Ormston 2011). In 2006, a higher number of Scots still identified themselves as working-class (64.7 per cent against 58.2 per cent in England) and support for redistribution has, on average, been higher than in England (42 per cent against 38 per cent from 2001 to 2008), but in both cases to a much lower extent than before.[9] Thus, societal differences do exist, but they are not so great as to justify the recent political divergence between Scotland and England and, in addition, have considerably decreased over the years (Harvie 1998, p. 213, Hassan and Warhurst 2001, McCrone 2012).

Why is that? Identity and the 'de-legitimation' of the Tories that occurred during the 1980s seem to play an important role. People with a predominantly Scottish identity are more likely to identify as left-wing than those with a predominantly British self-understanding. As concluded by Lindsay Paterson (2002, p. 33, see also Brown *et al.* 1999, pp. 100–105), 'appealing to left-wing sympathies in Scotland implies appealing to Scottish sympathies, and right-wing programmes similarly map onto British identity'. Furthermore, as argued by Michael Keating (2005, p. 458), the refashioning of Scottish identity as fundamentally in opposition to Conservative England led to the consequence that public policy has become less a matter of 'precise views' than a ' "moral economy" [...] summed up in the critique of neo-liberal excess' (Keating 2005, p. 458). In this connection, several authors have questioned the SNP's claim that the Scottish population utterly rejected Thatcher's neoliberalism, arguing that, in practice, many embraced aspects of her government's policies (Marr 1992, pp. 172–178, Finlay 2008). At a deeper level, despite all their criticism for the Conservatives' economic recipes, both Labour and the SNP have taken up at least part of the Tories' ideological heritage (Cuthbert and Cuthbert 2009, Torrance 2009, p. 175).

Finally, the Scottish Parliament has also played a role in furthering the political divergence between England and Scotland. As in the preceding case studies, it was conceived of as a nation-building tool aimed at assuaging conflict and reinforcing the cohesion of the British polity by showing understanding for the demands of its constituent units. This has had a clear impact on subjective national identification. While the share of Scotland's residents declaring themselves to be Scottish increased from 52 per cent in 1979 to 72 per cent in 1992 (Bennie *et al.* 1997, p. 132), since the establishment of the Parliament such growth has stopped while dual and prevalently British identities have caught up (Eichhorn 2015). At the same time (in line with SNP's claims), the Parliament was soon perceived as an inchoate step that needed to be reinforced. Already in 2001, the percentage of those who wanted its powers to be widened had increased to 66 per cent, up from 56 per cent the previous year (Paterson 2001, p. 89, see also Bond and Rosie 2002, p. 46). More fundamentally, as we will see more in detail in Chapter 9, Holyrood provided a completely new, and decidedly more favourable, opportunity structure to the SNP. Contrary to Westminster, at Holyrood the SNP can have an impact and the Scottish population has clearly realised it (Curtice 2009, pp. 63–65). Furthermore, different political systems shape the political debate in different ways and this has inevitably emphasised the divergence between Scottish and English politics (McCrone 2012, p. 76). Therefore, despite not being fundamental per se, the differences in attitudes mentioned above are amplified by the existence of different national identities and different political arenas.

Conclusion

The SNP is a deviant case in this study because, despite being a prosperous region by global standards, Scotland has consistently been confronted with the South-east of England's dominance within the UK economy. Also, although when including oil revenues Scotland's per capita GDP has generally increased considerably beyond the UK average, this increase remains only potential. As a consequence, the SNP's rhetoric of economic victimisation has not been centred around fiscal transfers from north to south, but rather on the better prospects that an independent and resource-rich Scotland would enjoy. Although the economic case for independence was incipiently formulated since the 1970s, Alex Salmond considerably improved it from the early 1990s, focusing less on oil and more on the detrimental consequences of the concentration of economic activity around London. Furthermore, by resorting to the rhetoric of small, dynamic and cohesive nations and playing on a representation of the Scots as skilled and talented people – tapping into the old Scottish myth of the lad 'o pairts – he stressed Scotland's several comparative advantages and promoted a positive instrumental case for independence, based on the country's bright future prospects, rather than on any accusations of deliberate harm on the part of London, or on principled considerations.

While the colonial metaphor was used sometimes in the 1970s, it was more often replaced by a claim of 'provincialisation' whereby Scotland's status as equal partner in the Union was often disregarded. This narrative was potently transformed during the late 1980s into that of the 'democratic deficit'. The SNP argued that the Tories imposed on the region their extreme neoliberal policies without having the legitimacy to do so. Since then, the SNP has consistently described Scotland as being a more 'caring' and 'compassionate' society, which, despite being competitive and highly skilled, rejected Thatcher's sheer individualism. Therefore, the party clearly conveyed the idea of Scotland as a more advanced society than Tory England, in the sense that, not only would it be prosperous, but also fairer.

The immediate context of the SNP's formulation of the nationalism of the rich is to be found in the beginning of the process of structural change experienced by Scotland at the turn of the 1960s. After a decade of unprecedented wellbeing, the Scottish growth rate slowed down while unemployment edged up. Traditional parties devised huge investment plans under regional policy, but could not stop structural change. While it is not clear where the claim that Scotland was subsidising England came from, after the discovery of oil it became a credible and appealing argument. The threat of Scottish independence now was real because oil had opened up the possibility of a constitutional alternative at a time when Britain seemed in utter decline. Prospects in Scotland were better than in England and the idea that the Union was holding Scotland back made sense. Still, most of Scotland's population did not call for independence, but for a bigger say on its own affairs within the Union.

During the 1980s oil production was in full swing and Scotland politically marginalised by Tory preponderance in the South-east of England. Factionalism prevented the SNP from taking advantage of this favourable conjuncture. Yet, that decade also supplied the ingredients necessary to decisively bolster the party's rhetoric of political marginalisation. Until then Scotland had tremendously profited from – and also certainly contributed to – Empire, first, and the British welfare state, later, while at the same time maintaining autonomous institutions.[10] For these reasons, until the SNP's rise, administrative autonomy and privileged access to the wider pool of British resources were considered more valuable than political autonomy. But when the perception that the Union was no longer advantageous for the region began spreading, self-government became a more attractive scenario.

By attacking the welfare consensus, which, after the Second World War, replaced Empire as the Union's main underpinning, Margaret Thatcher seriously jeopardised the relationship with Scotland. She portrayed the region's institutions as obstacles in her attempt to steer Britain away from decline. The Scottish defence of welfare mainly depended on the region's higher dependency on the state. It then evolved into a pattern of political divergence between Scotland and England that is only in part explained by existing – but shrinking – differences in attitudes, but rather by the fact that the anti-Thatcher narrative arising out of the 1980s favoured the partial conflation of ideological positions and national identity to the extent that left-wing tendencies are frequently identified with pro-Scottish leanings.[11]

There is little doubt that an independent Scotland would be a successful state, but whether it would profit or suffer from full sovereignty as compared to staying within the UK, it is probably impossible to say with enough certainty. This is due to the wide approximations inherent in any estimate of the regionalisation of general expenses as well as in the evaluation of the precise amount of oil revenues. What is sure is that such ambiguity has been a major weapon in the rhetorical arsenal of the British Government in countering the solidity of the SNP's economic estimates.

Finally, the establishment of the Scottish Parliament has offered the SNP a new and more advantageous opportunity structure, since there the party can have a decisive impact. In this way, it can be considered as one of the major factors explaining the recent party's transition from marginality to the mainstream and from opposition to power. It is also central to understanding how the SNP could win elections and organise an independence referendum in the absence of any major grassroots radicalisation in favour of full self-determination, as we will see in Chapter 9.

Notes

1 In general, gradualists are open to a limited form of self-government and willing to work with other forces, while fundamentalists campaign for outright independence and oppose any collaboration with other parties. This is a fracture that has characterised the party since its foundation.

2 At about the same time, in 1992, the Scottish Office began publishing a series of yearly studies on Government Expenditure and Revenues in Scotland (GERS) which consistently highlighted Scotland's dependence on transfers from the rest of the UK (see Keating 2009, p. 106).

3 On the use of oil in the 1970s as the panacea that could solve all evils see also Maxwell (2009, pp. 122–123).

4 For an analysis of this argument in a wider set of Scottish nationalist actors see Hearn (2000).

5 McCrone (1969, pp. 52–66) provided lower figures.

6 On the 'battle of numbers' between the SNP and the British Government, as well as for a wider discussion of the difficulties entailed in such calculations see Keating 2009, pp. 103–111.

7 These high deficits were due to the effects of the economic and financial crisis.

8 In 1974, 52 per cent of Scottish people lived in council houses, against 27 per cent in the UK as a whole (Miller 1981, p. 79). According to Buxton (1985, p. 49), Scotland was the fourth region for share on UK total public employment.

9 Redistribution measured as answers to the question 'How much do you agree or disagree that government should redistribute income from the better-off to those who are less well off?'. 'Strongly agree' and 'agree' answers collapsed. British Social Attitude Survey available from www.britsocat.com [accessed 22 February 2017].

10 Furthermore, with about 11 per cent of seats out of a share of the UK population of roughly 9 per cent, Scotland was over-represented at Westminster for most of its recent history.

11 Such divergence is also due to the consistent failure of the Conservative party in Scotland to recast its image as a party that can be trusted to defend the Scottish interest. The last general election, in 2017, however showed a revival of the Conservatives in Scotland, mainly due to a polarisation of positions for and against a second independence referendum and the collapse of Labour (see *The Economist* 2017a).

6 Cultural-determinism and welfare deservingness
The nationalisms of the rich compared

In the introduction I defined the nationalism of the rich as a type of nationalist discourse that aims to put an end to the economic exploitation suffered by a group of people represented as a wealthy nation and supposedly carried out by the populations of poorer regions and/or by inefficient state administrations. The core elements of this ideology are a claim of economic victimisation, according to which a backward core area holds back a more advanced periphery, and a denunciation of political marginalisation that takes different forms in each case, but that can generally be defined as a more subtle, and more subjective, kind of victimisation than open discrimination or deliberate exploitation. The previous chapters have further inquired into this proposition giving substance to my general definition, but also pointing out differences in the ways in which the parties have constructed their own arguments. Here, I discuss commonalities and differences in the specific versions of the nationalism of the rich formulated by each party. Table 6.1 summarises the main characteristics of each party's discourse for the two arguments mentioned above.

The fiscal victim

ERC, the LN, the N-VA and the VB have used different words – *geldstroom*, *expoli fiscal*, *rapina fiscale* – but they have all denounced the fiscal transfers between the region where their national constituency lives and the rest of the country (the SNP must be clearly treated as a deviant case and I will dwell on it below). This is the argument concerning which their rhetoric is most similar. Their reasoning can be broken down into the following logical steps:

1 there is uncontroversial evidence of sizable transfers between our nation and the rest of the country;
2 these transfers are excessive and unjust;
3 they are excessive because they are higher than in any other country – the parties usually do not provide clear comparative data – and because

Table 6.1 Party discourses compared

Arguments and sub-arguments	ERC	LN	N-VA	SNP	VB
Economic victimisation					
Fiscal transfers	C	C	C	S	C
Nation economically better off if independent	C	C	C	C	C
Need for tailored economic policy	C	C	C	C	C
Cultural-determinist explanation of economic success	C	C	C	S	C
Political marginalisation					
Lack of recognition	C	S	S	S	C/I
Cultural oppression	C	T	S	T	C
Critique of consociationalism	N/R	C	C	N/R	C
Critique of majoritarianism	S	N/R	N/R	C	N/R
Mismatch between economic and political power	C	C	C	C	C

Notes
C = core argument;
T = temporary argument;
S = secondary argument;
I = inconsistent, either argumentatively or across time;
N/R = not relevant.

they overcompensate the difference between donor and recipient, leaving the former worse off;

4   they are unjust because they are (a) obligatory, (b) non-transparent, (c) ineffective;

   a   the donor constituency cannot decide to stop donating at its will;[1]
   b   the transfers are deliberately non-transparent because in this way the centralist parties can use them to finance clientelist networks in other regions of the state, especially the poorer ones, by promoting subsidies, unemployment benefits, and oversized employment in the public sector;
   c   this solidarity promotes dependency rather than endogenous growth: on the one hand, this would be clearly shown by the lack of convergence since the beginning of the transfers; on the other, it is logically in the interest of the parties to keep the poorer regions dependent as, in this way, their role as mediators remains indispensable;

5   this solidarity is therefore a waste and a drag on the competitiveness of the donor nation; the money would be used better if kept in the nation's territory, allowing its members to enjoy better services and be more competitive.

Surprisingly, only the VB – in its thematic brochures the *Kostprijs van Belgie* – has provided detailed analysis of the transfers, while the other parties have tended to rely on studies carried out by external actors, often in academia or regional governments, or on anecdotal evidence. This might probably be due to the fact that the economic imbalance between the region and the poorest areas of the parent state is clear and the existence of sizable transfers largely accepted in the wider society. What is really at stake is their true size, causes and legitimacy.

The 'ambiguity' underlying the Scottish fiscal position is the main reason for treating the SNP as a deviant case. Scotland has only recently closed the gap with the British average income, which clearly fits uneasily with claims purporting the region as being wealthier and subsidising the Union. The potential wealth provided by oil revenues would have clearly boosted Scotland's economic prospects, although it is impossible to say precisely whether the region would have been better off as an independent state. Such ambiguous position within the UK economy did spur the SNP to provide detailed evidence of its net contribution to the rest of the country. The SNP has thus decided to fight the battle on economic grounds and rightly so, as electoral data suggests that this is the best way to convince the Scots to support constitutional change (see Chapter 9). The indeterminacy of the issue has allowed the debate to drag on almost indefinitely without any clear answers coming up. It has also led the Scottish economic case to rely a lot more than the others on alternative considerations. These mainly boil down to the accusation of too much centralisation and mismanagement of the Scottish economy on the part of successive London governments. More specifically, the SNP has argued that, from the post-Second World War period, Scotland suffered because policies tailored to the needs of the South-east of England, which were at odds with its own needs, were imposed on it. In the 1970s and 1980s the language of the party played on a double register, accusing London of deliberately sacrificing Scotland to the advantages of the South-east while pointing more to accusations of neglect, or to the structural consequence of being the junior partner in the Union, at other times. This latter approach has consistently prevailed from the 1990s onwards, in line with Salmond's idea of conveying a positive message about independence. Hence, the need for statehood has been predicated on the necessity to counter the gravitational attraction exercised by London on economic activity through the creation of a new centre of power in Edinburgh endowed with the fiscal competences required to set up a business-friendly environment in a globalised economy.

This argument concerning the need to devolve powers to set up policies more suitable to the local context reconciles the SNP with the other cases, as they all share a claim that the policies enacted by the centre have been detrimental to their own interests. In all cases, there is an assertion that the political and the economic centres of the country do not coincide. In other words, the most productive areas are deemed not to enjoy adequate representation within state institutions, thus the need to break away. Such reasoning relates to the accusations of political marginalisation that I will examine below. What is important to note here is that, again, this argument is less persuasive in the case of the SNP than in all other cases. And, yet, the party, and especially Alex Salmond, have consistently accused the South-eastern economy of being driven by the concentration of public employment, defence spending and mortgage tax relief to the disadvantage of the rest of the UK. Unlike the other cases, however, the SNP has not been able to convincingly portray the rest of the country as a 'cost' for Scotland.

One important element is shared by all parties in the sample and lies at the core of the nationalism of the rich. This boils down to a belief in the special talent and work ethic of the members of the nation. In the cases of the LN, the N-VA and the VB, such belief leads to an unambiguous cultural-determinist explanation of the nation's economic success, which is key for two reasons: first, it dignifies the nation's prosperity and turns it into a major marker of its members' identity; second, it allows them to reject solidarity on account of the reasoning that the areas they represent used to be less developed than the national average but were capable, through their hard-work, to build up their own current prosperity without state help. Hence, what the other regions of the state that 'live off the transfers' should do is simply to follow their example. Although they might tactically divert their attacks to the state administration and the central or local political elite, this cultural-determinist argument has led them to attribute opportunistic and parasitic behaviours to the rest of the parent state. In the case of ERC, we find such an argument but without denigration of the poorer regions of the country. While the Catalans are depicted as hard-working people who have made their way with no external support, and it is often implied that culture does play a major role in influencing patterns of economic development more in general, this does not involve any disparaging stereotyping of the regions of Spain that profit from the fiscal transfers flowing from Catalonia. The main targets of the party's rhetoric have been the Spanish state administration and the Spanish political elite. This reconciles the implicit cultural-determinism of its nationalism of the rich with the left-wing ideology of the party, since the intervention of the centralising and authoritarian Spanish state is identified as the main cause of the backwardness of the poorer Spanish regions. It certainly provides a more inclusive rhetoric with regard to the considerable Catalan population of Spanish origins – often coming precisely from Spain's most deprived regions. There is however a tension within the party's discourse, since by targeting traditional parties and their clientelist strategies, ERC has implicitly portrayed the inhabitants of poorer Spanish regions who vote for them as at least passively accepting these practices.

These four parties (ERC, the LN, the VB and the N-VA) have also claimed to represent the local constituency of SMEs, which would be living proof of the validity of the cultural-determinist argument they make. According to Jérome Jamin (2011, p. 27) this focus on the 'producing people' re-proposes, in a European context, the 'producerist narrative' used by populist parties in the United States, which suggests 'the existence of a noble and hardworking middle-class that is constantly in conflict with malicious parasites which are lazy and guilty, and found at both the top and bottom of the social order'. Such narratives have the undeniable advantage of explaining complex processes such as uneven development, lack of regional convergence, the persistence of the transfers and patterns of political divergence between regions with simple, compelling explanations. They also appeal to a wide section of the population – the working people – against enemies from above and below and can be justified with reference to widely shared values of merit, entrepreneurship, skilfulness and responsibility. Jamin further argues that such rhetoric is typical of right-wing parties. This might be true with regard to its complete form, where the producing people are squeezed from above and below, yet, as we have seen in the case of ERC, a left-wing version carefully limiting its attacks to unaccountable state bureaucrats and to those political elites that nourish dependence in other Spanish regions for their clientelist advantages (the enemies from above) is also possible. Yet, Jamin's formulation is mainly based on an adaptation of the rhetoric developed by American populist parties in the late nineteenth and early twentieth century, at a time when the welfare state was not yet a reality. On the contrary, the welfare state features prominently in the propaganda of the parties analysed here and is a key factor to understanding the formation of their arguments of economic victimisation – as I will argue more fully in the next chapter. Therefore, elaborating on Abts and Kochuyt (2013, 2014), I propose to link this producerist narrative to the wider literature on welfare state formation and criteria of deservingness, and to label their conditional conception of solidarity as 'welfare producerism'.

The moral economy of welfare

As argued by Mau (2003), the welfare state relies not only on rational self-interest assumptions whereby individuals seek forms of insurance against risk, but it also entails a 'moral economy' based on an entrenched consensus that people should pool resources to rebalance market inequalities that are deemed to be intolerable. However, redistribution is accepted conditionally and is based on ideas of reciprocity, trust and fairness. We can therefore think of the welfare state as a trust game in which people engage only if they do not perceive the recipients as abusing the system and in which they might disengage if they think that the system has negative collateral effects. More specifically, we can identify two social contracts undergirding welfare arrangements: a contract of mutual support between citizens, that is, between contributors and recipients (Mau 2003, p. 123); and a contract between citizens and the state, since the former formally delegate the organisation and delivery of welfare services to the latter, whose legitimacy has increasingly come to rely on its efficiency in carrying out this duty (Bommes 2012, p. 39). A widespread perception that these two contracts are being violated can lead to what Mau (2003, p. 123) has called the pathologies of mistrusting the recipients and that of mistrusting the system.[2]

With regard to the former, studies on welfare deservingness have identified five criteria widely used by Western European publics to identify the community of legitimate recipients of social support. Such criteria are: control, identity, need, attitude and reciprocity (Van Oorschot 2000, 2006). Control refers to the fact that people evaluate the reason why persons find themselves in need. The higher the perceived responsibility of the recipients for their own neediness, the lower their deservingness. Identity is linked to the 'bounded' nature of welfare, whereby people belonging to the 'relevant community' – usually identified with the nation – are seen as more deserving than outsiders. Need simply implies that people who are perceived as being more in need are deemed more deserving. Attitude is connected to the idea that although recipients cannot materially pay back for the help they receive, they should at least compensate symbolically, for instance, by showing gratitude and making a good effort to 'redress' their condition. Reciprocity means that, although a minimum of vertical solidarity is guaranteed, people who have contributed more should also somehow receive more (Van Oorschot 2000, 2006).

On the basis of these five criteria, we can identify two conditional conceptions of solidarity: welfare chauvinism, as a conditional conception of solidarity primarily based on 'identity'; and welfare producerism, which is prevalently based on the criteria of 'control', 'reciprocity' and 'attitude' (Abts and Kochuyt 2013, 2014). The two of them are not mutually exclusive and actors often draw on both, although to a different extent, when constructing their own understanding of the community of legitimate welfare recipients. It is however useful to distinguish them because the criterion of identity functions in a fundamentally different way as compared with the others and this because: it often – although not always – hinges on ascribed qualities (origin and/or ethnicity) rather than on behaviour; it is logically prior to the others since it relates to the definition of the community of social sharing to which the other criteria apply (see Deutsch 1975, p. 142, Opotow 1990, pp. 1–4). This is all the more relevant in my case studies, since dual identities are an important reality in the regions analysed. Hence, the argument of economic victimisation made by the parties studied here has relied considerably more on welfare producerism than welfare chauvinism. Although identity still lurks in the background, since the sub-state national community is clearly identified as the relevant 'collectivity of redistribution', the rejection of solidarity with the rest of the parent state is rarely justified solely on the basis of such criterion. On the contrary, welfare recipients are seen as undeserving because: they are not enough willing to work, hence they are responsible for (i.e. in control of) their neediness – or in some softer versions the parties they vote for are

responsible for that, although the fact that they vote for such parties suggests a kind of indirect responsibility; they often deliberately abuse the
system or, at least, they do not make a sufficient effort to get out of their
situation of need (attitude); they get more than what they would be entitled to on the basis of their contributions, while those who have contributed more do not get their fair share (reciprocity). This producerism
however is also strongly 'culturalised' in the sense that, by representing the
relevant nation as made up of hard-working, entrepreneurial people the
case-study parties have proposed a clear association between the imagined
'community of welfare producers' and the entire nation, which is therefore
portrayed as legitimately more deserving.

Their critique however has not only been limited to the contract
between citizens, but has also concerned the pathology of 'mistrusting the
system'. The main accusation has been that the parent state, and the traditional political elites with it, has inefficiently managed public resources,
leading to wastages, corruption, clientelism, fraud, rising taxes, deficit and
debt. In this aspect of their propaganda we can also see some populist
tendencies,[3] although present in different degrees in each case. Here is also
where the argument of economic victimisation links to that of political
marginalisation, since the state is described as mainly dominated by elites
who do not belong to the national community and therefore pursue other
interests.

The SNP is, once again, a deviant case. Especially in recent years, the
party has shared with the other cases a representation of the Scottish
people as a talented, ingenious and hard-working lot – building on the
much longer tradition of the 'lad o' pairts' and on Scotland's contribution
to the industrial revolution – yet, the party has had a hard time referring to
any SME constituencies because of its weakness in the region. On the contrary, it has consistently preached the need to reverse Scotland's low rates
of business start-ups as compared to England and to steer the economy
from one mainly based on big industry, first endogenous and later of multinational nature, to one with a higher number of SMEs. Another reason
why the cultural-determinist argument has been less prominent in the rhetoric of the SNP is because 'Scotland's wealth surplus' has mainly to do
with natural, rather than socio-cultural factors.

What is certainly common to all parties, however, and which arguably
is the main strength of the nationalism of the rich, is that the transfers and,
in the case of Scotland oil revenues, have been used as a 'trump card' to
project the appealing and credible image of a more prosperous society
combining competitiveness and welfare protection in a context of high
international competition due to processes of globalisation and European
integration. In this connection, it is interesting to note that even the right-
wing parties in the sample do not advocate radical welfare cuts to their
own community. Some of them – the VB and the LN at some point in their
history – have even presented themselves as the true defenders of the

working-class and have effectively expanded their electoral grip within this constituency. Hence, along the lines of what has been suggested by Keating (1996, p. xii), the nationalism of the rich can be seen as a rhetorical tool 'for reconciling economic competitiveness and social solidarity in the face of the international market', although the parties analysed here have clearly indicated different ways, some more exclusive than others, to reach this goal.

The nationalism of the rich also contains an important element of liberal communitarianism pointed out by Walzer (1990, p. 16), i.e. 'the dream of a perfect free-riderlessness', that echoes David Miller's (1995) argument according to which a strong national identity is a prerequisite for efficient solidarity. In other words, what these parties have suggested is that, to work, solidarity needs commitment and consensus on the basic norms and values shared by the society in which it is discharged, otherwise it leads to inefficiencies, free-riding, higher costs and lower quality. Since the economic success of the nations represented in this sample is portrayed as descending from the shared norms and values of their members, it follows – implicitly or explicitly – that where economic development has not materialised to the same extent other norms prevail. Hence, welfare and redistribution will be inefficient there. In this framework, changing the boundaries of the political community is the only possible solution because cultural change is deemed to be very difficult to bring about and, in any case, the rest of the population of the parent state is deemed not to have any willingness to effect it. In the cases of the VB and the LN, similar arguments are also directed at foreigners, while they are not in the other cases.

The above considerations might be less obvious concerning the SNP. The SNP's nationalism of the rich does not reflect the idea of Scotland being robbed by lazy parasites in England and/or corrupted bureaucrats – although it is worth stressing again that Salmond did accuse the South-east of being made up of 'subsidy junkies' living off state spending – but rather the image of Scotland as a different society, with a stronger social-democratic ethos, which should be free to use its 'extra-ordinary' human and natural resources to achieve its goals. Yet, one example of the anti-free-riding ethos mentioned above is provided by the arguments formulated in the 1970s about the use of oil revenues by the bankrupted British state, pawning away Scotland's wealth to cover its balance of trade deficit. It can be seen again in the recent decision of the SNP-led Scottish Government to charge pupils from the rest of the UK studying at Scottish universities tuition fees.[4]

The advanced periphery

The economic victimisation denounced by the case-study parties is directly linked to a perception of political marginalisation. Such an idea is more vague than the economic argument seen in the previous section, but it can be summed up as a subtler, and more subjective, form of victimisation than deliberate oppression or discrimination. In their analysis of secession in the twentieth century, Pavkovic and Radan (2007, pp. 47–50) have identified three types of grievances that appear in the propaganda of separatist movements: the unequal distribution of resources (economic and/or of status), harm, and alien rule, with the last one being the most important and common element. While grievances about resources do not require deliberate action on the part of the state or other groups within the country, but can simply stem from neglect, harm is always deliberate. Contrary to Pavkovic and Radan's description, when looking at the propaganda of the parties analysed here, we find plenty of arguments about the unequal distribution of resources, but few overt statements about harm and alien rule, which would, at least in part, confirm their peculiar character when compared to 'more traditional' separatist movements.

This assertion of course requires a number of qualifications, as the degree of its validity varies from one case to the other and, also, within each case over time. First, we can distinguish between parties such as the SNP, the N-VA and, in part, ERC that have tended to shift from a message centred around blaming central institutions towards one aimed at showing the positive prospects of independence and reassuring the population about the maintenance of good neighbourly relationships with the rest of the parent state after separation. Thus, the SNP has gone from using colonial metaphors in the late 1960s and early 1970s, to accusing the British Government of 'mismanagement' and 'undelivered results', rather than deliberate harm. The very same expression of democratic deficit, arising during the Thatcher years, points to a problem with British democracy, not its absence. Similarly, the N-VA has certainly been tough with the Walloon Socialist Party and sometimes – especially through personal declarations of some of its members rather than through official propaganda – delivered almost insulting statements with regard to the Francophones, but more consistently it has referred to the flaws of the Belgian consociational democracy as the main reason to 'divorce' the two halves of the country. ERC shows a more problematic outlook, especially in light of the constitutional crisis begun in 2010, which has rallied all nationalist parties behind the idea that self-determination is fundamentally about democracy and that the Spanish state's opposition to an independence referendum displays its authoritarian character. Yet, between the mid-1990s and the late 2000s, especially under Carod-Rovira's leadership, the party tried to spread a positive message based on the socio-economic advantages of independence and to soften opposition to the parent state.

The VB and LN are rather different in this respect, as they have generally showed a much stronger confrontational posture. Both parties have made reference to colonial metaphors in their early years and, in the case of the VB, accusations of francophone 'arrogance' have been recently voiced. Yet, in a fashion similar to the N-VA, since the second half of the 1990s, the party has more frequently underlined the flaws of Belgium's consociational democracy and the ensuing 'minoritisation' of the Flemish majority. Similarly, the League progressively abandoned claims concerning the eradication of local cultures and – like the VB – in the 1990s emphasised the corruption scandals that hit the country portraying itself as the only clean party and the representative of the working people against the 'corrupted political mafia'.[5]

More generally, all the case-study parties have confronted two main constraints with regard to the articulation of their grievances. The first has to do with the threat of violence and 'Balkanisation' that is often associated with nationalism and separatism – and that was arguably more salient in the first half of the 1990s, when the dissolution of Yugoslavia recalled the dangers of civil war. As we will see in Chapter 9, even if independence would probably be advantageous in economic terms, the populations of the regions analysed have shown a reluctance to support it massively. In such a context, when willing to expand their appeal to a wider constituency than a small clique of committed voters, the parties have made an effort to reassure the population that separation would be a smooth event. Expressions like 'orderly split', 'evaporation of the state', 'consensual separation', 'divorce', 'confederation' have thus been widely used along with examples of peaceful dissolutions such as those of the United Kingdom of Sweden and Norway (1905) and of the Czechoslovak Federative Republic (1993). All this points to the tight rope that these parties have to walk if they want to successfully voice grievances without sounding too aggressive or threatening.

The second constraint relates to the specific context where the parties have operated and, therefore, to the socio-economic and cultural material available to construct a credible narrative. Although in some cases there are historical experiences of harsh conflict and persecution – Franco's dictatorship probably being the clearest example – in their most recent history these parties have lived in quite stable and successful democratic regimes. Most of them have been plagued by corruption scandals and have displayed flaws in the functioning of their democratic institutions, but one could hardly conclude that they would not qualify as democratic regimes. Furthermore, all of them have also moved to a more decentralised architecture allowing for substantial forms of recognition of diversity and institutional autonomy. Therefore, in the longer term, exaggerated accusations of domination, oppression and authoritarianism could risk backfiring, all the more so because all these parties have accepted to bring about constitutional change from within those very same institutions, thus implicitly accepting their legitimacy. This is why I suggest using the label 'political marginalisation' to refer to the varied set of grievances concerning the political relationship with the parent state voiced by these parties. In this way, I do not want to downplay the importance of such grievances. On the contrary, it is precisely by putting them in a wider context of separatist claims and grievances that one realises how much the standard to judge political legitimacy is always relative (Linz 1973, p. 55).

That said, let us review in a more systematic fashion the core claims of political marginalisation made by each party. In a longer historical perspective, the SNP's main argument has concerned the centralisation of power in the London area. According to this narrative, while the Union was, in principle, a partnership among equals, the strength of the Southeast sidelined Scotland. During the Thatcher years such a situation evolved into a fundamental questioning of the nature of the Kingdom. The Iron Lady did not do anything undemocratic, strictly speaking, but she treated Britain as a unitarian instead of a union state, thus jeopardising Scotland's position as a constituent nation of the UK. Although the autonomous character of Scotland was later recognised, as has been, more recently, its right to self-determination, the narrative arising out of those years has had a lasting impact. ERC's main political grievance has similarly, although much more critically than in the Scottish case, had to do with its recognition as a nation endowed with a right to self-determination. Albeit linked to corruption scandals and specific institutional issues, accusations against the Spanish Government of being fundamentally undemocratic have revolved around the '*mentalitat radial*' of the Spanish political elite and its refusal to recognise the differential status of Catalonia. The LN on the contrary has not so much complained about the recognition of Padania as a nation, for the simple reason that this was far from being an uncontroversial concept in the North in the first place. What the League has rather consistently focused upon has been the underrepresentation of some northern constituencies – portrayed as representative of the entire North – within the purportedly southern-dominated state institutions and parties. During the 2000s, however, as the party was for most of the decade in power with Berlusconi's FI and PdL, it became harder to hold such an argument. This in part explains why the *Lega* gave more emphasis to immigration issues and strengthened its Eurosceptic position, while simultaneously demanding more powers for the northern regions and accusing its allies to hamper the devolutionist agenda. Finally, the VB and the N-VA probably are the most interesting cases of rhetoric of political marginalisation because they claim to speak on behalf of a demographic and political majority that is, however, purportedly made powerless by the constitutional guarantees granted to the francophone minority, which would constantly abuse them.

Therefore, what is clearly at stake in the discourse of these parties is the type of democracy, rather than democracy itself. Clear issues of recognition have been prominent only in the case of ERC – and even there, since the mid-1990s, they had begun to peter out until the recent crisis brought them back to the core of the party's discourse – and, to a much lower extent, of the VB. Yet, a general sense of neglect, the idea of being different and having diverging interests from the rest of the country have been sufficient to provide a breeding ground for these parties to formulate their arguments and obtain substantial support.

What is important to underline is that the claims of economic victimisation and political marginalisation must always be considered in conjunction: on the one hand, economic victimisation directly stems from the nation's political marginalisation; on the other, the nation's political marginalisation is more salient because of its exceptional economic power and unrealised potential, which would warrant not only equal but even special representation within the parent state. In other words, it is the perceived mismatch between the economic capabilities and the political power of the relevant nation that fuels the arguments of the nationalism of the rich. Such a mismatch coincides with a more general sense of 'relative deprivation' as defined by Ted Gurr (quoted in Tajfel 1978, p. 68), that is, as a discrepancy between an actor's 'value expectations' and its 'value capabilities' where 'value expectations are the goods and conditions of life to which people *believe* they are rightfully entitled' and 'value capabilities are the goods and conditions they *think* they are capable of getting and keeping' (my emphasis). As Gurr further suggests the emphasis 'is on the perception of deprivation; people may be subjectively deprived with reference to their expectations even though an objective observer may not judge them to be in want'.

Notes

1 While this is often couched as a democratic argument – i.e. 'the people should decide about the use of their own resources' – it in fact stems from the nationalist argument that a nation constitutes a distinct political community endowed with a right to self-determination and should thus always be free to decide how its money is spent.
2 Here, I am using Mau's two pathologies but reinterpreting them in combination with considerations from Bommes (2012, p. 39). When talking about the two pathologies, Mau refers to the belief that solidarity does not go to the truly needy (mistrusting the recipient) and that solidarity might have collateral long-term effects, such as sapping the poor's willingness to work (mistrusting the system). I rather propose here an actor-centred approach, whereby the two pathologies refer each to a contract between actors (citizens-citizens vs. citizens-state), since this is more suitable to identify the relevant Others singled out by each party, especially considering Jamin's distinction between enemies from above and below.
3 I refer to Mudde's (2004, p. 543) minimum definition of populism as being based on the antagonistic opposition between 'the pure people' and 'the corrupt elite'. Although, in practice, populism and nationalism often overlap, analytically one can distinguish between the vertical imbalance, which is internal to the nation, typical of populism, and the horizontal one between the nation and external others typical of nationalism. That is why, although it is certainly relevant especially to explain the electoral success of some of my case-study parties, in this work populism is not used as a major framework of analysis.
4 Although certainly required by the inefficiencies of its funding system, this policy was to remain in place even after independence.
5 ERC used a similar rhetoric in Catalonia in the first half of the 1990s.

7 Redistribution, uneven territorial development and identity

Although both domestic and international factors have contributed to the rise of the nationalism of the rich, the case studies reviewed in the previous chapters suggest that the former have played a primary role. In this chapter, I take a comparative look at the main findings concerning such factors and broaden my analysis to include centre-periphery relations in other European countries. The subsequent chapter will, then, focus on external processes such as globalisation and European integration.

Fiscal imbalances compared

The nationalism of the rich implies the existence of some form of economic drain on the part of central institutions, although this can also be potential and contested rather than actual and proven, as the case of Scotland shows. Relevant questions therefore are: whether there are similarities and differences in the extent and nature of fiscal transfers between the regions analysed; what has been the connection, in practice, between the origin of the transfers and the origin of the discourse about them; and whether other European regions have experienced similar fiscal imbalances, whether they have seen the rise of similar movements, and, if not, why.

With regard to Catalonia, Flanders and Northern Italy, the several studies reviewed in the previous chapters have shown great variance concerning the availability and quality of data, the methods used for the calculations and, as a consequence, the results obtained. This preliminary observation emphasises the fact that the contested nature of the transfers – notably regarding the methods for their estimation and the reasons why they arose and persist – has allowed the parties to selectively use data that best suits their arguments. Furthermore, although distortions have been pointed out, most studies emphasise the generally high correlation of regional fiscal deficits and GDP per capita, suggesting that they are mostly driven by automatic forms of interpersonal redistribution rather than by discretionary spending. In other words, these studies would suggest that redistribution is mostly 'colour-blind', while the case-study parties are not.

At the same time, the existence and relative stability over time of sizable transfers is undeniable (see Table 7.1 for a summary). Flanders' contribution has hovered around 4 per cent of regional GDP throughout the 1990s and early 2000s – and was arguably the same in the 1980s (Van Rompuy and Bilsen 1988, Van Rompuy 2010). When allowing for the effect of Spain's budget deficit, the Catalan contribution has remained around 5–6 per cent of the region's GDP between 1991 and 2005 (Uriel and Barberan 2007, p. 303). Although Maggi and Piperno's study (1998) did show a considerable increase in the fiscal deficit of the main Northern Italian contributor regions between 1989 and 1995, which might contribute to explaining the LN's breakthrough in those years, unfortunately, no longitudinal study of fiscal transfers is available. The analysis of the relation between primary and disposable income from 1995 to 2011 carried out in Chapter 4, however, can help obtain a rough idea of the fiscal deficit's evolution. This shows a quite stable picture, albeit with a slight deterioration in the case of Lombardy. All this has two implications. On the one hand, it cannot be argued that variability in the success of the parties in recent years is linked to any clear worsening of the regions' fiscal balances with the central administration. On the other, the persistence of the transfers is a powerful rhetorical weapon, since it can be used to underpin the claim that solidarity has not reduced the economic imbalances between different areas of the country and that the fiscal autonomy devolved to the regions is not sufficient. Although this argument betrays a conception of solidarity as a means to boost endogenous growth, rather than as a normative

Table 7.1 Summary of fiscal deficits in Catalonia, Flanders and selected Northern Italian Regions, selected studies (percentage of regional GDP)

Region	Monetary flow	Benefit flow
Catalonia	−7.5 (1985–2000)	−2.75 (1980–85)
	−8.6 (2001–09)	−5.2 (1991–2005)
		−6.2 (2001–09)
Flanders		−4.6 (1975–85)*
		−4.2 (1990–2003)*
Lombardy	−6 (1997)	−17.6 (1996–2002)
		−14.6 (2004–05)
		−11.6 (2005)
Piedmont	−4.5 (1997)	−8.6 (1996–2002)
		−5.1 (2004–05)
		−1.8 (2005)
Veneto	−9.8 (1997)	−11.1 (1996–2002)
		−7.6 (2004–05)
		−6.4 (2005)

Sources: see case-study chapters.

Note
* Mix of benefit and monetary flow methods.

obligation to provide a degree of equalisation between richer and poorer areas even in the face of persisting imbalances, it has not for this reason been less effective.

Unfortunately, most of the data just discussed does not account for the formative years of the nationalism of the rich in the 1970s and 1980s. During those years Flanders and, to a lower extent, Northern Italy substantially improved their relative economic position vis-à-vis the rest of the country, setting the ground for the formation of the transfers. Flanders overtook Wallonia in the mid-1960s with corresponding effects on the size and direction of inter-regional flows. While up to 1963 – according to some up to 1968 (Meunier *et al.* 2007) – Flanders was a recipient region (Dottermans 1997), from the early 1970s it became a net contributor and the fiscal deficit grew in the second half of that decade out of the widening gulf in revenues between the north and the south of Belgium. The situation is slightly more complicated with regard to Northern Italy, as the North has been richer than the South since national unification. Yet, Moioli (1990) and Diamanti (1994) emphasised how the constituencies of highest support for the northern regionalist leagues coincided with non-metropolitan areas of late industrialisation in Veneto, Lombardy and Piedmont of the type described by Arnaldo Bagnasco in his study on the Third Italy. The region of Veneto is emblematic in this respect. Between 1951 and 1981, it saw its per capita value-added going from 81 per cent to 109 per cent of the national average, recording the strongest improvement among all northern regions and the fourth strongest in the entire country. A symmetric evolution of the region's contribution to inter-regional redistribution is suggested by a longitudinal comparison of the data on fiscal transfers: while, in the mid-1970s, Veneto's fiscal deficit was equal to about –2 per cent of its primary income (Forte 1977, p. 110), all recent studies estimate the region's contribution at between –6.4 and –11.1 per cent of its GDP.

The Catalan case does not show a similar reversal of the economic conditions of the region or of some areas within it. Catalonia has consistently been one of the most prosperous Spanish regions since at least 1860 and, if anything, between the 1970s and 1990s, it saw its hegemonic position threatened by the Community of Madrid and the Balearic Islands. Accordingly, Catalan nationalism in the early part of the twentieth century already developed some of the economic arguments that later flowed into the nationalism of the rich in the late 1980s. Prominent among them was the idea that Catalonia was being held back by a more backward Castile after having recovered from the centuries of stagnation that had followed its decline in the fifteenth century, which provided a template for later elaborations on the subject (Llobera 2004, p. 66). Also, studies about the transfers were already carried out during the dictatorship and even more so in the first years of the transition. Hence, while one can easily understand why claims of economic victimisation were not vented openly until the death of Franco, when comparing the almost immediate coincidence of the early signs of the rhetoric of the nationalism of the rich in Flanders with the publication of the first academic studies on the transfers and the readiness of nationalist and separatist parties to use them, it is surprising that the same process took about a decade to occur in full form in the Spanish region. Two reasons can account for that. First, the trauma of the dictatorship forced a climate of consensus over the political elite that was aware of the need to ensure a smooth transition to a democratic state. The fiscal issue was thus overshadowed by the need to ensure the establishment of autonomous institutions and the protection of the Catalan language and culture. Second, at the time of the transition the weight of the Spanish state in the economy was meagre as compared to the European average. Yet, between 1970 and 1990, public spending increased from 20.1 per cent to 42.7 per cent of the country's GDP, with a parallel hike in taxes, deficit and debt that considerably increased the saliency of the transfers (Comin and Diaz 2005, p. 877).

The case studies however suggest that, by themselves, the fiscal transfers cannot explain the formation of the nationalism of the rich, since other regions within some of the countries analysed have experienced similar imbalances without seeing any such rhetoric of fiscal victimisation arising. Explanations for in-country variation have been provided in the relevant chapters. What is more interesting here is to have a look at patterns of inter-regional redistribution in Europe as a whole. This topic was examined for the first time by an EEC Commission established in 1974 with the purpose of drawing lessons for European integration. The same exercise was then repeated in 1998. Table 7.2 reports the fiscal deficits of specific contributor regions. The Northern Italian regions stand out for their very high contributions. If one takes the 1993 data, only Madrid, and to a lower extent the Balearic Islands and Stockholm, displayed similar imbalances. This might account for the peculiar nature of the Italian case, whereby the nationalism of the rich arose in a context in which there was no pre-existent national identity. Furthermore, when capital regions are taken out of the sample, only some German areas, notably Baden-Württemberg and Hessen are left along with the Italian and Spanish ones in which the nationalism of the rich arose – apart from the already mentioned exceptions of Emilia-Romagna and the Balearic Islands. Yet, neither Hessen nor Baden-Württemberg have experienced the rise of any regionalist and/or nationalist party of relevance, although some authors have referred to the latter as an example of active regionalism, of the bourgeois kind theorised by Harvie (1994), at the level of the institution of the *Land*. The absence, or low relevance, of the rhetoric of the nationalism of the rich here is probably due to the low cultural and ethnic differentiation from the rest of Germany (Harvie 1994, pp. 63–67, Keating 1998, p. 105).

In this connection, Bavaria is a more interesting case because it did show high regionalist activity, mainly based on a strong sense of cultural differentiation, and because it went through a process of economic ascent similar

Table 7.2 Inter-regional transfers in European countries, fiscal deficits of selected regions, 1960–75 and 1993 (percentage of regional GDP)

Region	McDougall Report 1977 (data from different years)		EU Study 1998 (1993 data)	
	BF	MF	BF	MF
Île-de-France (FR)	–10*	–7.7*	–6	–3
Baden-Württemberg (GE)	–	–5.4	–5	–4
Bavaria (GE)	–	–	–4	–3
North Rhine-Westphalia (GE)	–	–5.1	–	–
Hessen (GE)	–	–3.4	–4	–4
Stockholm (SW)	–	–	–9	–6
East Midlands (UK)	–7	–	–	–
South East (UK)	–9	–	–7	–5
Lombardy (IT)	–	–12	–14	–12
Piedmont (IT)	–	–8	–9	–8
Veneto (IT)	–	–	–8	–9
Madrid (SP)	–	–	–13	–9
Balearic Islands (SP)	–	–	–8	–7
Catalonia (SP)	–	–	–6	–5

Source: Commission of the European Communities 1977, European Commission 1998.

Notes

BF = benefit flow; MF = monetary flow.

* The report calculated the difference between expenditure and revenue from taxes and social welfare contributions in the Île-de-France, as a percentage of the region's revenue from taxes and social welfare contributions. Then French taxes and social contributions averaged 38.5 per cent of GDP. The balance has thus been recalculated in percentage of GDP by multiplying the above measures by 0.385.

to that experienced by Flanders and some Northern Italian provinces, becoming, during the 1970s and 1980s, a net contributor to the federal purse. The *Christlich Soziale Union in Bayern* (Christian Social Union, CSU), the local independent Christian Democratic Party that has continuously ruled the region since the Second World War apart from a short break in 1954–57, played a role similar to that of CiU in Catalonia, both by being a moderate regionalist party acting as a responsible partner in the German federation and defending the interests of Bavaria without demanding full independence (Hepburn 2008). The party has neither fundamentally put into question the federal system, nor lost substantial ground to separatist parties. Some peculiarities of the German federation probably account for this outcome. As Derek Urwin (2004 [1982], p. 240) argued before reunification, the Federal Republic 'is a country without a centre' – a condition that has lingered on after 1990 – and its institutional structure has so far struck a good balance between centrifugal and centripetal forces, leaving great autonomy to the *Länder* and providing them with a high level of participation into the policy-making process through the federal senate (the *Bundesrat*), which reduces room for claims of political marginalisation

(Keating 1998, p. 114). From a fiscal perspective, an aspect of the post-war German institutional architecture must be stressed. The federal role in financing inter-regional redistribution has been lower than in most central-ised countries and a substantial part of the levelling of differences in regional tax capacity is obtained through horizontal payments among *Länder*, whereby the richer ones compensate the poorer bringing their per capita fiscal capacity to, at least, 95 per cent of the national average. In the 1990s, this system came under attack for its in-built disincentives for the poorer states to increase their tax base. Yet, when compared to fiscal arrangements in the countries analysed here, it seems to provide two advantages: it entails a much more transparent form of redistribution – or at least of part of it – among the federal units; it foresees a guarantee whereby a contributor state can never see its fiscal capacity fall below the national average because of its contribution, thus ruling out, or at least limiting, overcompensation effects (see Commission of the European Communities 1977, Biehl 1994, Seitz 2000).

The case studies also show that in the 1970s and 1980s the saliency of the transfers increased in coincidence with situations of public policy failure, especially, the rise of public spending and taxes and the accumulation of budget deficits and debt in the parent states. This was by no means an iso-lated phenomenon. Public spending growth was a common trend across industrialised societies in the post-Second World War period due, first, to the general expansion of state intervention in the economy and welfare pro-grammes, and, since 1973, to the general process of stagflation triggered by the oil crisis. Yet, when looking at comparative figures on the growth of public spending as a percentage of GDP, in the period 1960–80 Belgium ranked second among western countries, while Spain and Italy recorded the quickest and second-quickest growth respectively in the 1980–90 period (my calculations based on Tanzi and Schuknecht 2000, pp. 6–7). Since the late 1970s, in Belgium and Italy this process was accompanied by spiralling debt/ GDP ratios, with the two countries topping the league of advanced eco-nomies – first and third respectively – by 1990 (my calculations on Alesina and Perotti 1995, p. 2). While Spain's debt remained low by western stand-ards, its increase was the largest among advanced countries between 1975 and 1990, going from 7.3 per cent to 42.5 per cent of GDP (my calculations on IMF-FAD 2012). Accordingly, tax revenues as a percentage of GDP also displayed higher than average rates, although with more variation: Belgium's tax revenue was the second fastest growing between 1960 and 1980, whereas Spain held first place in the 1980s. Italy remained at the high end of the ranking – in fifth position – during the entire 1960–90 period and then shot up to first place between 1990 and 1996, when most other countries were successfully reducing their fiscal pressure (my calculations on Tanzi and Schuknecht 2000, p. 52).

This data about fiscal trends roughly correlate with the different timing of appearance and development of the nationalism of the rich in the different regions. As Belgium's fiscal position deteriorated earlier as compared to Italy and, especially Spain, this, along with the growing imbalances resulting from Flanders' emergence as the strongest region in the country from the mid-1960s on, led to the formation of the nationalism of the rich already in the late 1970s. Although it was not the main reason for its electoral success, the persisting fiscal crisis of the country up to the mid-1990s contributed to de-legitimising traditional parties to the advantage of the VB. Italy showed a very similar profile in those years, although its better fiscal position at the beginning of the period – the debt/GDP ratio was only 35.4 per cent in 1965 compared to Belgium's 67.5 per cent – and its slower growth in public spending in the 1960s and 1970s, probably also due to more rudimentary welfare provisions, delayed the full development of the leagues' formulation of the nationalism of the rich into the second half of the 1980s. Finally, Spain is a more problematic case, as its fiscal evolution should be seen as a 'normalisation' with regard to the western average after a condition of extremely low intervention of the state in the economy during the dictatorship, rather than as a 'deterioration'. Yet, the process was undeniably radical and, as pointed out by Comin and Diaz (2005, pp. 893–894), 'due to its delay, the universal system of Social Security has been built in Spain when conditions were very unfavourable'.

Hence, although reflecting wider trends, the evolution of the fiscal position of Belgium, Italy and Spain's governments relatively to other western economies in the 1960–90 period does show more radical than average figures that, coupled with uneven regional development, weakened the legitimacy of central governments and opened up a window of opportunity for the successful development of the arguments of economic victimisation formulated by the parties analysed here. This does not mean that the fiscal vagaries of these countries were a sufficient condition. As already mentioned, fiscal strain was a general condition among advanced economies during the 1970–90 period, and other countries faced imbalances of similar magnitude, both in relative and absolute terms. Thus, these economic factors must be evaluated alongside identity, political and institutional variables. Yet, a comparison with Germany, which does show some similarities in terms of domestic cultural heterogeneity and uneven economic development, seems to confirm their importance. Although Germany's debt increased by 151.3 per cent of its GDP in the 1965–90 period – Italy's did so by 183.8 per cent – it remained much lower in absolute terms (43.6 per cent) (my calculations on Alesina and Perotti 1995, p. 2). During roughly the same time, public spending grew by 39.2 per cent or about 20 per cent less than the western countries' average, while the rate of growth of tax revenue was the second lowest after the US. Finally, its fiscal deficit during the 1973–89 years remained well below the OECD average (my calculations on Green 1993). In other words, Germany's fiscal performance clearly offered less ground for radical contestation and for the crystallisation of redistributive imbalances around regional/national lines than in Belgium, Italy and Spain.

To these considerations regarding the fiscal performance of the countries analysed, one should also add an efficacy problem. ERC, the LN, the N-VA and the VB have indeed suggested that the transfers have not helped but rather prevented economic convergence, by furthering dependence for electoral purposes rather than endogenous growth. In this respect, economic analyses suggest that such convergence has not been realised (in Flanders) (Van Rompuy 2010, p. 123) or did occur for some decades, but slowed down considerably or even stopped at some point (in the 1970s in Italy and in the 1980s in Spain) (Garcia-Milà and McGuire 2001, Padovano 2007, Ambrosiano *et al.* 2010). Whether this was due to fiscal transfers or not, it is not clear. Despite theoretical studies arguing that redistribution might hamper growth, the empirical evidence is mixed (Mulquin and Senger 2011, p. 21). Such mixed evidence however has not prevented the party from using such an argument and exploiting scandals concerning corruption and the discovery of widespread clientelistic networks in the poorer areas of the parent state as proof of their claims.

In many respects Scotland's recent history might be seen as the exact opposite of the situation depicted above. On the one hand, the United Kingdom was one of the most successful countries in reducing debt and containing public spending and tax revenue growth. On the other, the region's fiscal position within the British system of income redistribution has been ambiguous. Also, in 1960–90, Scotland went through a painful process of structural change from an economy over-reliant on heavy industry to a service-based one with a higher than average public sector, which entailed a stronger defence of welfare than in the South-east of England. In a provocative way, one could think of Scotland as a Wallonia endowed with the possibility of a constitutional alternative made attractive by the financial trump card of oil revenues. Yet, the situation is in fact more complex. The first wave of support for the SNP – which materialised before oil was discovered – had much to do with public policy failure. Although regional policy had diverted a disproportionate amount of resources to Scotland, the central government's 'stop-go' strategy badly hurt business formation in an economy more reliant than most of Britain on state spending. In this respect, the foundering of the Wilson government's promise to put an end to recurrent deflationary measures and the ensuing devaluation of the pound represented the proverbial straw that broke the camel's back. Furthermore, although it is true that, between the late 1950s and the early 1960s, Scotland's economy was underperforming compared to the rest of the UK, thanks to the effects of regional policy and declining growth in England, by 1965, and for the next decade, Scotland began closing the gap with the British average. Then, oil added a completely new dimension to the cause of Scottish self-determination, while the 1973 crisis further contributed to the idea that the region would be better off as an independent state, since the crisis simultaneously aggravated the UK's balance of payment hole – the UK being a net oil importer back then

– and multiplied by four the prospective revenues coming from the 'black gold'. The 'social-democratic utopia' depicted by *The Economist* in 1976 became indeed an attractive scenario. Also, although it did not experience spiralling debt, in those years the UK economy did show the highest inflation and lowest GDP growth rates of all the G-6 countries (see Maier 2010, p. 28). It also recorded the third worst budget deficit in the OECD between 1973 and 1976, behind only Italy and Belgium (Green 1993, p. 30). The 1976 loan from the International Monetary Fund (IMF) seemed the most evident sign of the inexorable decline of Great Britain.

Hence, despite remaining a deviant case, the rise of the nationalism of the rich in Scotland did share two similarities with the other cases, notably: a reversal of economic conditions with regard to the rest of the country, although suddenly brought about by the discovery of natural resources rather than by processes of endogenous growth; and a context of prolonged government mismanagement and public policy failure, especially in putting an end to balance of payment deficits in the late 1960s and early 1970s.

The welfare state and the end of the Glorious Thirties

In Chapter 1, I have argued that, apart from some embryonic appearances in the rhetoric of Catalan and Basque nationalism at the beginning of the twentieth century, the nationalism of the rich represents a recent phenomenon in the history of nationalism. However, I did not answer the question why this is so. There is no single factor accounting for the formation of the nationalism of the rich, but rather a complex mix of processes and events. Nevertheless, in a longer historical perspective, the post-Second World War years did mark a fundamental change in the normative, economic and social structure of Western European societies. This novelty lies in the rise of two linked phenomena: the establishment of comprehensive welfare systems based on an idea of national solidarity and providing unprecedented levels of insurance and redistribution; and the increasing acceptance of state intervention into the economy as a consequence of the rise of Keynesian economics to the status of dominant economic orthodoxy.

The welfare state was not invented ex nihilo in the years following the end of the conflict. Yet, the change obtained in the 25 years between 1945 and 1970 was radical both in quantitative and qualitative terms. The index of social insurance elaborated by Flora and Jens (1981, p. 54) clearly shows that this period, and especially the decade 1950–60, recorded a major and general expansion never encountered before. Contrary to the interwar years, wherein considerable divergence among countries was evidenced, the post-1945 period stands out for the remarkable display of convergence between them. European countries progressively moved away from the selectivity and differentiation that had characterised the various piecemeal legislations enacted since the last two decades of the nineteenth century towards a system based increasingly on a principle of universalism and equality. The transition was not smooth, but, at least up to the mid-1970s, the tendency was towards expansion (Fraser 1986, pp. 207–239, Hassenteufel 1996, Ferrera 2005, pp. 104–105). Furthermore, the welfare states established after 1945 differed from the previous 'experimentations' because, however audacious these latter had been, they were always defended as 'dispensations' from the 'orthodox' law of healthy economics that prescribed a limited role for the state. In the post-War period this scepticism progressively gave way to a reality in which 'that the national government should and could act was taken for granted' (Heclo 1981, p. 390).

Such interventionism was not limited to social policy but extended to the realm of macroeconomic management for the fulfilment of full employment. These two elements made up the pillars of the post-War socio-economic order. The triumph of Keynesian economics was in large part responsible for this change. The great innovation of Keynesianism lay in showing that, in time of crisis, the state could run budget deficits to stimulate demand, instead of contributing to deflation by balancing its budget as standard theories suggested. It thus provided a stabilisation of the economic cycle that promised steady growth. It also offered a series of tools that were supposed to enable governments to run an economy at full employment and redistribute wealth to unprecedented levels. The 'Keynesian revolution' broke out in the 1950s, although its diffusion was uneven both chronologically and with regard to its concrete applications (Bispham and Boltho 1982, pp. 289–292). It was based on the social consensus reached across Western Europe, and forcefully promoted by US administrations, around the 'politics of productivity', that is, the transformation of political and class conflict into a commitment to growth and efficiency (Maier 1977). As a result, political legitimacy has come to hinge fundamentally on governments' performance in managing the economy and ensuring growth (Postan 1967, p. 25). Although the capacity of politics to govern the economic cycle has been put into question since the end of the 1970s, the primacy acquired by economics in setting the ground on which to evaluate the action of elected executives has not disappeared (see Poggi 1990, p. 140).

The new responsibility of the state in ensuring growth and redistribution is a fundamental premise of the nationalism of the rich that goes a long way to explaining its virtual absence in previous decades. This new role created expectations that probably went beyond the actual capabilities of policy-makers (Mau 2003, pp. 8–11) and, in the presence of uneven development and cultural segmentation, it laid the ground for a crystallisation of fiscal protest around national lines. Yet, the nationalism of the rich began to emerge more than 20 years after the establishment of the welfare state and the 'Keynesian revolution'. This is because the 25–30 years following the end of the Second World War represented a period of enormous economic success. The Glorious Thirties displayed an unprecedented level of prosperity spreading across Western Europe. During this period, the welfare state was a fundamental and very successful nation-building tool, which aimed at keeping at bay both the risk of a slide back to fascist or radical socialist change and the disintegration of countries along social, national and ethnic lines (Esping-Andersen 2004, p. 27). Nevertheless, in many respects, those economic conditions were extraordinary and such exceptionality entailed that social policy expansion was virtually costless in political terms (Bispham and Boltho 1982, p. 298, Mishra 1984, p. 4). An example is given by the diversionary strategies that informed regional policy during the 1950s and 1960s. In a context in which western countries were able to ensure full employment, regional policy was seen as a method to guarantee jobs in deprived areas, thus boosting state legitimacy where dissent was more likely to develop, while at the same time relieving congestion in fast-growing areas. It was a win-win situation (Keating 1998, pp. 47–50) nourishing the 'welfare consensus' that prevailed over Western Europe for about three decades based on the 'mutual stimulation of economic growth and peaceful class relations' (Offe 1984, p. 194). In the 1970s, the growth machine stopped and welfare suddenly became a costly enterprise (Ferrera 2005, pp. 107–111, Rosanvallon, 2015 [1981], p. 55). Improvements in social coverage could no longer be paid out of revenues automatically increasing with growth, but rather through higher taxes. Inefficiencies within specific welfare systems became clearer than before (Heclo 1981, pp. 397–400).

All this has led to a higher stress on the conditionality of welfare arrangements in line with the principles of fairness and reciprocity informing them (Hemerijck 2013, p. 30). Yet, at the same time, many studies on the crisis of the welfare state have shown that despite complaining about its costs, voters have consistently supported the maintenance of the welfare state and often opposed welfare cuts (Pierson 1996, Van Oorschot 2000, p. 34, Mau 2003, p. 15). As Western European countries entered the age of 'permanent austerity' (Pierson 2001a), they started facing a dilemma largely unknown in the immediate post-Second World War decades: that between social solidarity and economic efficiency.[1] As argued by Ramesh Mishra in the early 1980s:

> the Keynes-Beveridge package of welfare implied that state policies would sustain both economic well-being (full employment and economic growth) and social welfare. With the eclipse of Keynesianism, the social has been cut loose from the economic and the two seem to be drifting apart. Increasingly, social expenditure and social welfare more generally are seen as having adverse consequences on the economy.
> (Mishra 1984, p. 19; see also Esping-Andersen 1982, p. 49, Rosanvallon 2015 [1981], p. 55)

Whether the crisis of welfare is due to in-built contradictions of the welfare state or to other factors is beyond the scope of this book. What must be stressed here is that social rights are different from civil and political rights in that they rely on considerable amounts of material resources that must be extracted from society. In this context, 'the matching of rights (entitlements) and duties (obligations to pay taxes and contributions) must be particularly accurate and stringent if fiscal bankruptcy is to be avoided' (Ferrera 2005, p. 47) and especially so in an age of slow growth and high unemployment that contributes to framing distributional problems as zero-sum games (Thurow 1980, pp. 3–25).

Since the mid-1970s, therefore, most advanced economies have confronted the thorny dilemma between the continuing popularity of – and even increased demand for – welfare among their public opinions and the challenge of ensuring its fiscal sustainability in the long term. All this has led to different political and ideological reactions, generally characterised by a need to increase the conditionality of welfare arrangements. Conditionality, and even retrenchment, was eagerly embraced by the neoliberal revolution that came to prominence with the governments of Margaret Thatcher and Ronald Reagan in the late 1970s and early 1980s. A left-wing version of a more conditional, although still inclusive, welfare state arose in the 1990s with the so-called social investment paradigm championed by the New Left, which emphasised empowerment and retraining over individual responsibility and moral hazard (Hemerijck 2013, pp. 36–39). The socio-tropic arguments of economic victimisation examined in the previous chapters can be seen as another alternative, although certainly a less sophisticated one, since the more or less explicit cultural-determinist argument concerning the economic success of the relevant community has allowed my case-study parties to criticise redistribution within the parent state without rejecting the welfare state altogether. This nationalist interpretation of fiscal protest has allowed even left-wing parties like the ERC to adopt such an anti-statist stand. Furthermore, the representation of the nation as endowed with an exceptional hard-work ethos and abundant excess financial resources embodied by the transfers has enabled the party to present independence as a way out of the dilemma between solidarity and efficiency. In a way, the transfers and the cultural-determinist argument hold the promise of reproducing the exceptional conditions of the Glorious Thirties in an independent country.

The role of national identity

In the Introduction, I have presented the distinction between nationalism as a form of politics and nationalism as a form of consciousness. I have also suggested that these two interpretations of the concept are not in contradiction but feed each other: it is the psychological process whereby people recognise themselves as being part of a specific community of sovereign equals, different from members of other communities, that provides a 'way of seeing the world' (Brubaker *et al.* 2004, p. 47) whereby individual choices and interests are mediated – although to different extents for different people and in different situations – through a specific set of values and interests that are deemed to be proper to the nation; this 'way of seeing the world' is exploited and constructed at the same time by specific actors, among whom political parties play a momentous role. Despite arguably maintaining some basic common features, national identities are protean realities, constantly reshaped by their holders as well as by external agents and events. All this makes it problematic to clearly establish national identity as a dependent or an independent variable. Most empirical studies of individual attitudes treat national identity as an explanatory factor and this because it is believed to be formed through processes of socialisation occurring early in the life-cycle and to remain quite stable (see Pinard and Hamilton 1986, Blais and Nadeau 1992, Howe 1998, Munoz and Tormos 2012). This is probably a correct assumption in individual analyses at specific points in time. It holds rather less when one deals with social groups in a longer historical perspective. Hence, one needs to carefully consider the ambivalent nature of national identity, especially in contexts of dual identity and in which two or more nation-building projects compete within the same social body.

Four of my five case-study parties – ERC, the N-VA, the SNP and the VB – did not construct a national self-understanding from scratch, but rather built upon pre-existing ones endowed with a large and consolidated set of myths, histories and cultural elements. Three of them – ERC, the N-VA and the VB – also took advantage of linguistic differentiation. All provided a reinterpretation of part of this cultural baggage, and more specifically denied the possibility, in the long term, of a partnership with the other people(s) inhabiting the parent state. One of them – the LN – tried to craft a new national identity building upon an entrenched, but vague, sense of cultural distinctness between territories of the parent state. Processes of nation-formation are usually long and uneven, therefore it is probably too soon to definitively say whether a Northern Italian nation will ever stem from this process. For the time being, the results are ambivalent.

Figure 7.1, 7.2 and 7.3 chart the evolution of subjective national identity in Catalonia, Flanders and Scotland. Stateless national identity (i.e. predominantly Catalan/Flemish/Scottish) is markedly stronger in Scotland than in Catalonia and Flanders. In the first, it has ranged between 53 per cent and 69 per cent of the local population, against 21–47 per cent in Catalonia and 27–36 per cent in Flanders during the period under study. As a consequence, dual and state national identity are stronger in these two and weaker in Scotland, although, state national identities seem to have been recently converging around similar levels in Catalonia and Scotland. On average, dual identities have prevailed in Catalonia and Flanders (42 per cent and 44 per cent respectively), while predominantly stateless national identity has prevailed in Scotland (61 per cent). In Catalonia and Flanders there has been a strengthening of the predominantly Catalan and Flemish identities to the disadvantage of

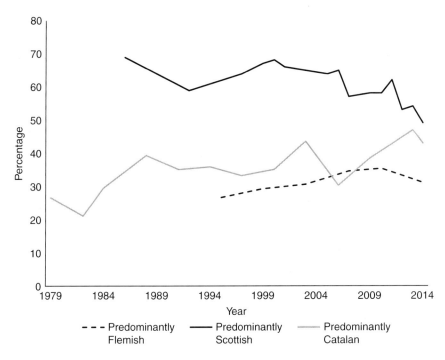

Figure 7.1 Predominantly stateless national identity in Catalonia, Flanders and Scotland, 1979–2014 (percentage of regional population).

Sources: my elaboration on ICPS 1991–2016, Bond and Rosie 2002, Argelaguet 2006, Moreno 2006, Swyngedouw *et al.* 2015, SSAS 2017d.

the predominantly Spanish one and the dual Belgian-Flemish one respectively. On the contrary, Scotland shows a clear weakening of the prevalently Scottish identity to the advantage of dual and predominantly British identity. Also, apart from the case of Catalonia, and there still very recently, there has not been any radicalisation around the extreme of uniquely stateless national identity.

Apart from the case of Catalonia, the data reported above does not go as far back in time as would be necessary to have a clear picture of its relevance at the time of formation of the nationalism of the rich. The historical literature surveyed in the relevant chapters however suggests that such identities were already well developed between the late 1960s and the early 1980s. Unfortunately, data on the evolution of the Northern Italian identity is fragmentary, but some studies reported by Biorcio (2010, pp. 40–41) would suggest that the League's nation-building effort has been in part rewarded, since the number of Northern Italians identifying with Northern Italy as their primary territorial identity has increased from 5.3 per cent in 1996 to 22.7 per cent in 2008. While this is remarkable, given

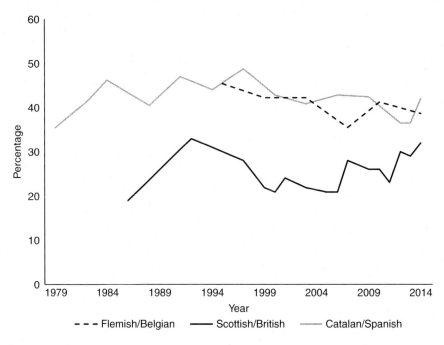

Figure 7.2 Dual national identity in Catalonia, Flanders and Scotland, 1979–2014 (percentage of regional population).

Sources: my elaboration on ICPS 1991–2016, Bond and Rosie 2002, Argelaguet 2006, Moreno 2006, Swyngedouw *et al.* 2015, SSAS 2017d.

the virtual inexistence of a Northern Italian identity until the early 1990s, it is not clear how consolidated such identity is and what its normative content is, especially in terms of self-government and self-determination claims.

Regardless of their relative strength, the existence – or construction in the Northern Italian case – of such stateless identities have made state legitimacy more problematic. Although dual identities are not necessarily troublesome for state legitimacy, 'where a people no longer identify with the political institutions governing them, the legitimacy of that system of government will be called into question' (McEwen and Moreno 2005, p. 6). This is especially the case for the solidarity undergirding welfare arrangements as confirmed by electoral research on welfare deservingness which highlights how 'identity' – most often coinciding with national identity – is the most important criterion used by European publics to identify the community of legitimate welfare recipients (Van Oorschot 2006, pp. 31–32). However, the opposite relationship can also obtain. Especially in their expansive phase, welfare states have been very successful nation-building

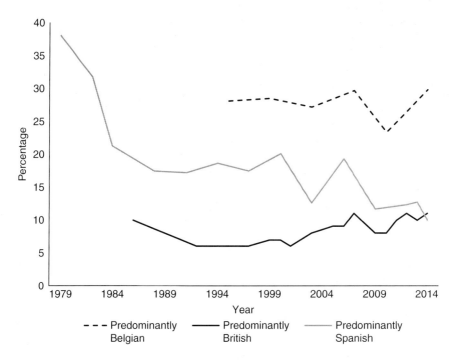

Figure 7.3 Predominantly state national identity in Catalonia, Flanders and Scotland, 1979–2014 (percentage of regional population).

Sources: my elaboration on ICPS 1991–2016, Bond and Rosie 2002, Argelaguet 2006, Moreno 2006, Swyngedouw *et al.* 2015, SSAS 2017d.

instruments that managed to bridge differences between national and ethnic communities and effect internal bonding by means of external bounding (Ferrera 2005, pp. 1–11, Bommes 2012).

The British welfare state in the 1950s and early 1960s did provide the population of Scotland with an unprecedented level of wellbeing and arguably replaced empire as the main rationale for the Union. Also, as argued by Finlay (2005), the British identity still had strong currency in Scotland in the 1970s, when the SNP's first breakthrough occurred, mainly on account of the achievements of the post-war welfare state. This is probably less the case in Belgium because Belgian welfare was almost totally managed by societal segments – Catholic, socialist and liberal – dominating Belgian society at the time (Deschouwer 2012, pp. 204–213). Therefore, the role of the state as the provider of benefits and services was hidden behind intermediate groups. Yet, although Belgium has become a highly decentralised federation, social security has remained a federal competence and is often considered as one of the last remaining pillars of state legitimacy (Dandoy and Baudewyns 2005).

The literature on Italian nation-building tends to stress the failure of such a process through the entire history of the country (Lanaro 1988, Graziano 2010, Cammarano 2011). Yet, the economic boom of the post-war period and the distribution of prosperity afforded by the welfare institutions established between 1962 and 1978 laid the ground for an unprecedented homogenisation of Italian society, both culturally, through the creation of a wider public for standardised products, and socially, by favouring the creation of a broad middle-class (Ferrera 1986, Lanaro 1988, p. 234, De Luna 1994, p. 42). At the same time, the Italian welfare was potently influenced by 'familist' practices to the disadvantage of universal protection that undermined the long-term stability of the system and consolidated North-South differences thus setting the ground, to some extent, for the later rise of the 'Northern Question' (Fargion 2005, Ferrera *et al.* 2012).

Spain is a peculiar case in this respect because the creation of the welfare state was delayed until the end of the dictatorship and coincided with the decentralisation of the country (Gallego *et al.* 2005). Decentralisation, and with it its welfare dimension, was thought of as a nation-building tool (Moreno and Arriba 1999, Martínez-Herrera 2002, Guibernau 2006) that was largely successful, as in less than two decades normalisation led the country to close the gap with the EU average in terms of social protection spending, playing a major role in ensuring a smooth transition to democracy and strengthening rather than weakening state legitimacy (Ferrera 1993, p. 28). The success of the democratic transition, the general stability of Spanish politics up to the mid-2000s and data on the reinforcement of dual identity until the late 1990s, would confirm this, although other dynamics, seen in Chapter 2, set in later.

Thus, with the exception of Northern Italy, at the time of formation of the nationalism of the rich in the regions analysed there were distinct state and stateless national identities. However, a substantial part of the population declared itself as having dual identities and accommodating stances, based on ideas of partnership and of negotiating forms of autonomy short of independence, were prevalent and remained such long thereafter. Yet, these distinct self-understandings still offered a frame that could be used to interpret regional fiscal imbalances in national terms. They thus opened a space for contestation within the sub-state national community that has been exploited for mobilisation purposes by 'ethnic entrepreneurs'. More generally, and in line with theoretical insights seen in the introduction and Chapter 6, one can conclude that in a context of dual or contested identity, issues of interpersonal redistribution can be framed as inter-territorial conflicts leading to calls for 'social closure', with regard to welfare arrangements, around the minority national community. If sub-state national cleavages coincide with economic imbalances such calls can be reinforced by cultural-determinist explanations of socio-economic development warranting the rejection of solidarity on widely accepted deservingness criteria of control, attitude and reciprocity embodying principles of meritocracy, trust and fairness.

The political marginalisation of the advanced periphery

Political marginalisation has assumed different forms in the five case-study parties and it is difficult to find a common pattern. Yet, we can see some symmetry between the arguments of ERC and the SNP, on the one hand, and those of the VB and N-VA, on the other, with the LN lying somewhere in between. This distinction mainly coincides with differences in the socio-political contexts in which these claims were developed. ERC's and the SNP's discourses represent pretty standard cases of minority nationalism in which the stateless community can trace its origins back to a history of independent statehood and conceives of itself as a constituent nation of a multinational state whose composition is made problematic by the presence of a titular nation enjoying a disproportional demographic and political weight – i.e. England in the UK and Castile in Spain. Yet, while Scotland has enjoyed a degree of formal recognition within the UK since the foundation of the latter in 1707, this was not the case for most of Catalan history since the abolition of the Principality's autonomy in 1714. On the contrary, the two twentieth-century dictatorships, along with older histories of defeat and repression, provided a wide reservoir of grievances for nationalist parties. Accordingly, in Scotland in the 1960s and 1970s, political marginalisation was mostly defined in terms of 'provincialisation', whereby Scotland was deemed to receive less attention – especially in terms of economic needs – than what it deserved as an official constituent unit of the UK. ERC instead complained that Catalonia was not being given the recognition it deserved both in actual and formal terms, as the Constitution did not clearly define it as a nation. These different degrees of recognition also go a long way to explaining why Scotland's population voted unconvincingly for political autonomy in 1979, while Catalonia's overwhelmingly accepted it in 1978. While the former did not necessarily need it and its population was more afraid of a separatist 'slippery slope', the latter was offered an opportunity to satisfy a demand opposed for many decades. Later, the compromise struck by the Spanish Constitution worked reasonably well for about 25 years, whereas the 1980s exacerbated the cause of Scottish political marginalisation through Thatcher's strictly unitarist interpretation of the British state. In both cases, it is important to note that political marginalisation has not been linked to the nation's representation in state parliaments. It has therefore been a demand for a special status rather than for equal representation within the existing central institutions.

The VB and the N-VA, by contrast, have operated in a very peculiar context, whereby a demographic and political majority has lamented the marginalisation caused by the constitutional guarantees granted to the francophone minority. Despite the virtual absence of a history of independent statehood, this argument could be potently fed by a history of linguistic discrimination within the Belgian state that led some observers to define the Flemings, certainly until the interwar years and arguably up to the 1960s, as a 'sociological minority' (Van Velthoven 1987, Devos and Bouteca 2008). This condition had progressively disappeared by the late 1970s, when the nationalism of the rich was formulated, but the ideological baggage inherited from the years of Flander's socio-economic subordination could be adapted to the new circumstances (Boehme 2008a, p. 558), whereby Belgian francophones have been granted constitutional guarantees that in some instances frustrate the majoritarian ambitions of Flemish parties.

The programme of the LN developed in a context that lies somewhere in between the Catalan and Scottish scenarios, on the one hand, and the Flemish one, on the other. The League has claimed the status of minority for the Padanian population (a point inherited from the previous regionalist leagues) and denounced the over-representation of southerners in the bureaucracy and the traditional political parties. Nevertheless, when taking into account an extended definition of Northern Italy, its population accounts for almost half of the population of the state, thus making its situation closer to that of the two Flemish parties. The *Lega* has indeed accompanied its demands for autonomy and independence with declarations that it would 'restore' northern control over the Italian state. In other words, both in Flanders and Northern Italy the imposition of a more assertive Flemish/Northern Italian policy within state institutions has been a more feasible alternative (for simple demographic reasons) than in Catalonia and Scotland, although only the LN consistently tried to implement it through repeated participation in government at the central level (see Chapter 9 for more detail).

In all cases – although in Catalonia and Northern Italy to a lower extent than in Scotland and Flanders – the claims of political marginalisation have been reinforced by subsuming left-right ideological positions within the centre-periphery cleavage through a representation of the relevant nation as sharing a specific ideological profile opposed to that of the rest of the country – i.e. right Flanders vs. left Wallonia, social-democratic Scotland vs. conservative England. Nevertheless, while survey data does show some differences in socio-economic attitudes, these are often much smaller than what debates between centre and periphery in the countries analysed would suggest, and frequently coexist with similar or even bigger intra-regional imbalances. The inclusion of ideological elements in the definition of relevant stateless national identities, especially with reference to events or historical periods that had a special influence on this process, has facilitated party attempts to make ideological and national differences coincide. Scottish identity, for instance, has largely been redefined during the Thatcher years, as an opposition to the relevant Other of Conservative England. This means that, in the collective imaginary, being Scottish and being left-wing are deemed to overlap to a large extent (Brown *et al.* 1999, Paterson 2002). Similarly, Catalan identity was heavily influenced by the dictatorship, to such an extent that being right-wing is still associated with memories of the Francoist regime, as proven by the Socialists' domination of general elections (in Catalonia) throughout most of the democratic period and CiU's careful positioning around the political centre – rather than the Right (Dowling 2005, p. 111). On the contrary, in Flanders, the nationalist tradition has historically been associated with the Right. Moderate Flemish nationalism has evolved more towards the centre, but, overall, Flanders is still politically more oriented towards the Centre-Right and this because of long-term processes of socialisation of the Flemish masses in which the Church played a prevalent role (Erk 2005b). In Northern Italy the association is less direct because the Northern Italian identity has been less clearly defined and because right-wing parties, such as Go Italy, have been widely voted for in the South. Yet, the values of thrift and entrepreneurialism, the hard-work ethic and the anti-statist ethos clearly attributed by the League to the North have generally been associated in the country with a right-wing tradition. This has gone along with a higher tendency of the three core northern regions of Lombardy, Piedmont and Veneto to vote for right-wing parties in the last 25 years (Feltrin 2010, Roux 2008).

Note

1 See also O'Connor (1973, p. 6). The question here is not so much whether such a dilemma is objectively true, but rather that, since the mid-1970s, it has been perceived as such by a broad spectrum of actors, both on the Left and on the Right, within advanced capitalist societies (Offe 1984, pp. 193–202).

8 The impact of globalisation and European integration

In the case studies the international processes of globalisation and European integration have often figured in the background without having been treated properly. The aim of this chapter is precisely to take a step back from the domestic context and focus on such larger phenomena to try to gauge what contribution they have made to the dynamics studied in the previous chapters.

The three-fold influence of globalisation

Globalisation can be defined as 'the intensification of world-wide social relations which link distant localities in such a way that local happenings are shaped by events occurring many miles away and vice versa' (Giddens 1994, p. 64). Yet, a stricter formulation centred on the economic dimension is often preferred in social sciences – arguably because it is easier to measure. Hence, economic globalisation can be formulated as 'the international integration of markets, goods, services, labour and capital' (Cameron *et al.* 2006, p. 1). In practical terms, this is often quantified as the sum of a country's imports and exports on GDP, or trade openness. Globalisation among advanced economies is clear when looking at the evolution of the average ratio of imports and exports of goods on GDP of 19 OECD countries, which went from 36.4 per cent in 1970 to 61.2 per cent in 2000.

It is almost commonplace to assert that the process of economic globalisation has weakened the power of the nation-state. Some scholars, such as Ohmae (1995), have even proclaimed the end of the nation-state as a meaningful economic unit in today's global economy, while Held (1988, p. 12) has argued that 'any conception of sovereignty which interprets it as an illimitable and indivisible form of public power is undermined'. Others, following Mann (1999, p. 267), have however downplayed the significance of the nation-state's loss of sovereignty by pointing out that its former power had largely been exaggerated. While an in-depth assessment of this debate is beyond the scope of this section, what is undeniable is that, since the 1970s, states, or at least advanced economies, have progressively opened their borders to foreign goods and services and have become more dependent on footloose global capital (Green 1993). The liberalisation of financial markets,[1] in particular, has had an extraordinary impact on state legitimacy. On the one hand, international capital mobility represented a boon for western governments, which could raise money to a level unprecedented before. On the other, as Yergin and Stanislaw have made clear, 'while the publics vote only every few years, the markets vote every minute', hence governments 'must increasingly heed the market's vote – as harsh as it sometimes can be' (Yergin and Stanislaw 1998, p. 371).

As the last quarter of the twentieth century has seen a rise of separatist movements and, at the same time, a clear expansion of economic globalisation, researchers have explored whether the two phenomena are correlated. The overall answer is that globalisation does not cause secession and, generally speaking, it even seems to quell it rather than fuel it. Analysing a wide sample of 116 countries, Zinn (2006, p. 271) claimed that open economies were less likely to develop political separatism than closed ones and concluded that 'this finding challenges the popular view that globalisation amplifies the intensity of subnational threats to state sovereignty and suggests that the increasing level of trade between countries is actually curbing parallel increases in the number of active self-determination movements'. Although agreeing with Zinn that globalisation per se does not cause secession, some authors have however argued that, in specific conditions where separatist parties and conflict already exist, trade openness can in fact have an inflammatory effect. The correlation between the two phenomena would be stronger in cases of inter-regional income inequality. As Sambanis and Milanovic (2011, p. 225) have pointed out 'self-determination is typically demanded when the economic benefits of membership in the predecessor state are low relative to the economic and political gains of independence', although this is likely to happen as 'an indirect result of globalization in countries with already active conflicts over self-determination' (see also Sorens 2004). Hence, globalisation does not seem to be a primary cause of secessionism, but it does seem to be relevant for the nationalism of the rich, since its impact would be most powerful among rich regions of countries affected by substantial inter-regional inequality, characterised by ethno-cultural difference and with active separatist parties.

The consequences of globalisation on the formation and development of the nationalism of the rich can be reduced to the following three elements: first, by intensifying international competition and providing more leverage to highly mobile capital as compared to less mobile labour, globalisation is deemed to have reduced the fiscal and monetary leverage of governments, as well as to have put under stress welfare expenses with negative consequences for national solidarity; second, trade liberalisation is said to have reduced the 'optimal' size of countries thus creating a more enabling environment for secession; third, coinciding with the transformation from

Fordism to post-Fordism and contributing to increasing inter-regional disparity, globalisation – it is argued – has promoted the development of
regional economies.

The idea that globalisation is correlated with welfare rollback might
only be the result of the fact that the sudden acknowledgement of 'interdependence' occurred during the watershed decade of the 1970s and was
immediately followed by the rise of neoliberal ideology preaching budget
austerity and monetary stability as the solution to the crisis of macroeconomic management that occurred in those years (Rhodes 1995, p. 6).
In other words, globalisation, the crisis of the welfare state and the spread
of neoliberal ideas might only be parallel trends. Nevertheless, the correlation seems to go deeper, although one should refrain from simple conclusions about the incompatibility of trade openness and generous welfare
systems. Heightened capital mobility – both in the form of portfolio and
foreign direct investments – along with the reduction of transport costs
and the rise of industrial capacity in the Third World, seems to have exercised strong competitive pressures on state budgets. The tension between
the logic of capital, seeking the most profitable locations, and that of
spatially-bound labour, trying to attract capital, has favoured attempts to
cut state spending and welfare provisions in order to make national economies more business-friendly (Keating 1998, p. 73, Esping-Andersen
2004). In practice, these attempts have been made difficult by slowing
growth rates, increasing unemployment, an aging population and strong
popular support for welfare arrangements, but a significant shift from progressively improving benefits and coverage to minimising the natural
expansion of existing commitments seem to have occurred in many countries (Cerny 1995, p. 612). Recent empirical studies have confirmed similar
trends, but also nuanced their extent. For instance, Cameron and Kim
(2006) have calculated that increased openness has led to small increases,
rather than reductions, in state spending, with countries suffering from
substantial balance of payment deficits recording large increases in
expenses. Furthermore, opinion surveys on trade liberalisation and social
protection in advanced countries show that citizens seem to generally
support globalisation as a general phenomenon, but are extremely wary
about asymmetric consequences in terms of employment and real salaries,
with low-skilled individuals as the category showing the highest anxiety.
This suggests that the 'labour-market policies of governments have substantial influence on how individuals view the costs and benefits of trade
liberalization' (Scheve and Slaughter 2006, p. 82) and that social protection and redistribution are still necessary prerequisites of support for globalisation in open economies. This would be confirmed by the strategies
adopted by some European countries, especially in Northern Europe,
which instead of wildly cutting the welfare state have tried to sustain substantial social protection with increases in labour productivity. Hence,
although there is evidence that globalisation has had an impact on

governments' macroeconomic and financial latitude, it should not be considered uncritically as a reason for the 'crisis of welfare' that began in the 1970s nor should we conclude that governments have been left with no leverage whatsoever (Garrett and Lange 1991). One also needs to question whether the path undertaken during the so-called Glorious Thirties would have been sustainable even in the absence of a transition to higher interdependence. Yergin and Stanislaw (1998, pp. 298–321), for instance, clearly attribute the welfare crisis to economic unsustainability, the end of the 'socialist spell' and the rise of neoliberalism, rather than to globalisation as such. Similarly, Pierson (2001b, pp. 98–99) emphatically downplays the role of globalisation when weighed against endogenous factors:

> the fundamental symptoms of declining governmental capacity and mounting budgetary stress would clearly be with us even in the absence of trends associated with globalization. This is not to suggest that increasing economic integration is unimportant, or to dismiss the linkages between international and domestic developments. Such links, however, are likely to be more modest, complex, and bi-directional than is commonly suggested. At the same time, we need to pay more attention than has recently been the case to profound social transformations that are essentially domestic in character. Societies are becoming more service-based, with a consequential decline in productivity growth. Social programmes have grown to maturity. Populations are getting older. Household structures are changing dramatically. These trends, loosely lumped under the label of post-industrialism, explain most of the strain facing the welfare states of affluent societies.

More importantly, a myth that should be debunked, and which is very relevant to our analysis, is that, in an age of ever-greater interdependence, the role of governments is growing increasingly superfluous. In fact, the opposite seems to be true. As capital is more mobile and competition higher, the performance of state institutions in delivering public goods in the most efficient way has become more salient than ever (Keating 1998, p. 74). This also stems from the rising importance of technological development and human skills, which are highly reliant on public goods, such as education and R&D, in driving growth (Porter 1990, p. 19). Yet, in this connection, the role of the nation-state has certainly changed, since 'the task is not to explain why a firm operating exclusively in the nation is internationally successful, but why the nation is a more or less desirable home base for competing in an industry' (Porter 1990, p. 69).

Another element that has put into question state legitimacy, especially in contexts of national heterogeneity, is that progressive market integration has reduced the large-scale advantages of political unity. In a paper – that has also been quoted by most of the parties analysed – Alesina and Spolaore (1997, p. 1041) have argued that 'the efficient and the stable number of countries are increasing in the amount of international economic integration' or, in other words, 'the benefits of large countries are less important if small countries can freely trade with each other'. In their model, the optimal size and number of nations are the result of a trade-off between the benefits of large-scale political jurisdictions and heterogeneity costs, in terms of citizens' public policy preferences. The former are mainly represented by a lower per capita cost of public goods, larger markets, better insurance against risk and security, while the latter boil down to the assumption that a bigger population will have a wider range of public policy preferences, thus making it harder for the government to satisfy them. As globalisation and, in the European context, common market integration provide small states with ever-easier access to wider consumer bodies, the benefits for state-less nations of remaining within their parent state would automatically shrink. While Alesina and Spolaore do not discuss them in-depth, the security advantages provided by EU and North Atlantic Treaty Organization (NATO) membership, along with the end of the Cold War, also seem to have contributed to present independence as a more advantageous goal than in previous decades (Meadwell 1999, p. 267).

These arguments are especially interesting in light of the evolution of territorial states and the role of war analysed in Chapter 1, but also when looking at nineteenth century debates about 'the correct size of nations'. Theorists such as Mazzini and Mill postulated that there was a minimum 'threshold' that states had to cross in order to call for self-determination (Hobsbawm 1990, pp. 14–47). Yet, in their paper, Alesina and Spolaore did not discuss the risk-sharing insurance element of the equation. Empirical studies conducted by Garrett and Rodden (2006) have questioned the conclusions reached by the two authors above, precisely on account of this function of larger political units. By analysing the degree of fiscal decentralisation of a wide sample of both developed and developing countries, they found that globalisation in the 1980s and 1990s correlated with increasing fiscal centralisation. The explanation lies in the instability brought about by trade liberalisation. As it is impossible to predict *ex ante* what sectors or regions will be hit by a shock, these will have an interest in sharing in a wider union providing better insurance, and such a dynamic would be exacerbated by the fact that increased competition promotes specialisation, thus making regions more vulnerable to exogenous factors. This is an argument that has featured highly in the debate over Scottish independence in the run-up to the 2014 referendum, with the Better Together campaign claiming that Scotland would be hit harder by a new financial crisis or a fall in oil prices as an independent country than as a part of the United Kingdom. Such criticism is probably less relevant to the other regions under study, where the economic imbalance with the centre is wider and less reliant on natural resources than Scotland's, but it is still an important caveat to be taken into account when assessing the impact of economic globalisation.

The final influence of globalisation on the nationalism of the rich lies in the development of so-called 'regional economies'. The 1970s were not only the decade in which the effects of 'interdependence' began being perceived, but also heralded the transition from Fordist to post-Fordist modes of industrial production. As the latter take huge advantage of the new opportunities offered by trade liberalisation and technological innovations in transport and information but, at the same time, require a high degree of horizontal integration and proximity among related firms in a specific area, they have increased the salience of economic disparities within nation-states. The penetration of the global market into national economies has created new links between international regions going beyond national borders (Scott 2001, p. 34). Hence, at the beginning of the 1980s, the economics literature rediscovered regions as meaningful units of analysis and fundamental actors in the post-Fordist world. Studies on the industrial districts of the Third Italy, Toyota City and the Silicon Valley, emphasised the flexible and vertically disintegrated organisation of these growth centres, but, even more importantly, they focused on some fundamental immaterial assets holding together dispersed networks of firms and explaining their global success. The introduction of concepts such as 'untraded interdependencies' (Storper 1995), 'institutional thickness' (Amin and Thrift 1994), 'embeddedness' (Granovetter 1985) and, later, 'social capital' (Putnam 1993) signalled the return of culture, identity and social institutions within theoretical thinking about economic development. The new economic regionalism thus came to 'see the market and systems of production as socially constructed rather than the product of perfect competition and in permanent equilibrium' (Keating *et al.* 2003, p. 14), while cultural norms and values came to be deemed to mediate interests and incentives of economic actors. Suddenly, regional cultures, which had until then been ignored at best and despised at worst, became a potential decisive asset to compete in the world economy. Although most studies focused on industrial districts or metropolitan areas that rarely coincided with political, cultural or institutional regions, the concept could be easily seized for nation-building purposes and to formulate the existence of stateless national interests at odds with that of other communities within the parent state. It could also be used to support cultural-determinist explanations about uneven development.

European integration: the opportunities of a new constitutional order

One could argue that the acceleration of the process of integration in a common European framework experienced by European countries since the early 1980s has run counter to Alesina and Spolaore's theoretical propositions about political disintegration going along with trade liberalisation. The authors, in fact, consider EU integration as only limited to its economic dimension. Although this is clearly an oversimplification required by theoretical parsimony, member states do remain the main gatekeeper of EU policy-making and the degree of economic integration certainly dwarfs the political dimension of the European project. Hence, along similar lines Sandro Sideri (1997) has suggested that the parallel processes of political fragmentation at sub-state level and integration at supra-state one are strategies to counteract the negative effects of globalisation. What is interesting in these insights is the idea that trade liberalisation has not spread evenly, but has rather tended to cluster around regional blocs running at different speeds. Institutional architectures and agreements such as the EU Treaties and the North American Free Trade Agreement (NAFTA) have gone very far along the way of internal trade liberalisation within regions, while, at the same time, negotiating more moderate openings to the outside world. In this perspective, European integration is a by-product of globalisation and, as such, has contributed both to the questioning and the reinforcement of state sovereignty.

This last point touches upon an old debate in the historiography of European integration, which focuses on whether states have remained in control (Milward 1992, Moravscik 1999) of the process or whether the process has gone much beyond what was originally meant (Haas 1958, Mitrany 1965). A compromise of a sort has been found around the middle-option proposed by Liesbet Hooghe and Gary Marks (2001) in the concept of multilevel governance. As Hooghe (1995, p. 176) clarified: 'national arenas are not going to be rendered obsolete by transnational interest mobilisation', but, at the same time, 'state executives have lost their monopoly [and] decision-making competences are shared among actors'. This points to a first way in which European integration has favoured the nationalism of the rich, and challenges to state power from below more generally: it has added a new layer of authority above the state that has, at least rhetorically, undermined its latitude and legitimacy.

One dimension of European policy that has had a direct impact at the regional level has been the EU Regional Policy, which 'aims to strengthen economic, social and territorial cohesion by reducing differences in the level of development among regions and Member States' (Eurostat 2008, p. 7). Initiated in 1975 with the establishment of the European Regional Development Fund (ERDF), it then evolved into the EU Cohesion Policy in 1988, which set in place a system of wealth redistribution across the continent that has accounted, on average, for about a third of the total EU budget. By involving regions in partnerships concerning the implementation – and in some cases even the conceptualisation – of cohesion projects, it has 'empowered' European regions informally involving them in the process of European integration and decision-making.[2] The establishment of the Committee of the Regions, in 1993, further contributed to regional mobilisation by introducing a dedicated political arena for regional actors in Brussels.[3] The most active and entrepreneurial among them have seized the occasion to establish missions in the European capital and carry out extensive lobbying activities.

Regional policy has had a direct bearing on the regional contexts in which our case-study parties have operated. In Belgium, federalisation was directly fed by the deepening of European integration and notably, the transition from EU Regional to Cohesion policy, as Flemish parties took advantage of it to speed up state reform (De Rync 1996). In Scotland, an existing tradition of partnership between local government and private actors accelerated the adaptation of the administrative structure of the region, notably the Scottish Office, to the instruments of the EU Cohesion Policy. After the establishment of the Scottish Parliament, a true multilevel governance was realised, with regional actors dealing directly with European officials in devising and implementing projects, although regional policy priorities have still needed the Treasury's agreement because of the low fiscal responsibility of the Scottish Executive (Bache 2004). Catalonia has largely tried to increase its power and visibility through its presence in Brussels. According to Morata and Popartan (2008, pp. 91–92) 'accession [to the EU] created the opportunity to affirm national identities in the European arena, eluding as much as possible the central government' and 'to develop a direct bilateral relationship with the EU institutions'. Italian regions have been latecomers in the process of mobilisation at the EU level, but the most active ones have quickly caught up. This trend has gone along with an important shift to regional devolution and, although the EU Cohesion Policy has not been a primary cause of such change, it has certainly accelerated it. Until the reforms of the late 1990s, Italian regions did not enjoy substantial autonomy to develop any significant activity. Before 1996, they were even forbidden to establish official representations in Brussels (Grote 1996). Since 1996, however, things began to change and especially so after the 2001 constitutional reform that considerably improved their competences. Reactions have been very uneven though. While most southern regions have paid lip service to regional mobilisation at the community level, some northern and central regions – in particular, Lombardy, Veneto, Emilia-Romagna, Tuscany and the autonomous provinces of Trent and Bolzano – have been ahead of the others: first, establishing offices even before the ban was lifted; and, later, by specialising progressively more in lobbying and networking, rather than just carrying out the basic functions of information and logistical support (Fargion *et al.* 2006).

All that produced two main outcomes: these regions came to have a 'taste' of what independence could be, in the form of an informal 'regional foreign policy'; and nationalist parties started calling for more representation powers vis-à-vis the EU. The idea of a 'Europe of the Regions' was widely exploited by the parties analysed in the previous chapters as a way to push for constitutional change in the domestic context. Such aspect points to a deeper influence exercised by the process of European integration, one that goes beyond the direct influence of Cohesion Policy and the erosion of state power brought about by the creation of multilevel governance. This plays out along three different dimensions: first, a debate has been initiated about new forms of sovereignty questioning the notion of indivisible sovereignty and introducing concepts like 'shared' sovereignty and 'constitutional pluralism'; second, the active promotion of subsidiarity has favoured devolution; third, new opportunity structures have opened up to minority nationalist parties in the form of the single market, the monetary union and the common security policy, which have presented independence as a less costly option than in previous decades (Elias 2009, pp. 1–6). Furthermore, the indeterminacy of the European project, especially in the decade between the late 1980s and the late 1990s, seemed destined:

> to rectify the incongruence between the political and the national that had consigned Europe's historic nationalities to the peripheries of sovereign states for far too long. For these reasons, it has been argued, minority nationalist parties have redefined their nation-building projects in such a way that the achievement of national self-determination has become inextricably linked to the future development of the European polity.
>
> (Elias 2009, p. 6)

This promise has remained a dead letter, though, and stateless nationalist parties have grown progressively disenchanted with the idea of a Europe of the Regions (Greenwood 2011, pp. 174–176). The EU has not given birth to new territorial hierarchies in which the regions can play as autonomous actors. Albeit weakened, state governments remain the gatekeepers of EU policy-making (Keating 2004, Elias 2009, p. 145). This may have caused a radicalisation of separatist stances among the strongest regionalist and nationalist parties, since the issue of representation at the EU level has been left unaddressed, emphasising further the need to obtain statehood as a condition to have a say in EU policy-making. Even more importantly, the principle of state integrity has clearly prevailed over national self-determination in EU practice and in its set of normative principles. The debate over Scottish independence, in which the European Commission repeatedly asserted that the issue was a domestic matter falling outside of the Union's jurisdiction, bore witness to the primacy of territorial integrity. The Commission also pointed out that any new member arising from an eventual process of separation should apply for membership like any other candidate and even hinted that some members could veto the entry of a country arisen from a process of secession (Carrell 2012, Pickard and Dickie 2014). Hence, although the EU has certainly offered a new opportunity structure to stateless nationalist parties, domestic factors have remained preponderant compared to the impact of the process of European integration (Elias 2009, pp. 140–167). Furthermore, in the long run, the EU has also revealed itself to be able to constrain the struggle for self-determination.

Notes

1 See Ferguson (2010) for more detail on this.
2 This has not been so much due to the amount of money transferred, but rather to the emphasis put on, and the opportunity structure offered for, regional mobilisation. Most authors agree that constitutional regions – often among the wealthiest ones – were those that mobilised most. In this respect, the principles of additionality, partnership and subsidiarity informing Cohesion Policy did play an important role in creating new avenues for regional mobilisation and empowerment (Hooghe and Marks 1996, Bomberg and Peterson 1998, Marks *et al.* 2002).
3 Although the Committee's lack of powers and poor performance have largely disappointed regional actors, it contributed to spurring their mobilisation in the 1990s (Borras-Alomar *et al.* 1994).

9 Beyond discourse

Support for independence, the political opportunity structure and party strategies

The arguments of economic victimisation and political marginalisation discussed in the previous chapters have constituted the core of the nationalism of the rich analysed in this study. The socio-economic factors that have favoured the formulation of this discourse however are not sufficient to explain the success (or not) of such parties. This will be briefly shown with reference to the two main dimensions along which we can measure separatist success: trends in support for independence and the electoral results of separatist parties.

It has been recently claimed that separatism has been on the rise in Western Europe in the last two decades (Palacio 2012, Bardos 2013, Campanella 2014). A look at Figures 9.1 and 9.2 suggests that this depends on how we define separatism. If we consider separatism as support for independence as a constitutional option offered to citizens within a range of alternatives including re-centralisation, the maintenance of the status quo and further devolution of powers, separatism in the last two decades has remained pretty stable except for a marked increase in Catalonia since 2008.[1] If we stop the analysis in 2007, that is, before the beginning of the recent economic crisis, the stability mentioned above appears even stronger across the three regions studied. With an average value of 29 per cent between 1991 and 2014, support for independence has been highest in Scotland, followed by Catalonia at 21 per cent. Support for independence has instead been surprisingly low – 8 per cent on average – in Flanders. This should be weighed against the fact that the Flemings are a majority within Belgium. Thus, although there is the perception of a problem with francophone vetoes, the imposition of a more majoritarian style of politics at the federal level is an option available to Flemish political parties, but not to Scottish and Catalan ones. Finally, because of lack of data in consistent form over a sufficiently long time period, I have not included Northern Italy in the chart. Fragmentary information about support for independence there, however, would suggest that between 1996 and 2011, it has hovered around 18–23 per cent of the Northern Italian population, although it is not clear whether by independence people mean full separation or some kind of far-reaching devolution of powers (Diamanti 1996, D'Alimonte 2011).

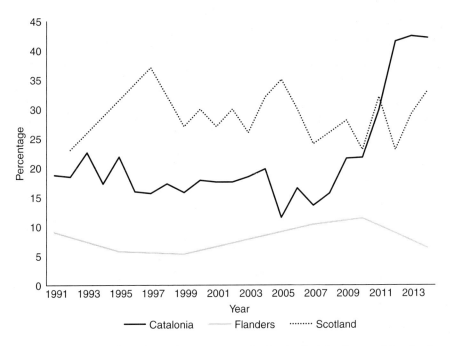

Figure 9.1 Support for independence compared, Catalonia, Flanders and Scotland, multiple constitutional options question, 1991–2014 (percentage of regional population).*

Sources: my elaboration on ICPS 1991–2016, McEwen 2002, p. 78, Swyngedouw and Rink 2008, Swyngedouw *et al.* 2015, SSAS 2017c.

Note

* For Flanders I have used data concerning position '0' along the 0–10 scale of the 'Flanders/ Belgium should decide everything' question until 2003 and regarding the independence option in the question on the constitutional future of the country between 2007 and 2014.

The perception of the evolution of separatism during about the same period is very different if we examine the electoral fortunes of the parties analysed in this study. Figure 9.2 suggests indeed a steady progression in Scotland, Catalonia and Flanders (when taking the VB and the N-VA together) along with stability in Northern Italy. The comparison between these two types of data indicates the need to clearly distinguish between support for independence and voting for separatist parties. Electoral studies confirm this conclusion. Public opinion researchers working on Flanders, have consistently shown that both the VB and the N-VA have won elections *despite* low support for independence (Swyngedouw 1992, Swyngedouw and Rink 2008, Swyngedouw and Abts 2011, Swyngedouw *et al.* 2014, 2015, p. 15). Contrary to Flanders, in Catalonia and Scotland, the pool of pro-independence voters has tended to be larger than the electoral constituency of separatist parties and voters have not automatically

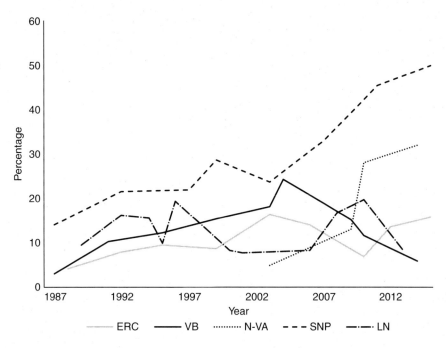

Figure 9.2 Electoral results of case-study parties compared, regional and general elections, 1987–2015 (percentage of regional vote).

Sources: my elaboration on Chamber of Representatives of Belgium 2003, 2014, Van Haute and Pilet 2006, Pauwels 2011, Beyens *et al.* 2015, *El Periodico* 2015, Audickas *et al.* 2016, Generalitat de Catalunya 2017, Ministero dell'Interno 2017.

identified with them. Data from ICPS (1991–2016), which however should be taken carefully because the samples are small,[2] suggest that, in the 1990s, 65 per cent of ERC's voters supported independence, a figure that shrank to 57 per cent in the following decade. At the same time, only 21 per cent and 31 per cent of total separatists sympathised with *Esquerra* in the 1990s and the 2010s respectively, while 33 per cent and 22 per cent sided with CiU instead (my calculations on ICPS 1991–2016). Similarly, during the 1990s, in Scotland, 'only' between 50 per cent and 75 per cent of SNP sympathisers supported independence. In the same period, 48 per cent of total independence supporters identified with the SNP and 42 per cent with Labour (McCrone and Paterson 2002, pp. 66–67). Labour even attracted more pro-independence voters than the SNP in 2001–06, although overall 40 per cent declared themselves closer to the SNP between 1999 and 2013 against 28 per cent who supported Labour (SSAS 2017e).[3] Hence, people supporting independence do not necessarily sympathise with separatist parties, which, at the same time, are able to attract voters who support other constitutional options. Similarly, the electoral fortunes of such parties do not necessarily depend on changes in support for independence and increases in grassroots support for this constitutional option does not automatically translate into a favourable electoral outcome for separatist parties. We thus need to look at these two phenomena separately.

Support for independence and the demand for regional autonomy

As suggested by the literature on support for independence in Quebec (Pinard and Hamilton 1986, Blais and Nadeau 1992, Howe 1998), the strength of subjective national identity and the perception of the economic consequences of independence are the two most important factors explaining support for independence. This has been confirmed by empirical studies in Catalonia and Scotland, although with some nuances in the latter. In 2013, 94 per cent of people who declared themselves as having an exclusively Catalan identity asserted that they would support independence in a hypothetical referendum (CEO 2005–14). Munoz and Tormos (2012) also found that, apart from national identity, the other variable that best correlated with support for independence was basing such support on instrumental economic considerations linked to Catalonia's fiscal deficit with the central administration. More interestingly, similarly to Howe's (1998) conclusion concerning support for sovereignty in Quebec, Munoz and Tormos were able to distinguish between two types of voters: those who would opt for independence in a hypothetical referendum even if the option of a Catalan state in a federal Spain were 'available' and those who preferred the federal alternative, if provided. While economic factors were quite irrelevant to the former, they were fundamental to the latter. In other words, there was a substantial body of 'conditional' supporters – at least 34 per cent of those supporting independence – for whom the belief in the equivalence between Catalan independence and better economic conditions was key in justifying their support for this constitutional option (see also Serrano 2013). This suggests that while grievances concerning the economic mistreatment of Catalonia were present much earlier than the recent rise of support for independence, the perception of the incentives associated with this constitutional option changed from 2008–09 onwards.

In Scotland, the perceived economic consequences of independence have been the most important variable influencing the Yes vote in the 2014 referendum. Already in 2012, 73 per cent of those who believed that the economy would become 'a lot better' after independence intended to vote Yes, along with 45 per cent of those who thought that it would become 'a little better'. In 2014, these percentages hit 88 per cent and 81 per cent respectively (Curtice 2013, 2014a). On the other hand, although important, national identity has been less decisive than in the Catalan case (see McCrone and Paterson 2002, pp. 73–75). In summer 2014, 'only' about 60 per cent of those identifying as 'Scots not British' said they would vote 'Yes' – as compared with 94 per cent in Catalonia as discussed above. Post-referendum results revealed that, by mid-September, the figure had increased to 88 per cent. Yet, this 28 per cent hike in the last weeks would still suggest that support for independence was not solely based on national identity. At least, it indicates that people made up their minds late in the process, which clashes with the idea of 'unconditional' support for independence (Curtice 2014a, 2014b).[4] Although figures on the determinants of support for independence in Flanders are fragmentary (while they are non-existent in Northern Italy), Swyngedouw *et al.* (2014) found a strong correlation, in 2010, between support for independence and a critical attitude towards inter-territorial transfers, thus confirming, at least partially, the importance of economic considerations.

Since, in the regions under study here, with the partial exception of Scotland, the economic prospects of independence may seem quite rosy, one might wonder why support for independence has been so low. Several explanations can account for this. First, dual identity has been prevalent in both Flanders and Catalonia. In Northern Italy, although there are signs of the appearance and reinforcement of a distinct Northern Italian identity, this is still far from being a consolidated reality. In Scotland, on the contrary, the predominantly Scottish identity has been consistently stronger than the dual (Scottish-British) one, but as mentioned above, it has had a less decisive impact over support for independence. Second, although by virtue of a simple economic cost-benefit analysis independence seems to be an appealing scenario, independence also is a risky option: it may lead to disruptions of trade flows and of economic relations, as well as to capital flights and higher interest rates, with ensuing effects on growth and employment. Third, secession might also threaten participation in the EU and forcing changes in the currency used, especially in the case of a unilateral secession. Furthermore, the very same economic primacy that, in theory, provides the inhabitants of these regions with a strong incentive to seek independence is also a powerful motivation for central governments of the parent state to oppose it. Hence, independence might be a less attractive option for relatively wealthy regions than it appears at first sight.

It is little wonder that, in all regions studied here, demand for more devolution of powers short of independence has generally been the preferred constitutional option of the local population. In Scotland, between 1992 and 2014, 54 per cent of the Scottish population on average supported devolution, as opposed to 29 per cent in favour of independence and 12 per cent of re-centralisation. Moreover, between 1999 and 2009, 64 per cent of residents on average have agreed that more powers should be devolved to the region (SSAS, 2017f). In Catalonia, between 1991 and 2014, an average 45 per cent of the region's residents have supported the status of autonomous community and 18 per cent have argued that Catalonia should become a state in a federal Spain, against 21 per cent calling for full independence. Also, between 2005 and 2013, 63.4 per cent on average declared that the autonomy enjoyed by the community was not sufficient (my calculations on ICPS 1991–2016 and CEO 2005–14). In Flanders, the situation has been more ambiguous, since the available statistics would suggest a demand for re-centralisation up to the late 1990s, followed by a trend in support for further autonomy to the regions and communities up to 2010 (Beyens *et al.* 2015, Swingedouw *et al.* 2014). By then, there was a clear majority of 52 per cent of the regional population calling for more devolution of powers and only a minority of 12 per cent demanding the split of the country, although calls for more autonomy were much lower in 2014 (Swyngedouw *et al.* 2014, 2015). In Northern Italy data about support for autonomy has been surprisingly scarce. However, in 2001, 71 per cent of inhabitants of the North thought that regions should administer all taxes and 86 per cent wanted regions to be given more autonomy (ITANES 2001). In 2011, 52.3 per cent of northern residents were in favour of a further federalisation of the country (D'Alimonte 2011).

Evidence from Catalonia would suggest that grassroots radicalisation would only occur in case of a major economic crisis. This conclusion is only partially true. Although it is reasonable to expect a higher salience of the inter-territorial transfers in the harsh conditions experienced by Catalonia since 2008–10, there is no straightforward reason why responsibility for the crisis should be attributed to the Spanish Government rather than to the EU or the financial markets, or even to the Catalan executive led by CiU. The reason why the protest has crystallised around the demand for self-determination is complex, but has much to do with the contemporaneous constitutional crisis, which began in 2005–06 and intensified in 2010. It also owes a lot to the framing activities of some civil society organisations that, borrowing heavily on ERC's discourse, have channelled protest into a demand for self-determination and presented independence as an option that would offer the region a more prosperous future. The strictly legalistic reaction of the Spanish state further reinforced such demands (Subirat and Vilaregut 2012).

This is also shown by similar events in Northern Italy and Scotland. In the former, although unemployment has been contained, the region was badly hit by the crisis, arguably much more so than Scotland and Flanders. At the end of 2011, Italy was on the verge of financial collapse, the technical government led by former EU Commissioner Mario Monti imposed harsh austerity measures and by December 2013 industrial production was only 76 per cent of its 2007 level (OECD 2017). Yet, this dramatic impact did not lead to a clear radicalisation around the North-South fracture. Although in 2011 the LN was on an upswing and seemed poised to launch another secessionist drive, the financial scandal that hit the party in 2012 plunged it into a year and a half of infighting from which it emerged only by fundamentally reformulating its propaganda. To save the party from virtual disappearance, the new leader, Matteo

Salvini, decided to sacrifice, at least temporarily, the northern profile to expand in areas beyond the North by channelling popular discontent primarily against the EU and immigration rather than against the South. Yet, a mobilisation along centre-periphery lines was not an unlikely scenario back in 2011–12, all the more so since a 2010 opinion poll showed around 60 per cent of the North's population expressing a favourable opinion about the region's independence (SWG 2010). Similarly, one would have expected a strong mobilisation for Scottish independence in the first half of the 1980s, when structural adjustment hit the region very hard and the Conservative government promoted harsh austerity measures that would later be remembered as distinctly 'un-Scottish'. Such an expectation is further warranted by the fact that, meanwhile, oil production reached its peak. Yet, until the later part of the decade, popular discontent was channelled in different directions. Politically, it mostly favoured the Liberal-Democrats. But, it also gave way to an unprecedented Scottish cultural renaissance, which, according to some, captured the energies of those who were disenchanted with the way in which mobilisation had ended in the 1970s (Finlay 2005, pp. 377–378). The troubles the SNP was going through during that decade certainly account for this outcome, but the 1979 referendum had also shown that the Scottish population was undecided about self-government and feared that it could lead to secession (Dardanelli 2005, Marr 1992, p. 163).

The electoral success of separatist parties: the political opportunity structure

As seen above, separatist parties can experience significant breakthroughs at specific elections, without any substantial change in popular support for independence. This has been the case with the VB and the N-VA throughout their histories, and with the SNP in most of the post-devolution period. Similarly, we can have situations in which support for independence increases, while the electoral results of separatist parties stagnate or even plunge, as it happened to ERC from 2008–11. The specific POS and the strategies deployed by separatist parties are useful tools to explain these outcomes.

The best formulation of the concept of POS was developed by Kriesi (2005) in the context of the study of social movements, as it is primarily relevant for the analysis of political challengers. Although they are not identical to social movements – defined as 'collective actors who are excluded or marginalized in the political order' and that organise 'new groups' or advance 'new political claims that have previously been ignored or excluded' (Jenkins 2005, p. 7) – my case-study parties share some of the traits associated with social movements, especially when considering the radical challenge of self-determination they present to the status quo. At the same time, these parties have always pursued their goals within representative institutions. Therefore, I will suggest some modifications to Kriesi's approach. Before discussing the POS in detail, it is important to stress that the aim of this section is not to provide a theory and empirical test of the reasons why separatist parties win elections, but rather to use existing theoretical and empirical insights to try to account for the electoral fortunes of my case-study parties.

According to Kriesi (2005, p. 83), the political opportunity structure available to a specific challenger at any given time can be defined as encompassing three main properties of a political system: 'its formal institutional structure, its informal procedures and prevailing strategies with regard to challengers, and the configuration of power relevant for the confrontation with the challengers'. The first dimension identified by Kriesi – the formal institutional structure – mainly refers to the 'points of access' available to challengers in a political system, of which the most important are the electoral system and the degree of state decentralisation.[5] With regard to the former, proportional systems tend to provide easier access to political challengers because they increase the chances that minor parties get seats and therefore encourage voters to cast a ballot for them (Meguid 2008, p. 7). At the same time, parties enjoying territorially concentrated support, as some sub-state nationalist parties, can profit from plurality systems as well (Sartori 1986, p. 59). My sample of case studies is evenly divided between proportional systems characterised by high fragmentation (Belgium and Italy) and regimes with majoritarian tendencies (the UK and, to a lesser extent, Spain).

Despite having a proportional electoral law since the end of the nineteenth century, Belgium was a two-and-half party system until the 1960s, when linguistic territorialisation led to the division of national parties along linguistic lines and, hence, to higher fragmentation. Proportionality and fragmentation were two outstanding features of the Italian system as well (Boogards 2005, Delwit 2009, pp. 327–332,). In both cases, proportionality allowed the parties to gain seats during their embryonic phases throughout the 1980s: the VB managed to hold seats in the low chamber when it polled below 2 per cent of the Belgian vote, the *Liga Veneta* and *Lega Lombarda* – predecessors of the LN – obtained representation in the Senate and the Chamber of Deputies despite obtaining less than 1 per cent. But, proportionality arguably played an even more important role at the time of breakthrough (in 1991 for the VB, in 1992 for the LN), as these parties could immediately transform their newly acquired electoral power into blackmail or coalition potential (the difference between share of votes and share of seats was 1 per cent and 0 per cent respectively) (my calculations on Deschouwer 2012 and Ministero dell'Interno 2017). The 5 per cent threshold at the district level introduced in Belgium in 2003 did not substantially affect the electoral performance of the VB, while the newborn N-VA did risk remaining out of the Chamber of Representatives and eventually did not make it into the Senate because of it. This influenced its decision to seek an electoral pact with the Flemish Christian Democrats for the 2004 regional and 2007 federal elections (Deschouwer 2012, pp. 120), but this institutional constraint to find allies did not penalise the N-VA in the long term (see below). In 1993, Italy adopted a more majoritarian system entailing a 4 per cent threshold to access the lower chamber, which promoted a bipolar electoral dynamic and urged the League to look for allies (except for the 1996 election). This need to compromise with other forces did penalise the LN, because it contrasted with its anti-establishment ethos. The Italian electoral law was reformed back to a more proportional formula in 2005, but the change did not have any substantial technical impact on the League's fortunes (Renwick *et al.* 2009, Passarelli and Tuorto 2012, chapter 1).

The difference with the extremely majority system in which the SNP has acted could not be starker. While the British first-past-the-post electoral system prized concentration, for most of its history, SNP's support has tended to spread out (Mitchell 2009, see also Curtice 2009). In 1970, for instance, at the time of its breakthrough in a general election, it obtained 11.4 per cent of Scottish votes, but only one out of the 71 Scottish Westminster seats, or 1.4 per cent (my calculations on Audickas *et al.* 2016). Hence, until the establishment of the Scottish Parliament, the party suffered from 'vote inefficiency'. Although it has a proportional electoral system, Spain has also been characterised by strong majoritarian tendencies. The system, however, falls short of pure bipartitism, as it has historically advantaged peripheral nationalist parties, which often offered their support to either PSOE or PP minority governments in exchange for advances in the process of devolution (Pallares and Keating 2003, Capo Giol 2008). Yet, the advantage enjoyed by Catalan parties has generally favoured CiU rather than ERC (see Field 2014). In effect, ERC remained a very marginal force in the Spanish Parliament until the mid-2000s, holding only one seat between 1977 and 2004 – even none in 1986–93 – and this not because of any major distortion in the electoral system, but rather because of CiU's preponderance in the region. What enabled ERC to play a role in Catalan politics before its breakthrough was the presence all along of the Catalan Parliament, where the party has been continuously represented and with a considerably higher share of seats than in Madrid.

This last consideration leads us to the second aspect of the formal institutional structure, i.e. the degree of state decentralisation. More decentralised states tend to provide more access opportunities to challengers (Kriesi 2005, pp. 82–83). Furthermore, the presence of devolved institutions – notably legislative assemblies and autonomous executives – plays a momentous role because they provide a more congenial POS to sub-state nationalist parties than that available at the centre.

Overall, regional devolved institutions have been a double-edged sword. On the one hand, they seem to have appeased conflict, provided better representation to minorities and gone along, at least for part of their recent history, with a strengthening of dual national identities (Guibernau 2006, De Winter 2007). On the other, nationalist parties have used them as platforms to promote nation-building policies (which might make residents more sensitive to centre-periphery issues, especially the youth through education), call for further devolution of powers and, in the case of separatist parties, further the independence agenda (see also Hepburn 2009a, p. 12). More fundamentally, devolution institutionalises 'territorial issues as a permanent feature of the electoral competition between parties' (Alonso 2012, p. 150). They have thus contributed to make sub-state nationalism 'normal', while at the same time keeping up, if not increasing, the salience of the centre-periphery cleavage. They have also constituted new political arenas that have shaped debates differently from those at the centre (McCrone 2012, p. 76) and allowed separatist parties to hold government positions at the regional level, hence showing that they can have an impact, while avoiding to have to compromise at the centre.

The SNP is an illuminating case in this respect. The party has been transformed by the Scottish Parliament, mainly because, thanks to its more proportional nature and to the obvious limitation of electoral competition to Scotland, this has enabled the SNP to overcome vote inefficiency. As a consequence, the SNP went from enjoying no governing potential and very little blackmail potential (Mitchell 2009, p. 33), to having a real impact at Holyrood, either as an opposition or a governing party (Curtice 2009, pp. 63–65). On the other hand, although the establishment of the Scottish Parliament and Executive have certainly reinforced the Scottish character of politics, nation-building has been more limited than in other minority regions (Keating 2010, pp. 254–262), or at least more 'unmindful' (Leith 2010). Such banal nation-building does not seem to have played a key role in increasing support for independence or for the SNP, notably by influencing the new generation of Scots socialised during devolution. Although there was an age cleavage at the 2014 independence referendum, the dividing line was between people younger and older than 55 (Curtice 2014c). Similarly, the SNP did receive more votes from young supporters than older ones in 2011, but this demographic variable did not differentiate it substantially from Labour (Johns *et al.* 2013, p. 169).

The importance of the Catalan Parliament for ERC in terms of representation has already been pointed out above. In the long run, *Esquerra* and its separatist agenda might have also profited in a more subtle way from the establishment of devolved institutions. Some commentators have indeed explained the current radicalisation of support for independence – which since 2012 did benefit ERC electorally – with the nation-building policies carried out by successive Catalan governments, mainly in the realm of education, culture and the media. These are deemed to have not only strengthened the Catalan language and identity, but, according to some, they have even promoted an oppositional definition of the Catalan self-understanding with regard to Spain (Tortella *et al.* 2016, pp. 310–425).

Although discussing the validity of such an argument goes beyond the scope of this chapter, empirical studies show that younger cohorts of Catalan residents, who have been more exposed to education in Catalan, are substantially more likely to vote for Catalan nationalist parties than older ones who have not (Aspach-Bracons *et al.* 2007).

The role of autonomous institutions is of less direct import in explaining the success of the VB, since the party rather profited from its anti-establishment position, its monopoly of the Flemish right (until the coming of the N-VA), and the cordon sanitaire raised around it by the other parties to play a 'whip role' (Mudde 2000, p. 111). Also, the character of demographic and political majority of the Flemish population, accompanied by the highly proportional Belgian electoral system, reduced the importance of the Flemish Parliament in providing better representation to Flemish parties in general. This point is also relevant for the N-VA, which, however, certainly profited from the multilevel governance offered by the existence of regional institutions. Between 2004 and 2014, this allowed it to continuously rule in Flanders, while playing a disruptive role at the federal level (see Sinardet 2010, pp. 363–369). Nation-building policies have been carried out by regional executives (see Slembrouk and Blommaert 1995, Osterlynck 2009, pp. 90–91), but, contrary to the Catalan case, there is no criticism of (nationalist) educational policies, nor empirical evidence of a link between age and identification with Flanders (Billiet *et al.* 2006, p. 917) or age and voting for the N-VA (Swyngedouw and Abts 2011). The VB used to be markedly over-represented among young voters, but less so in recent years, which seems to exclude a 'permanent' effect of devolved institutions (Abts *et al.* 2015).

The role of devolution in the case of the LN is ambiguous. Unlike the other parties in the sample, the *Lega* could not profit from a unified institutional structure governing the entire North on which to focus its electoral efforts without having to compromise in Rome. It has thus much more often combined participation in government at the regional level with alliances at the centre with parties defending interests often at odds with those of its constituency.

The second element of the POS listed by Kriesi is 'the informal procedures and prevailing strategies with regard to challengers'. As the challengers analysed here are political parties formally participating in representative institutions, rather than social movements, there is little informality about the strategies that the other actors – especially state parties – adopt to counter their challenges. In light of this consideration, it is more useful to analyse these strategies in conjunction with the wider configuration of power among relevant players in the political arena. The centre-periphery literature highlights two main tactics that state parties can adopt to deal with peripheral challengers: pro-periphery accommodation, and anti-periphery polarisation (Meguid 2008, pp. 22–40, Alonso 2012, pp. 24–40). These generally refer to the adoption of, or opposition to, the devolution

agenda by state parties, but it can also concern their willingness to collaborate in government with peripheral challengers. Pro-periphery accommodation is most likely to be used by a state party that feels directly threatened
by the challenger because the state party enjoys a relatively higher support
in that specific region. A rival state party that is less popular in the given
region, by contrast, is likely to adopt an anti-periphery polarisation strategy
to steal state-wide votes from its established rival. This game often takes a
left-right dimension because national identities frequently map over ideological affiliations (Alonso 2012, pp. 36–39).

As the Scottish identity has tended to be more easily associated with
left-wing political sympathies, Labour has generally felt more directly in
competition with the SNP and therefore keener on Scottish devolution,
while the Tories have generally opposed it (Hutchinson 2001,
pp. 131–148, Paterson 2002, p. 33). Such accommodation however has
not extended to collaboration in power in either Westminster or Holyrood. Although in Catalonia the subsuming of the left-right dimension
within the centre-periphery cleavage has been less clear than in Scotland,
right-wing positions have had a hard time getting rid of Francoism's
legacy. Hence, the Spanish Socialist Party (PSOE), notably through its
Catalan ally (PSC), has more easily competed with nationalist parties
there (notably CiU in the 1980s and 1990s, ERC from the 2000s) and
more eagerly embraced devolution (although mainly of a symmetric
nature), while the PP has given more limited support to it (Guibernau
2004, pp. 95–118, 2013, pp. 381–382, Dinas 2012). Both parties have
however been ready to collaborate in government with peripheral parties
at the central level when needed (although mostly to the advantage of
CiU). Flemish nationalism has a historical connection with the conservative Catholic movement – and in its most radical incarnations with the
extreme Right. For this reason, under the pressure of the *Volksunie*, the
Flemish Christian Democratic Party (CD&V) led the devolution process
in the 1970s and 1980s, while Flemish left parties (the Socialists and the
Greens) were more lukewarm. Accommodation however did not extend
as far as sharing in government with the VB. In this case, all Belgian
parties agreed to rule out any agreement with it at any level. Yet, this
decision was motivated with reference to the party's extreme Right positions, rather than to its separatist agenda (Pauwels 2011). Indeed, such
a ban did not touch the N-VA, since, in the second half of the 2000s,
the CD&V 'resurrected' its accommodative strategy by forming an electoral coalition with De Wever's party (Erk 2005b, Deschouwer 2013,
pp. 340–341,). The Italian case is peculiar because federalism has been
embraced by most parties in the country – although often only super-
ficially. While the Northern League has a clear right-wing profile, and
the Right has been electorally preponderant in the key Northern regions
of Lombardy, Piedmont and Veneto since the 1990s, the Italian Left and
Right have shown similar levels of support to the issue of regional

devolution, with the Left even carrying out the most extensive constitutional reform in this sense (Fabbrini and Brunazzo 2008, p. 114).

Accommodative strategies are often believed to be responsible for the 'demise of peripheral parties' on account of 'their own success' (Van Haute and Pilet 2006). As state parties adopt the devolution agenda – the argument goes – peripheral ones become increasingly irrelevant. This theory, contradicted by Figure 9.2, fails to take into account the existence of different types of peripheral parties (notably autonomist vs. separatist) and that peripheral parties can adapt to the accommodative and polarisation strategies of state parties. I will discuss such strategies in the next section. Before, however, we need to take a look at the configuration of powers among relevant actors in the political arena. Kriesi (2005, p. 89) defines it as 'the distribution of power among the various parties'. Being more concerned than I am with the initial access of challengers to the political system, he mainly associates the configuration of power with the electoral system. By contrast, I will mainly refer to it as the influence of the relative electoral power of the other actors in the political arena on the electoral chances of my case-study parties.

While for most of the 1990s ERC mainly occupied a niche and could not challenge CiU's dominant position in Catalan politics, in the first half of the 2000s the party profited from the 'exhaustion' of CiU's domination and the retirement of its historical leader Jordi Pujol (Davis 2004). Similarly, in the 1990s and the first half of the 2000s the SNP suffered from the electoral dominance of Labour in Scotland – due both to socio-structural and electoral reasons – as much as it profited from its decline since 2007 (Paterson 2006, p. 57, Hassan, 2011). The VB on the contrary could take advantage of an unexploited niche on the right-wing of the Flemish spectrum and, especially, of the virtual monopoly over the issue of immigration, until the rise of the N-VA, which provided a liberal-conservative alternative to the VB, more moderate along both the nationalist and ideological axes, but still radical enough to convince most of its voters that it could effectively defend the Flemish interest (Pauwels 2011, Swyngedouw and Abts 2011). Finally, the LN gained ground against traditional parties – especially the Christian Democracy – weakened by corruption scandals in the early 1990s, but later heavily competed with Berlusconi's Go Italy for northern liberal-conservative votes and had to move farther to the right, without great electoral success though (Biorcio 1997, pp. 1–28, Cento Bull and Gilbert 2001, p. 112). The revivals experienced in 2008 and, more recently, in 2014–2016, have equally been influenced by the activities of the other actors of the Italian Right. On the former occasion, the League collected the discontent of part of the constituencies of National Alliance and Go Italy after their merger into the People of Freedom (PdL) party. The latter instead has seen the LN partially filling the void left by the PdL's collapse (Biorcio 2010, pp. 68–80, Diamanti 2015b).

Parties' strategies to separatist success: gradualism, institutionalism, issue diversification and instrumentalism

Peripheral parties, and my separatist case-study parties more specifically, are not the passive objects of the influence of the formal aspects of the POS or the strategies of their competitors. They tend to adapt and to develop their own tactics. Although vote-maximisation is not always their only, or even main, goal, one can reasonably assume that such parties are generally driven by vote-maximisation aims, which in turn will contribute to giving them governing, coalition or blackmail potential (Sartori 2005, pp. 291–292). Yet, given their separatist nature and the distribution of preferences concerning constitutional reform in the regional population – which tend to favour devolution over full independence – they are especially prone to the following dilemma:

> in order to build an electoral constituency, peripheral parties need to be the preferred choice among voters with intense pro-periphery preferences. To maximize their vote shares, however, peripheral parties need to be the preferred party also among moderate centre-periphery voters [...] The problem is that dominating the centrist space and the pro-periphery extreme simultaneously implies a trade-off.
>
> (Alonso 2012, p. 221)

Most of the parties studied here have adopted four strategies – to varying degrees and at different points in time – to overcome this dilemma: gradualism, institutionalisation, issue diversification and instrumentalism.

Gradualism refers to the definition of independence not as an event to be achieved 'abruptly', but rather, or also, as a process to be reached in stages (Dalle Mulle 2016c, p. 2). This is important because it allows separatist parties to keep independence as their long-term goal, and therefore meet the requests of their most committed supporters, while, working, in the meantime, towards more easily achievable devolution goals and attracting a more moderate electorate. While the gradualist-fundamentalist fracture within the SNP seriously compromised the party's support for the 1979 referendum, by the late 1990s, the gradualist faction prevailed and, after the establishment of the Parliament, the party accepted 'devo-max' as an intermediate step to full independence (Lynch 2005, p. 524, Hepburn 2009b, p. 197). Similarly, the N-VA is committed to negotiating the transformation of Belgium into a confederation before obtaining its total 'evaporation' and establishing a Flemish Republic (Beyens *et al.* 2015, pp. 4–5), while the Northern League, despite keeping independence as its official long-term goal, has since the late 1990s put this option on the backburner and mostly focused on the achievement of more autonomy for the North (Biorcio 2010, pp. 34–49). ERC's case is a little more complicated because the recent increase in grassroots support for independence in Catalonia and the stand-off between the regional and state governments have almost completely precluded the possibility of a federal compromise. Yet, with the coming to power of Carod-Rovira in 1996 and throughout the 2000s, ERC moved to a more moderate position defined as a 'quiet and constructive sovereigntism' leading to the proposal to reform Spain into a confederation with Catalonia as an associated state, although still as an intermediate step towards full independence (Culla 2013, pp. 545–558).[6]

In most cases, gradualism has also entailed institutionalisation, i.e. the willingness to participate in government institutions, although almost exclusively at the regional level, to cater for the daily needs of the local population. Governing at the regional level, these parties have generally been able to show that they can have a direct impact on people's lives without having to compromise with state parties at the centre (and electorally pay for such compromises). As mentioned above, devolution has offered a very congenial opportunity structure, since it has allowed: the SNP to govern continuously at Holyrood since 2007, while remaining firmly in the opposition in Westminster; ERC to take part in two governing coalitions between 2003 and 2010 and contribute to initiating the momentous process of revision of Catalonia's Statute of autonomy without formally supporting Zapatero's governments in Madrid; and the N-VA to govern Flanders since 2004, while playing a disruptive role at the federal level up to 2014 (see Chapters 2, 3 and 5).[7]

The VB constitutes the most notable exception to these two strategies. The party never really campaigned to be truly in office, but rather openly accepted the role of 'whip party' and adopted a confrontational stand. It consistently portrayed itself as the true defender of Flemish independence and rejected confederalism. On the other hand, while being in government at the regional level, the LN also joined three government coalitions at the central level – in 1994, 2001–06 and 2008–11. The fragmentation of Northern Italy into a series of unconnected regions, which deprived the party of the unified platform that most other case-study parties could exploit to push forth their demand for more powers without compromising at the centre, probably accounts for this stronger tendency to participate in government at the centre.

This does not mean that participation in government, even if limited to the regional level, comes at no price. As pointed out by Elias and Tronconi (2011a, see also Hepburn 2009a, pp. 11–13), there is often a trade-off between policy and votes, because participation in government, or even simply legislative support to a governing majority, might impact badly on subsequent electoral performances. This was the case with ERC in 2008–10, when the party suffered a backlash of committed pro-independence militants and voters against its second coalition with the Greens and the Socialists (Culla 2013, pp. 648–717). Yet, restricting participation to the regional level offers the advantage of avoiding another danger, that of political impotency (i.e. to be seen as a party unable to achieve its goals because permanently in the opposition) which hit the VB in the late 2000s (Pauwels 2011), while at the same time limiting the potential damages of the policy-votes trade-off (see also Elias and Tronconi 2011b).

The third strategy – issue diversification – is linked to institutionalisation since, to convince people that they can govern efficiently at the regional level, separatist parties need to project a clearer and more varied ideological profile (either along the traditional left-right dimension or by taking up new 'unexploited' issues). This also allows them to react to the accommodation strategies of established parties and compete with them along different dimensions (Alonso 2012, pp. 26–29). Thus, from the mid-1980s on, the VB substantially emphasised its anti-immigration profile, which according to many studies explains most of its later electoral success (Swyngedouw 1992, 2001). Similarly, with the passage of the leadership from Colom to Carod-Rovira in 1996, ERC considerably strengthened its left-wing credentials (Culla 2013, pp. 286–505). Although a social-democratic profile was already visible within the SNP from the end of the 1960s, the party openly assumed this profile only from the late 1980s (Mitchell 1988, Lynch 2002, p. 14). The N-VA was not necessarily born as a centre-right party, but it clearly became such when compared to its immediate predecessor (the VU) (Beyens *et al.* 2015). Finally, when confronted with the challenge coming from other new centre-right parties and the failure of its independence agenda, the LN diversified its policy portfolio as well, focusing on immigration, security and globalisation issues much more than before (Albertazzi and McDonnel 2005, Zaslove 2011, pp. 193–205).

The final strategy, instrumentalism, has probably had a more subtle impact. Instrumentalism consists in the fact that most of my case-study parties, although to different extents at different moments of their history, have made an instrumental rather than a principled argument about independence, that is, they have portrayed independence as a means to achieve better standards of living and better democracy for their electoral constituencies, rather than as an end in itself (see Dalle Mulle 2016c). This is clearly the case with the SNP's idea of the 'economics of independence' and ERC's *catalanisme del benestar* (see Chapter 2 and 5). The N-VA (2001, p. 9) also openly defined its nationalism not as a 'goal, but a means to get to more democracy and better governance' (see Chapter 3). Although the LN is a slightly more ambiguous case in this respect, because the more ethnic definition of the Padanian nation has often been accompanied by a more principled rhetoric, the prevalence of a socio-economic understanding of the North mainly as a community of interests has gone hand in hand with demands for independence and/or more autonomy mainly on instrumental grounds (Diamanti 1994, pp. 56–60). The VB is an exception in this respect, as it has consistently evidenced a more principled rhetoric than all other case-study parties, further underpinned by its role as a 'whip' uncompromising party. Yet, as seen in Chapter 3, its arguments for self-determination do incorporate many instrumental elements linked to the better governance and welfare from which an independent Flanders could benefit.

Concluding remarks

An attentive reader might now wonder whether the elements of the political game seen above weigh equally in explaining the electoral evolution of my case-study parties. The answer is no and I will try here to provide a tentative ranking by order of importance. I will also link the party politics analysis to some structural factors examined in the previous chapters. Before doing that, however, I should recall that on the demand-side the general trend is a substantial support for further devolution of powers short of independence. Also, radicalisation can occur and, at least in the long term, drive separatist parties' success, as happened in Catalonia.[8]

As seen above, there are five major elements that can account for separatist parties' electoral outcomes: the electoral system, the presence of devolved institutions, the strategies of established parties against challengers, the configuration of power between relevant actors in the political arena and the strategies of the challengers themselves. The electoral system is certainly important, but, given the success of my case-study parties across the sample despite the presence of both very proportional (Belgium and Italy) and very majoritarian systems (the UK), it does not seem to play a decisive role and therefore is the least important factor. The strategies of established parties and the configuration of power in the electoral arena seem to come next in the ranking. These two elements are tightly linked since the strength of established parties relative to the challenger heavily influences their strategies towards it and, vice versa, their strategies do impact the configuration of power. The first two positions in this tentative ranking of factors are occupied by the existence of devolved institutions, first, followed by the strategies of the case-study parties. Instead of 'killing' my case-study parties, devolved legislative and executive institutions[9] have provided them (and often other nationalist parties in the same region) with better representation and a more congenial platform from which they could carry out nation-building activities and call for further devolution of powers. However, the fact that separatist parties in other devolved regions in Europe have not profited from them to the same extent (for instance, in Corsica, Sardinia and Bavaria) bears witness to the fact that the opportunities offered by any political structure must be seized upon by specific actors. This is why the specific strategies of separatist parties occupy second place in our ranking.

Given this conclusion, why do state parties grant devolution in the first place? Should we conclude with Alonso (2012, p. 41) that they do so only out of electoral calculations and that concerns over the integrity of the state do not play any role at all? I do not think so. Alonso argues that 'politicians know this, [that devolution strengthens peripheral parties] if only because they have seen it happen before'. Yet, she does not provide any historical evidence to support this claim. This is a retrospective and mechanical argument. Can we really argue that in the late 1970s Belgian politicians had such clear evidence that regional institutions would reinforce peripheral parties? And what about their Spanish colleagues a decade earlier? The VU had hit its electoral peak in 1970 and was slowly declining, the Walloon Rally collapsed much more quickly and the VB was still a marginal reality. One could certainly point to persistence of institutional reforms as a sign of the failure of devolution to stop the peripheral threat, but Belgium could also be considered a very peculiar case. The regionalisation adopted in Italy, for instance, did not seem to nourish any centrifugal dynamic at the time. Maybe British politicians could have looked more closely at the Spanish case and the continuing relevance of peripheral parties there in the 1990s. But it is also true that at that time separatist forces in Spain were still a minority phenomenon and the State of the Autonomies was generally considered a major success of the democratic transition (Guibernau 2013, p. 375). In other words, although electoral concerns certainly played a role, there is no evidence that parties deliberately sacrificed state integrity for their own advantage. It seems more likely that they tried to kill two birds with one stone: beating their state rivals, while also assuaging unrest in the periphery. Also, Alonso seems to ignore the demand-side, where support for devolution has been substantial. There are good reasons to believe that outright rejection of such demands – as was the case in Scotland through 1979–97, and in Catalonia more recently – would only nourish radicalisation.

Yet, at the same time, devolution triggers totally new dynamics that might advantage separatist parties. Whether this is the case seems also to depend on the level of regional income relative to the rest of the state. As seen in Chapter 8, several authors have concluded that separatist parties in relatively rich regions have been the most successful in recent years (Sorens 2004, Sambanis and Milanovic 2011). Separatist parties in relatively rich regions might be more successful simply because people are attracted by the economic incentives implicit in their arguments for self-determination. At the same time, it is as reasonable to believe that voters are likely be afraid to vote for separatist parties, since, as seen above, independence remains a risky option. Yet, at least in the cases of Scotland and Catalonia, there is some evidence of a momentous and often understated change: although support for independence has remained quite stable for most of the recent history of the regions analysed here, people appear more relaxed about an independence scenario. First, as shown in the case studies, independence is clearly not a taboo in political debates any longer. Second, there is also demand-side evidence of a less worried attitude. When comparing data from the 1979 and the 1997 referendum in Scotland, one can see that, although devolution remained the preferred option of the Scottish population in both, independence overcame the status quo, thus becoming the second best alternative (Dardanelli 2005). As further argued by Johns *et al.* (2013, p. 163) in their analysis of the 2011 SNP electoral landslide, 'what used to be thought of as a major deterrent to voting SNP – fear of independence – is no longer a widespread concern'. In Catalonia, while in 1991 67.4 per cent of residents believed that separatism could cause 'problems of coexistence' between the inhabitants of the region, in 2014, only 18 per cent thought that coexistence between locals would worsen as a result of independence (CEO 2005–14). The gradualist and instrumentalist strategies seen above might account for that, as well as the advances in the process of European integration, which arguably offer the reassuring prospect of a 'protective' constitutional umbrella to a hypothetical independent state – although the recent bid for independence in Catalonia and Scotland have strongly questioned this point.

Notes

1 The most recent data from the Scottish Social Attitude Survey (SSAS), not included here for issues of comparability with the Flemish series that stops in 2014, show a clear increase occurred after the 2014 independence referendum (see ScotCen 2017).
2 The chi-square test showed more than 20 per cent of cells with an expected count lower than five in each year of the series.
3 Unfortunately, we do not have enough data to make similar considerations with regard to Northern Italy.
4 The most recent data however shows the 'consolidation' of this stronger link between national identity and support for independence after the 2014 referendum (see ScotCen 2017).
5 Kriesi looks at the electoral system as an element determining the 'configuration of power' between established actors vis-à-vis the challenger. This is because he looks at protest movements that do not necessarily engage in direct political action within parliamentary institutions. Yet, my case-study parties were formed with the specific intent to pursue their agenda within such institutions. The electoral system is therefore directly relevant to their 'access' to the political system.
6 This observation concerning the move to gradualism of such parties nuances Alonso's (2012) prediction that peripheral parties will tend to radicalise their stand after devolution.
7 The N-VA supported a federal coalition in 2008, but after a few months it made the government fall on account of a lack of progress on institutional reforms. Since 2014, however, the party has played a key role in a federal government coalition with no institutional reform on the agenda. The new strategy followed by the N-VA is not yet completely clear, but the party seems willing to make a more muscular use of the Flemish majority in the federal institutions to push through some of the desired socio-economic reforms.
8 Recent data from the SSAS mentioned above suggests that this radicalisation scenario could be under way in Scotland as a consequence of the 2014 referendum, but unfortunately it is too early to draw any final conclusions on that.
9 The only partial exception is Northern Italy where, however, devolution did not bring about the creation of a single overarching northern region.

Conclusion

In a seminal contribution to the studies of nationalism John Breuilly (1993 [1982], p. 113) pointed out that 'no nationalist movement is based on pure sentiment. All nationalist movements build upon a variety of interests'. In many ways, the parties analysed in this study have gone much further and openly called for independence, or intermediate forms of self-government, prevalently on account of considerations of material interest.

This does not mean that interests trump identity. As we have seen throughout this book, identity is key for the formulation of a common interest along specific national lines. Adapting a well-known quote by Max Weber (1946, p. 277) on the relation between ideas and interests, one could say that 'not [identities], but material and ideal interests, directly govern men's conduct. Yet very frequently the "world images" that have been created by [identities] have, like switchmen, determined the tracks along which action has been pushed by the dynamic of interest. "From what" and "for what" one wished to be redeemed and, let us not forget, "could be" redeemed, depended upon one's image of the world'. At the same time, an identity that does not serve an interest is, in the long-term, doomed to lose legitimacy.

The power of the nationalism of the rich lies precisely in this virtuous combination of interest and identity. As prophetically argued by Stein Rokkan and Derek Urwin in the early 1980s:

> while the question of regional economic policy, when it first arose between 1930 and 1950, focused more on backward, more remote areas (the Italian Mezzogiorno was outstanding), these areas are not the home of the outstanding territorial problems of Western Europe. No matter what their cultural strength, economic weakness can easily provide the basis for arguments against the credibility and viability of self-sufficiency [...] The major territorial challenge may well come from economically superior or improving regions: these have an economic weight that more demonstratively can support independence and/or counterbalance the political resources of the centre.
>
> (Rokkan and Urwin 1983, pp. 134–135)

The previous chapters of this book can be considered an in-depth inquiry into Rokkan and Urwin's intuition: what is this territorial challenge precisely about? Is it something new? If yes, why? And what can explain its origins and evolution?

First, by reducing the nationalism of the rich to the basic idea of an advanced periphery held back by a more backward core, I looked for historical precedents of this phenomenon. Guided by theoretical works suggesting that nationalism often originated in backward peripheries, I searched for exceptions to this rule. Likely candidates such as Italian, Czech and Hungarian nationalisms in the nineteenth and early twentieth century Hapsburg Empire, or Belgian nationalism between 1815 and 1830, or, again, the Walloon-Flemish debate about child allowances a century later, did not stand up to scrutiny. What did represent instead a forerunner of the nationalism of the rich were the nationalist movements that arose in Catalonia and the Basque Country between the late nineteenth and the early twentieth century. There, we have clear claims by peripheries which considered themselves more modern than the respective centres, and which believed themselves to be held back by the latter. However, these manifestations of Catalan and Basque nationalism cannot be considered more than forerunners because their arguments only marginally concerned fiscal exploitation and rather referred to the traditional need to ensure protection of the local industry from foreign competition through trade tariffs, clearly conveying a 'dependence' on the wider market offered by the parent state that is nowhere to be found in – and is even in contradiction to – the discourse of the nationalism of the rich as defined here.

Next, I moved to the detailed analysis of the nationalism of the rich formulated by my case-study parties. The central claims of this discourse are: an argument of economic victimisation, whereby the relevant nation is exploited through the parent state's system of social redistribution; and one of political marginalisation, whereby the victimisation of the national community is carried out through more subtle means than open discrimination and oppression.

The most important discursive strategy adopted by the case-study parties consists of a cultural-determinist argument, resembling a popularised version of Weber's *The Protestant Ethic and the Spirit of Capitalism*,[1] whereby the economic success of the relevant nation would derive from its extraordinary work ethic and entrepreneurialism. This legitimises the nation's rejection to contributing to state solidarity, shielding it from accusations of selfishness. The notion of solidarity itself, as applied by the parent state, is called into question by the claim that the fiscal transfers generated by the system of social redistribution, and public spending more generally, have financed dependency and corruption, rather than true social support and endogenous growth. In this connection, the economic argument at the core of the nationalism of the rich has turned what in other contexts would be an interpersonal dispute over redistribution into an inter-territorial one.

As suggested by Jamin (2011, p. 27), to some extent, this argument of economic victimisation reproduces the rhetoric of the 'producing people' used by North American populist parties in the late nineteenth and early twentieth centuries, which centres around the idea of 'the existence of a noble and hardworking middle class that is constantly in conflict with malicious parasites which are lazy and guilty, and found at both the top and bottom of the social order'. While the LN, N-VA and VB clearly fit this category, ERC represents a left-wing version of the same, focusing on the 'enemies from above' represented by unaccountable state bureaucrats and political elites nourishing dependence in other Spanish regions. Yet, contrary to the rhetoric of the 'producing people' analysed by Jamin, the discourse examined here has grappled with one of the fundamental structural and normative novelties of the post-Second World War order in Western Europe: i.e. the welfare state and, more generally, the wider role of the state in the economy. Linking Jamin's consideration on American producerism to the existing literature on principles of welfare deservingness, I have suggested that most of my case-study parties have formulated a conditional understanding of solidarity prevalently based on the criteria of control, attitude and reciprocity which, borrowing from Abts and Kochuyt (2013, 2014), I have called 'welfare producerism'. This basically implies that the poorer regions of the parent state are not legitimate recipients of the inter-territorial transfers coming from the relevant nation because: they are responsible for their own state of need (control); they do not make enough of an effort to overcome their needy situation (attitude); and they receive too much relative to their contributions, while the relevant nation receives too little as compared to the efforts of its members (reciprocity). While 'identity' (usually understood as national identity) generally is the most relevant criterion of deservingness used by European public opinions to discriminate between legitimate and illegitimate recipients of social support (Van Oorschot 2006), my case-study parties have refrained from warranting their rejection of solidarity with the parent state solely on account of the identity criterion. The existence of strong dual identities in the relative regions might well account for this situation.

However, identity remains an important criterion, although often implicit: first, the (sub-state) national community clearly remains the primary community of legitimate solidarity; second, the combination of the cultural-determinist argument seen above and welfare producerism have given birth to a culturalised form of welfare producerism in which the 'imagined community of welfare producers' has discursively coincided with the 'imagined community of the nation'. This culturalised version of welfare producerism offers a less divisive form of producerist rhetoric than a culturally neutral one, since the self-understanding of the nation as a community of people endowed with an exceptional hard-working ethos and entrepreneurship conveys the image of a society naturally producing surplus resources that could be used to improve welfare without affecting the competitiveness of the national economy. Also, especially in the case of those parties that have openly stigmatised welfare recipients in other regions of the parent state and called for austerity measures to keep welfare and state spending under control, such culturalised welfare producerism allows for the portrayal of austerity and solidarity as compatible, since austerity will rebalance the distribution of benefits and burdens between the recipients (to be found outside the in-group) and the contributors (made up of the members of the in-group).

As mentioned oftentimes, the SNP is a deviant case, since despite having represented Scotland as a nation of hard-working and talented people and having accused the South-east of England of being the true subsidy junkie of the UK, factors linked to the economic structure of the region, the importance of oil revenues and its ambiguous fiscal position within Great Britain have made it difficult to sustain any strong form of culturalised welfare producerism. What is common to all cases however is that the transfers – oil revenues in the case of the SNP – have acted as a trump card that has enabled the party to present a bright future in an independent country endowed with unlimited resources to finance welfare and boost growth. In this way, to different extents, most of these parties have made an instrumental case in favour of independence that has postulated external self-determination as a means to ensuring solidarity and efficiency in a context of high international competition, rather than as an end in itself.

The arguments of economic victimisation have been accompanied by claims of political marginalisation that have assumed peculiar features in each case study. It is beyond the scope of this conclusion to review in detail the case of political marginalisation made by each party. What is fundamental, however, is to consider the two arguments in conjunction: the economic victimisation of the relevant nation is deemed to descend directly from its condition of political marginalisation; such political marginalisation is the element that justifies a call for constitutional change, since only through new institutions can this condition be reversed; and the nation's political marginalisation is even more obnoxious because of its economic primacy within the parent state, which should instead warrant some form of special treatment.

But, what explains the formation of the nationalism of the rich in the regions analysed here in the last quarter of the twentieth century? There is no easy answer to such a question and one has to look at a combination of several factors that, although generally present in most of the cases, do not appear precisely in the same way in each of them. Such a combination, however, can be broken down as follows: (1) the creation, from the end of the Second World War, of extensive forms of automatic redistribution to an unprecedented scale; (2) the beginning, from the mid-1970s, of an era of slow growth and even 'permanent austerity', exacerbated, in specific contexts, by situations of serious public policy failure and mismanagement of public funds; (3) the existence of national/cultural cleavages roughly squaring with uneven development and sharp income differentials among territorial areas of a given state.[2]

In a wider historical perspective, one cannot but stress the role played by the establishment across Western Europe, mostly in the 30 years between 1945 and 1975, of extensive forms of social redistribution and state intervention in the economy underpinned by the dominance of Keynesian economic theories. The welfare state was based on the idea of national solidarity and, at the same time, was used as a powerful nation-building tool. The unprecedented level of prosperity that it delivered, along with the faith in the capacity of the state to drive growth and achieve full employment, put economic performance at the core of government legitimacy. What is often forgotten is that most welfare states were built during a period of extraordinary economic growth that made the establishment of such extensive forms of redistribution virtually costless from a political perspective. Yet, when the growth engine began to falter in the 1970s, the costs became increasingly visible, while at the same time welfare arrangements continued to enjoy considerable social support. Since then, Western European countries have thus faced issues of welfare state sustainability and different ideological and policy alternatives have been devised to find a solution, from the neoliberal call to rolling back the state, to the empowerment-based approach to conditional solidarity embodied by the social investment paradigm (Hemerijck 2013, pp. 23–50). The nationalism of the rich can be considered a further, although less well-articulated, attempt to overcome the dilemma between solidarity and efficiency at the core of the crisis of welfare and consisting in the couching of fiscal protest in the form of the socio-tropic arguments of economic victimisation examined in the previous chapters. This nationalist interpretation has enabled the parties analysed to criticise redistribution within the parent state without rejecting the welfare state altogether.

Finally, I have pointed out that, while economic victimisation and political marginalisation make up the ethos of the parties, they do not necessarily explain their electoral success. The POS available to each party at any given point in time and the strategies they used to adapt to such structure are often more powerful factors to explain specific electoral outcomes. In this connection, the establishment of devolved institutions deserves special attention. While being aimed at assuaging unrest and strengthening state legitimacy in the periphery, devolution has also offered a suitable platform to separatist (and other nationalist) parties from which they can implement nation-building policies, call for further transfers of powers and play a role in government without having to compromise with state-forces at the centre. More fundamentally, devolved institutions have made the centre-periphery conflict a permanent feature of state politics and created distinct political arenas that frame debates differently from those at the centre. Most separatist parties have adapted to this new more congenial POS and used the strategies of gradualism, institutionalism, issue diversification and instrumentalism with the specific aim of satisfying the constituency of hard-core nationalists making up their members and most committed voters while, at the same time, expanding their support among the much wider moderate nationalist electorate.

Although the electoral success of these parties does not necessarily coincide with substantial changes in support for independence, it does seem to point to an often understated change, that is, there is evidence suggesting that voters have recently taken a much more relaxed attitude to independence. This does not mean that independence has become the preferred constitutional option in the regions analysed – so far this has been the exception rather than the rule – but independence is no longer a scary scenario, but rather a subject of discussion and even a possible outcome in the near future. In other words, what these parties have achieved is an unprecedented 'normalisation' of separatism. The acceptance of democratic means to bring this goal about, the reassurance that it would be implemented through a smooth and orderly process and the use of instrumental arguments in favour of independence, as well as the existence of a larger institutional structure embodied by the EU that, at least at the level of discourse, can be thought of as reducing the costs of separation go a long way to explaining such a significant change.

Notes

1 I am indebted to Michel Huysseune for this parallelism with Weber's work.
2 In Flanders, Northern Italy and Scotland, this last factor has been exacerbated by a recent reversal of economic conditions between the relevant nation and other areas of the parent state.

Annex 1

Interviews

Functions are intended as at the time when the interview took place.

VB

Gerolf Annemans, member of the Belgian Chamber of Representatives, 22/11/2012.
Frank Creyelman, member of the Flemish Parliament, 28/11/2012.
Filip Dewinter, member of the Flemish Parliament, 19/12/2012.
Bart Laeremans, member of the Belgian Senate, 03/12/2012.
Peter Logghe, member of the Belgian Chamber of Representatives, 12/11/2012.

ERC

Josep-Lluis Carod-Rovira, former party leader and vice-president of the *Generalitat* of Catalonia, 10/07/2013.
Cesc Iglésies, Vice-Secretary of General Political Action, 15/07/2013.
Jordi Solé, member of the Catalan Parliament, 09/07/2013.
Juan Manuel Tresserras, former minister of the *Generalitat* and Carod-Rovira's advisor, 13/07/13.
Alba Verges, member of the Catalan Parliament, 09/07/2013.

LN

Lorenzo Fontana, member of the European Parliament, 07/11/2012.
Oreste Rossi, member of the European Parliament, 15/11/2012.
Francesco Enrico Speroni, member of the European Parliament, 08/11/2012.
Gianvittore Vaccari, member of the Italian Senate, 03/03/2012.

N-VA

Paul de Ridder, member of the Brussels Parliament, 16/01/2013.
Jan Jambon, member of the Chamber of Representatives, 18/12/2012.
Kris Van Dijck, member of the Flemish Parliament, 18/12/2012.

SNP

Linda Fabiani, member of the Scottish Parliament, 03/12/2013.
Bill Kidd, member of the Scottish Parliament, 03/12/2013.
Stewart Maxwell, member of the Scottish Parliament, 02/12/2013.
Gordon Wilson, former Party Chairman, 04/12/2013.

Bibliography

Abts, K. and Kochuyt, T., 2013. 'De vreemde bedreiging van de verzorgingstaat'. *Tijdschrift voor Sociologie*, 34 (3–4), 227–249.

Abts, K. and Kochuyt, T., 2014. *Radical Right Voters and Welfare State. Between Welfare Chauvinism, Producerism and Welfare Populism*. Paper presented at the 'Welfare State and Radical Right' workshop. European University Institute, Florence, May 20–21.

Abts, K., Swyngedouw, M. and Meuleman, B., 2015. *Het profiel van de Vlaamse kiezers in 2014. Wie stemde waarom op welke partij*. Leuven: ISPO.

Abulof, U., 2015. 'Normative Concepts Analysis: Unpacking the Language of Legitimation'. *International Journal of Social Research Methodology*, 18 (1), 73–89.

Albertazzi, D. and McDonnell, D., 2005. 'The Lega Nord in the Second Berlusconi Government: In a League of Its Own'. *West European Politics*, 28 (5), 952–972.

Alesina, A. and Spolaore, E., 1997. 'On the Number and Size of Nations'. *The Quarterly Journal of Economics*, 112 (4), 1027–1056.

Alesina, A. and Perotti, R., 1995. *Fiscal Expansions and Fiscal Adjustments in OECD Countries*. NBER Working Paper n. 5214.

Alesina, A., Danninger, S. and Rostagno, M., 1999. *Redistribution through Public Employment: The Case of Italy*. National Bureau of Economic Research Working Paper 7387.

Algoed, K., 2009. *The Incentive Effects of the Belgian Equalization Scheme: Proposals for Reform*. VIVES discussion paper, 6.

Alimbau, J.R., 1995. *Catalunya, qüestió d'estat, vint-i-cinc anys d'independentisme català (1968–1993)*. Terragona: El Mèdol.

Alonso, S., 2012. *Challenging the State: Devolution and the Battle for Partisan Credibility*. Oxford: Oxford University Press.

Alquezar, R., 2001. 'Esquerra Republicana de Catalunya'. *In*: R. Alquezar *et al.*, eds *Esquerra Republicana de Catalunya, 70 anys d'història (1931–2001)*. Barcelona: Columna, 25–54.

Amat, J., 2009. *Els laberints de la llibertat. Biografia de Ramon Trias Fargas*. Barcelona: La Magrana.

Ambrosiano, M.F., Bordignon, M. and Cerniglia F., 2010. 'Constitutional Reforms, Fiscal Decentralization and Regional Fiscal Flows in Italy'. *In*: N. Bosch, M. Espasa and A. Sollé Ollé, eds *The Political Economy of Inter-Regional Fiscal Flows. Measurements, Determinants and Effects on Country Stability*. Cheltenham: Edward Elgar, 75–107.

Anderlini, F., 2009. 'Il mito dell'espansione leghista'. *Il Mulino*, 58 (5), 744–752.

Anderson, B., 1983. *Imagined Communities. Reflections on the Origins and Spread of Nationalism*. London: Verso.

Anderson, P., 2016. 'The 2016 Scottish Parliament Election: A Nationalist Minority, a Conservative Comeback and a Labour Collapse'. *Regional and Federal Studies*, 26 (4), 555–568.

Arachi, G., Ferrario, C. and Zanardi, A., 2006. 'Redistribuzione e ripartizione del rischio tra territori regionali in Italia: il ruolo dei diversi livelli di governo'. *In*: F: Barca, F. Cappiello, L. Ravoni and M. Volpe, eds *Federalismo, equità, sviluppo. I risultati delle politiche pubbliche analizzati e misurati dai Conti Pubblici Territoriali*. Bologna: Il Mulino, 93–123.

Argelaguet, J., 2006. 'Subjective National Identities in Catalonia'. *Nationalism and Ethnic Politics*, 12 (3–4), 431–454.

Argelaguet, J., Gómez-Reino Cachafeiro, M., and Pasquier, R., 2004. 'L'Esquerra Republicana de Catalunya, la troisième force de l'espace politique catalan'. *Pôle Sud*, 20 (1), 9–24.

Amin, A. and Thrift, N., 1994. 'Living in the Global'. *In*: A. Amin and N. Thrift, eds *Globalization, Institutions, and Regional Development in Europe*. Oxford: Oxford University Press, 1–22.

Aspach-Bracons, O., Clots-Figueras, I. and Masella, P., 2007. *Education and Political Behaviour. Evidence from the Catalan Linguistic Reform*, Departamento de Economia, Universidad Carlos III de Madrid, Working Paper 07–78.

Audickas, L., Hawkins, O. and Cracknell, R., 2016. *UK Election Statistics: 1918–2016*. Briefing Paper CBP7529, 7 July. London: House of Commons Library.

Avanza, M., 2009. 'The Northern League (Italy). A Party of Activists in the Midst of a Partisan Militancy Crisis'. *In*: M. Huysseune, ed. *Contemporary Centrifugal Regionalism: Comparing Flanders and Northern Italy*. Brussels, Koninklijke Vlaamse Academie van Belgie voor Wetenschappen en Kunsten.

Bache, I., 2004. 'Multi-level Governance and European Union Regional Policy'. *In*: I. Bache and M. Flinders, eds *Multilevel Governance*. Oxford: Oxford University Press, 165–178.

Bagnasco, A., 1977. *Tre Italie. La problematica territoriale dello sviluppo italiano*. Bologna: Il Mulino.

Bagnasco, A. and Trigilia, C., 1993. *La construction sociale du marché. Le défi de la Troisième Italie*. Cachan: Edition Cachan.

Balcells, A., 1991. *El Nacionalismo Catalan*. Madrid: Historia 16.

Balfour, S. and Quiroga, A., 2007. *The Reinvention of Spain. Nation and Identity since Democracy*. Oxford: Oxford University Press.

Barberan, R., 2006. 'Los estudios sobre la balanzas fiscales regionales en Espana (1960–2005)'. *Presupuesto y Gasto Publico*, 2 (43), 63–94.

Barberan, R., 2010. 'Comment V'. *In*: N. Bosch, M. Espasa and A. Solle Olle, eds *The Political Economy of Inter-Regional Fiscal Flows. Measurements, Determinants and Effects on Country Stability*. Cheltenham: Edward Elgar, 182–187.

Bardos, G., 2013. 'Spectre of Separatism Haunts Europe'. *The National Interest*, 17 January. Available from: http://nationalinterest.org/commentary/spectre-separatism-haunts-europe-7979 [accessed 18 April 2017].

Bartolini, F., 2015. *La Terza Italia. Reinventare la nazione alla fine del Novecento*. Roma: Carocci.

Bartolini, S., 2005. *Restructuring Europe. Centre Formation, System Building and Political Structuring between the Nation State and the European Union*. Oxford: Oxford University Press.

Begg, H.M. and Stewart, J.A., 1971. 'The Nationalist Movement in Scotland'. *Journal of Contemporary History*, 6 (1), 135–152.

Beland, D. and Lecours, A., 2005. 'Nationalism, Public Policy and Institutional Development: Social Security in Belgium'. *Journal of Public Policy*, 25 (2), 265–285.

Benford, R. and Snow, D., 2000. 'Framing Processes and Social Movements: An Overview and Assessment'. *Annual Review of Sociology*, 26 (1), 611–639.

Bennie, L., Brand, J. and Mitchell, J., 1997. *How Scotland Votes. Scottish Parties and Elections*. Manchester/New York: Manchester University Press.

Berend, I.T., 2003. *History Derailed: Central and Eastern Europe in the Long 19th Century*. Berkeley: University of California Press.

Beyen, M., 2009. 'Tragically Modern. Centrifugal Sub-Nationalisms in Belgium, 1830–2009'. *In*: M. Huysseune, ed. *Contemporary Centrifugal Regionalism: Comparing Flanders and Northern Italy*. Brussels: Koninklijke Vlaamse Academie van België voor Wetenschappen en Kunsten, 17–28.

Beyens, S., Deschouwer, K., van Haute, E. and Verthé, T., 2017. 'Born Again, or Born Anew: Assessing the Newness of the Belgian Political Party New-Flemish Alliance (N-VA)'. *Party Politics*, 23 (4), 389–399.

Biehl, D., 1994. 'Intergovernmental Fiscal Relations and Macroeconomic Management-Possible Lessons from a Federal Case: Germany'. *In*: S.P. Gupta, P. Knight and W. Yin-Kann, eds *Intergovernmental Fiscal Relations and Macroeconomic Management in Large Countries*. Washington: IBRD/WB, 69–121.

Billiet, J., 2011. 'Flanders and Wallonia, Right versus Left: is this Real?'. *In*: B. De Wever, ed. *Right-Wing Flanders, Left-Wing Wallonia? Is This So? If So, Why? And is it a Problem?* Re-Bel e-book 12, 1–24.

Billiet, J., Maddens, B. and Frognier, A-P., 2006. 'Does Belgium (Still) Exist? Differences in Political Culture between Flemings and Walloons'. *West European Politics*, 29 (5), 912–932.

Billig, M., 1995. *Banal Nationalism*. London: Sage.

Biorcio, R., 1997. *La Padania Promessa*. Milano: Il Saggiatore.

Biorcio, R., 2010. *La rivincita del Nord. La Lega dalla contestazione al governo*. Bari: Laterza.

Birch, A., 1989. *Nationalism and National Integration*. London: Unwin Hyman.

Bispham, J. and Boltho, A., 1982. 'Demand Management'. *In*: A. Boltho, ed. *The European Economy: Growth and Crisis*. Oxford: Oxford University Press, 289–328.

Blais, A. and Nadeau, R., 1992. 'To Be or Not To Be Sovereignist: Quebeckers' Perennial Dilemma'. *Canadian Public Policy*, 18 (1), 89–103.

Blockmans, W., 1994. 'Voracious States and Obstructive Cities: An Aspect of State Formation in Preindustrial Europe'. *In*: C. Tilly and W. Blockmans, eds *Cities and the Rise of States in Europe. AD 1000 to 1800*. Boulder: Westview Press, 218–250.

Bobbio, N. and Rusconi, G.E., 1992. 'Lettere sull'azionismo'. *Il Mulino*, 41 (6), 1021–1029.

Boehme, O., 2008a. 'Economic Nationalism in Flanders before the Second World War'. *Nations and Nationalism*, 14 (3), 542–561.

Boehme, O., 2008b. *Greep naar de markt*. Leuven: Uitgeverij LannooCampus.

Boix, R., 2012. 'Facing Globalization and Increased Trade: Catalonia's Evolution from Industrial Region to Knowledge and Creative Economy'. *Regional Science Policy and Practice*, 4 (1), 97–112.

Bomberg, E. and Peterson, J., 1998. 'European Union Decision Making: the Role of Sub-National Authorities'. *Political Studies*, 46 (2), 219–235.

Bommes, M., 2012. 'Migration in Modern Society'. *In*: C. Boswell and G. D'Amato, eds *Immigration and Social Systems. Collected Essays of Michael Bommes*. Amsterdam: Amsterdam University Press, 19–36.

Bond, R. and Rosie, M., 2002. 'National Identities in Post-Devolution Scotland'. *Scottish Affairs*, 40 (1), 34–53.

Bonomi, A., 1997. *Il capitalismo molecolare. La società al lavoro nel Nord Italia*. Torino: Einaudi.

Boogards, M., 2005. 'The Italian First Republic: "Degenerated Consociationalism" in a Polarised Party System'. *West European Politics*, 28 (3), 503–520.

Borras-Alomar, S., Christiansen, T. and Rodriguez-Pose, A., 1994. 'Towards a "Europe of the Regions"? Visions and Reality from a Critical Perspective'. *Regional Politics and Policy*, 4 (2), 1–27.

Bosch, N., Castells, A. and Costa, M., 1988. *Els fluxos fiscals del sector públic a Catalunya*. Barcelona: Centre d'Estudis de Planificació.

Brand, J., 1978. *The National Movement in Scotland*. London, Henley and Boston: Routledge & Kegan Paul.

Breuilly, J., 1993 [1982]. *Nationalism and the State*. 2nd edition. Chicago: Chicago University Press.

Brosio, G. and Revelli, F., 2003. 'The Political Economy of Regional Opting Out: Distributive Implications of a Prospective Europe of the Regions'. *Economics of Governance*, 4 (2), 127–142.

Brown, A., McCrone, D., Paterson, L. and Sturridge, P., 1999. *The Scottish Electorate. The 1997 General Election and Beyond*. Basingstoke: Macmillan.

Brown, G., 1975. 'Introduction: The Socialist Challenge'. *In*: G. Brown, ed. *The Red Paper on Scotland*. Edinburgh: EUSPB, 7–21.

Brubaker, R., 1996. *Nationalism Reframed, Nationhood and the National Question in the New Europe*. Cambridge: Cambridge University Press.

Brubaker, R., Loveman, M. and Stamatov, P., 2004. 'Ethnicity as Cognition'. *Theory and Society*, 33 (1), 31–64.

Bull, M. and Pasquino, G., 2007. 'A Long Quest in Vain: Institutional Reforms in Italy'. *West European Politics*, 30 (4), 670–691.

Buxton, N., 1985. 'The Scottish Economy, 1945–79: Performance, Structure and Problems', *In*: R. Saville, ed. *The Economic Development of Modern Scotland*. Edinburgh: John Donald, 69–78.

Buyst, E., 2000. 'Economic Aspects of the Nationality Problem in Nineteenth- and Twentieth-Century Belgium'. *In*: A. Teichove, H. Matis and J. Patek, eds *Economic Change and the National Question in Twentieth-century Europe*. Kindle edition. Cambridge: Cambridge University Press.

Buyst, E., 2011. 'Continuity and Change in Regional Disparities in Belgium during the 20th Century'. *Journal of Historical Geography*, 37 (3), 329–337.

Calhoun, C., 1997. *Nationalism*. Minneapolis: University of Minnesota Press.

Callatay, E. and Thys-Clement, F., eds 2012. *The Return of the Deficit. Public Finance in Belgium over 2000–2010*. Leuven: Leuven University Press.

Cameron, D.R. and Kim, S.Y., 2006. 'Trade, Political Institutions and the Size of Government'. *In*: D.R. Cameron, R. Gustav and A. Zinn, eds *Globalization and Self-Determination. Is the Nation-state under Siege?* London: Routledge, 15–50.

Cameron, D.R., Gustav, R. and Zinn, A., 2006. 'Editor's Introduction'. *In*: D.R. Cameron, R. Gustav and A. Zinn, eds *Globalization and Self-Determination. Is the Nation-state under Siege?* London: Routledge, 1–12.

Cammarano, F., 2011. 'Un ibrido fra stato e nazione'. *Il Mulino*, 60 (1), 72–78.

Campanella, E., 2014. 'Smaller is Better: Disintegrated Nations in an Integrated Europe'. *Vox*, 12 August. Available from: http://voxeu.org/article/disintegrated-nations-integrated-europe-alesina-spolaore-logic-applied [accessed 18 April 2017].

Camps i Arboix, J., 1961. *El tancament de caixes*. Barcelona: Rafael Dalmau.

Cannari, L. and Franco, D., 2012. 'La trasformazione economica del Nord Est'. *L'Industria*, 33 (1), 103–127.

Cantillon, B., De Maeesschalck, V., Rottiers, S. and Verbist, G., 2006. 'Social Redistribution in Federalised Belgium'. *West European Politics*, 29 (5), 1034–1056.

Capo Giol, J., 2008. 'Les élections en Espagne: continuité et changement'. *Pouvoirs*, 1 (124), 47–62.

Capron, H., 2000. 'The Sources of Belgian Prosperity'. *In*: H. Capron and W. Meeusen, eds *The National Innovation System of Belgium*. Heidelberg: Physica-Verlag, 21–41.

Carrell, S., 2012. 'Barroso Casts Doubt on Independent Scotland's EU Membership Rights'. *Guardian*, 12 September.

Carrell, S., 2017. 'Scottish Independence: Sturgeon to Press on with Referendum' [online]. *Guardian*, 29 March. Available from: www.theguardian.com/politics/2017/mar/29/scottish-independence-sturgeon-to-press-on-with-referendum [accessed 27 May 2017].

Cassese, S., 1977. *Questione amministrativa e questione meridionale: dimensioni e reclutamento della burocrazia dall'unità ad oggi*. Milano: Giuffré.

Cassese, S., 1998. *Lo Stato Introvabile. Modernità e arretratezza delle istituzioni italiane*. Roma: Donzelli.

Castells, A. and Parellada, M., 1983. 'Los flujos economicos de Cataluna con el exterior'. *In*: J.S. Dexeus, ed. *La economia de Cataluna, hoy y manana*. Bilbao: Banco de Bilbao, 402–470.

Castells, A., Barberán, R., Bosch, N., Espasa, M., Rodrigo, F. and Ruiz-Huerta, J., 2000. *Las balanzas fiscales de las Comunidades Autónomas (1991–1996). Análisis de los flujos fiscales de las Comunidades Autónomas con la Administración Central*. Barcelona: Ariel.

Cattoir, P. and Verdonck, M., 2002. Péréquation financière et fédéralisme. *In*: P. Cattoir, P. De Bruycker, H. Dumont, H. Tulkens and E. Witte, eds *Autonomie, solidariteit en samenwerking*. Brussels: Larcier, 307–353.

Cavallin, G., 2010. *La vera storia della Łiga Veneta*. Vigorovea: Zephyrus Edizioni.

Cazorla, J., 1994. *El clientelismo de partido en Espana ante la opinion publica. El medio rural, la administracion y las empresas*. Universidad de Grenada, Working Paper n. 86.

Cento Bull, A. and Gilbert, M., 2001. *The Lega Nord and the Northern Question in Italian Politics*. Basingstoke: Palgrave Macmillan.

CEO, 2005–14. *Baròmetre d'opiniò politica*. n. 304, 367, 404, 466, 544, 612, 661, 705, 733, 746.

Cerny, P., 1995. 'Globalization and the Changing Logic of Collective Action'. *International Organization*, 49 (4), 595–625.

Chamber of Representatives of Belgium, 2003. *Federal Parliamentary Elections On May 18, 2003* [online]. Available from: http://verkiezingen2003.belgium.be/index_uk.shtml [accessed 8 March 2017].

Chamber of Representatives of Belgium, 2014. *Election May 25 2014* [online]. Available from: http://polling2014.belgium.be/en/index.html [accessed 8 March 2017].

Checherita, C., Nickel, C. and Rother, P., 2009. *The Role of Fiscal Transfers for Regional Economic Convergence in Europe.* Working paper n. 1029, European Central Bank.

Colino, C., 2009. 'Constitutional Change without Constitutional Reform: Spanish Federalism and the Revision of Catalonia's Statute of Autonomy'. *Publius*, 39 (2), 262–288.

Colldeforns, M., 1991. *La balança fiscal de Catalunya amb l'Administració de l'Estat (1986–88).* Barcelona: Institut d'Estudis Autonòmics.

Colley, L., 1992. *Britons, Forging the Nation, 1707–1837.* New Haven: Yale University Press.

Colomer, J., 1998. 'The Spanish State of Autonomies: Non Institutional Federalism'. *West European Politics*, 21 (4), 40–52.

Comin, F. and Diaz, D., 2005. 'Sector publico administrativo y estado del bienestar'. *In*: A. Carreras and X. Tafunell, eds *Estadisticas historicas de Espana, Siglos XIX-XX.* 2nd edition. Bilbao: Fundacion BBVA.

Commission of the European Communities, 1977. *Report of the Study Group on the Role of Public Finance in European Integration.* 2 Volumes.

Conversi, D., 1993. 'Domino Effect or Internal Development? The Influence of International Events and Ideologies on Catalan and Basque Nationalism'. *West European Politics*, 16 (3), 245–270.

Conversi, D., 1997. *The Basques, the Catalans and Spain: Alternative Routes to Nationalist Mobilisation.* London: Hurst.

Crawford, R. and Tetlow, G., 2014. 'Fiscal Challenges and Opportunities for an Independent Scotland'. *National Institute Economic Review*, 227 (1), 40–53.

Cremonesi, M., 2013. 'La Lombardia basta a Maroni ma non alla Lega'. *Il Corriere della Sera*, 26 February.

Culla, J., 1999. 'La Catalogne: histoire, identité, contradictions'. *Herodote*, (95), 35–47.

Culla, J., 2013. *Esquerra Republicana de Catalunya 1931–2012: una història política.* Barcelona: La Campana.

Culla, J., 2017. 'Catalonia i el concert econòmic (un mite de la transició)'. *L'Avenç*, (434), 9–11.

Curtice, J., 2009. 'Devolution, the SNP and the Electorate'. *In*: G. Hassan, ed. *The Modern SNP, from Protest to Power.* Edinburgh: Edinburgh University Press, 55–67.

Curtice, J., 2012. 'Why No Tory Revival in Scotland?'. *In*: D. Torrance, ed. *Whatever Happened to Tory Scotland?* Edinburgh: Edinburgh University Press, 114–126.

Curtice, J., 2013. *Who Supports and Opposes Independence – and Why?* [online]. Edinburgh: ScotCen. Available from: www.scotcen.org.uk/media/176046/2012-who-supports-and-opposes-independence-and-why.pdf [accessed 4 May 2017].

Curtice, J., 2014a. *Has the Campaign Made a Difference?* [online]. Edinburgh: ScotCen. Available from: https://natcen.ac.uk/media/563071/ssa-2014-has-the-referendun-campaign-made-a-difference.pdf [accessed 4 May 2017].

Curtice, J., 2014b. *So Who Voted Yes and Who Voted No?* Blog post, 26 September. Available from: http://blog.whatscotlandthinks.org/2014/09/voted-yes-voted/ [accessed 18 April 2017].

Curtice, J., 2014c. 'It All Depends on Your Perspective: Economic Perceptions and the Demography of Voting in the Scottish Independence Referendum'. *Fraser of Allander Economic Commentary*, 38 (2), 147–152.

Curtice, J. and Ormston, R., 2011. *Is Scotland More Left-Wing than England?* [online]. Scotcen Brief, 42 (5). Available from: www.nuffieldfoundation.org/sites/default/files/files/scotcen-ssa-report.pdf [accessed 10 February 2017].

Cuthbert, J. and Cuthbert, M., 2009. 'SNP Economic Strategy. Neo-Liberalism with a Heart'. *In*: G. Hassan, ed. *The Modern SNP, from Protest to Power*. Edinburgh: Edinburgh University Press, 105–119.

D'Alimonte, R., 2011. 'Sì all'unità, divisi sul federalismo'. *Il Sole 24 Ore*, 20 February.

Dahl, R., 1982. *Dilemmas of Pluralist Democracy*. New Haven: Yale University Press.

Dalle Mulle, E., 2015. *The Nationalism of the Rich: Discourses and Strategies of Separatist Parties in Catalonia, Flanders, Scotland and Padania*. Unpublished PhD thesis. Geneva: The Graduate Institute.

Dalle Mulle, E., 2016a. 'Belgium and the Brussels Question: The Role of Non-Territorial Autonomy'. *Ethnopolitics*, 15 (1), 105–124.

Dalle Mulle, E., 2016b. ' "L'Altro positivo": un'esplorazione della relazione triangolare tra nazionalismi senza stato, stati sovrani e Europa'. *Nazioni e Regioni*, (8), 27–49.

Dalle Mulle, E., 2016c. 'New Trends in Justifications for National Self-Determination: Evidence from Scotland and Flanders'. *Ethnopolitics*, 15 (2), 211–229.

Dandoy, R. and Baudewyns, P., 2005. 'The Preservation of Social Security as a National Function in the Belgian Federal State'. *In*: N. McEwen and L. Moreno, eds *The Territorial Politics of Welfare*. London: Routledge, 148–167.

Dardanelli, P., 2005. 'Democratic Deficit or the Europeanisation of Secession? Explaining the Devolution Referendums in Scotland'. *Political Studies*, 53 (2), 326–328.

Davis, A., 2004. 'The November 2003 Election in Catalonia: A Landmark Change in the Catalan Political Landscape'. *South European Society and Politics*, 9 (3), 137–148.

De Boeck, E. and Van Gompel, J., 1998. 'Financiële Stromen tussen de Belgische Gewesten Opnieuw Bekenen'. *In*: Vanderveren, C. and Vuchelen, J., eds *Een Vlaamse Fiscaliteit binnen een Economische en Monetarie Unie*. Antwerp: Intersentia, 213–233.

De Boeck, E. and Van Gompel, J., 2002. 'Financiële Transfers tussen de Belgische Gewesten: Actualisering en Vooruitblik'. *In*: P. Cattoir, P. De Bruycker, H. Dumont, H. Tulkens and E. Witte, eds *Autonomie, solidarité et coopération, Autonomie, solidariteit en samenwerking*. Brussels: Larcier, 355–374.

De La Fuente, A., 2001. 'Un poco de aritmetica territorial: anatomia de una balanza fiscal para las regiones espanolas'. *Studies on the Spanish Economy*, 91, FEDEA.

De La Fuente, A., 2005. *Los mecanismos de cohesion territorial en Espana: un analisis y alguanas propuestas*. Fundacion Alternativas, documento de trabajo 62/2005.

De Luna, G., 1994. 'Dalla spontaneità all'organizzazione: la resistibile ascesa della Lega di Bossi'. *In*: G. De Luna, ed. *Figli di un benessere minore. La Lega 1979–1993*. Scandicci: La Nuova Italia, 21–80.

De Meo, G., 1992. 'Traslazione territoriale delle risorse in Italia'. *Rivista economica del Mezzogiorno*, 6 (2), 253–263.

De Riquer, B., 2000. *Identitats Contemporanies: Catalunya i Espanya*. Vic: Eumo Editorial.

De Rync, S., 1996. 'Europe and Cohesion Policy-Making in the Flemish Region'. *In*: L. Hooghe, ed. *Cohesion Policy and European Integration: Building Multi-Level Governance*. Oxford: Oxford University Press, 129–162.

De Schryver, R., De Wever, B. and Durnez, G., eds 1998. *Nieuwe Encyclopedie van de Vlaamse Beweging*. Tielt: Lanoo.

De Smaele, H., 2009. *Rechts Vlaanderen. Religie en stemgedrag in Negentiende-Eeuws België*. Leuven: Universitaire Pers Leuven.

De Standaard, 1979. 'Vlaanderen heeft een begrotingsoverschot'. 10 September, p. 1.

De Standaard, 1981. 'Vlaming en Franstalige op de weegschaal'. 6 March, p. 7.

De Wever, B., Verdoodt, F-J. and Vrints, A., 2015. 'De Vlaamse patriotten en de natie-vorming. Hoe de Vlaamse natie ophield klein te zijn'. *WT: Tijdschrift over de geschiedenis van de Vlaamse Beweging*, 74 (4), 217–248.

De Winter, L., 2007. 'La recherche sur les identités ethno-territoriales en Belgique'. *Revue internationale de politique comparé*, 14 (4), 575–595.

De Winter, L. and Türsan, H., 1998. *Regionalist Parties in Western Europe*. London: Routledge.

De Winter, L., Swyngedouw, M. and Dumont, P., 2006. 'Party System(s) and Electoral Behaviour in Belgium: From Stability to Balkanisation'. *West European Politics*, 29 (5), 933–956.

Deleeck, H., De Lathouwer, L. and Van Den Bosch, K., 1989. 'Regional Differences in the Distribution of Social Security Benefits in Belgium: Facts and Causes'. *Cahier économique de Bruxelles*, 123 (3), 265–310.

Delruelle-Vosswinkel, N. and Frognier, A-P., 1981. 'L'opinion publique et les problèmes communautaires (II)'. *Courrier Hebdomadaire du CRISP*, 122 (927–928), 1–28.

Delruelle-Vosswinkel, N., Frognier, A-P., Dawance-Goossens, D. and Grodent, J-J., 1983. 'L'opinion publique et les problèmes communautaires (IV)', *Courrier Hebdomadaire du CRISP*, 6 (991–992), 1–49.

Delwit, P., 2009. *La vie politique en Belgique de 1830 à nos jours*. Brussels: Edition de l'Université de Bruxelles.

Derks, A., 2004. 'Populism and the Ambivalence of Egalitarianism. How Do the Underprivileged Reconcile a Right Wing Party Preference with Their Socio-Economic Attitudes?'. *World Political Science Review*, 2 (3), 175–200.

Deschamps, R., Ernaelsteen, C., Mignolet, M., Mulquin, M.E. and de Streel, A., 2010. 'A New Structure for the Financing of Belgium's Regions and Communities through Personal Income Tax: The CERPE Model'. *In*: De Grauwe, P. and Dewantripont, M., eds *Towards a More Efficient and Fair Funding of Belgium's Regions*, Re-Bel e-book 5.

Deschouwer, K., 1997. 'Une fédération sans fédération de partis'. *In*: S. Jaumain, ed. *La réforme de l'Etat … et après: L'impact des débats constitutionnels en Belgique et au Canada*. Brussels: Edition de l'Univérsité de Bruxelles, 77–83.

Deschouwer, K., 1999. 'Comprendre le nationalisme flamand'. *Fédéralisme et regionalisme*, 1.

Deschouwer, K., 2006. 'And the Peace Goes On? Consociational Democracy and Belgian Politics in the Twenty-First Century'. *West European Politics*, 29 (5), 895–911.

Deschouwer, K., 2012. *The Politics of Belgium*. 2nd edition. Basingstoke: Palgrave.

Deschouwer, K., 2013. 'Party Strategies, Voter Demands and Territorial Reform in Belgium'. *West European Politics*, 36 (2), 338–358.

Dethée, M., 1984. 'Een regionale Analyse van de Sociale Zekerheid in België'. *GERV-Berichten*, n. 45. 47–90.

Dethée, M., 1990. *Regionale analyse van de Sociale Zekerheid 1985–1989*. Genootschap for Sociale Zekerheid, Antwerpen, 5 April.

Deutsch, M., 1975. 'Equity, Equality and Need: What Determines Which Value Will Be Used as the Basis of Distributive Justice?'. *Journal of Social Issues*, 31 (3), 137–149.

Devine, T.M., 2008a. 'The Challenge of Nationalism'. *In*: T.M. Devine, ed. *Scotland and the Union 1707–2007*. Edinburgh: Edinburgh University Press, 143–156.

Devine, T.M., 2008b. 'Three Hundred Years of Anglo-Scottish Union'. *In*: T.M. Devine, ed. *Scotland and the Union 1707–2007*. Edinburgh: Edinburgh University Press, 1–22.

Devine, T.M., 2012. *The Scottish Nation. A Modern History*. London: Penguin.

Devos, C. and Bouteca, N., 2008. 'Brussel-Halle-Vilvoorde: Voeren van de 21ste eeuw'. *Fédéralisme Régionalisme*, 8 (1), 1–13.

DGSIE (Direction Generale Statistique et Information Economique), 2017. *Population active (travailleurs et chômeurs) et inactive depuis 1999 basé sur l'Enquête sur les Forces de Travail, par année, province, sexe, classe d'âge et niveau d'éducation* [online]. Available from: https://bestat.economie.fgov.be/bestat/crosstable.xhtml?view=1c55b585-4710-431c-8996-df5cfd295d73 [accessed 27 January 2017].

Diamanti, I., 1988. 'Il politico come imprenditore, il territorio come impresa'. *Strumenti*, (2), 71–80.

Diamanti, I., 1994. *La Lega. Geografia, storia e sociologia di un nuovo soggetto politico*. Roma: Donzelli.

Diamanti, I., 1996. *Il male del Nord. Lega, localismo, secessione*. Roma: Donzelli.

Diamanti, I., 2008. 'Così sta nascendo l'identità nordista'. *La Repubblica*, 15 June.

Diamanti, I., 2014. 'Ora Marine fa scuola anche in Italia'. *La Repubblica*, 29 September.

Diamanti, I., 2015a. 'Padana, nazionalista e "personalizzata" ecco la tripla Lega alleata di CasaPound'. *La Repubblica*, 2 March, p. 9.

Diamanti, I., 2015b. 'Il Lega-forzismo che soffia a destra'. *La Repubblica*, 2 June.

Dinas, E., 2012. 'Left and Right in the Basque Country and Catalonia: The Meaning of Ideology in a Nationalist Context'. *South European Society and Politics*, 17 (3), 467–485.

Dottermans, G., 1997. 'Financiële stromen tussen de gewesten in België, 1955–1975'. *Bulletin de Documentation, Service d'études et de documentation, Ministère des Finances de Belgique*, 57 (6), 23–215.

Dowling, A., 2005. 'Convergiencia i Unio, Catalonia and the New Catalanism'. *In*: S. Balfour, ed. *The Politics of Contemporary Spain*. London: Routledge, 106–120.

Dury, D., Eugène, B., Langenus, G., Van Cauter, K. and Van Meensel, L., 2008. 'Transférts et mécanismes de solidarité interrégionaux via le budget des administrations publiques'. *Revue économique*, Banque Nationale de Belgique, September, 97–118.

Eichhorn, J., 2015. 'There Was No Rise in Scottish Nationalism. Understanding the SNP victory' [online]. *LSEBlogs*, 14 May. Available from: http://blogs.lse.ac.uk/politicsandpolicy/there-was-no-rise-in-scottish-nationalism-understanding-the-snp-victory/ [accessed 22 February 2017].

El Periodico. 2015. *Resultados Catalunya. Elecciones Generales 2015*. Available from: http://elecciones.elperiodico.com/resultados/generales/2015/comunidad/catalunya/?_ga=1.63195887.1988063708.1429135253 [accessed 18 April 2017].

Elias, A., 2009. *Minority Nationalist Parties and European Integration: A Comparative Study*. London: Routledge.

Elias, A. and Tronconi, F., 2011a. 'Introduction: Autonomist Parties and the Challenges of Political Representation'. *In*: A. Elias and F. Tronconi, eds *From Protest to Power. Autonomist Parties and the Challenges of Representation*. Vienna: Braumuller, 1–25.

Elias, A. and Tronconi, F., 2011b. 'Autonomist Parties from Protest to Power: A Comparative Overview'. *In*: A. Elias and F. Tronconi, eds *From Protest to Power. Autonomist Parties and the Challenges of Representation*. Vienna: Braumuller, 345–371.

Elias, N., 1975. *La dynamique de l'Occident*. Paris: Calmann-Lévy.

Elliott, J.H., 1963. *The Revolt of the Catalans. A Study in the Decline of Spain 1598–1640*. Cambridge: Cambridge University Press.

Elliott, J.H., 2002 [1963]. *Imperial Spain, 1469–1716*. Electronic ed. Harmondsworth: Penguin.

Erk, J., 2005a. 'From Vlaams Blok to Vlaams Belang: The Belgian Far-Right Renames Itself', *Western European Politics*, 2 (3), 493–502.

Erk, J., 2005b. 'Sub-state Nationalism and the Left–Right Divide: Critical Junctures in the Formation of Nationalist Labour Movements in Belgium'. *Nations and Nationalism*, 11 (4), 551–570.

Esman, M., 1975. *Scottish Nationalism, North Sea Oil and the British Response*. The Waverley Papers, n. 6.

Espasa, M. and Bosch, N., 2010. 'Inter-Regional Fiscal Flows: Methodologies, Results and Their Determinant Factors for Spain'. *In*: N. Bosch, M. Espasa and A. Sole Olle, eds *The Political Economy of Inter-Regional Fiscal Flows*. Cheltenham: Edward Elgar, 150–172.

Esping-Andersen, G., 2004. 'After the Golden Age? Welfare State Dilemmas in a Global Economy'. *In*: G. Esping-Andersen, ed. *Welfare States in Transition: National Adaptations in Global Economies*. London: Sage, 1–31.

Estrade, A. and Treserra, M., 1990. *Catalunya independent? Analisi d'una enquesta sobre la identitat nacional i la voluntat d'independència dels catalans*. Barcelona: Fundaciò Jaume Bofill.

European Commission, 1998. *Economic and Social Cohesion in the European Union: The Impact of Member States' Own Policies*. Regional Development Studies. Brussels: European Commission.

Eurostat, 2008. *Regions of the European Union, A Statistical Portrait*. Luxembourg: Eurostat Statistical Books.

Eurostat, 2017a. *Exchange Rates – Historical Data* [online]. Available from: http://ec.europa.eu/eurostat/web/exchange-rates/data/database [accessed 8 March 2017].

Eurostat, 2017b. *Population Change, Regional Data, Population on 1 January by Age, Sex and NUTS 2 Region* [online]. Available from: http://ec.europa.eu/eurostat/web/population-demography-migration-projections/population-data/database [accessed 8 March 2017].

Fabbrini, P. and Brunazzo, M., 2008. 'Federalizing Italy: The Convergent Effects of Europeanization and Domestic Mobilization'. *Regional and Federal Studies*, 13 (1), 100–120.

Fairclough, N., 2003. *Analysing Discourse: Textual Analysis for Social Research*. London: Routledge.

Fargion, V., 2005. 'From the Southern to the Northern Question: Territorial and Social Politics in Italy'. *In*: N. McEwen and L. Moreno, eds *The Territorial Politics of Welfare*. London: Routledge, 127–148.

Fargion, V., Morlino, L. and Profeti, S., 2006. 'Europeanisation and Territorial Representation in Italy'. *West European Politics*, 29 (4), 757–783.

Feltrin, P., 2010. 'La politica e gli interessi'. *In*: A. Picchieri and P. Perulli, eds *La crisi italiana nel mondo globale*. Torino: Einaudi, 113–173.

Ferguson, N., 2010. 'Crisis, What Crisis? The 1970s and the Shock of the Global'. *In*: N. Ferguson, C. Maier, E. Manela and D. Sargent, eds *The Shock of the Global. The 1970s in Perspective*. Cambridge: Harvard University Press, 1–24.

Ferrera, M. 1986. 'Italy'. *In*: P. Flora, ed. *Growth to Limits. The Western European Welfare States Since World War II*, Vol. 2, Germany, United Kingdom, Ireland, Italy. Berlin: De Gruyter, 388–482.

Ferrera, M., 1993. 'The "Southern Model" of Welfare in Social Europe'. *Journal of European Social Policy*, 6 (1), 17–37.

Ferrera, M., 2005. *The Boundaries of Welfare. European Integration and the New Spatial Politics of Social Protection*. Oxford: Oxford University Press.

Ferrera, M., Fargion, V. and Jessoula, M., 2012. *Alle radici del welfare all'italiana*. Padova: Marsilio.

Field, B.N., 2014. 'Minority Parliamentary Government and Multilevel Politics. Spain's System of Mutual Back Scratching'. *Comparative Politics*, 46 (3), 293–312.

Finlay, R.J., 1994a. *Independent and Free, Scottish Politics and the Origins of the Scottish National Party 1918–1945*. Edinburgh: John Donald Publishers.

Finlay, R.J., 1994b. *A Partnership for Good? Scottish Politics and the Union since 1880*. Edinburgh: J. Donald.

Finlay, R.J., 2005. *Modern Scotland, 1914–2000*. London: Profile Books.

Finlay, R.J., 2008. 'Thatcherism and the Union'. *In*: T.M., Devine, ed. *Scotland and the Union 1707–2007*. Edinburgh: Edinburgh University Press, 157–174.

Finlay, R.J., 2012. 'Thatcherism, Unionism and Nationalism: a Comparative Study of Scotland and Wales', in B. Jackson and R. Saunders, eds *Making Thatcher's Britain*. Cambridge: Cambridge University Press, 165–179.

Flora, P. and Jens, A., 1981. 'Modernization, Democratization, and the Development of Welfare States in Western Europe'. *In*: P. Flora and A. Heidenheimer, eds *The Development of the Welfare States in Europe and America*. New Brunswick: Transaction Books. 37–80.

Flora, P., Kuhnle, S. and Urwin, D., eds 1999. *State Formation, Nation-Building, and Mass Politics in Europe. The Theory of Stein Rokkan. Based on His Collected Works*. Oxford: Oxford University Press.

Fontana, J., 2014. *La Formacio d'una identitat. Una historia de Catalunya*. Vic: Eumo.

Forte, F., 1977. 'Italy'. *In*: Commission of the European Communities, *Report of the Study Group on the Role of Public Finance in European Integration*. Vol. 2.

Fortis, M. and Quadro Curzio, A., 2003. 'Alle prese con la concorrenza asiatica'. *Il Mulino*, 52 (6), 1103–1113.

Fossas, E., 1999. *Asymmetry and Plurinationality in Spain*. Working Paper n. 167, Institut de Ciènces Politiques i Socials, Universitat Autonoma de Barcelona.

Fossas, E., 2011. 'El Control de Costitucionalidad de los Estatutos de Autonomia', *Revesta catalan de derecho publico*, (43), 2–19.

Foucault, M., 1972. *The Archaeology of Knowledge and the Discourse on Language*. New York: Pantheon Books.

Fraser, D., 1986. *The Evolution of the British Welfare State*. Basingstoke: Macmillan.

Fusi, J.P., 1979. *El problema vasco en la II Republica*. Madrid: Ediciones Turner.

Fusi, J-P., 2000. 'Los nacionalismos y el Estado espanol: el siglo XX'. *Cuadernos de historia contemporanea*, 22, 21–52.

Gallego, R., Gomà, R. and Subirats, J., 2005. 'Spain: From State Welfare to Regional Welfare'. *In*: N. McEwen and L. Moreno, eds *The Territorial Politics of Welfare*. London: Routledge, 103–126.

Gamson, W. and Modigliani, A., 1989. 'Media Discourse and Public Opinion on Nuclear Power: A Constructionist Approach'. *American Journal of Sociology*, 95 (1), 1–37.

Garcia-Milà, T. and McGuire, T., 2001. 'Do Interregional Transfers Improve the Economic Performance of Poor Regions? The Case of Spain'. *International Tax and Public Finance*, 8 (3), 281–295.

Garrett, G. and Lange, P., 1991. 'Political Responses to Interdependence: What's "Left" for the Left?'. *International Organization*, 45 (4), 531–564.

Garrett, G. and Rodden, J., 2006. 'Globalisation and Fiscal Decentralization'. *In*: D.R. Cameron, R. Gustav and A. Zinn, eds *Globalization and Self-Determination. Is the Nation-State under Siege?* London: Routledge, 278–300.

Geertz, C., 1964. 'Ideology as a Cultural System'. *In*: D. Apter, ed. *Ideology and Discontent*. London: Free Press of Glencoe, 47–76.

Gellner, E., 1964. *Thought and Change*. London: Weidenfeld and Nicolson.

Gellner, E., 1983. *Nations and Nationalism*. Ithaca: Cornell University Press.

Generalitat de Catalunya, 2012. *Resultats de la balança fiscal de Caatalunya amb el sector public central 2006–2009*. Departament d'Economia i Coneixement.

Generalitat de Catalunya, 2017. *Resultats Electorals* [online]. Available from: http://governacio.gencat.cat/ca/pgov_ambits_d_actuacio/pgov_eleccions/pgov_dades_electorals/ [accessed 18 April 2017].

GERV (Gewestelijke Economische Raad voor Vlaanderen), 1983. *Regionalisering van de uitgaven en de ontvangsten inzake sociale zekerheid – periode 1975–1981*. Antwerp: GERV.

Giarda, P., 2004. *Decentralization and Intergovernmental Fiscal Relations in Italy: A Review of Past and Recent Trends*. Paper presented at the 60th Congress of the International Institute of Public Finance, Università Bocconi, Milano, 23–26 August.

Giddens, A., 1994. *The Consequences of Modernity*. Cambridge: Polity Press.

Giner, S., 1980. *The Social Structure of Catalonia*. Sheffield: Anglo-Catalan Society.

Ginsborg, P., 1996. 'Explaining Italy's Crisis'. *In*: S. Gundle and S. Parker, eds *The New Italian Republic. From the Fall of the Berlin Wall to Berlusconi*. London: Routledge, 13–39.

Goerlich, F., Mas, M. and Perez, F., 2002. *Concentración, convergencia y desigualdad regional en España*. MPRA Paper No. 15831.

Gourevitch, P.A., 1979. 'The Reemergence of "Peripheral Nationalisms": Some Comparative Speculations on the Spatial Distribution of Political Leadership and Economic Growth'. *Comparative Studies in Society and History*, 21 (3), 303–322.

Govaert, S., 1983. 'Le Vlaams Economisch Verbond (VEV) dans la Belgique des régions'. *Courrier Hebdomadaire du CRISP*, 18 (1003–1004), 1–50.

Govaert, S., 1993. 'La Volksunie'. *Courrier hebdomadaire du CRISP*, 31 (1416–1417), 1–85.

Govaert, S., 2001. *Les griffes du lion. Le nationalisme flamand à la veille de 2002.* Brussels: Labor.

Govaert, S., 2002. La Volksunie. Du déclin à la disparition (1993–2001). *Cahier hebdomadaire du CRISP*, 3 (1748), 5–32.

Grandinetti, R., 2010. 'I territori delle imprese nell'economia globale'. *In*: A., Picchieri, and P., Perulli, eds *La crisi italiana nel mondo globale*. Torino: Einaudi, 70–113.

Granovetter, M., 1985. 'Economic Action and Social Structure: The Problem of Embeddedness'. *American Journal of Sociology*, 91 (3), 481–510.

Graziano, M., 2010. *The Failure of Italian Nationhood. The Geopolitcs of a Troubled Identity.* New York: Palgrave Macmillan.

Green, C., 1993. 'From "Tax State" to "Debt State"'. *Journal of Evolutionary Economics*, 3 (23), 23–42.

Greenfeld, L., 1992. *Nationalism: Five Roads to Modernity*. Cambridge: Harvard University Press.

Greenfield, K.R., 1965. *Economics and Liberalism in the Risorgimento. A Study of Nationalism in Lombardy, 1814–1848*. Baltimore: The Johns Hopkins Press.

Greenwood, J., 2011. *Interest Representation in the European Union*. Basingstoke: Palgrave.

Grote, J., 1996. 'Cohesion in Italy: A View on Non-Economic Disparities'. *In*: L. Hooghe, ed. *Cohesion Policy and European Integration: Building Multi-Level Governance*. Oxford: Oxford University Press, 256–293.

GTABFC (Group de Treball per l'Actualitzacio de la Balança Fiscal de Catalunya), 2008. *Resultats de la balança fiscal de Catalunya amb l'administracio central, 2002–05.* Generalitat de Catalunya.

Guibernau, M., 1999. *Nations without States: Political Communities in a Global Age.* Cambridge: Polity Press.

Guibernau, M., 2004. *Catalan Nationalism: Francoism, Transition and Democracy.* London: Routledge.

Guibernau, M., 2006. 'National Identity, Devolution and Secession in Canada, Britain and Spain'. *Nations and Nationalism*, 12 (1), 51–76.

Guibernau, M., 2013. 'Secessionism in Catalonia: After Democracy'. *Ethnopolitics*, 12 (4), 368–393.

Gundle, S. and Parker, S., 1996. 'Introduction: the new Italian Republic'. *In*: S. Gundle and S. Parker, eds *The New Italian Republic. From the Fall of the Berlin Wall to Berlusconi*. London: Routledge, 1–15.

Haas, E., 1958. *The Uniting of Europe: Political, Social and Economic Forces.* Standford: Standford University Press.

Hale, H., 2008. *The Foundation of Ethnic Politics. Separatism of States and Nations in Eurasia and the World.* Cambridge: Cambridge University Press.

Hannes, J., 2007. *De mythe van de omgekeerde transfers. Fiscale prestaties van Vlaanderen, Wallonië en Brabant 1832–1912*. Roeselare: Roularta.

Harvie, C., 1994. *The Rise of Regional Europe*. London: Routledge.

Harvie, C., 1995. *Fool's Gold. The Story of North Sea Oil*. London: Penguin.

Harvie, C., 1998. *Scotland & Nationalism, Scottish Society and Politics 1707 to the Present*. 3rd edition. London: Routledge.

Hassan, G., 2007. 'Labour, Britishness and the Concepts of "Nation" and "State"'. *In*: G. Hassan, ed. *After Blair. Politics after the New Labour Decade*. London: Lawrence & Wishart, 75–93.

Hassan, G., 2011. 'Anatomy of a Scottish Revolution: The Potential of Postnationalist Scotland and the Future of the United Kingdom'. *The Political Quarterly*, 82 (3), 365–378.

Hassan, G., 2012. '"It's only a Northern Song": The Constant Smirr of Anti-Thatcherism and Anti-Toryism'. *In*: D. Torrance, ed. *Whatever Happened to Tory Scotland?* Edinburgh: Edinburgh University Press, 76–92.

Hassan, G. and Warhurst, C., 2001. 'New Scotland? Policy, Parties and Institution'. *The Political Quarterly*, 72 (2), 213–226.

Haussenteufel, P., 1996. 'L'Etat Providence ou les métamorphoses de la citoyenneté'. *L'année sociologique*, 46 (1), 127–149.

Hearn, J., 2000. *Claiming Scotland: National Identity and Liberal Culture*. Edinburgh: Polygon.

Hechter, M., 1977 [1975]. *Internal Colonialism: The Celtic Fringe in British National Development, 1536–1966*. Berkeley: University of California Press.

Heclo, H., 1981. 'Toward a New Welfare State?'. *In*: P. Flora and A. Heidenheimer, eds *The Development of the Welfare States in Europe and America*. New Brunswick: Transaction Books, 383–406.

Held, D., 1988. 'New Times. Farewell Nation State'. *Marxism Today*, December, 12–17.

Hemerijck, A., 2013. *Changing Welfare States*. Oxford: Oxford University Press.

Henderson, A., Delaney, L. and Lineira, R., 2014. *Risk and Attitudes to Constitutional Change*. Edinburgh: Scottish Centre on Constitutional Change.

Hepburn, E., 2008. 'The Neglected Nation: The CSU and the Territorial Cleavage in Bavarian Party Politics'. *German Politics*, 17 (2), 184–202.

Hepburn, E., 2009a. 'Introduction: Reconceptualizing Sub-State Mobilization'. *In*: E. Hepburn, ed. *New Challenges for Stateless Nationalist and Regionalist Partiesi*. London: Routledge, 1–23.

Hepburn, E., 2009b. 'Degrees of Independence: SNP Thinking in an International Context'. *In*: G. Hassan, ed. *The Modern SNP: From Protest to Power*. Edinburgh: Edinburgh University Press, 190–203.

Heremans, D., Peeters, T. and Van Hecke, A., 2010. 'Towards a More Efficient and Responsible Mechanism for the Belgian Federation'. *In*: P. De Grauwe and M. Dewantripont, eds *Towards a More Efficient and Fair Funding of Belgium's Regions*. Re-Bel e-book 5.

Hespanha, A.M., 1994. 'Cities and States in Portugal'. *In*: C. Tilly and W. Blockmans, eds *Cities and the Rise of States in Europe. AD 1000 to 1800*. Boulder: Westview Press, 185–195.

Heywood, P., 2005. 'Corruption, Democracy and Governance in Contemporary Spain'. *In*: S. Balfour, ed. *The Politics of Contemporary Spain*. London: Routledge, 39–60.

Hine, D., 1996. 'Federalism, Regionalism and the Unitary State: Contemporary Regional Pressures in Historical Perspective'. *In*: C. Levy, ed. *Italian Regionalism: History, Identity, Politics*. Oxford: Berg, pp. 109–113.

HM Revenue & Customs, 2017. *Statistics of Government Revenues from UK Oil and Gas Production*. January.

Hobsbawm, E.J., 1990. *Nations and Nationalism since 1780: Programme, Myth, Reality*. Cambridge: Cambridge University Press.

Hombravella, J.R. and Montserrat, A., 1967. *L'aptitud financera de Catalunya. La balança catalana de pagaments*. Barcelona: Edicions 62.

Hooghe, L., 1995. 'Subnational Mobilisation in the European Union'. *West European Politics*, 18 (3), 175–198.

Hooghe, L., 2004. 'Belgium: Hollowing the Center'. *In*: U. Amoretti and N. Bermeo, eds *Federalism and Territorial Cleavages*. Baltimore: John Hopkins Press, 55–92.

Hooghe, L. and Marks, G., 1996. ' "Europe with the Regions": Channels of Regional Representation in the European Union'. *Publius*, 26 (1), 73–92.

Hooghe, L. and Marks, G., 2001. *Multilevel Governance and European Integration*. Lanham: Rowman and Littlefield.

Hopkin, J., 2001. 'A "Southern Model" of Electoral Mobilisation? Clientelism and Electoral Politics in Post-Franco Spain'. *West European Politics*, 24 (1), 115–136.

Howe, P., 1998. 'Rationality and Sovereignty Support in Quebec'. *Canadian Journal of Political Science*, 31 (1), 31–59.

Hutchison, I.G.C., 2001. *Scottish Politics in the Twentieth Century*. Basingstoke: Palgrave.

Huyse, L., 1971. *Passiviteit, pacificatie and verzuildheid in de Belgische politiek*. Antwerpen: Standaard Wetenschappelijke Uitgeverij.

Huysseune, M., 2002. 'Imagined Geographies: Political and Scientific Discourses on Italy's North-South Divide'. *In*: B. Coppieters and M. Huysseune, eds *Secession, History and the Social Sciences*. Brussels: VUB, 207–226.

Huysseune, M., 2006. *Modernity and Secession. The Social Sciences and the Political Discourse of the Lega Nord in Italy*. New York: Berghahn Books.

Huysseune, M. and Dalle Mulle, E., 2015. 'Crisi economica ed evoluzione del regionalismo dei ricchi'. *Polis*, 29 (2), 191–220.

IBES (Instituto Balear de Estudios Socials), 2012a. *Barómetro de Opinión sobre la situación general de la Comunidad Balear*. 4th wave, December.

IBES, 2012b. *Ideologia politica y sentimiento identitario en el marco sociopolitico de las Islas Baleares*, June.

ICPS (Institut de Ciencies Politiques i Socials), 1991–2016. *Sondeig d'Opinio Catalunya*. Available from: www.icps.cat/recerca/sondeigs-i-dades/sondeigs/sondeigs-d-opinio-catalunya [accessed 18 April 2017].

IDESCAT, 2017a. *Population on 1 January. 1900–2017* [online]. Available from: www.idescat.cat/pub/?id=aec&n=245&lang=en [accessed 11 May 2017].

IDESCAT, 2017b. *Gross Domestic Product (Base 2010). Supply* [online]. Available form: www.idescat.cat/economia/?tc=5&id=5127&lang=en [accessed 12 May 2017].

IMF-FAD (International Monetary Fund–Fiscal Affairs Department), 2012. *Historical Public Debt Database* [online]. Available from: www.imf.org/external/pubs/ft/wp/2010/data/wp10245.zip [accessed 8 March 2017].

INE (Instituto Nacional de Estadisticas), 2017a. *Contabilidad Regional de España. Base 1986. Serie 1980–1996. Producto interior bruto regional* [online]. Available from: www.ine.es/jaxi/Datos.htm?path=/t35/p010/a1996/l0/&file=re002.px [accessed 12 May 2017].

INE, 2017b. *Contabilidad Regional de España. Base 2010. Producto interior bruto regional. Serie homogénea* [online]. Available from: www.ine.es/daco/daco42/cre00/b2010/homog/dacocre_base2010h.htm [accessed 12 May 2017].

INE, 2017c. *Tasas de paro por distintos grupos de edad, sexo y comunidad autónoma* [online]. Available from: www.ine.es/jaxiT3/Datos.htm?t=4247 [accessed 12 May 2017].

ISTAT (Istituto Nazionale di Statistica), 2011. *Valore della moneta – Coefficienti per tradurre valori monetari tra i periodi sottoindicati* [online]. Available from: http://seriestoriche.istat.it/ [accessed 20 March 2017].

ISTAT, 2013. *Formazione del reddito delle famiglie negli anni 1995–2011.*

ISTAT, 2017a. *National Accounts. Regional Accounts. Sequence of Accounts (millions of euro)* [online]. Available from: http://dati.istat.it/ [accessed 20 March 2017].

ISTAT, 2017b. *Rapporti caratteristici del conto economico consolidato delle Pubbliche amministrazioni – Anni 1980–2010* [online]. Available from: http://seriestoriche.istat.it/ [accessed 23 March 2017].

ISTAT, 2017c. *Rapporti caratteristici del conto economico consolidato delle Pubbliche amministrazioni – Anni 1995–2015* [online]. Available from: http://seriestoriche.istat.it/ [accessed 23 March 2017].

ISTAT, 2017d. *Conti e aggregati economici territoriali. Valori pro capite. Prodotto interno lordo ai prezzi di mercato per abitante. Valori concatenati con anno di riferimento 2010* [online]. Available from: http://dati.istat.it/ [accessed 23 March 2017].

ISTAT, 2017e. *Offerte di lavoro. Tasso di disoccupazione* [online]. Available from: http://dati.istat.it/ [accessed 23 March 2017].

Istituto Tagliacarne, 2011. *Reddito e Occupazione nelle province italiane dal 1861 ad oggi* [online]. Available from: www.tagliacarne.it/P42A220C205S204/Reddito-e-occupazione-nelle-Province-italiane-dal-1861-ad-oggi.htm [accessed 3 March 2014].

ITANES (Italian National Election Studies), 2001. *Inchiesta campionaria sulle elezioni politiche del 2001*. Bologna: Associazione Itanes.

Jamin, J., 2011. 'The Producerist Narrative in Right-Wing Flanders'. *In*: B. De Wever, ed. *Right-Wing Flanders, Left-Wing Wallonia? Is This So? If So, Why? And Is It a Problem?*, Re-Bel e-book 12, 25–35.

Janos, A., 1982. *The Politics of Backwardness in Hungary, 1825–1945*. Princeton: Princeton University Press.

Jenkins, J.C., 2005. 'Social Movements, Political Representation and the State: An Agenda and Comparative Framework'. *In*: J.C. Jenkins, ed. *The Politics of Social Protest: Comparative Perspectives on States and Social Movements*. Electronic version. London: UCL Press, 7–17.

Johns, R., Mitchell, J. and Carman, C., 2013. 'Constitution or Competence? The SNP's Re-election in 2011'. *Political Studies*, 61 (1), 158–178.

Jori, F., 2009. *Dalla Łiga alla Lega. Storia, movimenti, protagonisti*. Venezia: Marsilio.

Jurion, B. *et al.*, 1994. *Régionalisation de la charge d'intérêts de la dette publique (Rapport final)*. Liège: Conseil économique et social de la Région wallonne.

Kann, R.A., 1950. *The Multinational Empire: Nationalism and National Reform in the Habsburg Monarchy 1848–1918*. Vol. 1. New York: Columbia University Press.

Keating, M., 1996. *Nations Against the State: The New Politics of Nationalism in Quebec, Catalonia and Scotland*. Basingstoke: Macmillan.

Keating, M., 1998. *The New Regionalism in Western Europe. Territorial Restructuring and Political Change*. Cheltenham: Edward Elgar.

Keating, M., 2004. 'European Integration and the Nationalities Question'. *Politics and Society*, 32 (3), 367–388.

Keating, M., 2005. 'Policy Convergence and Divergence in Scotland under Devolution'. *Regional Studies*, 39 (4), 4543–463.

Keating, M., 2009. *The Independence of Scotland. Self-Government and the Shifting Politics of the Union*. Oxford: Oxford University Press.

Keating, M., 2010. *The Government of Scotland. Policy Making after Devolution*. 2nd edition. Edinburgh: Edinburgh University Press.

Keating, M. and Wilson, A., 2009. 'Renegotiating the State of Autonomies: Statute Reform and Multilevel Politics in Spain'. *West European Politics*, 32 (3), 536–558.

Keating, M., Loughlin, J. and Deschouwer, K., 2003. *Culture, Institutions and Economic Development. A Study of Eight European Regions*. Cheltenham: Edward Elgar.

Kemp, A., 2011. *The Official History of North Sea Oil: The Growing Dominance of the State*. Vol. 1. London: Routledge.

Kendrick, S., Bechhofer, F. and McCrone, D., 1985. 'Is Scotland Different? Industrial and Occupational Change in Scotland and Britain'. *In*: H. Newby ed. *Restructuring Capital: Recession and Reorganisation in Industrial Society*. London: Macmillan.

Kessler, A. and Lessmann, C., 2010. *Interregional Redistribution and Regional Disparities: How Equalization Does (Not) Work*. CEPR Discussion Paper n. 8133.

Kidd, C., 1993. *Subverting Scotland's Past*. Cambridge: Cambridge University Press.

Kinder, D. and Kiewiet, R., 1981. 'Sociotropic Politics: The American Case'. *Journal of Political Science*, 11 (2), 129–161.

Kossmann, E.H., 1978. *The Low Countries (1780–1940)*. Oxford: Clarendon Press.

Kriesi, H., 2005. 'The Political Opportunity Structure of New Social Movements: Its Impact on Their Mobilization'. *In*: J.C. Jenkins, ed. *The Politics of Social Protest: Comparative Perspectives on States and Social Movements*. Electronic version. London: UCL Press, 83–98.

Kuzban, R., Tooby, J., and Cosmides, L., 2001. 'Can Race Be Erased? Coalitional Computation and Social Categorization'. *Proceedings of the National Academy of Science*, 98 (26), 15387–15392.

Laclau, E. and Mouffe, C., 1985. *Hegemony and Socialist Strategy: Towards a Radical Democratic Politics*. London: Verso.

Lago-Peñas, S., Prada, A. and Vaquero, A., 2013. *On the Size and Determinants of Inter-regional Redistribution in European Countries over the Period 1995–2009*. MPRA paper n. 45406.

Laitin, D., Sole, C. and Kalyvas, S.N., 1994. 'Language and the Construction of States: The Case of Catalonia in Spain'. *Politics Society*, 22 (5), 5–29.

Lanaro, S., 1988. *L'Italia nuova. Identità e sviluppo 1861–1988*. Torino: Einaudi.

Lanaro, S., 1993. 'Le élites settentrionali e la storia italiana'. *Meridiana*, (16), 19–39.

Larosse, J., 2012. ' "New Industrial Policy" in Flanders: An Integrated Policy Framework for a New Productivity Revolution', *Reflets et perspectives de la vie économique*, 51 (1), 99–115.

Lee, C., 1995. *Scotland and the United Kingdom. The Economy and the Union in the Twentieth Century*. Manchester and New York: Manchester University Press.

Leith, S.M., 2010. 'Governance and Identity in a Devolved Scotland'. *Parliamentary Affairs*, 63 (2), 286–301.

Lepschy, A.L., Lespschy G. and Voghera, M., 1996. 'Linguistic Variety in Italy'. *In*: C. Levy, ed. *Italian Regionalism: History, Identity, Politics*. Oxford: Berg, 69–80.

Levy, C., 1996. 'Introduction: Italian Regionalism in Context'. *In*: C. Levy, ed. *Italian Regionalism: History, Identity, Politics*. Oxford: Berg, 1–30.

Levy, R., 1986. 'The Search for a Rational Strategy: the Scottish National Party and Devolution, 1974–79'. *Political Studies*, 34 (2), 236–248.

Linz, J., 1973. 'Early State-Building and Late Peripheral Nationalism against the State. The Case of Spain'. *In*: S.N. Eisenstadt and S. Rokkan, eds *Building States and Nations*, Vol. 2. Beverly Hills: Sage Publication.

Lipset, S. and Rokkan, S., 1967. 'Cleavage Structures, Party Systems and Voter Alignments: An Introduction'. *In*: S. Lipset and S. Rokkan, eds *Party Systems and Voter Alignments: Cross-National Perspectives*. New York: The Free Press.

Llobera, J., 2004. *Foundations of National Identity: From Catalonia to Europe*. New York: Berghan Books.

Lo Cascio, P., 2008. *Nacionalisme i autogovern*. Catarroja: Afers.

Lupo, S., 1996. 'The Changing Mezzogiorno'. *In*: S. Gundle and S. Parker, eds *The New Italian Republic. From the Fall of the Berlin Wall to Berlusconi*. London: Routledge, 247–260.

Luyten, D., 2010. 'L'économie et le mouvement flamand', *Courrier hebdomadaire du CRISP*, 31 (2076).

Lynch, P., 2002. *SNP. The History of the Scottish National Party*. Cardiff: Welsh Academic Press.

Lynch, P., 2005. 'Scottish Independence, The Quebec Model of Secession and the Political Future of the Scottish National Party'. *Nationalism and Ethnic Politics*, 11 (4), 503–531.

Lyttelton, A., 1996. 'Shifting Identities: Nation, Region and City'. *In*: C. Levy, ed. *Italian Regionalism: History, Identity, Politics*. Oxford: Berg, 33–52.

Mackay, C., 2009. 'The SNP and the Scottish Parliament: The Start of a New Sang?'. *In*: G. Hassan, ed. *The Modern SNP, from Protest to Power*. Edinburgh: Edinburgh University Press, 79–92.

MacMillan, M., 2009. *The Uses and Abuse of History*. London: Profile Books.

Maesschalck, J. and Van de Walle, S., 2006. 'Policy Failure and Corruption in Belgium: Is Federalism to Blame?'. *West European Politics*, 29 (5), 999–1003.

Maggi, M. and Piperno, S., 1998. *Dal risanamento all'Euro. Evoluzione del residuo fiscale nelle regioni italiane*. Contributi di ricerca, October. Torino: Fondazione Agnelli.

Maier, C., 1977. 'The Politics of Productivity: Foundations of American International Economic Policy after World War II'. *International Organization*, 31 (4), 607–633.

Maier, C., 2010. ' "Malaise". The Crisis of Capitalism in the 1970s'. *In*: N. Ferguson, C., Maier, E. Manela and D. Sargent, eds *The Shock of the Global. The 1970s in Perspective*. Cambridge: Harvard University Press, 25–48.

Maly, I., 2012. *N-VA. Analyse van een politieke ideologie*. Berchem: EPO.

Maly, I., 2013. *'Scientific Nationalism'. N-VA, Banal Nationalism and the Battle for Flemish Nationalism*, Tilburg Papers in Culture Studies 63.

Mann, M., 1999. 'Has Globalization Ended the Rise and Rise of the Nation-State?'. *In*: P. Thazha Varkey and J.A. Hall, eds *International Order and the Future of World Politics*. Cambridge: Cambridge University Press, 237–269.

Marks, G., Haesley, R. and Mbaye, H.A.D., 2002. 'What Do Subnational Offices Think They Are Doing in Brussels?'. *Regional and Federal Studies*, 12 (3), 1–23.

Marquand, D., 2008. *Britain since 1918. The Strange Career of British Democracy*. Kindle edition. London: Weidenfeld & Nicolson.

Marr, A., 1992. *The Battle for Scotland*. London: Penguin.

Martì, D. and Cetrà, D., 2016. 'The 2015 Catalan Election: A De facto Referendum on Independence?'. *Regional and Federal Studies*, DOI: 10.1080/13597566. 2016.1145116.

Martínez-Herrera, E., 2002. 'From National-Building to Building Identification with Political Communities: Consequences of Political Descentralisation in Spain, the Basque Country, Catalonia and Galicia, 1978–2001'. *European Journal of Political Research*, 41 (4), 421–453.

Martinez Shaw, C., 1985. 'La Catalunya del Siglo XVIII bajo el signo de la expansion'. *In*: R. Fernandez, ed. *Espana en el Siglo XVIII*. Barcelona: Critica, 55–131.

Mas, M., Maudos, J., Perez, F. and Uriel, E., 1994. 'Disparidades regionales y convergencia en las cc.aa. espanolas'. *Revista de Economia Aplicada*, 2 (4), 129–148.

Mason, J.W., 1997. *The Dissolution of the Austro-Hungarian Empire, 1867–1918*. London: Longman.

Mau, S., 2003. *The Moral Economy of Welfare States. Britain and Germany Compared*. London: Routledge.

Maxwell, S., 2009. 'Social Justice and the SNP'. *In*: G. Hassan, ed. *The Modern SNP, from Protest to Power*. Edinburgh: Edinburgh University Press, 120–134.

McAdam, D., McCarthy, J. and Zald, M., 1996. 'Introduction: Opportunities, Mobilizing Structures, and Framing Processes – Toward a Synthetic, Comparative Perspective on Social Movements'. *In*: D. McAdam, J. McCarthy and M. Zald, eds *Comparative Perspectives on Social Movements. Political Opportunities, Mobilizing Structures, and Cultural Framings*. Cambridge: Cambridge University Press, 1–20.

McCrone, D., 1992. 'Towards a Principled Society: Scottish Elites in the Twentieth Century'. *In*: T. Dickson and J.H. Treble, eds *People and Society in Scotland, 1914–1990*. Vol. 3. Edinburgh: J. Donald, 174–199.

McCrone, D., 2001. *Understanding Scotland. The Sociology of a Nation*. London: Routledge.

McCrone, D., 2003. 'Redesigning the UK: The Politics of Devolution'. *In*: A.G. Gagnon, M. Guibernau and F. Rocher, eds *The Conditions of Diversity in Multinational Democracies*. Montreal: Institute for Research on Public Policy, 135–150.

McCrone, D., 2012. 'Scotland Out of the Union? The Rise and Rise of the Nationalist Agenda'. *The Political Quarterly*, 83 (1), 69–76.

McCrone, D. and Paterson, L., 2002. 'The Conundrum of Scottish Independence'. *Scottish Affairs*, 40 (1), 54–75.

McCrone, G., 1965. *Scotland's Economic Progress, 1951–60*. London: Allen & Unwin.

McCrone, G., 1969. *Scotland's Future. The Economics of Nationalism*. Oxford: Blackwell, 66–67.

McCrone, G., 2013. *Scottish Independence: Weighing up the Economics*. Kindle edition. Edinburgh: Birlinn.

McEwen, N., 2002. 'State Welfare Nationalism: The Territorial Impact of Welfare State Development in Scotland'. *Regional and Federal Studies*, 12 (1), 66–90.

McEwen, N. and Moreno, L., 2005. 'Exploring the Territorial Politics of Welfare'. *In*: N. McEwen and L. Moreno, eds *The Territorial Politics of Welfare*. London: Routledge, 1–40.

McRoberts, K., 2001. *Catalonia: Nation-Building without a State*. Oxford: Oxford University Press.

Meadwell, H., 1999. 'Stateless Nations and the International Order'. *In*: P. Thazha Varkey and J.A. Hall, eds *International Order and the Future of World Politics*. Cambridge: Cambridge University Press, 262–282.

Meguid, B., 2008. *Party Competition between Unequals*. Cambridge: Cambridge University Press.

Meunier, O., Mignolet, M. and Mulquin, M-E., 2007. *Les transferts interrégionaux en Belgique: une approche historique*. Cahiers de recherche, Série politique économique, n. 11, Université de Namur.

Meynen, A., 2009. 'Economic and Social Policy since the 1950s'. *In*: E. Witte, J. Craeybeckx and A. Meyen, eds *Political History of Belgium. From 1830 Onwards*. Brussels: Academic and Scientific Publishers, 271–360.

Midwinter, A., Keating, M. and Mitchell, J., 1992. *Politics and Public Policy in Scotland*. Basingstoke: Palgrave MacMillan.

Mill, J.S., 1988. *Utilitarianism, Liberty and Representative Government, Selections from Auguste Comte and Positivism*. London: Everyman's Library.

Miller, D., 1995. *On Nationality*. Oxford: Oxford University Press.

Miller, W., 1981. *The End of British Politics? Scots and English Political Behaviour in the Seventies*. Oxford: Clarendon Press.

Milward, A., 1992. *The European Rescue of the Nation-State*. London: Routledge.

Ministero dell'Interno, 2017. *Archivio storico delle elezioni* [online] Available from: http://elezionistorico.interno.it/ [accessed 20 March 2017].

Mishra, R., 1984. *The Welfare State in Crisis. Social Thought and Social Change*. Brighton: Wheatsheaf Books.

Mitchell, J., 1988. 'Recent Developments in the Scottish National Party'. *The Political Quarterly*, 59 (4), 473–477.

Mitchell, J., 1996. *Strategies for Self-Government. The Campaign for a Scottish Parliament*. Edinburgh: Polygon Press.

Mitchell, J., 2009. 'From Breakthrough to Mainstream: the Politics of Potential and Blackmail'. *In*: G. Hassan, ed. *The Modern SNP, from Protest to Power*. Edinburgh: Edinburgh University Press, 31–41.

Mitchell, J., 2015. 'Sea Change in Scotland'. *Parliamentary Affairs*, 68 (1), 88–100.

Mitchell, J. and Convery, A., 2012. 'Conservative Unionism: Prisoned in Marble'. *In*: D., Torrance, ed. *Whatever Happened to Tory Scotland?* Edinburgh: Edinburgh University Press, 170–184.

Mitrany, D., 1965. 'The Prospects of Integration: Federal or Functional'. *Journal of Common Market Studies*, 4 (2), 119–150.

Moioli, V., 1990. *I nuovi razzismi: miserie e fortune della Lega Lombarda*. Roma: Edizioni Associate.

Mommen, A., 1994. *The Belgian Economy in the Twentieth Century*. London: Routledge.

Monasterio Escudero, C., 2002. 'El laberinto de la financiacion autonomica'. *Hacienda Publica Espanola*, 4 (163), 157–187.

Morata, F. and Popartan, L.A., 2008. 'Spain'. *In*: M. Baun and D. Marek, eds *EU Cohesion Policy After Enlargement*. Basingstoke: Palgrave MacMillan, 73–95.

Moravscik, A., 1999. *The Choice for Europe. Social Purpose and State Power from Messina to Maastricht*. London: UCL Press Taylor & Francis Group.

Moreno, L., 2001. *The Federalization of Spain*. London: Frank Cass.

Moreno, L., 2006. 'Scotland, Catalonia, Europeanization and the "Moreno Question"'. *Scottish Affairs*, 54 (1), 1–21.

Moreno, L. and Arriba, A., 1999. *Decentralization, Mesogovernments, and the New Logic of Welfare Provision in Spain*. Instituto de Estudios Sociales Avanzados (CSIC) Working Paper n. 99–01.

Mudde, C., 2000. *The Ideology of the Extreme Right*. Manchester: Manchester University Press.

Mudde, C., 2004. 'The Populist Zeitgeist'. *Government and Opposition*, 39 (4), 541–563.

Mulquin, M-E. and Senger, K., 2011. *Interregional Transfers and Economic Convergence*, CERPE Cahier de recherche n. 58.

Munoz, J. and Tormos, R., 2012. *Identitat o càlculs instrumentals? Analisi dels factors explicatius del suport a la independencia*. Centro d'Estudis d'Opinio, Generalitat de Catalunya.

Nagels, J., 2002. 'La situation économique de la Flandre et le Mouvement Flamand'. *Brussels Economic Review*, 45 (4), 95–136.

Nairn, T., 2003. *The Break-up of Britain*. 3rd edition. Edinburgh: Common Ground.

NBB (National Bank of Belgium), 2017a. *Public Finance: Receipts, Expenditure and Overall Balance* [online]. Available from: http://stat.nbb.be/ [accessed 8 March 2017].

NBB, 2017b. *Regional Accounts by institutional sectors – NACE 2008* [online]. Available from: http://stat.nbb.be/ [accessed 8 March 2017].

O'Connor, J., 1973. *The Fiscal Crisis of the State*. New Brunswick: Transaction.

OECD (Organisation for Economic Cooperation and Development), 2017. *Industry and Services. Production and Sales (MEI). Production in Total Manufacturing sa, Index* [online]. Available from: http://stats.oecd.org/ [accessed 23 March 2017].

Offe, C., 1984. *Contradictions of the Welfare State*. London: Hutchinson.

Ohmae, K., 1995. *The End of the Nation State, The Rise of Regional Economies*. London: Harper Collins.

ONS (Office for National Statistics), 2013. *A02 Summary of Headline LFS1 Employment, Unemployment and Economic Inactivity Series* [online]. February. Available from: www.ons.gov.uk/ons/rel/lms/labour-market-statistics/february-2013/table-a02.xls [accessed 22 February 2017].

ONS, 2016a. *Regional Gross Value Added (Production Approach)* [online]. December. Available from: www.ons.gov.uk/economy/grossvalueaddedgva/datasets/regionalgrossvalueaddedproductionapproachconstraineddatatables [accessed 7 March 2017].

ONS, 2016b. *Regional Gross Disposable Household Income (GDHI)* [online]. May. Available from: www.ons.gov.uk/economy/regionalaccounts/grossdisposable householdincome/datasets/regionalgrossdisposablehouseholdincomegdhi [accessed 22 February 2017].

ONS, 2016c. *GDP Deflators at Market Prices, and Money GDP* [online]. September. Available from: www.gov.uk/government/statistics/gdp-deflators-at-market-prices-and-money-gdp-september-2016-quarterly-national-accounts [accessed 22 February 2017].

ONS, 2017. *CPI All Items Index: Estimated pre-97 2015=100* [online]. March. Available from: www.ons.gov.uk/economy/inflationandpriceindices/timeseries/d7bt/mm23 [accessed 7 March 2017].

ONS and Scottish Government, 2016. *Regional Employment Patterns in Scotland: Statistics from the Annual Population Survey 2015*. *Web-tables* [online].

Available from: www.gov.scot/Topics/Statistics/Browse/Labour-Market/Local-Authority-Tables [accessed 22 February 2017].

Opotow, S., 1990. 'Moral Exclusion and Injustice: An Introduction'. *Journal of Social Issues*, 46 (1), 1–20.

Orridge, A., 1981a. 'Uneven Development and Nationalism: I'. *Political Studies*, 29 (1), 1–15.

Orridge, A., 1981b. 'Uneven Development and Nationalism: II'. *Political Studies*, 29 (2), 181–190.

Orte, A. and Wilson, A., 2009. 'Multilevel Coalition and Statute Reform in Spain'. *Regional and Federal Studies*, 19 (3), 415–436.

Osterlynck, S., 2009. 'The Political Economy of State Restructuring and the Regional uneven Transition to After-Fordism in Belgium'. *In*: M. Huysseune, ed. *Contemporary Centrifugal Regionalism: Comparing Flanders and Northern Italy*. Brussels: KVAB, 83–94.

Özkirimli, U., 2010. *Theories of Nationalism: A Critical Introduction*. 2nd edition. Basingstoke: Macmillan.

Padoa Schioppa Kostoris, F., 1996. 'Excesses and Limits of the Public Sector in the Italian Economy. The Ongoing Reform'. *In*: S. Gundle and S. Parker, eds *The New Italian Republic. From the Fall of the Berlin Wall to Berlusconi*. London: Routledge, 273–276.

Padovano, F., 2007. *The Politics and Economics of Regional Transfers. Decentralization, Interregional Redistribution and Income Divergence*. Cheltenham: Edward Elgar.

Page, E., 1978. 'Michael Hechter's Internal Colonial Thesis: Some Theoretical and Methodological Problems'. *European Journal of Political Research*, 6, 295–317.

Palacio, A., 2012. 'Europe's Regional Revolt', *Project Syndicate*, 5 November. Available from: www.project-syndicate.org/commentary/independence-calls-growing-in-catalonia-and-scotland-by-ana-palacio [accessed 18 April 2017].

Pallares, F. and Keating, M., 2003. 'Multi-Level Electoral Competition: Regional Elections and Party System in Spain'. *European Urban and Regional Studies*, 10 (3), 239–255.

Passalacqua, G., 2009. *Il vento della Padania*. Milano: Mondadori.

Passarelli, G. and Tuorto, D., 2009. 'La Lega Nord oltre il Po'. *Il Mulino*, 58 (4), 663–670.

Passarelli, G. and Tuorto, D., 2012. *Lega & Padania. Storie e luoghi delle camicie verdi*. Electronic version. Bologna: Il Mulino.

Paterson, L., 1994. *The Autonomy of Modern Scotland*. Edinburgh: Edinburgh University Press.

Paterson, L., 2001. 'Does Consultation Work? The Scottish Parliament's First Two Years'. *Scottish Affairs*, 37 (2), 85–90.

Paterson, L., 2002. 'Is Britain Disintegrating? Changing Views of "Britain" after Devolution'. *Regional and Federal Studies*, 12 (1), 21–42.

Paterson, L., 2006. 'Sources of Support for the SNP', in C. Bromley, J. Curtice, D. McCrone and A. Park, eds *Has Devolution Delivered?* Edinburgh: Edinburgh University Press, 46–70.

Patriarca, S., 2001. 'Italian Neopatriotism: Debating National Identity in the 1990s'. *Modern Italy*, 6 (1), 21–34.

Patriarca, S., 2011. *Italianità. La costruzione del carattere nazionale*. Bari: Laterza.

Pauwels, T., 2011. 'Explaining the Strange Decline of the Populist Radical Right Vlaams Belang in Belgium: The Impact of Permanent Opposition'. *Acta Politica*, 46 (1), 60–82.

Pavkovic, A. and Radan, P., 2007. *Creating New States: Theory and Practice of Secession*. Aldershot: Ashgate.

Payne, P., 2003. 'The Economy'. *In*: T.M. Devine and R. Finlay, eds *Scotland in the 20th Century*. Edinburgh: Edinburgh University Press, 13–45.

Payne, S., 1975. *Basque Nationalism*. Reno: University of Nevada Press.

Peden, G., 1993. 'An Agenda for the Economic History of 20th Century Scotland'. *Scottish Economic and Social History*, 13 (1), 5–26.

Pellistrandi, B., 2006. 'L'Espagne et sa pratique democratique'. *Etudes*, 405 (1), 21–31.

Persyn, D. and Algoed, K., 2009. *Interregional Redistribution, Growth and Convergence*, UNU-CRIS working paper n. 13.

Peters, B.G., 2006. 'Consociationalism, Corruption and Chocolate: Belgian Exceptionalism'. *West European Politics*, 29 (5), 1079–1092.

Petit Fonseré, J., 1965. 'Unas notas breves sobre la actuacion del sector publico y las relaciones economicas entre Cataluna y el resto de Espana'. *Moneda y Credito*, 95, 61–76.

Picchieri, A. and Perulli, P., 2010. 'La crisi Italiana e il Nord'. *In*: A., Picchieri, and P., Perulli, eds *La crisi italiana nel mondo globale. Economia e società nel Nord*. Torino: Einaudi, 3–35.

Pichler, R., 2001. 'Economic Policy and Development in Austrian Lombardy, 1815–1859'. *Modern Italy*, 6 (1), 35–58.

Pickard, J. and Dickie, M., 2014. 'EU Commission President Says Scotland Membership Not Automatic'. *Financial Times*, 16 February.

Pierson, P., 1996. 'The New Politics of the Welfare State'. *World Politics*, 48 (2), 143–179.

Pierson, P., 2001a. 'Coping with Permanent Austerity: Welfare State Restructuring in Affluent Democracies'. *In*: P. Pierson, ed. *The New Politics of the Welfare State*. Oxford: Oxford University Press, 410–456.

Pierson, P., 2001b. 'Post-Industrial Pressures on the Mature Welfare States'. *In*: P. Pierson, ed. *The New Politics of the Welfare State*. Oxford: Oxford University Press, 80–104.

Pinard, M. and Hamilton, R., 1986. 'Motivational Dimensions of the Quebec Independence Movement: A Test of a New Movement'. *Research in Social Movements, Conflicts and Change*, (9), 225–280.

Poggi, G., 1990. *The State: Its Nature, Development and Prospects*. Cambridge: Polity Press.

Poirier, J. and Vansteenkiste, S. 2000. 'Le débat sur la fédéralisation de la sécurité sociale en Belgique: le miroir du vouloir-vivre ensemble?'. *Revue belge de sécurité sociale*, (2), 331–379.

Pons, J. and Tremosa, R., 2005. 'Macroeconomic Effects of Catalan Fiscal Deficit with the Spanish State (2002–2010)'. *Applied Economics*, 37 (13), 1455–1463.

Porter, M.E., 1990. *The Competitive Advantage of Nations*. Basingstoke; MacMillan.

Postan, M., 1967. *An Economic History of Western Europe, 1945–1964*. London: Methuen.

Pujas, V. and Rhodes, M., 1999. 'Party Finance and Political Scandal in Italy, Spain and France'. *West European Politics*, 22 (3), 41–63.

Putnam, R., 1993. *Making Democracy Work. Civic Traditions in Modern Italy.* Princeton: Princeton University Press.

Quévit, M., 2010. *Flandres-Wallonie. Quelle solidarité?* Brussels: Couleurs livres.

Renwick, A., Hanretty, C. and Hine, D., 2009. 'Partisan Self-interest and Electoral Reform: The New Italian Electoral Law'. *Electoral Studies*, 28 (3), 437–447.

Rhodes, M., 1995. *'Subversive Liberalism': Market Integration, Globalisation and the European Welfare State.* European University Institute Working Paper 95/10.

Ricolfi, L., 2010. *Il sacco del Nord. Saggio sulla giustizia territoriale.* Milano: Guerini e Associati.

Rochtus, D., 2012. 'The Rebirth of Flemish Nationalism: Assessing the Impact of N-VA Chairman Bart De Wever's Charisma'. *Studies in Ethnicity and Nationalism*, 12 (2), 268–285.

Rokkan, S., 1973. 'Cities, States and Nations: A Dimensional Model for the Study of Contrasts in Development'. *In*: S.N. Eisenstadt and S. Rokkan, eds *Building States and Nations*. Vol. 1. London: Sage, 73–98.

Rokkan, S. and Urwin, D., 1983. *Economy, Territory, Identity. Politics of West European Peripheries.* London: Sage.

Roller, E., 2001. 'The 1997 Llei del Català: A Pandora's Box in Catalonia?'. *Regional and Federal Studies*, 11 (1), 39–54.

Roosma, F., Gelissen, J. and Van Oorschot, W., 2013. 'The Multidimensionality of Welfare State Attitudes: A European Cross-National Study'. *Social Indicators Research*, 113 (1), 235–255.

Rosanvallon, P., 2000. *The New Social Question. Rethinking the Welfare State.* Princeton: Princeton University Press.

Rosanvallon, P., 2015 [1981]. *La crise de l'Etat-Providence.* Paris: Le Seuil.

Roux, C., 2008. 'Italy's Path to Federalism. Origins and Paradoxes'. *Journal of Modern Italian Studies*, 13 (3), 325–339.

Rudolph, R., 1976. *Banking and Industrialization in Austria-Hungary, the Role of Banks in the Industrialization of the Czech Crownlands, 1873–1914.* Cambridge: Cambridge University Press.

Rusconi, G.E., 1993. *Se cessiamo di essere una nazione.* Bologna: Il Mulino.

Sahlins, P., 1989. *Boundaries. The Making of France and Spain in the Pyrenees.* Berkeley: University of California Press.

Sala, G., 2014. 'Federalism without Adjectives in Spain'. *Publius*, 44 (1), 109–134.

Sambanis, N. and Milanovic, B., 2011. *Explaining the Demand for Sovereignty.* World Bank Policy Research Working Paper n. 5888.

Sartori, G., 1986. 'The Influence of Electoral Systems: Faulty Laws or Faulty Methods?'. *In*: B. Grofman and A. Lijphart, eds *Electoral Laws and their Political Consequences*. New York: Algora, 43–68.

Sartori, G., 2005 [1976]. *Parties and Party Systems. A Framework for Analysis.* Colchester: ECPR Press.

Savage, R., 2005. *Economie belge, 1953–2000. Ruptures et mutations.* Louvain: UCL Presses.

Scheve, K. and Slaughter, M., 2006. 'Public Opinion, International Economic Integration and the Welfare State'. *In*: D.R. Cameron, R. Gustav and A. Zinn, eds *Globalization and Self-determination. Is the Nation-state under Siege?* London: Routledge, 51–94.

Schmidt, V., 2008. 'Discursive Institutionalism: The Explanatory Power of Ideas and Discourse'. *Annual Review of Political Science*, (11), 303–326.

ScotCen, 2017. *From Indyref1 to Indyref2? The State of Nationalism in Scotland* [online]. Scottish Social Attitudes report. Available from: www.ssa.natcen.ac.uk/read-the-reports/scottish-social-attitudes-2016/from-indyref1-to-indyref2.aspx [accessed 3 May 2017].

Scott, A.J., 2001. *Les régions et l'économie mondiale*. Paris: L'Harmattan.

Secretary of State for Scotland, 1966. *The Scottish Economy, 1965 to 1970. A Plan for Expansion*. Edinburgh: Scottish Office.

Segatti, P., 1999. 'Perché é debole la coscienza degli italiani'. *Il Mulino*, 48 (1), 15–23.

Segura, A., 2001. 'Esquerra Republicana de Catalunya, 1997–2000: la lenta consolidacio'. *In*: R., Alquezar, A. Francesc-Marc *et al.*, eds *Esquerra Republicana de Catalunya, 70 anys d'història (1931–2001)*. Barcelona: Columna, 171–184.

Seitz, H., 2000. 'Fiscal Policy, Deficits and Politics of Subnational Governments: The Case of the German Laender'. *Public Choice*, 102 (3), 183–218.

Serrano, I., 2013. 'Just a Matter of Identity? Support for Independence in Catalonia'. *Regional and Federal Studies*, 23 (5), 523–545.

Sideri, S., 1997. 'Globalization and Regional Integration'. *The European Journal of Development Research*, 9 (1), 38–82.

Sinardet, D., 2008a. 'Belgian Federalism Put to the Test: The 2007 Belgian Federal Elections and Their Aftermath'. *West European Politics*, 31 (5), 1016–1032.

Sinardet, D., 2008b. 'Territorialité et identités linguistiques en Belgique', *Hermès, La Revue*, (2), 141–147.

Sinardet, D., 2010. 'From Consociational Consciousness to Majoritarian Myth: Consociational Democracy, Multi-Level Politics and the Belgian case of Brussels-Halle-Vilvoorde'. *Acta Politica*, 45 (3), 346–369.

Slembrouck, S. and Blommaert, J., 1995. 'La construction politico-rhétorique d'une nation flamande'. *In*: A. Morelli, ed. *Les grands mythes de l'Histoire de Belgique, de Flandre et de Wallonie*. Brussels: Vie Ouvrière, 263–280.

Smeyers, K. and Buyst, E., 2016. *Het Gestolde Land*. Antwerp: Polis.

Smith, A.D., 1979. *Nationalism in the Twentieth Century*. New York: New York University Press.

Smith, A.D., 1999. *Myths and Memories of the Nation*. Oxford: Oxford University Press.

Sorens, J., 2004. 'Globalisation, Secessionism, and Autonomy'. *Electoral Studies*, 23 (4), 727–752.

Sperber, D., 1985. 'Anthropology and Psychology: Towards an Epidemiology of Representations'. *Man*, 20 (1), 73–89.

Spruyt, H., 1994. *The Sovereign State and Its Competitors: An Analysis of Systems Change*. Princeton: Princeton University Press.

SSAS (Scottish Social Attitude Survey), 2017a. *Do You Think England's Economy Benefits More from the Union, Scotland's or About Equal?* [online]. Available from: http://whatscotlandthinks.org/questions/do-you-think-englands-economy-benefits-more-from-the-union-scotlands-or-about-5#line [accessed 15 May 2017].

SSAS, 2017b. *Does Scotland Get More, Less or Pretty Much Its Fair Share of Government Spending?* [online]. Available from: http://whatscotlandthinks.org/questions/does-scotland-get-more-less-or-pretty-much-its-fair-share-of-government-spendi-5#line [accessed 15 May 2017].

SSAS, 2017c. *How Should Scotland be Governed (Three Options)* [online]. Available from: http://whatscotlandthinks.org/questions/how-should-scotland-be-governed-five-response-categories-collapsed-to-three#line [accessed 15 May 2017].

SSAS, 2017d. *Moreno National Identity* [online]. Available from: http://whatscot landthinks.org/questions/moreno-national-identity-5#line [accessed 15 May 2017].

SSAS, 2017e. *Party Political Identification Broken Down by 'How Should Scotland be Governed (Five Response Categories Collapsed to Three)'* [online]. Available from: http://whatscotlandthinks.org/questions/party-political-identification-5/ explore/ScotPar3/#explore [accessed 24 May 2017].

SSAS, 2017f. *How Much Do You Agree or Disagree That the Scottish Parliament Should Be Given More Powers?* [online]. Available from: http://whatscotland thinks.org/questions/how-much-do-you-agree-or-disagree-that-the-scottish-parliament-should-be-given-6#table [accessed 24 May 2017].

Staderini, A. and Vadalà, E., 2009. 'Bilancio pubblico e flussi redistributivi inter-regionali: ricostruzione e analisi dei flussi fiscali nelle regioni italiane'. *In*: Banca d'Italia, *Mezzogiorno e politiche regionali, seminari e convegni*. Roma: Banca d'Italia, 597–621.

Statistics Belgium, 2017. *Indice des prix à la consommation et indice santé* [online]. Available from: http://statbel.fgov.be/fr/statistiques/opendata/datasets/prix/ [accessed 8 March 2017].

Stella, G.A., 2000. *Schei. Dal boom alla rivolta, il mitico nordest*. Milano: Mondadori.

Stengers, J., 2004. 'Histoire de la législation électorale en Belgique'. *Revue belge de philologie et d'histoire*, 82 (1–2), 247–270.

Storper, M., 1995. 'The Resurgence of Regional Economies, Ten Years Later: The Region as a Nexus of Untraded Interdependencies'. *European and Regional Studies*, 2 (3), 191–221.

Subirats, J. and Vilaregut, R., 2012. 'El debat sobre la independència de Catalunya. Causes, implicacions i reptes de futur'. *Anuari del Conflicte Social*, 2, 514–527.

Sullivan, J., 1988. *ETA and Basque Nationalism: The Fight for Euskadi, 1890–1986*. London: Routledge.

SWG, 2010. *Affari italiani. Federalismo e secessione*. 25 June. Available from: www.affaritaliani.it/static/upl/aff/affari-italiani-rel-14.pdf [accessed 27 May 2017].

Swyngedouw, M., 1992. 'L'essor d'Agalev et du Vlaams Blok'. *Courrier heb-domadaire du CRISP*, 17 (1362).

Swyngedouw, M., 2001. 'The Subjective Cognitive and Affective Map of Extreme Right Voters: Using Open-Ended Questions in Exit Polls'. *Electoral Studies*, 20 (2), 228–238.

Swyngedouw, M. and Abts, K., 2011. 'Les électeurs de la N-VA aux élections fédé-rales du 13 juin 2010'. *Courrier Hebdomadaire du CRISP*, 40 (2125), 5–31.

Swyngedouw, M. and Ivaldi, G., 2001. 'The Extreme Right-Wing Utopia in Belgium and France: The Ideology of the Flemish Vlaams Blok and the French Front National'. *West European Politics*, 24 (3), 1–22.

Swyngedouw, M. and Rink, N., 2008. *Hoe Vlaams-Beglischgezind zijn de Vlamin-gen?* CeSO/ISPO/2008-6.

Swyngedouw, M., Abts, K. and Galle, J., 2014. 'Vlamingen en de communautaire kwestie', in K., Abts, M., Swyngedouw, J., Billiet and B., Meuleman, eds *Vlaan-deren kiest. Trends in stemgedrag en opvattingen over politiek, staatshervorming en kerk*. Leuven: Lannoo Campus, 219–245.

Swyngedouw, M., Abts, K., Baute, S., Galle, J. and Meuleman, B., 2015. *Het Com-munautaire in de Verkiezingen van 25 Mei 2014. Analyse op basis van de pos-telectorale Verkiezingonderzoeken 1991-2014*. Leuven: ISPO.

Tajfel, H., 1978. 'Social Categorization, Social Identity and Social Comparison'. *In*: H. Tajfel, ed. *Differentiation between Social Groups. Studies in the Social Psychology of Intergroup Relations*. London: Academic Press, 61–76.

Tambini, D., 2001. *Nationalism in Italian Politics. The Stories of the Northern League, 1980–2000*. London: Routledge.

Tanzi, V. and Schuknecht L., 2000. *Public Spending in the 20th Century. A Global Perspective*. Cambridge: Cambridge University Press.

Taylor-Gooby, P., 1988. 'The Future of the British Welfare State: Public Attitudes, Citizenship and Social Policy under the Conservative Government of the 1980s'. *European Sociological Review*, 4 (1), 1–19.

Teti, V., 2011. 'L'invenzione della questione settentrionale, la cancellazione della questione meridionale e nuove forme di razzismo'. *In*: V. Teti, ed. *La razza maledetta. Origini del pregiudizio antimeridionale*. Roma: Manifestolibri, 7–47.

The Economist, 1976. 'Decline and Fall'. 3 January.

The Economist, 2017a. 'Uniting the Clans'. 11 May.

The Economist, 2017b. 'Scotland's Government Focuses on Policy not Freedom'. 7 September.

Thomas, P-H., 2014. 'La Wallonie plus dynamique que la Flandres?'. *Trends-Tendances*, 23 Janvier, 32–35.

Thurow, L., 1980. *The Zero-Sum Society. Distribution and the Possibilities for Economic Change*. New York: Basic Books.

Tilly, C., 1990. *Coercion, Capital and European States, AD 990–1990*. Oxford: Basil Blackwell.

Tilly, C. 1994. 'Entanglements of European Cities and States'. *In*: C. Tilly and W. Blockmans, eds *Cities and the Rise of States in Europe. AD 1000 to 1800*. Boulder: Westview Press, 1–27.

Torrance, D., 2009. 'The Journey from the 79 Group to the Modern SNP'. *In*: G. Hassan, ed. *The Modern SNP, from Protest to Power*. Edinburgh: Edinburgh University Press, 162–176.

Tortella, G., 2000. *The Development of Modern Spain. An Economic History of the Nineteenth and Twentieth Centuries*. Cambridge: Harvard University Press.

Tortella, G., Garcia Ruiz, J.L., Nunez, C.E. and Quiroga, G., 2016. *Cataluña en España. Historia y Mito*. Madrid: Gadir.

Trias, R., 1985. *Narracio d'una asfixia premeditada*. Barcelona: Tibidabo Edicions.

Trigilia, C., 1992. *Sviluppo senza autonomia*. Bologna: Il Mulino.

Uriel, E. and Barberan, R., 2007. *Las balanzas fiscales de las comunidades autonomas con la Administracion Publica Central*. Bilbao: Fudacion BBVA.

Urwin, D., 2004 [1982]. 'Germany: From Geographical Expression to Regional Accommodation'. *In*: M. Keating, ed. *Regions and Regionalism in Europe*. Cheltenham: Edward Elgar.

Vaillancourt, F., 2010. 'Inter-Regional Fiscal Flows: Interpretation Issues'. *In*: N., Bosch, M. Espasa and A. Solé Ollé, eds *The Political Economy of Inter-Regional Fiscal Flows, Measurements, Determinants and Effects on Country Stability*. Cheltenham: Edward Elgar, 39–58.

Van den Berghe, P., 1981. *The Ethnic Phenomenon*. Westport: Praeger.

Van der Essen, L., 1920. *A Short History of Belgium*. Chicago: University of Chicago Press.

Vandermotten, C., 1997. 'Two Hundred Years of Change in the Industrial Geography of Belgium'. *In*: H. Van der Wee and J. Blomme, eds *The Economic Development of Belgium since 1870*. Cheltenham: Edward Elgar, 146–174.

Van der Wee, E., 1997. 'The Economic Challenge Facing Belgium in the 19th and 20th Century'. *In*: H. Van der Wee and J. Blomme, eds *The Economic Development of Belgium since 1870*. Cheltenham: Edward Elgar, 52–66.

Van Goethem, H., 2010. *Belgium and the Monarchy*. Antwerp: University Press Antwerp.

Van Haute, E. and Pilet, J-B., 2006. 'Regionalist Parties in Belgium (VU, RW, FDF): Victims of Their Own Success?'. *Regional and Federal Studies*, 16 (3), 297–313.

Van Hecke, A., 2010. *Balancing Public Debt Division in Belgium: How to Assign (Part of the) Federal Debt to the Region?*, Centre for Economic Studies, KULeuven.

Van Oorschot, W., 2000. 'Who Should Get What, and Why?'. *Policy and Politics*, 28 (1), 33–49.

Van Oorschot, W., 2006. 'Making the Difference in Social Europe: Deservingness Perceptions among Citizens of European Welfare States'. *Journal of European Social Policy*, 16 (1), 23–42.

Van Rompuy, P., 2010. 'Measurement and Practice of Fiscal Flows: The Case of Belgium'. *In*: N. Bosch, M. Espasa and A. Solé Ollé, eds *The Political Economy of Inter-Regional Fiscal Flows, Measurements, Determinants and Effects on Country Stability*. Cheltenham: Edward Elgar, 108–124.

Van Rompuy, P. and Bilsen, V., 1988. *10 jaar financiële stromen tussen de gewesten in België*. Leuven: KUL.

Van Rompuy, P. and Verheirstraten, A., 1979. 'Regionale herverdelings- en financieringsstromen'. *Leuvense Economische Standpunten*, (14), 1–23.

Van Velthoven, H., 1987. 'Historical Aspects. The Process of Language Shift in Brussels: Historical Background and Mechanisms'. *In*: E. Witte and U. Baetens Beardsmore, eds *The Interdisciplinary Study of Urban Bilingualism in Brussels*. Clevedon: Multilingual Matters, 15–45.

Vandelli, L., 2011. 'L'unificazione italiana e il rapporto centro-periferia'. *Il Mulino*, 60 (3), 415–424.

Vantemsche, G., 1994. *De beginjaren van de sociale zekerheid in België, 1944–1963*. Brussels: VUB Press.

Verdonck, M. and Deschouwer, K., 2003. 'Patterns and Principles of Fiscal Federalism in Belgium'. *Regional and Federal Studies*, 13 (4), 91–110.

Viesti, G., 2003. *Abolire il Mezzogiorno*. Bari: Laterza.

Vilar, P., 1962. *La Catalogne dans l'Espagne moderne. Recherches sur les fondements économiques des structures nationales*. Paris: SEVPEN.

Vos, L., 1993. 'Shifting Nationalism: Belgians, Flemish and Walloons'. *In*: M. Teich, ed. *The National Question in Europe in Historical Context*. Cambridge: Cambridge University Press, 128–147.

Walzer, M., 1990. 'The Communitarian Critique of Liberalism'. *Political Theory*, 18 (1), 6–23.

Weber, E., 1976. *Peasants into Frenchmen: The Modernization of Rural France, 1870–1914*. Standford: Standford University Press.

Weber, M., 1946. 'The Social Psychology of World Religion'. *In*: H.H. Gerth and C. Wright Mills, eds *From Max Weber: Essays in Sociology*. New York: Oxford University Press, 267–301.

Wils, L., 1992. 'Introduction: A Brief History of the Flemish Movement'. *In*: T. Hermans, L. Vos and L. Wils, eds 1992. *The Flemish Movement: A Documentary History, 1780–1990*. London: Athlone Press, 7–23.

Wils, L., 2010. *Van de Belgische naar de Vlaamse Natie. Een geschiedenis van de Vlaamse Beweging.* Leuven: Acco.

Wilson, G., 2009. *SNP: The Turbulent Years 1960–1990.* Stirling: Scots Independent.

Winters, S.B., 1969. 'The Young Czech Party (1874–1914): An Appraisal'. *Slavic Review*, 28 (3), 426–444.

Witte, E., 1993. 'Language and Territoriality. A Summary of Developments in Belgium'. *International Journal on Group Rights*, 1 (3), 203–223.

Witte, E., 2009a. 'Breakthrough of a Liberal Constitutional State (1830–1848). *In:* E. Witte, J. Craeybeckx and A. Meynen, eds *Political History of Belgium: From 1830 Onwards.* Brussels: ASP, 19–60.

Witte, E., 2009b. 'Increasing Tensions Between the Communities and the Creation of a Federalised Belgium'. *In:* E. Witte, J. Craeybeckx and A. Meyen, eds *Political History of Belgium. From 1830 Onwards.* Brussels: Academic and Scientific Publishers, 361–391.

Witte, E., 2009c. 'Mechanisms of Post-War and Present-Day Political Systems'. *In:* E. Witte, J. Craeybeckx and A. Meyen, eds *Political History of Belgium. From 1830 Onwards.* Brussels: Academic and Scientific Publishers, 420–432.

World Bank, 2017. *World Bank Development Indicators. GDP Deflator* [online]. Available from: http://databank.worldbank.org/data/reports.aspx?source=2&series=NY.GDP.DEFL.ZS&country=BEL# [accessed 8 March 2017].

Yergin, D. and Stanislaw, J., 1998. *The Commanding Heights.* New York: Simon & Schuster.

Zaslove, A., 2011. *The Reinvention of the European Radical Right.* Montreal: McGill-Queen's University Press.

Ziblatt, D., 2006. *Structuring the State. The Formation of Italy and Germany and the Puzzle of Federalism.* Princeton: Princeton University Press.

Zinn, A., 2006. 'Economic Integration and Political Separatism. Parallel Trends or Causally Linked Processes?'. *In:* D.R. Cameron, R. Gustav and A. Zinn, eds *Globalization and Self-Determination. Is the Nation-State under Siege?* London: Routledge, 233–246.

Zolberg, A., 1974. 'The Making of Flemings and Walloons: Belgium: 1830–1914'. *The Journal of Interdisciplinary History*, 5 (2), 179–235.

Primary sources

Agudo, C., 2010. 'Només Esquerra defensa la IP per la independència', *Esquerra Nacional (EN)*, 181, p. 6.

Ambrosetti, G., 2002. 'Otto mesi di lotta e di governo'. *Il Sole delle Alpi (SdA)*, VI (1), pp. 7–10.

Annemans, G., 1993. 'Grondslagen van een sociale politiek'. *In:* VB. *Arm Vlaanderen?* Congress, Hasselt, 5 December.

Annemans, G., 1994. 'Geen Vlaams Blok-pottekijker by Augusta', *VLB (Vlaams Blok)*, 2, p. 3.

Annemans, G. and Builtinck, K., 1997. *100 vragen aan en antwoorden van Vlaams-Blokpropagandisten.* Electoral brochure, VBA (Vlaams Blok archive).

Annemans, G. and Smout, W., 1997. *De kostprijs van België. Nord-Zuid-transfers in België anno 1992.* II edition. Electoral brochure, VBA.

Annemans, G. and Utsi, S., 2011. *After Belgium, the Orderly Split-Up*. Brussels: Uitgeverij Egmont.

Aragones, P., 2012. 'La Suècia del Mediterrani?'. *EN*, 204, p. 9.

Arckens, E., 1996. 'Het Volk beslist'. *VLB*, 8, pp. 10–11.

Arcucci, F., 1992. 'I valori della nostra cultura'. *Lombardia Autonomista (LA)*, X (10), 8 May, p. 5.

Bain, M., 1975. *Scotland – Europe's Industrial Slum*. Press release. 21 April, Acc. 10090/141, NLS (National Library of Scotland).

Ballarin, A., 2012a. ' "Oberate dalle tasse PMI in pericolo" '. *La Padania (LP)*, 3 July, pp. 4–5.

Ballarin, A., 2012b. 'Salvi gli Ospedali al Sud, su l'Iva al Nord', *LP*, 6 July, pp. 2–3.

Bassi, P., 2005. 'Governo, torna Bossi "escono" An e UDC'. *LP*, 12 March, p. 5.

Bonometti, G., 1998. 'Iri 2 la vendetta'. *SdA*, II (13), 28 March, pp. 15–19.

Bossi, U., 1982. 'L'autonomia dei popoli. Il più avanzato modello sociale. Nuovo determinismo', *LA*, I, March, p. 1.

Bossi, U., 1986. '29 maggio di lombardità', *LA*, IV (8), June, p. 1.

Bossi, U., 1991a. 'L'Italia fuori dall'Europa', *LA*, IX (26), p. 4.

Bossi, U., 1991b. 'Lega Nord per la libertà'. *LA*, IX (5), p. 4.

Bossi, U., 1996. 'Padania sovrana'. *Lega Nord (LeN)*, XIV (31), 29 July, p. 2.

Camps Boy, J., 1990a. 'El sistema de finançament autonomic ara (1)'. *La Republica (LR)*, 8, pp. 4–5.

Camps Boy, J., 1990b. 'El sistema de finançament autonomic ara (2)'. *LR*, 9, pp. 6–8.

Carcano, F., 2006. 'La strada che porta al federalismo passa dal Mezzogiorno'. *LP*, 12–13 February, p. 6.

Carcano, F., 2012. 'Un altro regalo per il solito sud…'. *LP*, 13 September, p. 4.

Carod-Rovira, J-L., 1986. 'Una necessitat vital: refundar ERC?'. *L'Avui*, 1 November, p. 9.

Carod-Rovira, J-L., 1991. *La via democratica a la independencia nacional*. Unpublished paper. Catalan Parliament Library.

Castellazzi, F., 1990. 'L'industria dei sequestri'. *LA*, VIII (3), p. 3.

Castelli, R., 2011. 'Pagano sempre solo i Padani'. *LP*, 6 December, p. 1.

Cestonaro, B., 1987. 'Come hanno tentato di farci diventare italiani'. *Mondo Veneto (MV)*, VI (2), p. 4.

Cobbaert, P., 2014. 'Wij gaan voor een besparingslogica'. *De Zondag*, 27 April, pp. 12–13.

Colom, A., 1989. 'Per la llibertat del presos Catalans', *LR*, 4, p. 3.

Colom, A., 1995. *Contracte amb Catalunya*. Barcelona: Columna.

Cornali, A., 1998. 'La Lega corre da sola'. *SdA*, II (41), pp. 16–19.

Crawford, D., 1975. *Letter Sent to the Chancellor of the Exchequer, Denis Healey*. Press release. 7 April. Acc. 10090/141, NLS.

D'Haeseleer, G. and Bultinck, K., 2003. *Vlaams Blok, sociale volkspartij*. Electoral brochure, VBA.

De Man, F., Laeremans, B. and Van Hauthem, J., 2005. *Zwartboek Splitsing*. Electoral brochure, VBA.

De Wever, B., 2009. 'Er zijn verschillen…'. *Nieuw-Vlaams Magazine (N-VM)*, October, p. 3.

De Wever, B., 2010. 'Weg van het chaos-denken'. *N-VM*, May, p. 3.

De Wever, B., 2013. 'Gedaan met lachen'. *N-VM*, March, p. 3.

De Wever, B., 2014. 'Historisch'. *N-VM*, February, p. 3.

Decoster, F., 1980. 'La Belgique, qu'elle crève'. *De Vlaams Nationalist (DVN)*, June.

Dekker, N., 1972. *The Reafilty of Scotland's Oil*. Edinburgh: SNP.

Delfi, S., 1997. 'Spremuta d'IRAP'. *SdA*, I (9), pp. 31–37.

Della Torre, C., 1990. 'Marcheno ICIAP alle stelle!'. *LA*, VIII (19), p. 4.

Dillen, K., 1983. 'Wij staan niet alleen', *VLB*, 2, p. 4.

Dillen, M., 2012. 'Een menswaardig pensioenstelsel voor alle Vlamingen'. *Vlaams Belang Magazine (VBM)*, 5, pp. 34–35.

Dussin, L., 2008a. 'Gli ultimi operai indecisi abbandonano la sinistra comunista per il Carroccio', *LP*, 30 March, p. 10.

Dussin, L., 2008b. 'Federalisti e no global: così battiamo la crisi'. *LP*, 10 December, p. 4.

Dussin, L., 2011a. 'Italia, una "famiglia" da cui bisogna uscire', *LP*, 23 August, p. 8.

Dussin, L., 2011b. 'Zavorra Sud, zavorra Italia'. *LP*, 13 September, p. 8.

Dussin, L., 2011c. 'Se la Padania si confedera l'Italia può avere un futuro'. *LP*, 18 September, p. 9.

Eisen, E., 2003. ' "Rispettate il giuramento!" '. *SdA*, VII (8), pp. 34–37.

ERC, 1977. *Sintesi Programatica*. Spanish election manifesto's summary, ERC archive (ERCA).

ERC, 1989a. 'Entrevista', *La Humanitat*. 0, p. 1.

ERC, 1989b. *L'Esquerra, la nova frontera, vota Esquerra Republicana de Catalunya*. Spanish election manifesto, ERCA.

ERC, 1990. 'Espai entrevista: Heribert Barrera i Costa'. *LR*, 6, p. 16.

ERC, 1992a. '18e Congrés Nacional Extraordinari d'ERC'. *LR*, 15, p. 11.

ERC, 1992b. *Cap a la independència*. Catalan election manifesto, ERCA.

ERC, 1993a. 'ERC pel Concert econòmic'. *LR*, 16, p. 8.

ERC, 1993b. *Ideological declaration of the Esquerra Republicana of Catalonia*. Centre Maurits Coppieters.

ERC, 1993c. *Pels Catalans, per Catalunya. Cap a l'independència*. Spanish election, ERCA.

ERC, 1994. *Països Catalans, Unio Europea, Per l'Europa de les Nacions*. European election manifesto, ERCA.

ERC, 1995. *Força cap a la independencia*. Catalan election manifesto, ERCA.

ERC, 1996. *La teva veu, cap a la independencia*. Spanish election manifesto, ERCA.

ERC, 1998. 'ERC pel dret a l'autodeterminacio i la reforma de la Constitucio'. *EN*, 8, p. 1.

ERC, 1999a. 'ERC presenta Josep-Lluis Carod-Rovira com a candidat a la preidència de la Generalitat de Catalunya'. *EN*, 11, p. 1.

ERC, 1999b. 'ERC vol que la nova legislatura signifiqui un canvi real per a Catalunya'. *EN*, 16, p. 6.

ERC, 2000a. *Programa marc*. Spanish election manifesto, ERCA.

ERC, 2000b. 'Puigcercos evidencia les discriminacions de l'Estat cap a Catalunya'. *EN*, 20, p. 7.

ERC, 2000c. 'ERC vol modificar la llei de caixes d'estalvi per tal d'impedir la sortida del pais de 500.000 pessetes anuals dels estalvis depositats'. *EN*, 20, p. 13.

ERC, 2001a. 'La politica industrial d'ERC'. *EN*, 32, p. 13.

ERC, 2001b. 'Pacte Nacional per Catalunya'. *EN*, 28, p. 5.

ERC, 2002. 'Espanya: un estat, una nacio, una capital'. *EN*, 30, p. 4.

ERC, 2003a. *Un pais actiu i equilibrat, eleccions al parlement de Catalunya 2003.* Catalan election manifesto, ERCA.

ERC, 2003b. 'Una constitucio per a Catalunya'. *EN*, 42, p. 5.

ERC, 2004. *Parlant la gent s'entén.* Spanish election manifesto, ERCA.

ERC, 2005. 'El català, de Brussels a Madrid'. *EN*, 64, p. 5.

ERC, 2006a. *Un pais de gent emprenedora amb treball per a tothom_emprenedors.* Catalan election manifesto, ERCA.

ERC, 2006b. *Ara toca no. Catalunya Mereix Més.* Campaign brochure, ERCA.

ERC, 2006c. *Un pais compromès amb la millora de la qualitat de vida de les persones, programa 2006_benestar.* Catalan election manifesto, ERCA.

ERC, 2006d. *Preguntes entor a l'estatut.* Campaign flyer, ERCA.

ERC, 2008a. 'L'Estat es queda 2.622 euros de cada ciutadà català'. *EN*, 87, p. 8.

ERC, 2008b. *Objectiu: un pais de 1a (per aixo volem la independència).* Spanish election manifesto, ERCA.

ERC, 2011a. 'De la crisi no se'n surt només amb retallades'. *EN*, 191, p. 5.

ERC, 2011b. 'Inconformistes devant les retallades socials'. *EN*, 191, p. 4.

ERC, 2012a. 'Ni espoli fiscal, ni espoli social'. *EN*, 204, p. 13.

ERC, 2012b. *Un nou pais per a tothom.* Catalan elections manifesto, ERCA.

ERC, 2015. *Programa Electoral.* Spanish election manifesto, ERCA.

Favere, P., 1979. 'Barst de Belgische Frank?'. *DVN*, September.

Franco, P., 2011. 'Capitale reticolare, indice delle democrazie mature'. *LP*, 26 May, p. 10.

Front d'Esquerres, 1977. *Declaracio.* March, ERCA.

Garibaldi, I., 2014. 'Legge stabilità: la Lega cancella 100 milioni PER LSU DEL SUD'. *LP*, 31 October, p. 8.

Geens, G., 1981. *Volksverbonden, vastberaden.* Electoral flyer, folder 6.2.10.2, KADOC, Leuven.

Girardin, S., 2013. 'Buchi di bilancio e malagestione: la sanità che spacca in due il Paese'. *LP*, 24 January, p. 8.

Gubetti, F., 1992. 'Cosa succede nella Sanità?'. *LA*, Special issue, 10 March, p. 6.

Halliday, J., 1959. *Don't Waste Your Vote on London Controlled Politicians.* Campaign leaflet, Acc. 7295/23, NLS.

Hiers, S., 2015. 'Taalwetgeving: een voodje papier?'. *VBM*, 4, p. 10.

Joseph, B. and Leen, L., 2003. *De kostprijs van België. De financiële plundering van Vlaanderen.* Electoral brochure, VBA.

Junts pel Sì, 2015. *Programa Electoral.* Catalan election manifesto, ERCA.

JVS, 1979. 'Walen buiten! En België mee!'. *DVN*, May.

Laitem, J., 1980. 'Cijfers om bij te tollen'. *DVN*, March.

Leen, L. and Van Den Troost, T., 2005. *175 jaar België, 10 vraagen en antwoorden over dit kunstmatige land. Deel I.* Electoral brochure, VBA.

LN, 1992. *Programma elettorale.* General election manifesto, Lega Nord's archive (LNA).

LN, 1994. *Programma elettorale.* General election manifesto, LNA.

LN, 1995. 'Tutti dal Sud i prefetti del Nord'. *LeN*, XIII (45), p. 3.

LN, 1996a. *Programma elettorale per la Padania, elezioni politiche del 21 aprile 1996.* General election manifesto, LNA.

LN, 1996b. 'Nord: paga cento, incassa uno'. *LeN*, 18 March, p. 3.

LN, 1996c. 'Quattro opzioni'. *LeN*, 15 July, p. 5.

LN, 1996d. 'Lega mediatrice tra due legalità', *LeN*, XIV (36), p. 5.

LN, 2001. *Ragionamenti per la campagna elettorale*. Electoral brochure, LNA.

LN, 2012a. 'Sud, accanimento terapeutico'. *LP*, 8–9 July, p. 2.

LN, 2012b. 'Così la ricchezza che produciamo potrà restare sul nostro territorio'. *LP*, 16–17 September, p. 5.

LN, 2013a. 'Le Regioni del Sud e quelle a Statuto speciale fanno concorrenza sleale', *LP*, 28 January, p. 11.

LN, 2013b. 'Franz: "Il 75% delle tasse al Nord è l'unica soluzione per salvare l'intero Paese"'. LP, 20 February, p. 6.

LN, 2014. 'Pensioni d'invalidità, al SUD sono il DOPPIO rispetto al NORD'. *LP*, 27 September, p. 10.

Macintosh, S., 1966. *100 Home Rule Questions*. Forfar: SNP, SNP archive (SNPA).

Magri, A., 1992. 'Più soldi in busta paga, meno allo stato'. *LA*, 5 March, p. 5.

Mariani, G., 2008. 'La Corte dei Conti bacchetta l'INPS'. *LP*, 27 March, p. 11.

McIlvanney, W., 1987. *Stands Scotland Where it Did?* Second lecture chaired by Gordon Wilson, SNP's Annual National Conference, Dundee, SNPA.

Michiels, A., 2007. 'Naturlijk Vlaams!'. *VBM*, 4, p. 19.

Moltifiori, A., 1990. 'Schiavitù lombarda'. *LA*, VIII (8), p. 5.

Montero, G., 2000. 'L'Italia incompiuta'. *SdA*, IV (7), pp. 22–23.

Murray, G., 1977. 'Scotland's Oil Wealth Enigma'. *The Free Scot*, May, 7, NLS.

N-VA, 2001. '21 haakse ankerpunten voor een nieuw beleid. Manifest van de N-VA'. *Volle Manen*, 1 (10), 9–15.

N-VA, 2002a. *De Nieuw-Vlaamse Alliantie in vraag en antwoord – Deel I*. September, p. 4.

N-VA, 2002b. 'Ondernemen, bouwsteen voor onze samenleving'. *Volle Manen (VM)*, October, p. 8.

N-VA, 2003. *Waarom N-VA? 18 redenen voor zes miljon Vlamingen*. Federal election manifesto, 18 May.

N-VA, 2004a. 'Jaarlijks 11,3 miljard euro Vlaamse "solidariteit"'. *VM*, November, p. 4.

N-VA, 2004b. 'Om over na te denken voor u in het stemhokje stapt!'. *VM*, May, p. 3.

N-VA, 2004c. *Voorstellen voor het Vlaanderen van de 21ste eeuw*. Regional election manifesto, 13 June.

N-VA, 2004d. 'Geert Bourgeois: Samen de Vlaamse staat dichterbij brengen'. *VM*, April, p. 8.

N-VA, 2005. 'De N-VA onderbouwt onafhankelijkheidsgedachte'. *VM*, July, pp. 8–9.

N-VA, 2007a. 'Nu hervormen of morgen verdrinken. Sociaal-economische hefbomen voor deelstaten'. *N-VM*, December, p. 8.

N-VA, 2007b. *Voor en sterker Vlaanderen*. Federal election manifesto.

N-VA, 2007c. 'Rien ne va plus'. *N-VM*, September, pp. 8–9.

N-VA, 2008. 'Federale overheid armlastig door paars begrotingsbeleid'. *N-VM*, February, p. 8.

N-VA, 2009a. *Afrit Vlaanderen, uitrit crisis*. Regional and European election manifesto.

N-VA, 2009b. 'Vlaamse begroting: besparen en investeren'. *N-VM*, December, p. 11.

N-VA, 2009c. 'Een Vlaming bestaat wel'. *N-VM*, December, p. 5.

N-VA, 2010. *Nu durven veranderen. En sterk sociaal en economisch perspectief voor Vlaanderen en Wallonië*. Federal election manifesto.

N-VA, 2011. 'Bart de Wever: Vlaams-nationalisme, de grondstrom van Vlaanderen'. *N-VM*, September, p. 9.

N-VA, 2012a. 'Vlaamse begroting in evenwicht'. *N-VM*, October, p. 11.

N-VA, 2012b. 'Brusselse dienst voor arbeidsbemiddeling (Actiris) werkt niet'. *N-VM*, May, p. 12.

N-VA, 2013a. *New-Flemish Alliance* [online]. Party presentation. Previously available from: www.n-va.be/english [accessed 21 April 2013].

N-VA, 2013b. 'Confederalisme is de sleutel voor een beter beleid'. *N-VM*, May, p. 9.

N-VA, 2014a. 'Bart de Wever: "25 mei is van historisch belang" '. *N-VM*, May, pp. 4–8.

N-VA, 2014b. *Verandering voor Vooruitgang*. Federal, regional and European election manifesto.

N-VA, 2014c. 'Verandering voor Vooruitgang'. *N-VM*, January, pp. 6–9.

N-VA, 2016. *The N-VA's ideology and purpose: Is the N-VA a nationalist party?* [online]. Available from: https://english.n-va.be/frequently-asked-questions [accessed 10 March 2017].

Neri, S., 2013. 'Cassa in deroga, il sud bara e il Veneto resta all'asciutto'. *LP*, 2 February, p. 6.

Orestilli, D., 1991. 'Le poltrone del Sud', *Lega Nord Emilia Romagna*, supplement to *LA*, IX (10), p. 1.

Pagès, P., 2009. 'La darrera gran Diada autonomica?'. *EN*, 153, p. 4.

Pagliarini, G., 2006. 'Federalismo fiscale o il Paese colerà a picco'. *LP*, 14 February, p. 10.

Paini, P., 1996. 'Un referendum per la Padania'. *LN*, XIV (3), p. 3.

Parisi, M., 2002. 'Come stare al governo'. *SdA*, VI (38), p. 1.

Pas, B., 2009. 'Financieel doemscenario'. *VBM*, 5–6, p. 11.

Pas, B., 2013. 'Er is in Vlaanderen slechts één partij die klaarheid biedt'. *VBM*, 5, pp. 10–12.

Peeters, J., 1982. 'Devaluatie het zoveelste bewijs'. *VLB*, 3, p. 2.

Pellai, P., 2008. 'Abbiamo le scatole piene e le tasche vuote'. *LP*, 22 March, p. 3.

Penris, J., 1994. 'Allen Vlaamse Onafhankelijkheid biedt de oplossing'. *VLB*, 2, p. 13.

Petra, G., 2012. 'L'urlo di Cota: "Per noi solo tasse e bastonate. Taglino le spese di Roma" '. *LP*, 13 July, p. 10.

Peumans, J., 2012. *Kieskoorts in gemeenten is geen excuus voor een leeg Vlaams Parlement* [online]. Press release. Available from: www.n-va.be/nieuws/kieskoorts-in-gemeenten-is-geen-excuus-voor-een-leeg-vlaams-parlement [accessed 10 March 2017].

Piazzo, S., 1996. 'Basta soldi ai falsi invalidi'. *LeN*, XIV (8), p. 6.

Piazzo, S. and Malaguti, C., 1996. 'Paga solo la Padania!'. *LeN*, 20 May, p. 4.

Reid, G., 1975. *Speech at St. Andrews University*. Press release, 25 February. Acc. 10090/141, NLS.

Reina, P., 2002. 'Sotto il Sole di Pontida …'. *SdA*, VI (26), p. 1.

Ruspoli, S., 2002. 'L'Italia federale, la leva per cambiare'. *SdA*, VI (44), p. 61.

Salmond, A., 1977. 'The Economics of Independence'. *West Lothian Standard*, Spring, Acc. 10090/195, NLS.

Salmond, A., 1993a. 'Towards a Prosperous Scotland'. *In*: SNP, ed. *Horizons Without Bars. The Future of Scotland. A Series of Speeches*. SNPA.

Salmond, A., 1993b. 'Rosyth – Scotland's Turning Point?'. *In*: SNP, ed. *Horizons Without Bars. The Future of Scotland. A Series of Speeches*. SNPA.

Salmond, A., 1993c. 'Independence and Scottish Democracy'. *In*: SNP, ed. *Horizons Without Bars, The Future of Scotland. A Series of Speeches*. SNPA.

Salmond, A., 1998. 'Speech to the Scottish Council Development & Industry'. *In*: SNP, ed. *A Collection of Recent Economic Speeches*. SNPA.

Salmond, A., 2003. *The Economics of Independence*. Edinburgh: SNP, SNPA.

Salvini, M., 2001. 'Pontida di lotta e di governo'. *SdA*, V (25), p. 1.

Savoini, G., 2000. 'Un accordo per la Padania'. *SdA*, IV (10), pp. 8–9.

Scottish Government, 2013a. *Scotland's Future. Your Guide to an Independent Scotland*. Edinburgh: The Scottish Government.

Scottish Government, 2013b. *Building Security and Creating Opportunity: Economic Policy Choices in an Independent Scotland*. Referendum campaign brochure.

Sillars, J., 1989. *Independence in Europe*. SNPA.

Slootmans, K., 2015a. '11 juli campagne'. *VBM*, 7–8, p. 6.

Slootmans, K., 2015b. 'Huurindexering: toonbeeld van asociaal beleid', *VBM*, n. 4, p. 14.

SNP (Scottish National Party), 1961. *Vote McDonald for Bridgeton*. Campaign leaflet. Acc. 10090/176, NLS.

SNP, 1967. *21 Wasted Years*. Campaign leaflet. Acc. 10090/176, NLS.

SNP, 1968. *SNP&You*. Campaign leaflet, SNPA.

SNP, 1972a. *Oil Campaign Action Pack*. 11 August. Acc. 10090/160, NLS.

SNP, 1972b. *The Price of the United Kingdom*. Campaign flyer, Acc. 7295/23–24, NLS.

SNP, 1972c, *England Expects Scotland's Oil* [online]. Campaign flyer, Scottish Political Archive, University of Sterling. Available from: www.scottishpoliticalarchive.org.uk/wb/ [accessed 2 February 2014].

SNP, 1972d. 'Another Paper Tiger?'. *SNP Research Bulletin*, 2 (11), Acc. 10090/140, NLS.

SNP, 1973. *It's His/Her Oil*. Campaign flyer, Scottish Political Archive, University of Sterling. Available from: www.scottishpoliticalarchive.org.uk/wb/ [accessed 2 February 2014].

SNP, 1974. *Scotland's Future*, SNP Manifesto. Acc. 10090/200, NLS.

SNP, 1978. *Return to Nationhood*. Electoral brochure, NLS.

SNP, c.1980s. *No Wonder She's Laughing. She's Got Scotland's Oil. Stop Her, Join the SNP*. Campaign poster, Acc. 13115/1, NLS.

SNP, 1984. 'Nats Expose Watford Gap'. *Free Scot*, Autumn. Acc. 13099/50, NLS.

SNP, 1989. *Screw up the poll-tax*. Campaign leaflet, University of Stirling, Scottish Political Archives. Available from: www.scottishpoliticalarchive.org.uk/ [accessed on 9 February 2017].

SNP, 1992. *Independence in Europe. Make it Happen Now*. General election manifesto, SNPA.

SNP, 1995a. *For the Good of Scotland – Towards a Better Scotland*. Edinburgh: SNP, SNPA.

SNP, 1995b. *For the Good of Scotland – Counting the Benefits of Independence*. Edinburgh: SNP, SNPA.

SNP, 1995c. *For the Good of Scotland – Paying Our Fair Share, and More!*. Edinburgh: SNP, SNPA.

SNP, 1996. *Scotland Pays Her Way*. Edinburgh: SNP, SNPA.

SNP, 1997. *Yes We Can Win the Best for Scotland*. General election manifesto, SNPA.

SNP, 1999a. *Taking Scotland into the 21st Century. An Economic Strategy for Independence.* Electoral brochure, SNPA.

SNP, 1999b. *Enterprise, Compassion, Democracy.* Scottish Parliament election manifesto, SNPA.

SNP, 2001. 'Policy Question Time'. *Snapshot*, Spring, SNPA.

SNP, 2002a. 'The Scottish Economy – Your Top Ten Questions Answered'. *Snapshot*, Summer, SNPA.

SNP, 2002b. 'Five Myths That Need to be Exploded'. *Snapshot*, Summer, SNPA.

SNP, 2003. *Talking Independence.* Electoral brochure, SNPA.

SNP, 2005. *If Scotland Matters to You Make it Matter in May.* General election manifesto, SNPA.

SNP, 2007a. *Let Scotland Flourish. An Economic Growth Strategy for Scottish Success.* Edinburgh: SNP, SNPA.

SNP, 2007b. *A Platform for Success: A Wealthier Scotland Benefiting All.* Edinburgh: SNP, SNPA.

SNP, 2010. *Elect a Local Champion.* General election manifesto, SNPA.

SNP, 2011. *Re-elect. A Scottish Government Working for Scotland.* Scottish election manifesto, SNPA.

SNP, 2012. *Choice. An Historic Opportunity for Our Nation.* Referendum campaign brochure, SNPA.

SNP, 2015. *Stronger for Scotland.* General election manifesto, SNPA.

SNP Research Department, 1975. *Scotland's Oil: The Background.* August. Acc. 10090/140, NLS.

Sol, S., 2012. 'Sense espoli ens en sortim'. *EN*, 207, pp. 4–7.

Sol, S., 2013. 'Ofec Economic'. *EN*, 211, pp. 4–7.

Speroni, F., 1991. 'Una confederazione contro il centralismo'. *LA*, IX (5), p. 6.

Staglieno, M., 1994. 'L'Italia nel nuovo contesto internazionale'. *LN*, XII (12), p. 2.

Stucchi, G., 2010. 'Sistema allo sfascio, solo col federalismo si esce da questa crisi', *LP*, 25 June, p. 8.

Sturgeon, N., 2013. 'No more "what ifs" ', *Scotland on Sunday*, 17 March. Available from: www.scotsman.com/scotland-on-sunday/opinion/comment/scotland-decides-eight-essays-on-independence-1-2841425 [accessed on 14 February 2014].

Truyens, E., 1980. 'Sociaal-ekonomische rubriek. Nationalisme en ekonomie'. *DVN*, n. 8.

Valkeniers, B., 2011. 'Grieks scenario'. *VBM*, 12, p. 3.

Valkeniers, B., 2012. 'Buitenspel', *VBM*, 1, p. 3.

Vallanz, M., 1990. 'Nord: colonizzati in casa'. *LA*, VIII (4), p. 3.

Van Gorp, G., Truyens, E., Dillen, M., Gerits, L. and Van Raemdonck, F., 1980. *Vlaams-Nationale ekonomie: Financiële perspektieven voor een zelfstandig Vlaanderen.* First VB Congress, 22–23 March, VBA.

Van Hauthem, J., 1989. 'Vlaanderen by de bok gezet'. *VLB*, 2, p. 3.

Van Hauthem, J., 1996. 'Verkiezingen broodnodig'. *VLB*, 12, p. 1.

Van Hauthem, J., 2007. 'Een unitaire kieskring?'. *VBM*, 4, p. 6.

Van Hauthem, J. and Verreycken, W., 1990. *Onafhankelijkheid, moet en kan. Deel II, Brussel and state reform.* Congress brochure, VBA.

Van Osselaer, W., 2015. 'Vlaams Belang wil betaalbare rusthuizen'. *VBM*, 7–8, p. 20.

Van Overmeire, K., 2002. *Le Vlaams Blok, le parti nationaliste flamande*, Electoral brochure, VBA.

Vanhecke, F., 1979. 'Terug naar de middeleeuwen'. *DVN*, November.

Vanhecke, F., 1998. 'Vlaamse strijd, sociale strijd!'. *VBM*, 4, p. 3.

Vanhecke, F., 2000. ' "Een revolutionaire partij: de enige partij die opneemt voor de belangen van de kleine man" '. *VBM*, 5, p. 2.

VB, 1980. 'Belgie, een misverstand?'. *DVN*, February.

VB, 1983. 'Fijn erbij te zijn', *VLB*, 7, pp. 4–5.

VB, 1984. 'Happart eruit!', *VLB*, 2, p. 8.

VB, 1988. *Grondbeginselen. Manifest van het rechtse Vlaams-nationalisme.* 2nd edition. Deurne: Vlaams Blok.

VB, 1989. 'Doen!!!', *VLB*, 2, p. 1.

VB, 1992. *The Vlaams Blok: Facts and Objectives.* Publicity brochure, VBA.

VB, 2001. *Congres 'Vlaanderen Onafhankelijk'.* VB Congress, Gent 15 December, VBA.

VB, 2005. *Synthesetekst – t.b.v. het economisch congres van het Vlaams Belang – 'Ondernemend Vlaanderen: welvaart voor iedereen!'.* VB Congress, Brussels, 26 November, VBA.

VB, 2007. *Toekomstplan voor Vlaanderen.* Federal election manifesto, VBA.

VB, 2009a. *VLeerst!.* Regional election manifesto, VBA.

VB, 2009b. 'Wil u 2.000 euro extra verdienen?'. *VBM*, 2, p. 5.

VB, 2009c. *Vlaams Geld, in Vlaamse Handen*, Electoral brochure, VBA.

VB, 2010a. 'Uitstel als oplossing'. *VBM*, 2, pp. 18–19.

VB, 2010b. *Vlamingen 1st*, Federal election manifesto, VBA.

VB, 2013a. 'Werken tot de dood aan minimumtarief'. *VBM*, 12, p. 9.

VB, 2013b. 'Er is in Vlaanderen slechts één partij die klaarheid biedt'. *VBM*, 5, pp. 10–12.

VB, 2014. *Uw stok achter de deur*, Federal and regional election manifesto, VBA.

VU (Volksunie), 1977. *Gedaan met geven en toegeven. Uw enige Vlaamse waarborg: Volksunie.* Electoral flyer, folder 6.2.8.4, KADOC, Leuven.

VU, 1978. *Zes miljoen Vlamingen.* Electoral flyer, folder 6.2.9.2, KADOC, Leuven.

Wienen, W., 1998. 'Werk, Identiteit, Veiligheid'. *VBM*, 4, p. 4.

Wilson, G., 1988. *The Scottish Paradox.* Andrew Lang Lecture, University of St. Andrews, SNPA.

Wolfe, W., 1972. *Scotland Now. Conference Speech.* Press release, 27 May. Acc. 10090/141, NLS.

Wouters, L., 1982. 'Happart aan de poorten van Brussel'. *VLB*, 2, p. 2.

Zaia, L., 2010. 'È il riscatto dell'identità veneta. Mai più sudditi'. *LP*, 30 March, p. 9.

Index

Page numbers in *italics* denote tables, those in **bold** denote figures.